THE
PERSONAL SESSIONS
Book 6 of
The Deleted Seth Material

Sessions

12/15/80–5/10/82

THE EARLY SESSIONS

The Early Sessions consist of the first 510 sessions dictated by Seth through Jane Roberts. There are 9 books in *The Early Sessions* series.

THE PERSONAL SESSIONS

The Personal Sessions, often referred to as "the deleted sessions," are Seth sessions that Jane Roberts and Rob Butts considered to be of a highly personal nature and were therefore kept in separate notebooks from the main body of the Seth material. *The Personal Sessions* are expected to be published in 7 volumes.

"The great value I see now in the many deleted or private sessions is that they have the potential to help others, just as they helped Jane and me over the years. I feel that it's very important to have these sessions added to Jane's fine creative body of work for all to see." –Rob Butts

THE SETH AUDIO COLLECTION

Rare recordings of Seth speaking through Jane Roberts are available on audiocassette and CD. For a complete description of The Seth Audio Collection, request our free catalogue. (Further information is supplied at the back of this book.)

For information on expected publication dates and how to order, write to New Awareness Network at the following address and request the latest catalogue. Also, please visit us on the Internet at *www.sethcenter.com*.

New Awareness Network Inc.
P.O. BOX 192
Manhasset, N.Y. 11030

www.sethcenter.com

THE
PERSONAL SESSIONS
Book 6 of
The Deleted Seth Material
Sessions
12/15/80–5/10/82

Published by New Awareness Network Inc.

New Awareness Network Inc.
P.O. Box 192
Manhasset, New York 11030

Opinions and statements on health and medical matters expressed in this book are those of the author and are not necessarily those of or endorsed by the publisher. Those opinions and statements should not be taken as a substitute for consultation with a duly licensed physician.

Cover Design: Michael Goode
Photography: Cover photos by Rich Conz and Robert F. Butts, Sr.
Editorial: Rick Stack
Typography: Raymond Todd, Michael Goode

ISBN 0-9768978-0-6
Printed in U.S.A. on acid-free paper

I dedicate The Personal Sessions
to my wife, Jane Roberts,
who lived her 55 years
with the greatest creativity
and the most valiant courage.
-Rob

A NOTE ON THE COVER DESIGN PHOTOGRAPHS

June 2003. A note about the photographs Michael Goode used in his strik-ing cover design for The Personal Sessions *series.*

The central colored photograph of Jane and the lower right-and-left-hand shots of her and myself were taken by my father, Robert F. Butts, Sr., in Sayre, PA a year or so after our marriage in December 1954. The upper right one of Jane in trance for Seth was taken (among many others) by Rich Conz, a photographer for the Elmira, NY Star-Gazette, while he witnessed Session 508 on November 20, 1969. (See Volume 9 of The Early Sessions.*)*

I don't know who photographed the young Jane shown on the upper left, but she saved that picture all of those years for me to inherit upon her death in September 1984, when she was 55.

My inventive and versatile father had always taken photographs, and in his later years turned professional, photographing many weddings and other events in the Sayre area (and also Jane's and my wedding at the home of my younger brother Loren and his wife Betts in Tunkhannock, PA). To help my father, my mother Estelle trained herself to hand-color his black-and-white photographs, for color film was not available then—and so she colored Jane's portrait. Now I won-der: do my long-deceased parents, and Rich and the unknown photographer of the young Jane, all know that their creativity will grace the covers of a series of books that I so lovingly dedicate to them, as well as to Jane and each reader? I believe that they do, each in his or her own way.

—Rob

DELETED SESSION
DECEMBER 15, 1980 9:45 PM MONDAY

(Jane felt very relaxed before the session, as she had most of the day: "The first day I've had it made in a month," she said. Still, she'd become blue temporarily in the bathroom after supper. She did want to have a session, though. After our meal I'd reread some of these late private sessions, and had planned to go over some of those from 1973, but various distractions prevented me from doing the latter.

(The mail was very heavy last week, and Jane still has a batch of Christmas cards to reply to yet, as well as a dozen "regular" letters, even after answering better than 35 letters.

("I'm just waiting," she said at 9:35. "Actually my ankles are doing all kinds of things, releasing.... I'm so relaxed I could go right to bed...." So could I for that matter.

(As we sat waiting I read to Jane pages 4 and 5 of the private session for October 22, 1973—excellent material concerning the contrasts displayed by Jane's parents. Seth had discussed her father's laxness, and her mother's drive toward purpose, power, and control, and how Jane had felt that she must make a <u>choice</u> between the two modes of behavior. Not realizing that she could choose her own independent course. The session and others dating from that time offers very good insights into Jane's choice of actions over the years. "Well, I guess he's gotten turned on by what you just read," she said now—for now she felt that Seth was ready to come through. She'd been waiting impatiently for some time for you-know-who to put in an appearance.)

Now—

("Good evening.")

—good evening.

Ruburt should read that session *(for October 22, 1973)* and ones immediately previous. The attitudes still stand to some important degree. The contrast represented his own interpretation of his private reality, of course—yet they also represent the main issues involved right now in your society at large.

The same issues underlie your own attitudes, the tension between effort and relaxation, discipline and spontaneity has applied, say, in the creative area as far as painting is concerned. Ruburt set out, of course, to handle his own purposes and challenges, but he chose those in the context of your world, so that in encountering them personally he would encounter them for your society as well. In such ways, the species does handle psychological and psychic issues.

Everything I said recently about the disclaimer stands. Be aware, however, of the sudden reassurances from Framework 2. *(Also at Prentice)*—The news program invitation *(from ABC)*, which places you in a context, however small, of national interest—an invitation that you did not court; these, plus many excellent letters of late, should show you of course the beneficial aspects of your work that you <u>can</u> at times overlook *(with irony)*. You have at the very least a very large extended family, people whose lives you have touched for the better.

The ability to reach people in such a fashion is a gift. The disclaimer itself will be creatively utilized—something else that can escape your notice when you become too shortsighted. I am still in the process of trying to teach you both that <u>trust</u> is also a spiritual and physical imperative. It is indeed a condition of biological life—this of course despite all of your upbringing. That kind of trust is behind all of man's curiosity, for without a trust in the world he would never have the courage to explore it.

(10:00.) When you make love you are entrusting yourself to someone else, making a spiritual and biological statement of openness that is understood through all the levels of your experience—even to the cellular. Under such loving conditions healing energies are spontaneously released. In its own fashion such acts of love are beneficially related with the spontaneous behavior of animals. That is, you can behave to some extent at such times with a creature-like sense of trust and spontaneity, and of loving openness of a kind that animals at their best often display. Again, I mentioned that you could both benefit far more from more such encounters. They generate trust.

Your morning discussion, concerning Ruburt's past, was also beneficial, for it is good to remind yourselves of your <u>own</u> (underlined) backgrounds, rather than ever comparing yourselves with other people whose own backgrounds may have little to do with yours. You have both done remarkably well from that viewpoint. When you seem to suffer in contrast to the development or situation of any other specific or generalized persons, it is when you are trying to live up to artificial pictures of yourselves—of people who should have been as knowledgeable years ago as they are now, and who therefore now should be at much greater stages of development.

In others words, you often expect too much of yourselves. This makes you dwell upon any difficulties, so that any blemishes are overly emphasized, any accomplishments taken for granted, and you are left with a sense of disapproval. *(Pause.)* Then you lack trust in yourselves because you try to live up to images that are not connected with your backgrounds, and often ignore them. What you have learned seems as nothing, because you forget how your attitudes changed.

In a fashion you recognized much of this in your morning discussion about Ruburt's problem, but it applies to each of you. The idea of Ruburt doing some work in the near future on *Rich Bed* is therefore a good one.

(Long pause.) Love-making reunites you with your own pasts, and unconscious bodily memory carries you backward to your earliest responses to your own body and that of others. To some extent then the child with all of his wonder about his own body is aroused in each act of love-making, whatever its variety. With those memories come feelings of biological exuberance, the body's faith in itself, all highly important, and far more therapeutic than is ever realized in your society.

(10:20.) Again, it goes without saying that in your situations you largely overlook such benefits. Ruburt's remarks in his essay on love apply here, in regard to its specific nature. That is *(pause)*, it arouses memories from your own most intimate moments in the past, and therefore in its own way records the development of ideas and attitudes that you might otherwise completely overlook. You had friends lately disappointed in marriages and relationships *(Sue and Claire)*. Your own relationship is itself quite extraordinary, precisely in the light of your own backgrounds—not as you think those backgrounds <u>should</u> have been, but as they were.

When you ask why you did not understand when you were young what you know now, you are ignoring the validity of your own past to some extent, and denying the accomplishments that have resulted—because it seems that you should now be much further on, so that you create a kind of artificial self who began where you are now, and with whom it seems you can never catch up.

At Ruburt's end, it almost seems as if he had our material at hand magically without effort, and therefore should have put it to use at once, learning the lessons of half a lifetime in a few years, and graduating to solve all of his own problems and half of the world's as well. Against that image of course he feels inadequate, and of course such an image would make him lose faith in himself to some degree; so it is very important that you realize how well you have both done in many areas of activity, and that you reinforce each other in those directions.

<u>If you did</u>, other issues would take care of themselves.

(It had been snowing very finely ever since suppertime. Now as Jane paused in her delivery I heard the town sander moving powerfully up Holley Road past our kitchen windows. Its rotating red light flashed briefly into our living room.)

There is no need saying Ruburt would be in better physical condition <u>perhaps</u> if the psychic development has not happened—since that development was a part of his natural growth processes. While it may sound unrealistic, the fact remains that much of Ruburt's problems are indeed caused by a constant comparison with the self that he is, and the self that he and you think he should be *(long pause)*, and to some extent by too much concern about what the world may think or not think.

Again, you have evidence of his body's willingness to change for the better. His faith is growing, and both of you can help reinforce it. The sessions on work discuss the relaxation and work aspects thoroughly, and should not be forgotten. Many of your accomplishments *(long pause)* are allowed to fade when you do not pay attention to the large bulk of your mail, for it does involve people whose lives you are indeed helping to change for the better.

Love-making, like dreams, returns you to yourselves, and initiates beneficial Framework-2 activity. It regenerates your energies, and indeed clears the passageways for creativity.

End of session—a potpourri.

("Thank you. Very good.")

A fond good evening.

("Thank you. Good night."

(10:40 PM. I told Jane that she's come through with another excellent session. Her delivery had been quite steady and mostly low key, but definite.)

JANE'S NOTES
DECEMBER 27, 1980

(Our 26th Wedding Anniversary. Notes.

(Yesterday while proofreading the Mass Events *galleys I got the feeling that that book really bothered me, served as a focal point. My eye troubles started the same spring that Seth started dictating it; I was doing* James*; Frank L. was building the porches; and the Gallery of Silence people were bugging us. Before though, the fact escaped me that Seth had started* Mass Events—*representing his and my direct attack on official dictums—or so it seemed to me. Before we sort of did it by inference. I accept everything in the book—his opinions on medicine, etc.—but I think I felt that if I was going to tell it like it was—and I was, was determined to, then I also needed more protection from the world—and began cutting down mobility again. My idea is that the eyes get bad after the muscular strain reaches a certain point. This idea also came back, reading a book on William James Peggy G. gave me for Xmas—his attitudes and mine so often seem similar—that he was determined to be daring, press ahead no matter what, explore consciousness—while at the same time being attracted to safety, disliking controversy, wanting peace, etc. I think I am that way. The long breaks when Seth didn't dictate may have come when I got particularly concerned about the material, the wisdom of presenting it to the world, etc. In fact Seth gave us Frameworks 1 and 2 stuff in there, to help me. I did grab hold*

several times, and with the God *of* Jane *book, the new inspiration there—and stuff on following impulses, made some very good improvements. But far more than Rob, from the beginning I was nervous and anxious—about directly coming out with many of the ideas—which at the same time I fervently and even passionately believe in.... I may fear that if you go too far.... telling it like it is.... that the establishment will just cut off your platform.... or that people will or would stop buying the books.... something like.... biting the hand that feeds you—you can only go so far. Yet I've always known that these ideas conflicted with official ones—it's just that before the "attack" was less direct....*

(Lately I've really been working with ideas of safety, saying and believing that I am safe, secure and supported and that I do trust my natural spontaneous motion.... Now as I write some old dumb stuff comes emotionally to mind—my mother saying that I'd destroy those I loved or some such nonsense.... but as if I always felt that spontaneously, left alone, I'd end up taking away people's comfort blankets and I felt bad about that, even while I knew that those philosophic blankets were wormy, had to go. And I do see that I'm offering something far better.

(We have a lovely quiet Xmas—Gallaghers here Xmas Eve—four inches or so of snow, Joe and Margaret here last PM—pleasant—I give Rob his planter thing; we get the bed. He surprises me with a great white sweater for an anniversary gift....)

DELETED SESSION
JANUARY 7, 1981 9:23 PM WEDNESDAY

(Jane was bleary—really "out of it"—when she said that she'd try for a session at 8:55. She didn't feel Seth around and had no idea what he might talk about, or whether the session would be long or short. As we waited I explained to her a few things about the political fighting in San Salvador; I'd just finished typing the last, 930th session, wherein I'd referred to the attached news clippings about that country's travails. I thought the session, on the behavior of nations, excellent, and that San Salvador could almost be a test example of what Seth had talked about.

(The evening was very cold—10° —as we sat for the session. The house was quiet except for the rumble of the furnace. The cats were asleep. "Well, I'm waiting," I said to Jane, joking, at 9:17. She made a face. We waited. "Force it," I said at 9:20, still joking, and Jane protested in good humor. Finally, she said she felt "him a little bit"....)

Ruburt is correct: it will be a fairly brief session. I would like to make several comments – of, I hope, a helpful nature.

Ruburt has indeed made excellent strides, of late, in dealing with beliefs, and in switching orientation, so that he is beginning to learn to use the magical approach—which is, again, the natural one. Of late, when he says that he is out of it, or very relaxed, he is involved at certain levels of awareness, in which indeed mental and physical tensions are being relieved and drained away.

In your terms he would be in the alpha state, fluctuating, sometimes, between several states of consciousness and orientation. The body is responding in its own way, and with its own sense of order, its own inner spontaneous logic. As a result he has had some valuable nightly experiences, two in particular, though there are others that he does not recall.

In those states, while his body is resting, he is learning greater agility both physically and in natural manipulation of the magical approach in general. He is also given at such times immediate physical feedback: he realizes at once that his body is more at ease, more agile, and so forth. His state of mind during the day then varies, so that with his files (of poetry) today he was in a highly relaxed, creative, productive, mental level, one that served to cushion his mind from the critical reproaches he can often give himself, and therefore bodily relaxation could continue.

The festival incident of the dream state was highly fascinating, and it did represent a particular state of consciousness above all—one in which reality is perceived in a different fashion. The dream (last night) reflected and updated old Sumari traditions that honored God as a god of festivals, of celebration, traditions, that built upon the idea of life itself as a celebration.

The dream also served as a framework allowing him to intuitively and psychically and biologically perceive the emotional reality of Framework 2. That is, he participated in its emotional content. The healing processes were then accelerated.

(9:36.) You should both to some extent have further experiences now in all areas of your life with the magical or natural kind of orientation to physical events. That orientation does indeed "tip the balance" in terms of probabilities on your behalf. You will (underlined) experience feelings of effortlessness as the goals once considered, say, quite difficult are achieved—seemingly they occur by themselves.

It seems you need certain practical instructions that involve direct experience, immediate feedback, and Ruburt has been receiving some of that in the dream state, and also to some extent in his waking reality, as he begins to trust the feelings of support and relaxation.

Remember again that the intellect can see only so far, and that it uses the cause-and-effect kind of logic, while magical events leapfrog that kind of orientation. A small note: Your new (TV film) equipment is fine with me, and can if you wanted to serve us all quite well. Ruburt's dream, by the way, also signaled him that he is now approaching what the Sumarians used to call "the time of festivals," or a time of grace. All of their ceremonies were joyful and life-giving.

There will be more on your nations, for I will fill out the picture to some extent, and did not mean to imply that such people could not change—but that the changes would come in their own fashions, through their own characteristics as they blended, say, the helpful advice of others with their own needs and desires. They will always love pageantry, for example, symbolism and excitement, so that their public political events will stress such facts far more, say, than your own.

Ruburt should relax for the rest of the evening. I simply wanted to add these comments, and bid you both a magical good evening.

(*"Thank you, Seth. Good night."*

(*9:49 PM. Jane was still very relaxed, even during the session her eyes had closed often as she spoke for Seth, or she had stared at me beneath very heavy lids.*)

DELETED SESSION
JANUARY 26, 1981 9:30 PM MONDAY

(*This afternoon I mailed to Prentice-Hall the corrected page proofs for* The God of Jane.

(*This is the first session Jane has held since giving the deleted one for last January 7. Once again, she was very uncomfortable as she sat in her chair across the coffee table from me. Earlier today—as she reaffirmed now—she'd said more than once that she wanted to "get back to the sessions, no matter what," or how she felt. Her bodily condition presented rather large contrasts: Her upper body was very relaxed, her eyes bleary. Her arms were longer, as they had been for some time now. Her backside was sore, as well as her hips and inner thighs at the groin; she couldn't move forward easily. At the same time her upper legs above the knees were "soft and mushy," while below the knees the muscles were hard and tight. Yet her feet were in good shape. These are the highlights of her condition. This morning she'd slept for an hour before lunch.*

(*This week especially has also been one of emotional turmoil for us, and for many others, on the national scene: the inauguration of President Reagan; the freeing of the American hostages by Iran, and their return to this country in stages. Steve and Tracy Blumenthal have also lent us a complete videotaping set, and we've experimented a little bit with filming Jane reading poetry. The Gallaghers have also been featured. We're waiting for an extension cord from Steve for the TV camera so we can try to record sessions. I've wanted to try to film Jane reading poetry in the meantime, but each time I think of asking her —usually at night—I can see that she's so uncomfortable that I let it go.*

(Jane has had some interesting nighttime experiences in connection with the hostages, and has written the brief note attached to the session. She hasn't been able to really explain them yet; perhaps Seth will comment. My own guess is that she's touched upon some probable events.

(Jane said she felt Seth around by 9:20, but that she thought the session would be a short one. I told her I was primarily interested in but two things, both personal: her reactions to Mass Events *and* God of Jane *in connection with her symptoms, and what was going on in her backside and hips. She hasn't "walked" for weeks now—since last year—and the hip problems especially have persisted now for a number of months. I wanted to hear from Seth something about why her body was taking so long to respond in those areas.*

(Tomorrow, the hostages meet President Reagan at the White House. See my files for much material on the whole hostage question of recent months.

(The night before this session was held Jane suggested that each day we read over a session, or talk or review some notes, as a way to give ourselves a "pep talk" and to lead us into the day. So the day of the session, after breakfast this morning, we reread the deleted session for January 7, 1981, which is a very good one. And this morning—Tuesday—I read last night's session to Jane from my notes, since I didn't have it typed yet.)

Good evening.

("Good evening. Seth.")

Now: every individual alive is intimately concerned at certain levels with all of the national and global challenges in the political and social and religious arena.

I do not want to oversimplify, but it is as <u>if</u> each generation or group of generations seeks it own overall themes, about which the world will be organized. Those will appear in the private lives of citizens and in private dreams and in national events, or global ones, so that both arenas of activity are always intimately involved.

You knew ahead of time the kind of world you would be entering. The challenges that you and Ruburt both accepted have been discussed often, and to some extent they mirrored the challenges of the world at large. It is only of late, relatively speaking, that some of those issues have begun to rather clearly show themselves in the arena of public events, however.

Ruburt found it very difficult to take a public stand, as separate from, say, a private one. My book and his—that is, *Mass Events* and *God of Jane*—both do take public stands. They comment clearly on issues that affect individual and private, and national or community behavior. The importance of impulses was stressed in particular, and the acceptance of such an idea is important to Ruburt's recovery, of course—but also vital in the behavior of nations.

It may seem that nations behave only too impulsively, that for example the just-released American hostages were kidnapped as a result of highly impulsive behavior. In fact, that event might only seem to prove that impulsive behavior is basically aggressive, undependable, and chaotic. As a matter of fact, the students took such regrettable actions not because they gave into impulsive behavior, but because the road to true impulsive expression had been blocked so long that such actions became one of the few possible ways of giving vent to certain expressions. When you are a hostage you cannot express your own impulses, of course. Your free will is highly curtailed for all practical purposes. It is curtailed because the number of impulses are so drastically reduced by circumstance.

Whenever, and for whatever reasons you block the normally free flow of impulses, you also curtail the exercise of free will, for free will involves you in the experience of choosing between the actualization of one impulse or another. The captors then cut down on the freedom of the hostages by reducing the number of impulses to which the hostages could respond. This is all so clear that it is difficult to express step by step. The telling itself makes the affair seem complex—but whether or not you are dealing with private behavior, with the treatment of one person in regard to his or her own impulses, or whether you are dealing with a mass event of political nature, involving the enforced blockage of impulses on the part of one group toward another, you are necessarily cutting down on the exercise of free will.

(Long pause at 9:49.) In a way, the external politics of the situation within your country is helping Ruburt to understand his own position far better than he did earlier. It is helping him clarify some issues. There were always two faces to his endeavors—the private search for understanding, and the public expression as a writer. In a fashion this applies to most endeavors of a creative kind. The painter's painting is a result of a private search, but in a gallery it becomes a public expression.

Largely—for I am simplifying here to some considerable degree, but largely—Ruburt felt little difficulties to be encountered in his private search, but in their public expression he was far more cautious. It is impossible, of course, to really separate the two, but as his work became better known, the private search became more of a public issue.

Years ago, when the Gallery of Silence people began to bug him, he felt threatened, afraid that he would become the brunt of fanatics or extremists. He was nevertheless determined to take some kind of a public stand—for not to do so would mean not to express himself through his books at all. He knew he would never give into <u>that</u> course, but he felt that some of that dates back to childhood habits and beliefs, when his very food and bed was given him by the auspices of the public.

He was taught to be very cautious lest that livelihood be taken away. The only private fears he had were also old ones, having to do with the whole false-prophet syndrome, the fear of leading people down the garden path, and so forth. Those private and public arenas became connected, however. *(Long pause.)* He was worried that his natural expression and search, publicly expressed at that point in history, was dangerous because it put him in the gaze of a growing band of fanatics on the one hand, and also roused old fears of a private nature, having to do with the overall validity of revelatory information.

(10:05.) He would not stop expressing himself, but immediately felt he needed greater protection. To some extent he doubted his own vision—see the connection with his eye difficulty. Despite this he went on with some considerable courage, determination and vigor in my book and his own to encounter the nitty-gritty, so to speak, to bring out the issues clearly to himself and to the world.

The information in *Mass Events* and in our sessions helped him use impulses to a far better degree than he had before, and helped him keep some balance, let him advance in understanding despite the period of difficulty. Still at various times and throughout the period, he used <u>what he thought of as</u> that additional protection: the symptoms kept him inside, where it seemed he could indeed express himself with the least duress. At the same time he was learning that expression denied at one level means expression denied to some extent at <u>all</u> levels *(louder)*—so that of course his creative work also suffered to some degree.

Realizing that, he made considerable efforts to change his attitudes and beliefs. The national situation has somewhat changed. The challenges are more out in the open now. He does not feel that he is involved alone, as he did before: the fanatics, for example, are everywhere—quite visible, and if they might find his work offensive, he is hardly alone. He has, therefore, been involved in the nitty-gritty. This means that he has been encountering his own beliefs, arguing with them—<u>changing</u> them at very elemental levels.

You have definite signs of the body's overall <u>positive</u> response: the arms are straighter, the feet stronger, the ankles more flexible, and overall adjustments are constantly being made. With all this you have the changes in the thighs and hips, so that the muscular rigidity has definitely given away. The entire stance is altering and the circulation improving.

(10:20.) At the same time, he has been extremely uncomfortable. Each day the entire body is learning to relax more. The flesh becomes more pliable, and as that occurs in response to his newer beliefs in safety, still he must reassure himself that all is (underlined) well, and give permission for further release.

This is a stage, then, in that process—one in which he is holding his own. The period, however, can and should be shortened. Your free and open communication with each other on this subject can be of far more value than either of you realize, and it is really the only primary point of contention right now. That is, he is dispensing with the beliefs behind the problems fairly well, so it is only on the issue of safety, and the safety of relaxation, that he is still concerned.

There is considerable experimentation on the body's part when he sleeps, and it does try out positions that as yet he does not take when waking. Helpful massage on your part will also be of value, because of what it implies.

There is much material, of course, dealing with the hostage situation, for as it in a fashion echoes Ruburt's own situation, so it also symbolizes the situations of many people, which is why the affair captures the attention of the world. Have Ruburt use his recorded suggestions again for a while. *(Pause.)* Ruburt feels that some of the threats he felt hidden in the world are now out in the open. They actually seem less dangerous than they did before for that reason. To some extent or another there are always social as well as private aspects to a person's state of health.

(10:30.) The understandings that Ruburt is now achieving are precisely the ones needed. What is left is reassurance that each step along the way is safe and supported. It is important for him to remember the effortlessness with which increased flexibility can come. It can come as easily as your income does *(with humor, referring to my work on taxes the last two days)*. It is important that he not worry, or project his difficulties into the future—and while he does much better at that than he did, he still needs the reminder.

End of session.

("Can I ask a question?")

You may.

("I know we've gone over it many times, but I need some refreshing on why he's equated the lack of mobility with protection. Is it because the immobility keeps him inside the house, where he feels safe, or....?"

(Seth gave me a half-pitying look combined with one of willingness and understanding. I'd expected the reaction, but still wanted a concise definition that we could refer to.)

The material has been given countless times. Give us a moment....

He thought that immobility kept him at his desk working, free from any impulses to do otherwise, since for many years he believed that the spontaneous self must be harnessed toward creativity, and that left alone it would have too many other interests.

At the same time he feared that the spontaneous self could get him into difficulties *(long pause)*, because he had no way of knowing where his own search might lead him—and particularly he feared that it might lead him into conflict with the rest of the world.

The immobility protected him, so he thought, from encountering any such outside conflicts, and insured his continuing creativity by cutting down other interests and distractions, and by organizing his time in a most economical fashion—or so it seemed. That is a simplified answer. The nuances, which are important, appear in many groups of sessions, given in the past, and also include his reaction to attitudes of your own, which to some extent helped form and solidify his own ideas in those regards.

End of session.

("Thank you very much.")

I bid you a fond good evening.

("The same to you. Good night."

(10:42 PM. Jane closed her eyes as Seth, and when she opened them that personality was gone. The session had hardly been a short one; I told her it was excellent.

("I was hardly aware of my ass or anything else," she said. "I felt a whole lot of stuff there on the hostages—stuff it would take forever to get, darn it...." So we talked about what a great book Seth could do on the hostage question. "Before you got through it would cover history, religion, science—the whole works," Jane said. I agreed that it would certainly encapsulate our whole civilized world structure before Seth finished it. "Forget it," Jane said. "We've got one half done now." She wanted to know what would happen to Seth's book on dreams in the meantime, and I explained that it would only wait until the other project was finished. After all, it was waiting now for us to get back to it.

(Jane had been restless during the session, but felt pretty good now. I thought the session contained many good things. It's Wednesday as I finish typing it. I typed half of it Tuesday night; but Tuesday morning, in keeping with our idea to ground ourselves in new ideas each day, I read the full session to her from my notes.

(As I finished it this evening, however, I can see now that the session is even a better one that I'd thought. Actually, it contains the key to Jane's recovery, and her progress continues. I massaged her thighs after supper. This afternoon, when I told

her it was okay to relax, "even to walk," she said "something melted" inside her, and she became more relaxed. In fact, she slept for over an hour this morning. She planned to try for a session this evening, she said, as I went back to my typing.

(I might add that Seth's capsule commentary on the reasons for her symptoms is just what I wanted, and that we ought to keep copies of it available for easy reference. The thought came to me after supper that Jane's doing the ESP classes probably contributed to the symptoms over the years, since the class situation was one in which she advanced her unconventional ideas to the public. I haven't had a chance to discuss this with her, but it seems possible that her disseminating her ideas to a large number of people, in person each week, could have struck her deep-seated need for protection.... If Jane reads this material before holding a session tonight, perhaps Seth can comment.)

JANE'S NOTE ABOUT THE HOSTAGES

(Today is Friday, January 23. The American hostages were released Tuesday, January 20. That day we watched the events on television. That night, all night it seemed, I was concerned with the hostages, uneasy, though I don't recall actual dreams. The next morning we learn on TV that they'd been badly mistreated....

(Last night [Thursday] slept great. Again though all night it seemed I was involved someway with the hostages. All I recall was bewilderment that the world and everyone in it thought that the events were taking place now, while they weren't in my time scheme at all. I think they were in the past from my viewpoint. The difference bothered me. Finally I decided that I'd just have to go along with the mass belief that the events were happening now and act as if they were, even if I knew better....

(After watching the televised events from all over the world, Tuesday night I dreamed that in the future all households would be connected to interconnecting computers, keeping track of all inhabitants, actions, goods, and so forth. Thursday in the mail receive a letter all about the new home-sized computers, how they worked, and how one could be used to work with our records and sessions....)

DELETED SESSION
JANUARY 28, 1981 8:55 PM WEDNESDAY

(I finished typing last Monday's session just before we sat for this one. At my request Jane read the page of notes I'd attached to the end of the session. I didn't ask

that she or Seth comment on the notes, but at least I'd made it possible for either one to do so. Among other things I'd written that Monday's session was even better than I'd thought it was.

(Once again—by 8:47—Jane was very uncomfortable, trying again and again to find a tolerable position in her chair so that she could hold the session. "Yet I'm having trouble keeping my eyes open," she said.

(At 8 PM tonight ABC TV News had begun a three-hour dissertation on the whole American-Iranian-hostage situation, narrated by Pierre Salinger. The program was fascinating, and was actually a sequel to a previous program of equal length that ABC had broadcast a few days ago; we'd seen much of that one, too. I heard Jane listening to this evening's segment while I was working in the writing room. What a tale of intrigue, personalities, and beliefs it was. And as soon as Seth opened the session, I understood at once how he was going to link that tale with Jane's own hassles.

(Whispering:) Good evening.

("Good evening, Seth.")

Now: Your documentary rather neatly shows two portions of the world's mind operating at odds, rather than in complementary ways—almost as if they were surgically separated, or somehow functionally impaired, as in many ways they have been through misunderstandings throughout the years.

Both portions of this world mind, or world brain, therefore, operate in exaggerated fashions, so that their own characteristics are almost caricatured, untempered as it were by other portions, as if perhaps in an individual the left and right portions of the brain were artificially functionally separated.

What is perfectly clear to one portion of that world brain may not be perceived at all by the other side, and vice versa. For the purposes of this discussion, we must simplify, so we will say that generally speaking your own country aligns itself with the world of reason, while in the same fashion Iran allies itself with the world of emotion. Both react, again, by exhibiting exaggerated versions of the characteristics involved, however. The same applies in any personality who attempts to separate the intellect and the emotions from their necessary unity within psychological structure. In either case, you end up with the need for negotiators, who attempt to bring the two sides into at least some alignment, or to correct the vision and perception of each side until the situation of the other side is at least <u>perceived</u> with some clarity.

Now under many situations people, again, behave in the same manner. They use portions of themselves as hostages—or as in Ruburt's case they use a portion of themselves not so much as hostages, but they take a part of the self under "protective custody." This almost always occurs when there are misunderstandings in particular areas between the picture of the self or the world as painted by the intellect, and the picture of the world or of the self painted by the emotions.

At the basis of almost all problems of any nature there is a point where value fulfillment is being denied. The point is not so much to search for what is wrong, but to discover what underlined expression is denied, even while it is sought for. That is, the individual has a problem because there is a blockage of value fulfillment in a given area.

The person seeks a certain kind of expression while also feeling that the same expression is either dangerous, forbidden, or for one reason or another impossible to achieve. This applies to human personal problems and to political ones in which entire peoples are involved.

Many of the methods used to find solutions actually involve the setup of negotiations on the part of nations—the third party or parties—who in the beginning can communicate with each side, explaining one side's viewpoint to the other. The setting up of communication with individuals, communication between the various portions of the self, is highly desirable then. This is often accomplished quite automatically as other portions of the self form themselves into negotiative postures, inserting various thoughts and ideas and feelings to the opposing psychological camp.

Ruburt took a portion of himself into protective custody—not wishing to do that portion any damage, but simply to restrain it, to teach it discipline. Some people take portions of themselves, again, as hostages, restraining such portions with the idea of punishing them for imagined wrongs, or for actions not understood.

(Pause at 9:20.) In either case, however, portions of the self are hampered, restrained, and their expression drastically reduced, and there are bound to be repercussions. Ruburt's body suffered whether or not he intended it to, because value fulfillment was being further denied. In the case of hostages and those in protective custody, a certain kind of enforced isolation is also bound to happen —and to some degree or another, the individual involved will display in certain areas the same kind of exaggerated postures between various portions of the self, as the Americans and the Iranians display in their behavior together.

One side will be unable to see or understand the behavior of the other side. Each will seem foreign to the other. The American response—generally, now, speaking—to Iranian emotionalism is to become still more self-righteously reasonable, cooler, more superior. The Iranian's response to the Americans' reason involves new outbursts of emotionalism and behavior that appear utterly irrational to the American view. So we are often indeed faced with a lack of

communication between various portions of the self, or between various portions of the world.

In between you have the nations' concerns about world approval or disapproval, and endless versions of face-saving devices. With the individual, of
course, you have personal versions of the same issues.

Ruburt's intellect and his emotions, working together, work joyfully in his
writing, his psychic endeavors, and his subjective experience in general. They
unite and stimulate his creative abilities so that he does what comes naturally,
easily and vitally to him, searching out his own view of reality—but in certain
areas the intellect and the emotions begin to separate in their visions of the picture of the world. The intellect *(long pause, eyes closed)* disapproves of certain feelings and emotions because the intellect, allied with *(pause)* the social aspects of
reality, thinks in terms of a public face, or respectability, of its position with
other adults in the world.

Some of this is difficult to clarify, because affairs are not really all that
clearly cut *(emphatically)*. *(Long pause.)* When united, the intellect and intuitions do well. The intellect, however, wants the emotions to be perhaps more
respectable than they are, neater, held better in check, well-dressed. It wants
approval from the world. In Ruburt's case, it began to worry that the exuberant,
spontaneous, emotional parts of the self would allow their search for truth and
creativity to get out of bounds, bringing some danger, perhaps, rather than
honor—or at the very least scorn and criticism.

(9:37.) Over a period of time you ended up with two exaggerated postures
—artificial ones—with the spontaneous elements of the personality straining
for the full use of their abilities (in parentheses: value fulfillment), and the reasoning one determined to pursue such endeavors—but with caution. The intellect's reasons, however, were not entirely its own, but only appeared to be
because the opposing camps were so out of communication. The intellect actually quite unknowingly made those reasoning deductions on an emotional basis
from an outdated picture of the world, held jointly by emotions and intellect
years ago in Ruburt's childhood.

(Long pause.) By the very fact that a portion of the self is kept, say, in a sort
of protective custody, it is kept in isolation, which means that it is not kept up
on current events. Like political hostages, it does not get all of the mail—or the
mail it does get is apt to be censored, so it is not operating with a full set of facts.
That alone of course prolongs the difficulty.

The portions of the self kept in protective custody develop certain characteristics just to get by—modes of behavior that perhaps serve to take off some
of the pressure, while ever seeking ways to escape the situation. This applies to

all such instances, of course.

We are now involved with reassuring Ruburt that it is safe to move, and ultimately that it is safe to _relax_. We are trying to reassure him that relaxation is indeed a part of a creative process, and that it also makes all other motion possible. _(Pause.)_ Such a statement can be accepted by all portions of the self, but it must be emphasized time and time again. In the meantime, there can seem to be other reasons, different ones, that crop up to make his attitudes seem more rational. These are part of the modes of behavior adopted by the portion of the self held in custody, so to speak.

At any given time, then, he may not feel it right to relax, because he has thus-and-thus a chore to perform, or because of the hour, or for any other reasons that will all serve to hide the fact that he is _afraid_ of relaxing. He _thinks_ he fears relaxing because then he will do nothing—but instead he is afraid of letting go _because he fears he will go too far_, and put himself in an unsafe position in the world. Some of your own earlier attitudes should help you relate to that kind of rationale.

When you spoke to him this afternoon, telling him it was safe to relax, you helped break his isolation. The person held in protective custody had someone to talk to, and another party to help in the negotiations. A trusted party, a highly important point.

(Long pause at 9:55.) Because the two of you are so involved, your own position is bound to change, and in years previous—_to some extent_, now—you also felt that certain portions of Ruburt's personality should indeed be held in protective custody. For some time you were alarmed only because the _treatment_ given that portion was more severe than you thought it should be. Now you are actively acting as a trusted party, working for the release of the portion held in relative captivity, and your assurances at this point can be extremely important.

Ruburt has also managed to set up a better system of communication, and whenever you begin to pay more attention to your impulses again, you are bound to get off-center at any point. You begin to change the situation. Your impulses immediately begin to broaden your picture of reality, to _uncensor_ the mail, so to speak. Ruburt will naturally seek your aid, however, and your helpful hand, as he moves out of those limited corridors of activity—and so he is. End of session—

("Yes.")

—and a fond good evening.

("Thank you very much, Seth. Good night.")

(10:01 PM. Another excellent session, I told Jane. Her delivery had been mostly fast and emphatic. At the same time she'd acted very uncomfortable, often sitting *ramrod straight as she spoke for Seth; however, she didn't remember any of that behavior now. She'd known Seth was ready to come through strongly, though, and he had.)*

DELETED SESSION
FEBRUARY 4, 1981 8:56 PM WEDNESDAY

(This session may mark the beginning of the most important group of sessions Seth has given so far. Certainly we hope so.

(It came about because of several factors I'll try to list in at least rough chronological order. The first of these would be Jane's nearly extreme physical changes over the past few months, her ups and downs as far as mobility, feelings, aches, restless sleep, etc., are concerned. Seth has said again and again that these changes represent improvements growing out of our better understanding of our beliefs, our artistic/creative work, and indeed our whole life-style. We have tried to go along with his pronouncements, but also have felt numerous misgivings, as may be quite natural.

(Jane's sessions have been very irregular also, and she hasn't worked on Seth's latest book for some months now. Therein lay one of those clues that was right in front of us, yet invisible at the same time. In each Seth book there have been layoffs, so to speak—long or longish periods in between certain sessions, while, usually, we held personal sessions in the interim; these were usually devoted to trying to get at the root causes of Jane's symptoms. This pattern was most pronounced while Seth was producing Mass Events, *but without checking at the moment we remember similar if shorter layoffs while the previous books were being produced. This has always bothered me to some extent, but I usually told myself that was Jane's way of working, and to forget it. It did make for some tricky work writing notes for* Mass Events, *say, to explain these long periods in between certain sessions in the book.*

(I didn't fully grasp the significance of these interludes while working on Mass Events, *not until I reread the other night Jane's paper of December 27, 1980. She'd written that treatise at my request following some remarks she'd made. I'd read it, but it hadn't penetrated sufficiently at the time. In it she tied her eye trouble and other symptoms with her fears about public reactions to her Seth work—her fears of its rejection, etc., and that she might—indeed, has—found herself outside the accepted realms of science, religion, etc., because of her psychic work.*

(As soon as I reread her paper the evening before last, I was reminded of the two excerpts I'd copied from recent deleted sessions—those for January 26 and 28, 1981. In them Seth briefly explained how Jane had created her symptoms as protection against the spontaneous self going too far: this fear was the real reason for the

symptoms—not, as we usually thought, her fear that she would do other things besides work if she had normal mobility. The latter idea is a cover-up for the previous one. To Jane, going too far means that she would find herself in an unsafe position in the world. And to me, as I began to put all of this together, it meant that although she did the Seth books, which we think so highly of, she also drags her feet in resistance with each one—hence the long intervals of non-work that crop up during the production of each one. Again, without checking, I think that an examination of our records would show that her symptoms flared up, indeed worsened, as she worked on each Seth book, and that behind her labors on each book there lay this fear that she was going too far with each one she produced. This fear may be based on outmoded ideas—as Seth has mentioned at various times—it may make no sense, or whatever, yet as long as it exists it must be dealt with. This present session represents, then, our latest attempt to come to terms with all of our personal, public, and creative aspects involved with the Seth material—not just those we'd chosen to deal with in past years.

(Yesterday morning, then, while painting, the thought came to me clearly: Jane does the Seth books just to please me. I knew at the time that this was likely to be an oversimplification, yet I also knew at once that it contained the key to the puzzle; this rather simple idea helped me assemble all of the information already described in these notes, half of it in ways I cannot consciously describe. But it did lead to the discussion I had with Jane this noon [on the 4th], and this session. All at once I had several ideas I wanted to talk over with her.

(Coupled with all of this is the statement Seth made recently to the effect that we "have made no major errors." This is one of those bits of data that I return to much later and begin to question, after having let it pass at the time. "Well, if we've made no major errors," I said to Jane recently, "what do you call the hassles we do have?"' I was—am—quite aware of the humor implicit in the whole situation. At times I for one can agree with Seth, but at other times I have strong doubts.

(This noon after lunch, then—on the 4th—Jane and I had a discussion about the ideas mentioned above. My latest efforts to cope with our challenges involve her letting go of Seth's latest books. Dreams, for some time. That is, we can work on it if we want to, but with no thought of deadlines or signing a contract, which would commit Jane to additional public exposure. The idea is that she'll be free to do what she wants with the Seth material, for as long as she wants to, without our adding fuel to her fears until we've had a chance to work things through. I told her I was sure I was on the right track here, without knowing positively that I was, and without having pat answers that would solve all of our hassles.

(Putting off Dreams, it seemed to me, was a necessity at the moment because I now believed that the long interlude in her dictation was, again, a clear sign of

resistance to the project on Jane's part. The idea is an attempt to at least call a halt to something that she has resisted from the start, or so it seems in retrospect—and I mean the start of the sessions, not just Dreams. *I reminded her that I was the one who first suggested we start publishing the Seth material, and that she'd had reservations about doing that. It seemed to me now that a clear course of hanging back had been displayed by Jane all though our psychic endeavors, and that it could be easily charted if we took the time to do so. I said that she would have probably used her psychic gifts in some fashion in her writing, but that the Seth books might very well have not come into existence except for my own interest—hence my mental insight this morning that Jane did the Seth books to please me. I know things aren't that simple, but I do feel that the fact of public exposure represented by the Seth books has always bothered Jane. And currently she has been bothered more than ever, as she has described in her December 27, 1980 paper. This upset includes her work on her own latest,* The God of Jane.

(I explained that in their different ways both Jane's ESP classes, and the mail, reflect other aspects of public exposure, and that these too must have engendered resistance over the years. [Jane remarked last week to the effect that she wondered how she could get out of answering the mail, for example.] Class had always seemed to offer much, and has helped many people, yet implicit in its very existence was the fact of public exposure concerning unacceptable psychic abilities, in Jane's eyes, I told her. My idea is that both class and mail have had an unfortunate reinforcing effect over the years as far as the symptoms and their attendant fears go.

(Like class, Jane has often been threatened by the mail, only more overtly, as well as by personal visitors who sought us out. Another example of this occurred at noon, when we were visited by two beautiful young ladies—who, unfortunately, were using the Seth material in ways we wouldn't have. All such incidents, I told Jane, reinforce individual actions on the part of readers that would be quite rejected by the establishment: further signs of how far outside accepted thought Jane has found herself over the years. I explained here that I thought this has always bothered her deeply. No reviews in accepted journals, no welcome in the universities by academia, as she herself wrote in God of Jane. *And of course the whole lengthy disclaimer bit for* Mass Events *beautifully sums up the situations: Even our own publisher seeks to protect itself from possible legal action because of the material within the Seth books. Jane sees this as a threat, although she doesn't say much about it. And I for one wonder about disclaimers for future books—or even having them added to past works.*

(Even today's mail, which we read after finishing our discussion, contained several beautiful examples of points I've described above. This brought up another matter—our being confronted with the work we have published, as well as by Mass Events *and* God of Jane. *No way to get away from those fifteen books of the past, I*

said, so to that extent we have to live with the results they engender. I too wondered about dispensing with answering the mail, while being very reluctant to do so, since many of the letters are openly laudatory, and we save them for reference [although we haven't actually used any for such purposes]. But therein lies trouble, too, I said, because they would reflect Jane's concern about public exposure, her fears about leading people astray.

(Putting off the publication of Dreams, *then, is only a ploy to gain some time to defuse the present situation, while Jane's body struggles to right itself as much as possible. We do believe Seth's assessment, to the effect that her body is righting itself in numerous areas after years of disuse, of being held down, but at the same time it's very difficult not to have qualms and doubts about what's happening at the same time. At Christmastime I discussed with Jane the idea of seeking medical help, and asked her to tell me what she thought of this idea later, but she has yet to bring up the subject. I knew she's not in favor of it, but as I said at the time, this seemed to mean that she was indulging the idea of spending the balance of her life sitting down —quite immobile for all practical purposes. I'd told her at the time that I had no great hope that medicine could help much, but still I wondered often enough if the medical profession might be able to offer some sort of help. I didn't want Jane to get so bad that she was forced to turn to doctors, before at least considering outside help. At times I feared something like this would happen if she wasn't able to "pull out" of her symptoms on her own—that is, with her own, Seth's, and my help.*

(I repeated in our discussion that it was perfectly all right with me if Jane chose not to publish any more Seth books, but concentrated on her own works, and she said she understood this. It's my personal opinion, at least of the moment, that it will be quite a while before Dreams *is either finished or printed. At least Jane now has some breathing space, and the cycle of resistance may be interrupted, say, if not reversed yet. We now have time for Framework 2 to operate. In this interim I may do some work on* Dreams *myself, or start something of my own.*

(I also learned during the discussion that Jane didn't like the Seth book material being tied too closely to current events, as witness Mass Events *and Jonestown and Three Mile Island. She reminded me also that even the title of* Mass Events, *when Seth had given it, had alarmed her, or at least aroused some sort of defensive mechanism in her—something I'd forgotten. On the other hand, I'd taken it for granted that the way Seth had used current events in* Mass Events *had been quite natural and extremely informative, offering a much broader view of human affairs. This little dilemma also pointed up some of Jane's other reactions to remarks I would make, innocently enough, I thought, to the effect that Seth could do a great book on any number of current events—the latest being the whole hostage question. She hadn't really been in favor of such endeavors, then, even when she discussed them with*

me.

(Nor, I might add, had I ever pressed her to do books with Seth on current events. It's clear now that she would see such efforts as leaving her too open to public attack. The same goes for appearances on TV—as note our recent involvement with the ABC news offer—and, probably, on radio. In short, then, it seems that any overtures she may choose to make about encountering public reaction to her abilities will —and should be—of her own choosing. Perhaps if she attains a sense of inner peace and protection she will come to naturally make such choices; doing which will encourage her feeling of personal freedom and safety instead of threatening it.

(Perhaps our biggest challenge from now on will be how to deal with the "fallout" from work we've already done—those 17 books out there that are constantly drawing a very mixed group of reactions from people "across the board." Not all of this is bad, of course, and I trust that here again Jane will gradually come to an accommodation with such responses, seeing them not as implied threats, but as true reinforcements of her abilities, which, as we have learned, really do have the power to move others in a variety, and often profound number of ways.

(I've taken the time to write the above notes as much as for a reminder to myself as for anything else, and to start off this session as something special. I did not know whether Jane would have a session or not—yet I was still somewhat surprised when she did offer to hold one tonight. Once again, she'd been "so far out of it," sitting on the couch and watching TV, that I'd given up on hearing Seth comment upon our latest ideas. Jane had been "out of it" for most of the day, except during our talk, which lasted over an hour. I must admit that at this time I'm pretty well puzzled as how to best help her. She was still very uncomfortable each day as bodily changes swept through her. Her backside and legs in particular have bothered her recently. Yet last night it had been her arms and elbows—I'd say that during the night she'd wake me up over a dozen times crying in her sleep at the discomfort in her arms. This morning I discovered that the knots of muscle beneath her left elbow had almost disappeared—an effect I'd never seen before. Instead the elbow was full of fluid. Was this the latest attempt by the body to heal itself by flooding afflicted areas with soothing liquid, say as lubrication, or what?

(As I covered her up for a nap at 4:30 this afternoon, I asked her "how one person could raise so much hell?"—meaning that in line with our talk today I now believed that the whole Seth business, and especially the books, had been conducted in the face of a steady, fierce resistance. One foot dragging the other after it, was a way I'd put it recently. That resistance is the state that we absolutely must dissipate, I think.

(By 8:52, then, Jane said she felt Seth around. She'd perked up a little, although she was still quite bleary-eyed. At the same time she sat quite upright in her

chair, not leaning back, and I read this posture as a sign that she was still very uncomfortable sitting there. She began the session at her usual pace of delivery, but after a few paragraphs slowed down considerably.)

Now—

("Good evening.")

—I will end up covering all of the areas you discussed this afternoon —of course, in my own fashion. We will call this discussion one.

There is some difference, of course, in Ruburt's mind between his attitude toward his books and mine. To some extent this is more than understandable. He would *(pause)*, had I not emerged, written books of his own in any case. He would have encountered no <u>unusual</u> obstacles as far as his public stance was concerned, in that he would have felt the rather characteristic dilemma of some creative writers, who must assimilate the private and public portions of their experiences. He would have had no unusual difficulty, however, in, say, standing up for his own ideas—holding his own, so to speak, in any arguments or philosophies.

He would have been in that case operating himself within the recognizable framework of psychological identity, being himself within the context of personality structure as it would be defined by all. He feels quite competent with his own books. They begin by giving some verbal tribute to old definitions, and then <u>take off from there</u>, having firmly established the fact that he is more or less in the same kettle of fish. In that regard there is little ambiguity.

Now, <u>my</u> books do not pretend to even accept those conventions, but start out from a different viewpoint entirely. That viewpoint alone makes a difference. That viewpoint alone establishes a different kind of pattern. It assumes to know. It speaks of knowledge that is self-evident from my point of view. It offers no apologies for itself. It presupposes a vaster structure of personality and identity, period.

(Now slowly at 9:13:) Ruburt is very highly gifted—extraordinarily so in many respects. The nature of his gift generally speaking, however, presupposes or implies the existence of vast reaches in the psyche—reaches that if *(pause)* unwisely compared to the usual portions of the self, can seem to leave the usual self in a position of inferiority by contrast.

(After breakfast on the morning of the 5th I read this session to Jane before typing it in the afternoon. Seth's statement stopped me in what seemed to be a new way personally—for I don't think I've considered that Jane might even see Seth's own material as in competition—or as even a threat, although I don't care for that word —to her. This whether the material was published or not. Yet Jane said she'd had such thoughts occasionally. I don't recall her telling me

about them, though.)

The books that I have written are excellent conveyors, not only of content but of essence. In a fashion, as far as the psyche is concerned, they come from a portion that is indeed immersed in knowledge that is self-evident.

If I were only—only—a portion of Ruburt's larger psyche, then I would be the portion that knows what it knows: the portion that is concerned with spontaneous knowledge.

Now. Your social systems have very few frameworks that even take such experiences into consideration. *(Pause.)* There are the esoteric schools, for example, the spiritualistic societies, the Eastern traditions. Overall they involve a very small esoteric group. The mainspring of society becomes touched by such groups now and then—but in the world of, say, the usual public encounter there are no accepted frameworks for such experiences.

You have first of all to explain your definition of personality, to attempt redefinitions of a very emotional kind, for when you are speaking of, say, space and time, that is one thing. When you are asking people to reexamine the whole matter of personal identity, you are setting conditions that may frighten many of them. Ruburt feels that he could, for example, explain any of his own books from his own framework quite well. To explain my books is something else again, and in that manner of speaking, my books are self-evident also.

(Long pause at 9:27.) Give us a moment.... There are few people in such a position. He is not cowardly in that regard *(as Jane had speculated during our discussion)*. He was, in fact, quite daring in refusing to accept the conventional spirit-guide dogma—which would at least have given him a kind of psychological covering *(all emphatically.*

(Pause.) He is appalled with the way that many people interpret my material. Sometimes it seems he would prefer even a smaller but more select group of readers *(with amusement)*—readers who were tops in their fields, or who in one fashion or another earned his respect. The point is that our books reach all kinds of readers in all walks of life. That is because all kinds of people are innately acquainted with the nature of self-evident knowledge.

They may misinterpret its nature, project it outside of themselves, turn it into a hobby, a chore, a religion, an art, a rigorous set of laws—but reading my books, they recognize the authority of the inner psyche.

Ruburt and you live in a world with its own cultural taboos, its own assumptions. The idea of personhood is a highly vital one, uniting peoples and societies. The idea of personhood held by the Roman Catholic Church affected the history of the world for centuries, and that idea of personhood is intimately involved, of course, with the idea of personhood's source.

Now Ruburt understood quite well in a fashion that his own experiences were taking him outside of that cohesive framework, not simply outside of science's or religion's dictums, but outside of those areas that science and religion ignored, deplored, or denied (all very intently).

(9:40.) In that regard he felt that he was violating an important cultural taboo, and embarked upon a program that would necessitate caution, self-protection, and a certain detachment. He was determined to go ahead, because his own value fulfillment sought those directions—such was his nature. My published works, however, presented him with what he felt to be a public stance in a different fashion than his own would (louder). My books automatically seemed to suggest a framework of reference to which few others could have access.

(Jane was speaking very intently for Seth through this material. The night was very cold; a bitter wind struck at the house again and again, rattling the blinds in the heavy metal awnings on the western side of the living room where we sat.)

Again, definitions of personality are important here. Ruburt could read poetry without first having to define the nature of a poet. He could meet any criticisms with suitable explanations, since any audience was not about to question the poet's psychological validity. Any arguments would take place within an implied framework of definitions.

Before even hearing the poetry no such audience, Ruburt felt, would question the fact of poetry itself—its techniques, traditions or value. My books, however, by their very existence appear in a world that largely does not concern itself with anything but the most surface elements of psychological reality. (Long pause.) The matter of duplicity almost immediately arises. Ruburt feels the existence of innumerable barriers in that regard—having, he feels, to fend with the questions that ensue.

(Pause.) I must be, as Seth, true or false, fiction or nonfiction, personality essence—spirit, if you prefer—or Ruburt's own psyche in definitions usually accepted, playing at best a dubious role. And to a large degree those questions would be there even if our material quite agreed with the established knowledge of your world—but it does not. It contradicts much of the world's knowledge.

If Ruburt wants to disagree with the world's knowledge, he feels that it is his right—and again, would defend such ideas forthrightly. They would be based upon experiences that are his own—many that you have shared as a result of your own personal experiences together. But Ruburt is not aware of my subjective experience. My self-evident knowledge comes even if I were no more, again, than a part of his larger psyche, from reaches that would be inaccessible in those terms to him *(all emphatically)*. That is, in those terms I would be delivering self-evident knowledge to him, revealing it *(long pause)*, delivering it. I could not hand over the psychological quality of self-evident <u>knowing</u>, however. <u>In that regard</u> he does not have the same kind of inner experience with which to back up my words.

To some extent he lacks the kind of faith in people that I have, because of the belief systems that surround you. It bothers him that some people, he thinks, consider that our books make up another bible or its equivalent, and it seems to him that their lack of <u>understanding</u> in that regard hampers his own creativity.

His attitude <u>can</u> hamper his creativity. Theirs, of course, cannot.

The success of the books brings such questions into prominence, of course, and I will discuss more of those allied concerns.

Give us a moment.... the books themselves—mine as well as his—are themselves indications of achievements *(pause)* that are not easily broken off, since they represent the natural, creative development of his own abilities and growth. They also provide, if you realize it, the solutions to your dilemmas, as I hope you shall shortly see. That is, they provide you with that larger framework of understanding, for the old frameworks of understanding force you to continue to explore your reality for larger definitions. In those areas of concern, then, Ruburt is still involved with too-small definitions.

I will have far more to say, but that is enough for discussion one. I know that it is difficult to understand, but the challenge is one of growth, one that exists in a fashion because you <u>have</u> moved into an ever-expanding framework —but in an uneven course.

In larger fashions you have made no grievous errors. That will become clear as we proceed with this discussion. End of session—

("Thank you, Seth." I said when that worthy paused.)

A fond good evening. This should help relieve some of Ruburt's stress. Read the session of course together. I will also give some pertinent comments more specifically, involving interviews, television, classes and so forth.

("Thank you."

(10:15 PM. Jane came out of trance very heavy-lidded. Then: "I guess it's me —but write this down, if I can get it quickly enough—about creativity and dogma. I think it's in relation to my book dictation."

(I told her the session was excellent, as I'd known it would be. "Yes." she said. "I had the feeling that he was going to get into deeper stuff." All through the session she'd sat stiffly upright in her chair; hardly relaxed. I urged her now to get back on the couch. "I wish I'd done the dishes," she said. There was a day's accumulation of them in the sink. The bitter wind banged the metal awnings outside;

the local forecast was for a temperature of zero degrees to five/ten below. I told Jane I'd do the dishes—and read the session to her from my notes tomorrow morning after breakfast.

(Now it's Friday night [the 6th] as I finish typing this session. Seth's reference to "grievous errors" was obviously in answer to my own comment as recorded in the opening notes. At first when I asked her, Jane said the session hadn't done anything to "relieve some of Ruburt's stress." But then we decided that it had helped her somewhat Thursday and Friday. On Wednesday night she'd had a dream involving our Instream-Oswego experience, and a copy of that is attached under February 5. And she had a pair of positive healing dreams that afternoon during her customary nap. These dreams were quite good.

(Jane's dream about Oswego reminded me of a little episode that I think of every so often, and that I've referred to in a note in one of the books, I think— probably Mass Events: *When I'd asked her once years ago what she wanted to do more than anything else in life, she'd answered quickly, "Change the world." Her conflict can be easily seen, then, manifesting between that idea and her deep-seated need for protection.*

(These notes at the end of the session are meant to round out the opening notes, and to suggest new questions for us and for Seth. The other day I'd told Jane that I had given up on the idea of donating our work and assets to Yale University Library —indeed, that in the year since we'd had our will made out I hadn't sent them any material at all. Jane agreed that the idea of Yale had made her uneasy. I hadn't even answered Larry Dowler's long letter of acceptance beyond sending him a short note of thanks for all his work. Jane, now, did not urge that we contribute to Yale. Our will still commits us in case of accident, say, but that document can be changed.

(After this session was held we briefly talked about things we might do in order to ensure privacy, should we decide to be more active in the pursuit of that quality. There would be moving to a new location, perhaps, or doing something about the mail—answering labors each week. I suppose we might use the post office's impending rate increases as an excuse to save on postage, and either cut way down on, or eliminate, answering the mail, if this will help. I'm willing to do most anything, but our ideas here as yet are very vague, and I haven't discussed with Jane yet whether she thinks a move would do any good, really.

(That topic ties in with my idea that I mentioned to her this afternoon, about it hardly being a coincidence that many events in our lives are coming to a head at the same time: Our deep upset about Jane's condition; the trouble with the disclaimer idea for Mass Events; *Prentice-Hall's reorganization into the General Publishing Division, in which all of their narrative books will be phased out, thus*

eliminating any real need for Tam and his job; indeed, Tam is looking at other job offers even now. [It's been my position for some time now that Tam will end up leaving Prentice-Hall, or will be let go.] If and when he does go, we will be without our friend there, and will have to make decisions based on that departure. But we may be in the process of making such decisions even now, I suspect. I doubt if we would follow Tam helter-skelter to another publishing house if he left Prentice-Hall tomorrow—especially in light of our decision to hold off on Dreams. *And the irony of the situation is that, even though we detest the idea of the disclaimer for* Mass Events, *we see it as another means of protection in the public arena....*

(We are making small decisions about protection along the way, however. Today I mailed Jane's letter to Meredith Wheeler of ABC News, declining MW's second recent invitation to be on that show; and when Tam called this afternoon to tell Jane that a British journalist was at CBS in NYC, and wanted to interview her for a newspaper article, we decided to not call back and okay the interview.

(Today I also reminded Jane about a question we've thought about at other times: Why does the portion of her that's raising such a fuss about protection not understand the damage it's doing to the whole personality—including itself? The circle becomes self-defeating, of course, and as far as I'm concerned reached that status years ago. Yet it persists.... Any hope we have in all of this is that our new stance will allow us to focus on the good things we have in life, and to create a synthesis of old and new ideas that will result in Jane returning to normal mobility. In this session Seth referred to Jane's need for value fulfillment as she explored her psychic gifts. He also stated that our old frameworks of understanding force us to continue to explore reality for larger definitions. All very well, if such explorations can be carried out with a reasonable feeling of safety or protection, evidently, but if that essential ingredient or feeling is missing, then more caution must be used by us— and as I see it, that's where we stand now. The hope is that our hiatus as far as encountering the public goes will give us some valuable time to organize new approaches to our lives.

(I remarked to Jane today that if I'd known what I think I know now, today, a month ago we could have withdrawn Mass Events *from Prentice-Hall, using the disclaimer dispute as an excuse, and delayed its publication for as long as we wanted to. I added that although we'd talked about doing so—and had even mentioned doing so in our letter to the legal department last December—I'd also felt that she wouldn't stand for such an action. Now, it seems that we will have to deal with the public as far as* Mass Events *goes. All of these kinds of reasons apply to* God of Jane *also, as far as I can tell, though probably to a lesser degree.*

(I doubt if finances are a problem, incidentally, as I explained to Jane. We have two books coming out this year; when they earn back their advances there will

be income from them. Many of Jane's other books also produce a yearly royalty income in the meantime. She may do other books than on matters psychic, and these will earn money also. If our income dropped because we committed ourselves to no new books, the royalty and the interest on our savings would be much more than adequate to live on, for then state and federal taxes would melt away. Financially, then, now is an ideal time to experiment with any changes we may want to put into effect. Jane's poetry book is due in 1981; she's started a "Seven."

(As for myself, I have more than enough to do to keep me busy indefinitely. Helping Jane, taking care of the house, typing sessions, working on taxes and other correspondence, filing, painting—these things and many others are more than enough to keep me going indefinitely. And since I will not be doing the formal notes for another Seth book for some time, it now seems impossible that I managed to find as much time as I did to work on the previous books.

(So. we'll take it from here....)

JANE'S NOTES
FEB. 5, 1981

(We had a Seth session for me last PM. Early this morning I awakened, quite sore, and with the vague memory of a dream. It involved a cold unwelcoming room which represented I think the reception of my work or writing. There were things I could do to rectify this though; and in the dream I did this, and awakened....a card table was involved somehow.

(Seth's session may have been in my mind. Anyhow I got the following thoughts at once: that when we were in Oswego so many years ago visiting Instream at the university I discovered that.... my experiences put me outside the pale; on the other side of the fence from, say, the academic circles that I'd so respected; that my experience with other people was going to be vastly different; I thought I was looking for truth, but I'd be one of those under suspicion because of the kind of person into which I'd developed.... This meant.... I'd need protection, some distance from the world.... I'd thought such things before but this was full of emotion.... [Also see healing dream later in the day].... I began to doubt myself, feeling that my natural leanings would lead me into areas considered suspect by others; that instead of rewards, there would be tinges at least of dishonor. (The rewards are considerable though, I admit.)

COPY OF INSPIRATIONAL TYPE MATERIAL
RECEIVED SATURDAY, FEBRUARY 6
AFTER READING PORTIONS OF MY 1973 NOTEBOOK

*Seth as a "master event." As the Mona Lisa is "more real" than, say, a nor-
mal object or the canvas that composes it, so is all good or great art more than its
own physical manifestation. Consider art as a natural phenomena constructed by
the psyche, a trans-species of perception and consciousness that changes, enlarges
and expands life's experiences and casts them in a different light, offering new
opportunities for creating action and new solutions to problems by inserting new,
original data.*

*To confine such creativity to solve life's problems <u>primarily</u> or to direct it pri-
marily in that fashion, limits it and holds it in an improper focus; shackles it.*

*So after getting to the position that yes, these ideas <u>are</u> factual (or even, larg-
er than facts) is okay, good—but only part of the picture, and the premise could
actually be misleading and limiting....*

*We have to go beyond that—the point of problem-solving or problem-focus
—back to stressing the creative larger-than-life aspects, otherwise all we have is a
better problem-solving framework. Nothing wrong with that of course but we're
still in the same arena only our explanations are better than official ones.*

*I've rejected all that kind of hash projected onto Seth's books by others or
myself—the assumptions that Seth must prove himself as a problem solver— or the
importance of functionalism over art.*

*The larger view is that art by being itself, is bigger than life, while spring-
ing from it; that Seth and my books go beyond that simply by being themselves.
They automatically put people in a different vaster psychological space, another
frame of reference, in which a good number of problems vanish or simply do not
apply....*

*To do that, I have to drop those old feelings of responsibility as a primary
focus (to get the ideas out quickly so they can help people, etc.) because those feelings strain the Seth-book framework particularly when I demand that in each
book Seth answers all questions and so forth.*

*Again as with master events, we're dealing with a different framework of
action entirely, where the Mona Lisa is "more real" than the physical properties
that compose it, which is not to deny the validity of the canvas, say. But to discuss
Seth or Seth's ideas primarily from the true-or-false framework is the same thing as
considering the Mona Lisa only from the validity of the physical properties of paint
and canvas; very, very limiting. To "just" say that Seth's ideas are true is to limit
him and us....*

For Seth to comment on our world is okay, but for me to somehow insist that his material offer solutions to all of men's problems is not— instead it limits the sessions creative thrust. The Seth material is supposed to put us in a different psychic position where the problems are solved automatically or are at least diminished or do not apply.... Only not concentrating on the problems brings in the needed extra material to solve them.

The mechanics of publishing have to come last. I've felt that I should "push" the material, go on television or whatever to demonstrate and promote it, but that is the "wrong" level for me.... The strong ideas of responsibility are limiting too; they put you in a less creative framework, stifle creativity. I've hampered my own psychic development and possible new books by such focuses which generate their own paranoiac-like fears.

My "work" is not adjacent to the world or parallel exactly but at a different level.... and speaking engagements, etc., would limit it to specifically to human problems.... I don't have to "live up" to anything, I don't have to "make the material work" or prove through my actions that it does because it proves itself in the way that creativity does, by being beyond levels of true-false references. Otherwise, I'm at cross purposes with myself.

DELETED SESSION
FEBRUARY 9, 1981 10:05 PM MONDAY

(We almost didn't have the session. An unexpected visitor arrived at about 8 PM—Walter from Connecticut—and Jane talked to him for at least half an hour. Then she did the dishes, and so forth. All this time she was so uncomfortable in her chair that I thought she'd pass up the session, although I'd been hoping she'd get at least a little something on herself; I thought we shouldn't be losing any chances to do so at this time.

(Finally she called me for the session at 9:40 PM. Again she struggled to get comfortable, just as she'd done for last Wednesday night's session. Walter is a nice young man. I went back to working on taxes while Jane talked to him, and at the same time found myself wondering whether his unexpected visit might symbolize one of the very facets of Jane's dilemma about privacy versus the public life—at least as I understand it: Her vulnerability and availability to anyone who chooses to come here. We can't get away. Others must know this, by whatever means, and may take advantage of her immobility. Walter, for example, told us that when he woke up this morning he decided to go see Jane Roberts—so he just came. [This was his second visit, the first being a couple of years ago.]

("Walter wants to be 'a great psychic teacher' like me or Cayce," Jane said as we waited for Seth to come through. He therefore expressed an attitude typical of many visitors or those who write—attitudes that really bother Jane. "I didn't feel good when he came in." Jane continued, "but at the same time I enjoyed talking to him. He energized me and I forgot my troubles...." Walter didn't stay too long, as noted, because I'd asked him not to. In this case at least, then, Jane had reacted positively to someone drawn to her by a public aspect of her abilities.

(Jane had remarked the other day that she thought Seth would talk about her reaction to class and the mail—topics discussed in the opening notes for the last session. I was also still thinking about her reaction to the sessions themselves: the idea that she could feel inferior to Seth and/or the material was, as I noted, a pretty new one for me, and somewhat surprising. Yet Jane had said recently that such thoughts had come to her. See page 289 of the last session. I noted there that I didn't recall her telling me about such feelings.

(She'd spent considerable time today looking over her 1973 notebook/journal, and combining new notes with fresh insights arising from that old material. We went over it together; she is to type it together before long, when it will be added to a session.

(I suggested now that Seth talk about Jane's very uncomfortable state concerning her backside, hips and legs. At the same time, her neck was so relaxed that her head kept dipping down. I said I felt that her fears were behind much of her hip discomfort, and she had admitted to feelings of fear several times lately—including today when she did her notes. She finally felt Seth around at 9:55. She still sat stiffly upright in her chair as we talked a bit and waited. Finally: "I guess I'm about ready, but I think it'll be short....")

Good evening.

("Good evening, Seth.")

Now: Ruburt for a while should write his own impressions of encounters such as this evening's, or such as the visit of the two girls *(from Columbus, Ohio a few days ago).*

Through writing such notes, and exploring his <u>feelings</u>, his own attitudes will come more clearly to mind. In any case he should begin again writing about his feelings. He is in a way a different kind of psychologist, examining the nature of psychological reality from different viewpoints. He did not simply accept "mediumship" at its face value, so to speak. *(Long pause.)* Most people, generally speaking, have one more or less familiar notion of a self that they try to actualize within physical reality. *(Pause.)* They do not have visions or experience, again generally speaking, with any characteristics that cannot be actualized more or less within the framework of established experience.

They try to actualize that self within the known world. Ruburt uses abilities that do not fit that known world's categories—abilities that by their nature strad-dle many dimensions of activity, none of them normally conventional, normally established, none of them easily defined. As a <u>physical person</u> Ruburt can only actualize himself through the properties of his creaturehood, yet he is aware of those other tantalizing activities.

He encounters the invisible organization of my books, say, the effect of those books upon others. He recognizes the vast complexity that lies behind our rela-tionship, and therefore is ever aware of psychological issues encountered by few other people, relatively speaking. His relationship with me, and mine with him, is bound to be interpreted in multitudinous ways by our readership, the public and so forth. To some extent *(pause)*, there can be a feeling of inferiority on his part *(pause)*, one that he does of course not deserve. He focuses in the world, and I do not.

(So here again, we have a reference to Jane's possible feelings about Seth and what he does, regardless of whether his labors may be eventually published as "a Seth book."

(10:20.) A good portion of my abilities, knowledge, and so forth, is avail-able to me because I am <u>not</u> focused within your world. My abilities are put together in a different fashion. I have a certain freedom by nature that is *(pause)* "traded in" by mortal people in return for life's brilliant focus. *(Long pause.)* Ruburt is <u>not</u> responsible for other people's conceptions of who or what I am, or who or what he is. They will make such interpretations on the basis of their own devel-opment and understanding, interpreting it through their own systems of value.

He is dealing with still-largely unknown phenomena, so that he has, of course, no pat answers to fall back upon. I will return to this subject later. What it means in the context of tonight's discussion is that he feels there is no established framework that he will accept to explain our relationship in, say, the public arena <u>outside of the books</u>, which allow him to make considered statements, and pro-vide room for reasoned thought.

Public interviews involve him, therefore, in far more than the selling of books, you see, connected with the tours of people who are merely writers. To that degree he feels at a certain disadvantage. If he simply did not want to make any public statements outside of the books themselves, there would be no problems there. He simply would refuse. If he were poorly equipped to speak in public there would be no problem. He found out, however, that he <u>could</u> (underlined) speak well.

The trouble is that he tries to live up to an idealized image. That image in a way is a potpourri, picked up from his readers, even other books, the culture in general. He thinks that ideally he should want to be a public person, to give and enjoy giving interviews to the press or television, that he <u>should</u> (underlined) carry our message out into the world, have sessions on television so that people can see how I operate *(with amused emphasis)*. If he were not frightened, it seems to him that is what he would and should do.

(Pause at 10:35.) He also feels he should (underlined) be able to display at least enough healing ability to help those in dire straits *(pause)*, and he expects himself to display such a deep understanding and compassion for the world and its people that any divergence from such an attitude seems to make him appear more inferior by contrast. In that regard, tell him that my own fine tempered consideration of men's foibles is somewhat easier to come by, since I do not deal with them daily. He feels pressured, therefore, to become a public person, forgetting his own background and temperament.

He thinks that that background and temperament should no longer apply. That is, if once he disliked crowds, a new purpose and understanding should let him rise above such nonsense—but there has always been a kind of singularity there *(long pause)*—a characteristic need to go his own way. This does not mean that he has no need for expression. Small groups are one thing, large ones something else. The private context was the home, when you had classes. He likes encounters with other people, naturally, but he does not like crowds nor speaking to a kind of mass mind, directly encountered.

(Long pause.) He felt that he was supposed to be a different kind of person than he is. We will deal with some of this under the heading of responsibility later. In all probability, however, someone who was that publicly attuned would not be able to have our own kind of sessions to begin with, for the mixture of abilities would be of a different sort.

Ruburt should do some small amount of writing each day—for his own pleasure and expression. It is disconnected from ideas of publishing, though later it may be published. *(Pause.)* The responsibility for each person's life lies with that person. That (underlined) is one of our main messages. The books offer their own continuing educational process for people to follow if they choose, and the process of self-discovery is one of the most valuable aspects of such growth. So Ruburt is not to be taken in by people who come here or write, expecting him to solve their problems in the flesh, or expecting me to do it. Nor is he obligated to answer mail.

A note: Ruburt's discomfort is indeed aggravated by fears. This I mentioned in particular some time ago *(long pause)*. He feels he is facing the nitty-gritty, determined for a way out, yet still at times he is afraid the worst possibilities will occur instead, and he is suspicious of changes in the body unless they are of obvious improvements. You have been of considerable help, assuring him that he is indeed protected, and he has been making strides there himself.

He tried too hard at times, however, so that again he concentrates upon the problem in an attempt to solve it, which aggravates the fears. Motions are being restored in terms of circulation and activity—joints, ligaments, nerves and muscles all being involved. Even a very brief massage on your part in the night when he is bothered would help. Your reassurances then are also invaluable.

Moist heat will also help as an aid, but mainly the entire idea of the body's good intent and support. The writing down of feelings, and some free writing, will also benefit along with the discussions of feelings you have embarked upon. A lighter hand, however, on Ruburt's part: We are not looking for realms of negative feelings in particular, but for the honest expression of <u>feelings</u>, whatever they are.

End of session, and I bid you a fond good evening. He should feel quite a bit better shortly.

("I hope so. Good night."

(11:02 PM. "I remember some—not much," Jane said. And once again, I told her, she had given an excellent session.

(In some way portions of Seth's material tonight triggered an awareness of my own—not a new one, yet it seemed somehow that it was quite significant. Simply that the whole hassle Jane and I are involved in first showed itself—clearly—when we met with Instream in Oswego, and encountered the disbelieving young nameless psychologist. I found myself reviving Jane's hesitation on the jungle gym at the park on the lake at Rochester; we'd stopped there on our way home from Oswego, and brother Dick had taken us to the lake.

("I didn't trust myself up there at the top of that thing," Jane said. "That was the first time I had trouble with my physical body, that I didn't trust it. And I knew we were going to go home and start that series of tests for Doctor Instream...."

DELETED SESSION
FEBRUARY 11, 1981 10:00 PM WEDNESDAY

(Yesterday evening, when I began to massage Jane's calf muscles, I discovered that those areas were looser, more "floppy," than I'd found them to be in some years. Their new state didn't yet match that of her thighs, but it was much better nevertheless. I thought that if her legs attained equality in their states of looseness, that she would find it much easier to straighten and strengthen them.

(My "discovery" cheered Jane considerably, and she mentioned it several times today. Especially did she comment upon the fears she encounters at bodily changes. Seth has mentioned her fears at times recently; so have we; still, I asked that if she had a session tonight Seth might give some information on the fears. Easing them, I said, would certainly help her body generally.

(Jane had spent a lot of time today either on the couch or the bed [in the latter case making notes], and seemed to be better, generally speaking. After supper she grew particularly relaxed on the couch. I tried to let her know, without pushing, that a session tonight would be helpful, that I wanted to take advantage of the opportunity to learn more. Jane decided to have a session by 9:30, then. "I'm so sleepy I could go right to bed. If only I could just feel him around. It's sure quiet...."

(She tried to get comfortable in her chair. It was quiet in the house, and outside, too. We've been undergoing extremes of weather lately. Today it was raining at 52 degrees; now it's 25 above and snowing, with a low close to zero predicted. The new snow covered the bare ground evenly and whitely.

(A reminder: Each morning after breakfast we've been reading a session and having a discussion about it and matters in general. All our own sessions have been beneficial, I'd say. In these recent sessions Seth has several times referred to points he wants to go into in more detail later. My next project is to start a list of these points so that we make sure they're covered.

(I've also thought of making a list of pertinent points—one liners, say —that are especially good, from these sessions. Seth comes through with great statements like that in just about every session, I'd say.

("Well, I guess I'm about ready," Jane finally said, "but I do really think this will be short." She'd said something very similar before launching into the last session, too. Re 458 below: The number of "our" apartment house in Elmira, NY.)

Now—

("Good evening.")

—there are hidden aspects involved with creativity, of course—stages of development that do not show.

In one way or another many artists of whatever kind seek to physically express these innermost overtones. As Ruburt mentioned, years ago in Sayre he would find someplace in your apartment that seemed somehow secret for his workroom. He would then momentarily, for a while, withdraw from the workaday world. On other occasions he would write nighttimes, letting those hours by themselves create their own moods of secrecy and isolation from the social environment.

Sometimes back then he would not even tell you of projects until he was certain they had jelled. He did not want to talk them out ahead of time.

(Pause.) In later life the trend continued, as per many examples at 458 *(and as we have discussed today)*. That creative kind of withdrawal is quite healthy, psychologically pertinent, and creative. As some of his other less auspicious ideas came into prominence, however, that natural healthy withdrawing tendency was also used <u>to some extent</u> (underlined) as a framework that was

overextended. As the feeling that he needed protection grew, the need for relative isolation grew also. You live in a social world, so the symptoms also served as face-saving devices.

Ruburt had a reason for not going on tour, for example—one that was certainly acceptable enough in a world of conventional understanding. He was saved, so it seemed, from endless explanations; so with a kind of psychological economy that worked far too well for a time the symptoms served to keep him writing at his desk, to regulate the flow of psychic activity, making sure of its direction, and to provide a suitable social reason to refrain from activities that might distract him—from tours or shows, and also even from any onslaught of psychic activity that might follow any <u>unseeming</u> (underlined) spontaneous behavior.

The fact that some isolation suits you both made the affair palatable enough in the beginning. The idea of a public life—to some extent, now—has hung over his head, so to speak, <u>almost</u> like a threat. He told himself that if he were using his abilities as he should, he would then naturally seek out their public expression.

He took it for granted that, ideally speaking, he <u>should</u> do such public work, that it was his responsibility, but also that it represented a natural <u>expression</u> of abilities that he was denying because of his fears. So often he told himself that if he got better he would only be too glad to go on television or whatever, or to do whatever he was supposed to do.

(Pause at 10:20.) It goes without saying that this is all black and white thinking. He writes his own books because writing is such a natural part of his expression. It is his art. Ideally it is his play as well, and his books serve as his own characteristic kind of public expression, fulfilling the most private and the most public poles of his psychological activity.

He did not start out being a public speaker, for example. He likes the distance between himself and the public that books provide *(emphatically)*. He is excellent at communicating ideas in writing or vocally, gifted in understanding people—so those abilities do come to his aid in public speaking engagements.

(Long pause.) In such engagements, however, for him at least, that necessary private threshold is crossed, endangered. The inner psychological distance must become surfacely portrayed, instantly translated to the audience, so that for him there is the same kind of reaction that he might have in talking to others overly much about a book of his own in progress—as if he might <u>talk out the book</u>, and therefore not need to write it, while at the same time losing much of the inner development that might otherwise give the book its own deeper meanings.

So while he can indeed speak well publicly, that kind of contact does not come easily for him. He might plunge into it at the occasion, but not naturally seek it out. This does not mean he does not enjoy discussing his work with others, with individuals or small groups, carefully chosen or at home, or that he does not enjoy reading poetry, say, on those occasions.

He has, however, held it over his head that if he improved he should then do such work—and that only fear held him back. He was afraid that the spontaneous self would go overboard in that direction. It is the spontaneous self, of course, as much as any other portion of the personality, that often <u>spontaneously</u> holds back when such issues are considered—the part that is somehow spontaneously offended—a very important point to remember. So the reasoning: "Get better, then you can go out into the world to go on television or whatever," or "Once you get better, you will be delighted to go on television and tell your story"—those directives simply make the issues more muddy.

(Long pause at 10:35. This turned into a one-minute pause.) The public arena *(pause)* is not so frightening. It is more factual to say that it goes against the grain as far as Ruburt is concerned. On top of that, however, you have the unconventional aspects of his own work that involves at least some controversy. *(Long pause.)* If Ruburt wrote other kinds of books—mysteries, for example, or straight novels—he would of course have no trouble explaining them in the public arena. But he would not find that arena <u>anymore to his overall liking</u>.

The important point is that he has felt that he should perform publicly, to promote our ideas, and also because he felt <u>he should do so, since he obviously could do so</u> *(all intently)*.

Added to that you have the issue mentioned earlier, of my relationship with him and vice versa, and his idea of an idealized self. Now it is that idealized self he is seeing in his mind that should find it so easy and natural to triumph in the public arena, solve people's problems, always be compassionate and understanding, and certainly not critical of mankind's foibles.

In that area of thinking, any one interview that is offered becomes a testing ground. The news broadcast *(for ABC)* for example: Suppose he did say yes, he has thought, and even managed to get by with it in his present condition—how many other such interviews might then be offered? With Sue's book there have been other opportunities—people who wanted the story from the horse's mouth, so to speak, and the talk from Prentice of a new campaign publicizing Ruburt's work. Ruburt didn't feel free to simply admit that he did not like the public arena. He felt he needed excuses, or in his own eyes and the eyes of others he would seem to be a coward.

Now this idealized self was primarily Ruburt's—but <u>to some extent also</u>

you contributed to it, feeling that anyone as gifted as Ruburt, if he were sure enough of himself, would indeed want to go out in that arena and press forward. You both felt a sense of schism between Ruburt's physical condition and a hypothetical image of Ruburt as someone getting my material and ideally embodying it, so that if not perfect at least the main aspects of the life were smoothed out without contrasts. *(Long pause.)* In that regard indeed Ruburt felt as if he could not live up to my creative work—as if his physical being must embody all of the knowledge that came to him through our sessions—another important point.

(A very important point, I think. See my note at the end of the session.

(10:55.) Some of the members of your readership added to the pressure, of course *(long pause)*. Behind all that you have earlier aspects of Ruburt's life, involving habits of secrecy developed in childhood, the need for protection and so forth, that simply served to help build the framework. The young woman *(Jane)* found herself extremely uncomfortable to find your family members living together in one house—astounded by the thought of the family together in a trailer, frightened of the camp get-togethers. She could be expected to have some difficulties when presented with the thought that she should speak to gatherings of perhaps a thousand people or more, and that this was indeed her responsibility, all other feelings to the contrary.

If Ruburt had wanted to join the public arena, nothing would have kept him out. The feelings of resistance do not signify cowardice, but quite spontaneous objections to activities that largely go against his grain, and certainly when they are presented in such a black or white framework to begin with.

He is not expected by me to set up an organization. *(Long pause.)* He does not have the responsibility to see to it that as many people as possible view a session.

Now spontaneously he would give more sessions for others, quite happily and easily, but in the framework of the situation, the black or white aspect holds back such expression. *(Pause.)* He would probably see more groups, as you both did at 458 together, were it not for the black or white thinking, but this would be in response to quite spontaneous urgings to do so. *(Pause.)* The spontaneous self can quite spontaneously say no—and most of his spontaneous feelings toward the public arena are those of quick natural rejection.

The radio shows from the house pleased him for some time, but they also became taboo because he feared they might lead to other engagements of a more public venture that would be difficult to refuse. We are getting some of this through to him—hence the bodily responses, and relaxations. The last few sessions should be read carefully and kept in mind.

End of session, unless you have a question.

("Nope." I had some, actually, but could see that it was time for Jane to get out of her chair.)

I bid you then a fond good evening.

("Thank you, Seth. Good night."

(11:12 PM. "It's amazing," Jane said with a laugh, after I said she really got going in the session. "I kept waiting and waiting and waiting—so I thank you for helping me have the session."

(It's Thursday night [2/12] as I finish typing this session. As I typed the paragraph on page @38-39 of the material, I had the insight described below. I think it came to me because of my concern recently over the new idea I'd come across—concerning Jane's ideas about her relationship with Seth, her feelings about her abilities versus his, etc. I must admit that I am still rather surprised to understand, finally, that Jane has entertained feelings of inferiority about her abilities as related to those of Seth.

(I made quick notes about my insight just now. and transcribe them below without much elaboration. I would say they represent simplistic thinking to some degree—but that, again, I've hit on something here that hasn't been expressed in just this way before. I feel the same mechanisms for understanding operated here as did when I had the insight of February 3—see the deleted session for February 4 [the first in this new series], wherein I wrote that Jane "does the Seth books just to please me." I think that insight is connected to the following:

("The issue is, basically, that Jane feels and fears that Seth—the Seth phenomena—could overwhelm her and take over eintirely if she ever permitted it to—subjugating all else that she holds dear; her own talent, her own personality even, so that she would become merely a spokesperson for Seth."

("Naturally, she wouldn't ever let Seth say this, especially without coaxing. All else would come after this primary, basic fear—her dislike of going public, especially when she found out that Seth could easily win a large audience in the country, and perhaps the world. The opposition of science and religion would only reinforce her own personal fears, then—a very important point. She knew she had the ability but feared the consequences of its use socially and personally. At the same time she wanted to use the ability but keep it under control."

("It would be easy for her to transpose that basic fear of the psychic abilities and Seth into a fear of spontaneity going too far, and of not working at her desk. The intellect wouldn't dare give too much leeway to the psychic expression, while at the same time being fascinated by the affair and wanting to study it all. But the intellect would insist upon keeping rigid control, fearing that if Jane let her spontaneous self hold sway that it would go whole hog psychically, in the worst way, and destroy

all other elements and activities of the personality."

("Jane then wanted to do the Seth books and not do them. All of this reflects black or white thinking, of course. Jane could have ended up in as much trouble by not doing the Seth books as she did by doing them, then. As long as repression was used in either direction the whole personality would suffer. What is vital is that the whole personality understands each of its portions, accepts and believes in them, and trusts in their expression. All else in life would flow from that balanced creative free state of being. All portions of the personality will automatically integrate themselves with the others to the benefit of all. Then decisions can be easily made about what activities to pursue in daily life: what books to write, how to deal with the public, etc."

(Much could be added to all of this, of course. I want to get Jane's comments, and have Seth discuss it. Beneath the familiar parts I think there is something new here.

DELETED SESSION
FEBRUARY 17, 1981   9:51 PM TUESDAY

(See the attached material that Jane received on February 6. It's very good, of course, and as far as I can tell contains the key to Jane's problems. She's received more on her own like this material, yesterday and today, but hasn't typed it yet from her notes.

(No session was held last night, obviously, because Jane was so relaxed. She'd felt better through the day, and had slept well the night before. She also slept well last night, and felt better today. Earlier she'd mentioned having a session to make up for last night, but as 9 PM passed I thought she'd decided to let it go once again because of her relaxed state. Once again she was very comfortable on the couch after supper, watching the news on television; in fact, for some days now she'd had her best times, as far as feeling better go, while relaxing after supper.

(Note that tonight's session refers to the notes I wrote "on inspiration" at the end of the last session, for February 11. These concern my insight—a simplistic one to be sure—that one of Jane's hassles results from her fear that Seth would take over if given the chance. My notes bothered her somewhat when she first read them, and she'd mentioned them several times since. Note, however, that I wrote that she feared Seth would take over—not necessarily that he would if given the chance—a big difference. But Seth seems to lay to rest our concerns here this evening.

(At the same time, Jane also liked my concluding material in the notes, regarding the integration of each portion of the personality into one whole, and so thus

attaining the freedom to follow any chosen course of action in the world.

(I mentioned black and white thinking in the notes, and Seth has also used that phrase several times recently. I remarked to Jane today, then, that what we need is more insight into the phenomenon of such thinking itself—for after all, that approach to life's challenges has led to our problems, it seems to me. I meant, of course, that all of us indulge in such black and white thinking at times, on some subjects, and I added that I periodically have to catch myself when I overreact to certain events. The question is why the personality would choose to use black and white thinking to begin with, when the results are so often deleterious to the whole personality, if we can just dissolve such approaches.... I'd like Seth to comment.

(Once again Jane said the session would be short; she began speaking for Seth at a good pace.)

Now: generally speaking, Ruburt enjoys our sessions, and considers them with a natural zest.

This applies—again, generally speaking—whether or not actual book dictation is involved. Difficulties arise, however, in book dictation on those occasions when he becomes too heavy-handed and worries about the responsibility of helping to solve the world's problems—about his or my capacities in that regard, and when he considers the possible and various objections that any given subject matter might activate on the part of any given group of people. So if the area becomes too sensitive we let dictation go for a while. Sometimes I insert the particular material in your private sessions first of all, so that he becomes somewhat acclimated to it.

The only other times there is any such difficulty also involve responsibility when he concentrates upon his responsibility to hold the sessions—that is, when he focuses upon need, function, or utility <u>as separate from</u> other issues involved. Such feelings can then for a while override his natural inclinations and his natural enjoyment and his natural excitement with which he otherwise views our sessions.

(Rather intently:) He would not have had the sessions to begin with over this period of time for your sake alone, or even for your sake <u>primarily</u>—they simply would have petered out. You do have a large role to play, however, and I will go into that more clearly along with the way that you might have sometimes misread some of your own attitudes. Nothing, however, would have kept him at the sessions for this amount of time unless he wanted them.

There are, also, natural rhythms, as I have mentioned, and it is understandable enough to take breaks now and then whether or not you even understand why you want them. When you are concentrating upon responsibility, however, then each lapse becomes a lapse from responsible action, and complicates the inner spontaneous rhythm that to a large degree is automatically maintained.

Use your abilities (underlined); a fine idea, a good policy, an excellent course—but not when it is considered a commandment.

(10:05.) Ruburt's abilities—and your own, for that matter—came to light because they are natural characteristics of your beings. They bring you enjoyment, fulfillment, understanding, excitement, discovery. Now that can be said of your painting and of Ruburt's poetry. Ruburt writes poetry by himself, but left alone, enjoys reading it later to others. *(Pause.)* In a strange fashion he does not feel a responsibility to write poetry—he doesn't use the ability because he thinks that <u>he should</u>. In fact, sometimes he writes poetry when he thinks that he should not be doing so, but instead doing something more responsible.

Now basically he has the sessions because he enjoys them, and so do you. On top of that, however, the whole idea of responsibility has played an over-heavy hand, and it is this idea of responsibility—<u>overplayed</u>—that is to a large degree responsible for the idealized image of the public person with which Ruburt has unsuccessfully tried to compete.

It seems to him as if he would—<u>if he were using all of his abilities as he should</u>—be a public figure. He would also be far more capable of helping people solve their problems through some kind of therapeutic framework. *(Pause.)* He would see to it that as many persons as possible had the opportunity to see a session, and he would furthermore also be developing his own psychic experience at a far greater rate. Against that kind of image, he feels inferior.

(Pause.) You had some time ago an old newspaper article you had saved, on the dangers of using the words "should" or "would" too often—and there is perhaps nothing else you could do that is as detrimental to the true development of the natural self. Part of the difficulty in what Ruburt thinks of as the development of his abilities, or the more frequent insertion of inspirational work of his own, is the very fact that he feels so responsible to so thusly perform. All of these issues are highly important. The idea of responsibility, as described here, blocks creativity, hampers natural psychic and physical flow: "I <u>should</u> be doing thus and so." "What do I like to do? What do I feel like doing? What makes me feel good?" Those questions are far more pertinent. When you want to do something truly there are usually few real impediments. Desire flows freely into action.

(10:20.) Our books and sessions are primarily a celebration of life, not a justification of it, or an excuse or apology for the conditions of physical reality.

Ruburt's own material of late is excellent, and will help enlarge the picture. It came spontaneously and clearly. His body has been attempting to relax.

When he feels like so doing, then such activity or lack of it is precisely what is needed at the time, and he need not feel that he <u>should</u> be doing something else.

I will go into the question of Ruburt's attitude toward me very shortly, as per your own question in a note. There is some application there, but the larger one applies to his own ideas of what someone in his position <u>should</u> (underlined) be doing, and the idealized image is partially a construct to which you also added details unwittingly in the past.

If you would remember natural selves, and your <u>own</u> characteristics, you would have a much better, clearer idea of what to realistically expect from yourselves, and you would let other ideas go when they conflict with your own quite definite inclinations. The full potentials of Ruburt's abilities and of our work will result from following the natural contours of your beings, from whose resources your own individual and joint problems can also be eradicated.

An organization is obviously not characteristic of two people who are very largely loners. Any kind of <u>extensive</u> public life cannot be reasonably expected from two people who value privacy to the extent that you both do. This does not mean, again, that black and white thinking is not involved. Ruburt has been straining to live up to an unreasonable image—<u>sometimes</u> with your unwitting assistance—an attempt that certainly has made him drag his feet, and one that is exhausting.

Again, the old feelings about spontaneity of course apply, so read this session remembering other ones. I have myself in the past given a good deal of information about the conflicts that can arise when Ruburt overemphasizes the idea of work as opposed to creativity.

(*Pause.*) Most people work so many hours, then relatively speaking follow their pleasures to whatever extent possible. Because you have no set hours in that regard, Ruburt has filled all of them with "I should do this," or "I should be doing that," or "What should I be doing now?" —and that alone blocks creative flow.

It is further inhibited if that sense of responsibility is wedded to solving the problems of the world or of correspondents, or when such an attempt is allowed to tinge any book sessions. I am not here referring to *Mass Events*, which was indeed directed toward the condition of the world, but to matters—whatever they may be—where Ruburt feels a responsibility <u>on his part</u> (underlined) for me to dictate specific material that might answer questions he thinks scientists or others might have in mind about any given subject matter; for I write from a different viewpoint, and our material is of course not to be dictated in any (*pause*) <u>important way</u> by the statement of your official knowledge at any given time. It is to rise beyond such categories. It is to present a larger thematic framework, which then can be used to put the world together in a different fashion for those who want to do so.

(Pause at 10:40.) In that regard Ruburt's material is correct; simply by being itself our material serves its purpose—and its purpose is multitudinous.

Remember what I told you some time ago, though you have made excellent strides in that regard, apropos natural man, in contrast to what you may think you <u>should</u> (underlined) be doing, in terms of any idealized self with characteristics that are not your own.

End of session. Now Ruburt had the session because he spontaneously felt like having it—and my heartiest regards to both of you.

("Thank you very much, Seth.")

(10:42 PM. "Well, I'm glad I did that," Jane said. "I sat there thinking about it for fifteen minutes before I called you. I thought I should be doing the dishes.... I really want to read that one—I think there's stuff in it that will help me right away....")

(And as usual, I told her, I'd read it to her at the breakfast table.)

JANE'S SILVER DREAM FRAGMENT
FEBRUARY 14, 1981

I awakened toward morning with my body quite sore and with the memory of an earlier dream scene. I had come into a room to find some kind of religious talk going on, people in folding chairs; I'm rather surprised. I'm obviously interrupting so I sit down gingerly till the affair is over. Later a woman puts me in charge of cleaning up the silverware—perhaps used for refreshments at the meeting. I tell the "help" that this isn't my cup of tea, they will have to help; at the same time I discover that this isn't the best silver as I'd thought but serviceable enough stuff. I don't think the good silver had been used. My body hurt from polishing the stuff....

Just before awakening I'm aware of my body's soreness and think it's from caring for the silverware, which wasn't even the best silverware; that somehow the silver represented my psychic ability.... or just abilities in general, and being so careful of them turned me into their servants....

The dream comes to mind several times but don't type it up till the weekend. I did jot it down immediately though, feeling that it was significant. There was a feeling of disappointment connected and I'd say that it represents some feelings about my abilities—I thought they were sterling—really terrific—and wore myself out caring for them, but I fear that they are only very good serviceable ones after all, their earlier promise not proving true.... or that my over-care of them has turned them into functional serviceable tools.... implements for nourishment rather than the elegant more artistic connections of sterling silver—which is itself beautiful while also serving a function.... The earlier religious scene suggests that I was appalled to find my abilities leading me anywhere within the realm of religious ideas at all to start with. By being so careful with the abilities—actually because I valued them, I end up being their servant, but actually end up using my abilities at the service of others—to help save the world, solve problems, etc.... gain being overly concerned with their utility....

DELETED SESSION
FEBRUARY 18, 1981 9:55 PM WEDNESDAY

(I was typing the first portion of last night's session when I heard President Reagan giving his anxiously awaited first address to Congress; he spoke on economic issues mainly. I took a break at 9:15 to watch some of his speech on TV. Jane was relaxed on the couch as usual. Eventually, however, she surprised me by saying she'd try for a session. Earlier today she'd said she would have one tomorrow night instead.

(The president finished speaking. As the minutes passed and we sat waiting, I asked Jane what she was thinking about. She said she'd decided to hold the session because she "should" have it—whereas last night's session had been quite spontaneous: she'd wanted to do it. Which raised some intriguing questions about the sense of responsibility she would still feel—indulging that very quality we're supposed to be so on the lookout for. On the other hand, given our present work orientations the sessions would have to happen sometime during the week—at least twice—and it didn't seem reasonable to think that Jane would have every one of those on the spontaneous spur of the moment. Somehow, somewhere along the line, some sort of responsible decision to have them would be made....

(I'll note my question here so that it won't be forgotten, although actually I mentioned it to Jane after tonight's session had been held. Simply, I thought it would be a good idea if Seth would tell us about what <u>good things</u> we've managed to accomplish through the years as far as Jane's symptoms go. It would be nice to know what hassles we've surmounted, that no longer apply. This would seem to imply that others had come along, or been developed by us, to take their place—at least something had been created to take their place. But surely we've accomplished some beneficial things too.

(Jane's delivery as Seth was quite animated and brisk.)
Now—

("Good evening.")

—there are different kinds of value systems, each quite workable according to the types of individual who holds them.

People are propelled to act in highly individual ways: what makes one man go forward can make another go backward. As a general rule the production of any kind of art is a private one <u>initially</u>. That art may add to the richness of society, to culture—but art always possesses its own secretive inner nature, and with that nature each artist of whatever kind must always relate.

At its very basis, regardless of all tales to the contrary, art is indeed love's production. Ruburt writes because he <u>loves</u> to write—the activity of itself is intriguing, again, it is a method of discovery and accomplishment, of celebration. It is natural for him to be inspired.

There are manuals that are written <u>primarily</u> (underlined) as textbooks or as guides to help others, in which there is no attempt made to create an art, but to state a case. In a way these are the result of two different kinds of value systems: art for its own sake, produced out of love, or texts produced primarily for the benefit and instruction of others. In the second case the value is first of all to help others by stating as clearly as possible known facts about particular subject matters such as health or what have you.

Ruburt is involved with the production of art. It subverts art's nature to some extent when it is asked to serve another master, however beneficial that master may seem to be—for art by its nature will always come up with surprises, and deals not so much with specifics or with directions as with overall patterns that must always be free to fall in fresh and unexplored directions.

(An excellent definition....)

If you are overconcerned with helping others, then you must first of all begin to question whether or not your creative material, still forming, will serve that purpose, and if not, or if there is a question, you give birth to hesitations and doubts that—again—subvert art's free flow. An overhanded sense of responsibility leads in the same direction.

(Pause at 10:08.) So true art must in a vital fashion be divorced from utility, or from its function outside of itself, or you will end up with something else entirely. Left alone, Ruburt's creative life falls into inspirational patterns that spring from their own secretive sources. If the "products" help people, that help is an additional feature flowing naturally from the art itself, and not applied <u>to</u> it with a heavy hand.

(Pause.) Ruburt has felt too responsible to develop his psychic abilities, to produce another "psychically inspired" work of his own. The sense of responsibility of that kind stifles love, which must be free to form its own creativity in

its own fashion. Therefore, left alone, Ruburt writes freely, and in an inspired nature because that is (underlined) his nature. It is what he loves to do. When he becomes overly concerned with ideas of responsibility to use his talent, then the love beneath them is smothered to some extent and denied its flow.

When that flow is relatively unimpeded then he is naturally attracted to subjective activity and to performance in the natural world as well. He enjoys seeing people then. To enjoy seeing people is a different thing than expecting yourself to be a public personality, however. Ruburt has been trying out a system of values that is not naturally his own. He has told himself that his art must be used to help people primarily—as if that had been his main goal all along. Art then becomes a method of doing something else—and that idea runs directly contrary to the basic integrity of art, and to art as he truly understands it to be. He therefore often felt forced to do what before he had done because he wanted to.

(Pause.) This led certainly to conflict. The idea of the public image coming through the correspondence, and as it was interpreted by Ruburt, further deepened the feeling of responsibility. Certainly "a great psychic teacher" had a responsibility of some weight (ironically humorous), and therefore it seemed imperative to Ruburt that he not make errors, that he live up to the characteristics generally ascribed to such an image. Thus, some experimentation was cut out (such as?). He began to think that anything less than this public personality was cowardly.

He felt that your visitors came to see the public image (as they certainly did, I'd say), and felt inferior by contrast. To some extent he became divorced from some of his own feelings, for they seemed now beneath him.

He had always enjoyed being somewhat disreputable—had seen himself and you prowling around the edges of society (as Jane had said earlier today)—not simply observers of it but to a large extent apart from its foibles, and certainly not mired in all of its conventional misunderstandings. He enjoyed dealing with it by sending the written word out into the public arena. He insisted upon that—the publication of his work. The books were to be his public platform.

(10:28.) He is proud of that translation of private creative experience into the artistic public act of publication. He is not a performer, however, in the same way that an actor is, whose art requires for its best execution the lively responsive immediately present audience. He did not want to be a public personality of that kind.

It seemed that this would be thrust upon him, however—that it was expected, and that indeed furthermore he should expect such performance from himself. *(Long pause.)* His own earlier attitudes about such matters began to seem cowardly, so he tried to divorce himself from them. That idea, however, together with the idea of responsibility, you see, was always in the background.

In a fashion, the fears became substitutes for the earlier natural feelings that he had been in contact with before. There were reasons then not (underlined) to go out into the world: it was dangerous, and so forth. Those feelings of fear were reactivated to provide a seemingly reasonable explanation for the earlier natural feelings he was no longer in touch with.

(Long pause at 10:38.) The earlier ones saw the two of you as apart from society's inner workings—not divorced, now, from society—but you had both pursued policies of not following society's mores. You prided yourselves on not having regular jobs, and being apart from certain portions of the culture. You recognized the importance of community without joining any of its organizations.

Ruburt made gestures of unconventionality. To go on public television, join the workshops and so forth would not be Ruburt's way, even while he felt that such a course was expected of him. He thinks in terms of individuals. He distrusts crowds. *(Long pause.)* He has no use for congregations—but all of those feelings remained largely unexpressed in later years.

(Long pause.) Beside this, he felt that such a performance would alter the direction his work would take in ways that would be detrimental overall, for the broadening quality of that kind of discourse could only be as extensive in scope as the quality of his audience's understanding, so that the material might become too tailored to public need or consumption—tied up in answering conventional questions—an excellent point, by the way.

(Yes. And one that Jane and I soon became aware of even on that first very limited tour we took to help publicize The Seth Material.*)*

It would do you both good if you took some time to become better acquainted with your own feelings about who you are or what you are, as opposed to who or what you think you should be, and why you think you should be different.

Ruburt's nature leads to periods of painting and poetry and subjective exploration of unconventional thought. He felt that he should be doing other things, however: he should be using (underlined) his time better.

His body is relaxing because it needs to, and he is finally allowing it. He was able to see the quality of his poetry today for his book. The poetry adds to the world simply by its being. Art is not meant to be a prescription. It is a celebration. People who celebrate do not need prescriptions.

This will be a brief session. I want you to read over the last sessions, however, for your own edification. If you want to, note down any particular questions you want to ask—knowing of course that I will answer them in my own fashion. Ruburt's material last night in the dream state was excellent, bringing feelings to the surface, and rearousing some attitudes he had forgotten.

This was a session Ruburt enjoyed—also one he had out of a sense of responsibility—but at least with some <u>understanding</u> of the issues involved. I bid you then a fond good evening.

("Thank you. Seth. It's very good.")

(10.55 PM. Jane thought the session had been short. She was surprised to learn that an hour had passed. She'd also been "a little more comfortable" in her chair.

(Attached is more of her own material that "came" to her. She's just finished typing it, although she received it last Monday and Tuesday. It's excellent material, as Seth said, and is a continuation of that she received on February 6; see the end of the last deleted session [for February 17].

(I intend to now begin compiling a list of questions for Seth that grow out of his recent sessions—hence his remark above about such a list. We've talked about this a number of times, and I've also mentioned it in session notes. Coupled with this will be my compilation of brief quotes from the sessions—making points for Jane's quick perusal that I think are especially good. This list can also be used as a guide to refer us back to the body of material from which any particular quote is taken.)

JANE'S NOTES
FEBRUARY 16, 1981 MONDAY

Each person or act has his or its "proper stance," or platform of intention from which to operate. There are healers, for example, who respond primarily to the needs of others. In the nonpsychic arena these correspond with your doctors and nurses and even to, say, social reformers. The framework is an excellent one for those who find it a natural extension of inner intent. It deals with utility, function, need, and the "righting of wrongs."

Beyond that platform (which is <u>not</u> your own native one) is another that operates as "high art," in which activity is for its own sake, for the joy and discovery of the performance or execution, a high play that sets the needs of the world at least momentarily aside, rises up above specifics into those vaster realms from which specifics emerge.

(<u>Note</u>: As I type this, I see the copy better and better.)

You've been largely operating from a base that isn't naturally yours but was taken on as a result of your sympathy for the world and for the problems of others. But that base doesn't provide the kind of springboard or the thrust you need or your abilities require. It's as if, at usual levels, you tried to be a doctor instead of a writer. At psychic levels, the qualities you need for sessions and your own work do not mesh with the overriding need to help others. You need the free joy of performance. Then, helping others follows naturally as your work helps others help themselves. In fact this is the only true kind of help.

(Became very relaxed when I got this material.)

JANE'S NOTES
FEBRUARY 17, 1981 MONDAY

At more mundane levels the same kind of problem arises when art is considered according to its utility, function, or social value—as opposed to the idea of art for its own sake. Instead, of course, art must first of all be a private adventure, sought for itself.

In a fashion, you consider the public arena of TV and tours in the same way that Joseph views the world of art galleries, shows, and auctions. You disdain it, while considering publishing acceptable. Besides this, it seems to you that such encounters involve a simplification and distortion by their very nature as far as your work is concerned, along with a unique kind of psychological disclosure that could be humiliating, lacking the proper frame of understanding. In a world in which women are considered passive and the trance largely feminine, you feel that the performance of a session could be too easily misread. This offends your sense of privacy while reading poetry to others does not.

At the same time you've felt a strong responsibility to perform publicly, to sell books, get your message across, let people see that—yes, the sessions do happen—there is no fraud involved. You were also afraid that spontaneously you would want to do public encounter work, that you'd be tempted, that once begun, you'd be swept along and that the circumstances would be volatile.

That is, trance work you feel requires a safe framework and stresses a private stance even though its messages can be shared. Even then the question arises of public response to trance messages when they contradict official thought—and your questions about how the material might be misused as you explained in God of Jane *very well, and—How "responsible" is the conscious mind for trance messages?—How responsible are you for Seth's messages? That is the kind of question with which few people contend. The very phrasing of the question and the word,* responsible, *shows its loaded nature. Actually the sessions show a remarkable synthesis of conscious and unconscious abilities, a creative blend that fulfills all portions of the psyche....*

DELETED SESSION
FEBRUARY 23, 1981 9:07 PM MONDAY

(*Jane was again very relaxed after supper as she sat on the couch watching TV. Indeed, she'd been quite relaxed for much of the day, alternating with periods of soreness in her backside. She hasn't done too much, other than some typing on her poetry book this morning; she slept for several hours today. The changes continue in her body.*

(*For the first time in a very long while, most of last week's mail remains unanswered—sitting in the basket on the table at the end of the couch. Another batch of letters arrived from Prentice-Hall today, adding to the pile. Some of the letters are great, others very depressing. In other words, they range over the usual human situations we encounter. One even took us to task for "obscenities" in Volume 2 of "Unknown." Jane and I have been talking about how best to deal with the implications of the mail—it often bothers her—but haven't reached any conclusions. There may not be any simple one way to handle the situation. I ask a question or two about it in my list of questions for Seth.*

(*Yes, I've started my famous list of questions for that "personality energy essence;" it's based on this latest group of private sessions, that began on February 4, 1981. Jane has read the first two pages of questions. A few may contain new insights into our challenges. Next comes my list of "pithy quotations" from the same group of sessions—positive statements from Seth [usually] that we can quickly review. I can already see that both lists could be almost endless....*

(*"Well, at least I'm somewhat comfortable in the chair tonight," Jane said as we waited at 8:58. "I can lean back somewhat—but I'm always the most uncomfortable in the chair. I don't know what I'm doing here instead of being in bed. Well, I'll be ready in a minute...." Yet at the same time she sat stiffly forward, her body canted to her left; she didn't look comfortable, and she decided to try the foam rubber pads beneath her thighs, a move that sometimes "helps relieve the pressure on those [pelvic] bones back there, and keeps me from feeling that I'm falling forward. They also help me when I move around in the chair." Her talk reminded me, paradoxically, that last night while sitting on the couch she'd been able to cross her legs in a way she hadn't been able to do for a long time.*

(*At 9:00 she told me she thought Seth would discuss my questions #5 and 6, about black-and-white thinking, and touch upon "that article" about micro metal-*

bending, or psychokinetic metal bending. I was surprised to hear this, for even though I'd been quite interested in the article I'd forgotten it for the moment. It appeared in the PSI News *bulletin of the Parapsychological Association. Vol. 4, No. 1 for January 1981. She'd read the article this noon at lunch when I called her attention to it. Until I'd first read the piece a couple of days ago, I hadn't realized that much progress had been made scientifically in the detection of psychic metal-binding on a micro scale. The presentation of information seemed to be very straight-forward, though I'm sure that it will be attacked by the skeptics in a variety of ways. Perhaps we'll learn more about the situation as it develops. I'm attaching a copy of the article to this session, for Seth came through with some unique insights concerning healing and micro metal-bending, or PKMB.)*

Good evening.

("Good evening, Seth.")

Now: the conscious mind <u>legitimizes</u> physical reality. It puts its stamp of approval upon those probabilities that are considered to be actual and real in your world. It does so according to your beliefs, and the <u>mass mold</u> of your beliefs is formed as you learn from parents and teachers what to expect in the nature of events.

(Jane kept shifting around in her chair....)

In that fashion, as you mature from infancy you become neurologically responsive to certain pathways of activity, while ignoring other quite valid neurological phasing. To an extent you develop habitual patterns of reference in that regard, so that certain <u>cues</u> in the environment automatically trigger the familiar neurological activity.

From a very small amount of physical data, then, certain kinds of developments are deduced, and almost automatically such passageways are activated. *(Pause.)* A very small example: the smell of an orange may instantly provide you with a mental image of one, so that that received from one sense is picked up in a fashion by the others—all serving in one way or another to give you a more completed picture of the object or event involved.

These habits become quite ingrained. They operate very smoothly. Now when anyone is involved particularly in formal experiments dealing with, say, PK, you run into <u>cross activity</u> in that respect. The conscious mind is set up by your belief systems to believe that PK effects are impossible, or at the best highly improbable.

(Pause.) If such an individual can convince himself or herself that somehow the entire affair is more in the nature of a game, then you can have at times some success, because in a game the conscious mind is willing to make allowances, and to "pretend." In a good variety of cases, however, the formal

experiment itself sets up a barrier, for the conscious mind is being asked to cooperate in a venture that it considers <u>nearly</u> an impossibility.

(Pause at 9:20.) This opinion is backed up, you see, by the habitual use of
accustomed neurological activity, and even while such an individual may agree
that PK is possible at certain levels, there is a kind of neurological prejudice built
in. Added to that is the conscious mind's position as the arbiter of actuality. This
in particular applies to events like metal bending of silverware or whatever.

To some extent the physical senses themselves are scandalized. In <u>micro-
scopic</u> experiments, however, the senses themselves cannot perceive such altered
behavior <u>in the same fashion</u> (underlined). They are not used to dealing with
such miniature events to begin with, nor do they identify with them. To that
extent there is great freedom.

The same applies to the conscious mind itself, which is not programmed
in the same fashion to be the arbiter of microscopic events. It does not feel overly threatened, then, despite this, in many instances there will still be some blockage of PK effects. That blockage may still allow a kind of displacement target-
ing, however, in which case inner abilities are allowed to operate, but in a rather
sabotaged way—not hitting the target with which the conscious mind is so
familiar or concentrated upon, but hitting another microscopic target instead,
in which effects are then noticeable.

It is the conscious mind as it is trained in your society that deals with black
and white thinking, apropos of one of your questions. The connection between
black and white thinking and creativity is legitimate, but it exists the other way
around: as a rule the artist or creative person <u>is</u> (underlined) creative to the
extent that he or she escapes black and white thinking, for the creative person
deals with syntheses, original versions of reality and the consideration of <u>differ-
ent groups</u> of probabilities—groups that appear otherwise very unlikely together from the standpoint of black and white thinking.

(Long pause at 9:31.) The displacement target effect is highly important,
for it operates in many other fashions. In all natural healing, of course (as Jane
mentioned this noon), you are involved with PK activity—as you are <u>ultimately</u>
with any physical act, and with any motion, microscopic or otherwise. <u>Too
much</u> concentration, however, upon the desired end—too much concentration
—can bring about a displacement target effect.

You might have, for example, poor eyesight while you are concentrating
upon trying to heal yourself of something else—a broken leg: your eyes might
be healed in a displacement effect, while the healing of your leg or whatever
might be put off immediately because it is blocked by your own overconcern.

(Long pause.) The motion of microscopic events always involves probabilities, which are at the heart of your world, and healings always involve activity at that level also. To divert the conscious mind can therefore be of great import —enjoying television, relaxing in whatever fashion, <u>allows</u> the desired activity to occur. That is why such diversions are so beneficial. On some occasions company can provide the same service. Ruburt should therefore try to divert his mind more. His ink sketches serve that capacity. Television also.

(*Pause.*) In your creativity you both largely avoid black and white thinking, and automatically leap out of that framework. The conscious mind is quite willing to let go in that regard, for art not only provides it with enjoyment but fulfills its own framework of action. It does not regard art as a game, exactly, but it does not expect the same rules to apply, either, to a painted apple on a canvas and a real one.

(*Pause at 9:45.*) The changed pattern of activity <u>is</u> helping Ruburt. It <u>is</u> (underlined) an excellent idea for him to write down any and all improvements he notes in each day. They become part of the physical evidence of the world.

His body is changing at microscopic levels—highly important. (*Pause.*) The major issue is indeed the reminder that he <u>can</u> trust his own native rhythm and motion—that it is safe to express himself in his natural life. The main point also is to be relieved of comparison with a super image, with thoughts of what he should be, and an acknowledgement of his <u>own</u> (underlined) feelings about any event or situation. He did indeed identify with his own tensions, so that as these are relieved he <u>is</u> sometimes frightened.

You can help by reminding him that there is no reason to be fearful in that regard.

His eyes have improved reading. I will try to answer all of your questions in one way or another. Ruburt is working through many issues now well, however I do want to mention that Framework 2 often involves such "displaced" targets, when one desired event may be blocked in one area, but a beneficial event of like consequence instead happens in an area seemingly quite divorced from it.

Ruburt's body is changing while he sleeps. The areas involving motion are highly involved. He is sleeping better—all issues that should be remembered. That will be enough for this evening, and I will go into some of your questions next session.

(*"Thank you."*)

Then I will bid you a fond good evening.

(*"Thank you very much, Seth. Good night."*)

(*9:56 PM. Jane's delivery had been quite good, although she hadn't appeared to be too comfortable in her chair. I explained to her that this session offered valu-*

able clues as to how to use suggestion: If one could learn how to direct the suggestions —even through the use of <u>misdirection</u>—much could be accomplished. The use of that misdirection would certainly have it funny connotations, too, I thought.

(I also think there are clear connections between Seth's material this evening and that given in Appendix 4 in Volume 1 of "Unknown." In that material I quoted Jane's own material on other "sidepools" of neurological activity. I wrote later in "Unknown" that I thought Appendix 4 contained some of the best material in that work, and I still think so.)

DELETED SESSION
FEBRUARY 25, 1981   9:05 PM WEDNESDAY

(7:30 PM. I'm starting these notes in advance of tonight's session without being really sure that Jane will hold one—although I think she plans to. Once again she slept several hours in the middle of the day. Right now she's sitting on the couch, feeling quite relaxed after eating supper, watching the TV news. As for myself, I want to try to reconstruct our after-breakfast discussion of today.

(As we began to reread Monday's session this morning, Jane said something that triggered a reaction on my part that I felt was based on material Seth gave in that session: "I tell my body every day that I trust it, that it can bear my weight when I go to the john, for example," or words closely to that effect. Suddenly it came to me that she had it backwards—that her body didn't need any additional trust, that it was perfectly willing to do her bidding at any time, including healing itself. What she should be stressing, I said, was that she trusted her spontaneous self—<u>then</u> the body would automatically react to the release of tension, to her trust in that spontaneous self. Put another way, the intellect then must learn to cooperate in that trusting by relaxing its near-paranoid protective cover.

(All of this is a simplification, of course, for we had a rather lengthy discussion about it. Yet I could see that I confused Jane somewhat: for she'd used that typical suggestion about trusting her body for years, and I had agreed with it, at least tacitly, besides using similar suggestions myself at times.

(But with a new insight growing out of this month's series of private sessions, I explained, I now felt that one could more directly get at the heart of one's challenges, instead of trying to cajole the body into behaving differently—after all, the body's condition was the <u>result</u> of certain ways of thinking, not the <u>cause</u> of the trouble. In addition, it was obvious that the body hadn't responded to those habitual suggestions over the years, so something else was needed. The cause of Jane's symptoms is her fear of the spontaneous self—that is the area that needs treatment. One might better

address the fears of being the public person, for example, rather than trying to futile-ly patch up a body that was only faithfully following mirroring habits of deep and long standing.

(Now Jane agreed with all of this at the time, but later while painting I wondered whether I'd been too vehement in what I'd said. I didn't want her to feel bad. And I learned during the day that our talk had upset her considerably, even though I'd told her I felt that there was "a lot of hope" in the ideas expressed in our discussion. Jane further echoed my concern when she said later that she didn't know what suggestions to give herself when she went to the john, and later got onto the bed. Yet I felt that I was on to something good, and asked Jane pretty definitely to see that Seth discussed the subject tonight. I also wanted him to talk about the subject we'd mentioned for Monday night's session, but which hadn't been covered: the reasons for her sore backside, and what she could do to help ease her hip and leg discomfort. Somehow we got totally off that subject when Seth went into the interesting topic of PKMB, or psychokinetic metal bending. But at this time in these sessions we've got to get all the new data we can to help in our own hassles.

(At lunchtime Frank Longwell dropped off a medical device that's used to transfer moist heat to the body. After lunch I fussed with transplanting a cutting of Swedish ivy while Jane slept. I also wanted to try to make up some of the painting time I'd lost this morning. As I finished cleaning up the planter I came up with another of the "insights" I've been getting since we started this series of private sessions on February 4, 1981; see my notes at the end of the session for February 11.

(I wrote down my intuited data, but strangely enough I forgot to show it to her when she got up around 2 PM. I'll either read it to her before tonight's session, or discuss it with her after breakfast tomorrow, when I read her tonight's session. Here are my notes:

("Insight, February 25, 1981, 1:20 PM. Although Jane enjoys the sessions, as Seth himself said in the session for February 1, 1981 She is still somewhat afraid of what he will produce in the future—new theories and ideas that either might or will place her in further confrontation with the major tenets of our ordinary world—meaning science, religion, medicine, history, whatever. She fears then, Seth going too far as an expression of her creative and spontaneous self. This expression then must be kept within strict, safe limits. This fear of future developments ties in very well with her natural concerns about becoming a public figure, one that should be able to solve the world's problems. Once more, I know I'm on to something here, while agreeing in advance that I've expressed the insight in simplistic terms."

("The insight also reminds me of one of my questions for Seth: I plan to ask him for hints about what sort of ideas he would advance if he's given the freedom to do so by Jane. He's already alluded to this notion through a rather recent reference to

the fact that he "toned down" some of his material for Mass Events *in order to make it more acceptable. I now wish I'd asked him at the time, acceptable to whom? Jane and me, Prentice-Hall, the world, critics, the post office?"*

(I should add, too, that this latest insight ties in well with the paragraph of Seth's that I've copied from the deleted session for January 28, 1981, to add to my list of quotations from these recent private sessions: Seth discussed Jane's fear of letting go —not because she is afraid of relaxing per se, but because she fears she will go too far.

(Jane called me for the session at 8:25. "I don't feel Seth around and I don't feel like a session," she said, "but I guess I'd better...." We sat waiting for some time. I showed her my rough notes on the latest insight, and took pains to explain to her that it wasn't a negative statement, but one that I saw as having only beneficial connotations. "What I think would happen if Seth were free to do anything he wanted to, would be great," I said. "Whether it was ever published or not. We can talk about it later." We agreed the insight represented something of a new idea.

("I might have bitten off more than I can chew," Jane said at 8:43. "But I assume Seth would have said a lot more about things like UFO's, Atlantis and reincarnation if I'd let him.... I replied that it hardly mattered, that the time element entered in, that we'd still want material on the subjects we were interested in, that Atlantis was "way down the list."

(Finally, as Jane sat quite upright in her chair, she began feeling Seth around. At the same time she talked about how upset she was at sleeping during the day; and added to her upset now was the question of what suggestions to use. She talked about having a "breakthrough" session to clear up her hassles. Then:)

Now—

("Good evening."

—for our friend. *(Pause.)* He has indeed of late made a decision to let go of a good deal of his bodily armor.

The body is softening. The affair frightens him nevertheless because, as mentioned earlier, he identifies strongly with his own bodily tensions. Letting them go brings him into a more or less constant encounter with many of the fears that helped generate them. Some of these have to do with an erroneous idea of relaxation in general, of course, with his father, and with spontaneity.

It often seems to him that to relax is to be lax, to let down, do nothing, achieve nothing, as if spontaneously left alone he would be lazy, unambitious, and again lax. He has those feelings and fears. *(Pause.)* At the same time there are feelings that to relax would be to let go too much *(louder)*—slide into overly spontaneous behavior, to lack control over one's life, to lose the observer's fine focus. As his body begins to relax—as indeed it has—those feelings become more prominent than before. Under the circumstances he is handling them rather well.

They do present difficulties, however, and are the cause of the panicky emotions he feels at times. The body's relaxation is as of now uneven. Certain muscles relax for the first time in recent times, while others might momentarily contract so that balance is maintained—so the body is in a state of constant change.

The change itself, and the relaxations, give him a feeling sometimes of having no firm support *(as Jane said earlier today)*. He should try to talk with you, however, when he is anxious, to foreshorten such periods. The fears do indeed prolong this particular period.

(9:20.) Ruburt, far more than other people, is involved in a life that utilizes conscious and unconscious activity, so that any dilemmas in that regard are certainly physically reflected. *(Pause.)* Anything that I may say in a session is relatively agreeable to him, though its publication in book form may at times cause difficulty as he wonders how the material will be interpreted by others.

Taking some kind of writing or sketchbook or whatever into the bedroom will help, so that he can do some creative work there if he wants to. The same applies to the couch.

As far as physical therapy is concerned, if you gave hot water packs—plain towels, or Frank's gadget—either one—the same or even half the attention you gave the cold water baths, this would now be of excellent immediate benefit. There are reasons why the body might at one time respond to the cold, then the hot water.

The idea that it is indeed safe to relax is important, coupled with the realization that all creativity is <u>basically now</u>—basically—effortless, and that this applies to the body's motion also. When he is effortlessly creating a poem he is not worried that he is relaxing too much, or going too far, or giving up control. Instead, he is letting go by going with himself *(all intently)*—and that attitude makes all the difference.

(Pause.) The rigidity that was a general characteristic <u>is</u> breaking up, you see, so that by contrast portions of his body do feel vulnerable to him—soft, unprotected—but those feelings were to a large degree covered over before. Now he is physically aware of them, and mentally also. They can be encountered far more directly then, and as they are the body will feel more and more able to respond more, and let go the other <u>stops</u> that still do operate.

I admit that it is somehow sometimes difficult to attain proper balance, so that you are not concentrating upon the problem exclusively again. Those early autumn sessions, and the late summer ones, are of help here to balance what we are doing now, for they remind Ruburt of the magical framework and its operation, and assure him that relaxation is one of the best methods that release Framework 2 and its creativity.

(Pause at 9:32.) The particular paper of suggestions—he will know what I mean—does contain a good variety of suggestions for him, couched in terms that are highly beneficial. Again, certain suggestions couched one way will work at one time, according to the circumstances, while the same group may be rather adverse to fit other circumstances. Overall suggestions do of course give excellent leeway, so that the pressure can be taken off any specific areas of overconcern.

(Long pause at 9:35.) Give us a moment.... the displacement aspect mentioned *(in the last private session)* helped in the improvement of Ruburt's lumps on the arm. For example *(gesturing to the area)*, when he had simply momentarily forgotten about them in other concerns about his condition.

It is very important that Framework 2 be remembered, that overall suggestions be creative while open *(intently)*, rather say than at this time too closed-ended. Talking with you is highly important now, many of the feelings that the rigidity <u>hid</u>, you see, now come into consciousness—an excellent situation because they can be and are being encountered. The entire arena of public endeavor brings up questions about the differences between spontaneous and controlled behavior, of course *(long pause)*—an issue we will go into another time, but thoroughly.

I am trying to give information that will be of practical benefit immediately, since Ruburt was so concerned. There are a few other suggestions that he knows of, on a pad, that are also good now. He looks for your approval and reaction, and your own responses have been excellent in that regard *(leaning forward stiffly)*. I have mentioned quite a few different issues here, and they involve recommendations, including Ruburt's reading of those prior sessions <u>frequently</u>.

They do not have to be studied every day, but kept in mind. The entire rationale as expressed in some of those sessions concerning the rather paranoid tendencies of the conscious mind, should also be remembered. Such issues help place certain of Ruburt's reactions in perspective.

I am trying to hit all important points. *(Pause.)* I will in <u>time</u>, along with your questions, give some material, again, on Ruburt's attitudes toward both of his parents as these relate to his difficulties. For now, however, I will bring the session to a close, though he may hold brief spontaneous sessions, you know, at other nights than our usual ones. I bid you a fond good evening.

("Thank you, Seth."

(9:47 PM. "That was short," Jane said, "but I wanted something that will help now." Her delivery had been okay. I said I'd read it to her in the morning before

I had it typed.

(Actually it's Friday night as I finish this typing, and I read the untyped portions of the session to Jane each morning as I had it in progress. It has been a lot of help. She's sleeping better, and yet is still uncomfortable on her bottom and legs. The fears continue to surface. I'd say she's doing very well, and it seems that this time we are really making progress. Another brief insight came to me yesterday, which I told her about: simply that she'd given up her <u>own volition</u> to one part of her personality. I mentioned it because she discussed the question of volition in God of Jane; she thought the insight made sense.)

DELETED SESSION
MARCH 2. 1981 9:25 PM MONDAY

(I had another of my "insights" while painting this morning, and talked it over with Jane after supper tonight. It was, simply, that we were wrong to blame imagined excesses of the spontaneous self for her problems—that really the trouble lay in her discovery that with the psychic abilities she was destined to find herself outside conventional creative authority: a person who learned that she would have to protect her very integrity as a person against charges of fraud. Publishers don't put disclaimers on novels or poetry, I said. I added that Seth—and we—must have covered this ground many times over the years; yet now I felt that once again I was "on to something important."

(Our talk lasted almost an hour in spite of myself, for I didn't want her to get upset before a session. I felt that we couldn't afford to miss sessions these days. Her reading the NY Times Book Review *each week had reminded me recently that her intent perusal of that publication represented a striving toward something she was not about to achieve—conventional recognition in creative writing.*

(She'd obviously, I thought, expected recognition by her peers in the writing field when she matured, with her obvious talents. Yet she'd found this deep yearning snatched away with the advent of her psychic abilities—goodbye to all of those accepted reviews, the critical success, even the money, that would go along with the conventional acceptable public image of the successful writer of good quality poetry and/or fiction. I said that most "successful?" poetry and fiction might not penetrate very deeply into the human condition, compared with the understanding her own psychic gifts offered, but it would have been safe and accepted by her peers. What more could anyone ask of life, I demanded ironically?

(The insight, such as it was, offered many clues to our present situation. I asked that Seth discuss it if she held a session tonight. Jane had been quite blue after sleep-

ing for a couple of hours late this afternoon—and after she'd already slept for two hours this morning. It wasn't that her psychic work, and the books, weren't good, I said, or that they didn't help people, but that they didn't fit into the world as she saw it. Seth himself had referred to her dilemma in the excerpt I've taken from the private session for January 26, 1981, very well.

(Her challenge, then, is that she's never integrated fully her psychic orientation, the true source of all of her gifts, with her views of the rest of her world. I think, I added, that it was an error to blame fear of the spontaneous self going too far if given free reign—I didn't think nature would arrange things that way, for the organism couldn't survive for long that way. The behavior of Instream, the other psychologist at Oswego, the demand for credentials from Fell and others, the letters asking for help of various kinds—especially those from the unbalanced—all of these things and more added up in her eyes to an indictment, one might say, of one's very nature. Clear indications that left alone without safeguards one would go too far for one's own good.

(No wonder, then, the retreat from the world, <u>even the refusal to leave the house</u>. Protection from the world must be had at all costs, even while she, with my help, persisted in using her abilities to some extent at least through the books. I wondered how much about all of this she'd never let Seth say. No wonder we sought privacy more and more: any public exposure came to be avoided automatically, as part of the protective coloration.

(Jane didn't react overly much to any of this, beyond implying at least a general sort of agreement. I was rather surprised when she agreed to hold the session. "Well, I guess I'm about ready," she said at 9:15. "You must have got me going...."

(She's been sleeping much better, but with interspersed bouts of restlessness and discomfort in her backside and legs. Right now she was also uncomfortable as she waited for Seth to come through. Earlier today I'd told her I realized how cleverly she'd engineered her activities so that she didn't go to the john very often. Right then, she hadn't been to the bathroom since noon. "I'd go if I had to," she protested, but I answered that she'd simply trained her body to wait as long as possible for such natural acts; then she could avoid all the discomfort of getting into the bathroom and on the john, etc. I added that I supposed now she'd work it so that she only went to the john once before going to bed after the session. I wondered if she was trying to set a record for holding it. By way of contrast, I wanted to ask Seth to comment on the <u>good things</u> her psychic abilities have accomplished. But right at this time she can barely get from her chair to sit on the john or the bed—literally.)

Good evening.

("Good evening, Seth.")

You are in charged waters indeed with your discussion. Most of the ideas that you stated were highly pertinent, applying specifically to Ruburt's situation

—but very touchy for him. As a child, couched in the Catholic Church, his poetry was a method of natural expression, a creative art, and also the vehicle through which he examined himself, the world as he knew it, and the beliefs of the Roman Catholic Church.

His creative abilities led him beyond the precepts of that church, creatively speaking, at a fairly early age—though the actual breaking-off point did not occur in fact until he was in his teens. He was fairly young, then, however, when he first encountered conflicts between creativity as such, intuitive knowledge, and other people's ideas about reality.

I have mentioned this on occasion—that he felt quite different from his contemporaries. Many gifted children do, and he used various kinds of protective coloring. No matter what he was taught in Catholic school or later in the public one, his intuitions, wedded to his creative capacities, led him to question established views.

Poetry was not considered fact, of course. It was a kind of concealed knowledge, apparent but not apparent. Later he tried straight novels, but when he let himself go his natural fiction fell into the form of fantasy, outside of the novel's conventions into science fiction's form—and at that time further away from the mainstream. He managed to get some of his work published, however, so that as he reached his early 30's he had some apprenticeship under his belt.

His earliest dreams were simply to be a poet. The American novelist was laid on as a more acceptable and practical framework.

(9:32.) Again, his natural abilities kept leading him, so it seemed, away from the straight novel framework into the science fiction format, where at that time he discovered that science fiction was not given any particular honor in the literary field. He decided to break away from it. Again he tried some straight novels. At the same time his abilities were examining the world at large, and your own worlds, as they were unfolding.

You both had more questions at that time than you had ever had in your lives before, and your growing practical knowledge of the world made you each realize how little the species knew in vital areas. It was more or less at that point that Ruburt's abilities seemingly started, or that his psychic initiation began suddenly.

There are multitudinous elements operating against such an initiation in your society, and particularly these operated back in those days when the sessions first began. There is a natural desire to want the respect of one's fellows, to avoid social taboos or ostracism. Those issues were encountered at that time because Ruburt's abilities thrust them through their surfaces. His abilities grew despite the society's inhibiting factors. It did take Ruburt some time to fully understand how his work might perhaps be regarded. The fact that I could also write books was of the greatest benefit, of course *(dryly, almost with a smile)* — and no one was more surprised than Ruburt to discover that I could do so.

(A long, uncomfortable pause at 9:41.) Ruburt could have said, "I bear no responsibility for Seth's words, since they are not mine in the usual fashion." On the other hand, while he did critically examine our material, he insisted in those terms "that he must be responsible for it," in that he and everyone else must take normal responsibility in a fashion for "subconscious" actions or revelatory information.

He could have tried to publish the material in camouflaged form through fiction, and he was far more tempted to take such a line than perhaps you realized. Had one of his straight novels been accepted at that time, the story might be different somewhat. He recognized, however, the excellent quality in his own newer writings and in my own work also. He recognized the elements of mystery and creativity involved in the entire affair, and realized that he could not after all camouflage all of that, and so took the course upon which you both embarked.

He was very unsure of himself, since the entire dimension of activity was new, and at that time extremely rare in your country. The whole idea of being a "psychic" was completely new.

As he continued with his books and mine, he became more bewildered, in that there seemed to be no literary framework in which they were legitimately reviewed. It was as if he were considered a writer no longer, or as if the writing itself, while considered good enough, was also considered <u>quite beside the point</u>—of secondary concern, and in the psychic field the very word "creative" often has suspicious connotations. Many such people want <u>the truth</u>, in capital letters, in quite literal form, without creativity slurring the message, so to speak, or blurring the absolute edges of fact and fiction.

(Pause at 9:44.) There was a necessary period of time in which Ruburt and yourself experimented in several areas of psychic exploration, quite rightly picking and choosing those areas that suited you best, and ignoring others that you found for whatever reasons unsuitable. Ruburt quickly discovered that the public image of a psychic was quite different than that given to a writer, and so was the social image. As our readership grew, as you heard from readers or from some members of the media or whatever, it seemed to Ruburt that what he did best—have sessions, write his books—was not enough, that he was expected to do far more.

At the same time, he was to be denied his rightful place as a writer *(as I'd said earlier)*, to defend this new position—a position moreover that seemed to change all the time—for beside my books there was *Seven*, Sumari, and later *Cézanne* and *James*. Each one flying in the face of one kind of conventional misunderstanding or another. He felt that he could hardly keep up with the spontaneous self: what was it about to do next?

Now in *Mass Events* and *God of Jane* he courageously went still further, letting it all hang out, as they say—a necessary part of his own growth and development. That is, he is better off for producing those two books than he would be otherwise.

At the same time, however, over a period of time he began to <u>hold back</u> creatively to some extent on inspiration itself, wondering where it might lead him, and this caused part of his physical difficulties *(long pause)*, the physical blockage of course reflecting the inner one. Part of that blockage was also directly related to his ideas of work and responsibility.

(Pause at 10:05.) Even poetry did not seem to be work for a while, for example, nor did psychic activity <u>for its own sake</u> *(Long pause.)* All of this in its way fits together with other material—but no writers of merit, for example *(intently)*, outside of Richard Bach, have written him to applaud his work, and to the writing community it seems he does not exist. The psychic community is a hodgepodge to which he feels no natural leanings, as far as its organizations or affiliations are concerned.

This is because his position <u>is</u> unique, in that he is dealing in areas that serve as thresholds, where ordinary creativity is accelerated and goes beyond itself, where fact turns into fiction, and fiction into fact. In those unknown realms, from which all psychological events are formed, he <u>wants</u> to fly ahead theoretically—that is, to delve through my books and through his own into ideas that still await, and feels somewhat angry because it seems that excellent theoretical material is overlooked by others to a large extent, while being used as a Band-Aid to help the current problems of the people.

He has held back his inspiration, though, out of confusion, wondering about experiences that cannot be put directly into beneficial use, and also out of concern, again, that the spontaneous self and its intuitional insights will put him in further conflict with the world.

When you want to be a landscape painter, at least you know what a landscape is. You have your brushes and colors to work with. In Ruburt's case, there are no definite boundaries, in certain ways, to the dimensions of that creativity —no specific methods, no specific pathways, and it is for that reason that he tried to exert such balancing force.

Experiment is a poor word—<u>excursions</u>—into the library while the two of you sit at the table, for example, would be excellent. Your joint dream episodes are always of benefit. The encouragement of such inner mobility also releases the bodily mechanisms. It is safe to move: he can get off dead center.

(*Long pause at 10:20.*) The public image is bound to make him feel inferior if he takes it too seriously. That always stimulates his idea of responsibility. It is his public image as a psychic, of course, not as a writer, that here is the issue. In a fashion we are delivering source materials for each person to interpret and enjoy. It may serve as the source material for several different kinds of disciplines, or schools or whatever. (*Pause.*) It will serve to inspire others, but each person is responsible for his or her own life, and Ruburt does not have a private clientele, nor is he temperamentally suited to use his psychic abilities to track people down or to serve as a therapist. That narrows his abilities too specifically and holds him down from other kinds of explorations for which he is highly equipped and quite proficient.

A focus upon natural inspiration, spontaneous creativity, psychic exploration, will automatically help relieve the physical situation, if this is done with some understanding.

End of session.

(*"May I ask a question?"*)

You may.

(*"How is he going to come to terms with the lack of public recognition that he wants so much as a writer?"*)

That is only a part of the picture. He was not particularly thinking of any great fame to begin with, but the just-enough recognition—

(*"That's what I mean."*)

—of work well done. That recognition in a fashion comes from several fronts—from people in all walks of life, from professors, members of different professions rather—than specifically from other writers (*pause*), and in time that situation itself will improve. It is the public image as he thinks he has as a psychic that bothers him, more than the one he feels is lacking as a writer.

The psychic public image (*long pause*) is a composite, of course, composed in your minds largely from your correspondence, and in that regard you both often exaggerate certain elements over others. Concentrate upon certain kinds of mail. That issue can be understood with some help from me, and your own common sense.

End of session. I have not forgotten your questions, but also try to keep these sessions kindly, and to respond to your intuitions as you express them. A fond good evening.

(*"Thank you, Seth. Good night."*

(*10:35 PM. Jane's delivery had been surprisingly good, much more emphatic and paced than I'd expected it to be. She'd not been comfortable in her chair, though. She was pleased with the session, which I told her we ought to memorize. She even said she was going to the john after ten-and-a-half hours: "I could hold it another hour, though," she said. I told her that kind of thing was out—that each day I planned to keep after her to go at decent intervals.*

(The wind was strong, rattling the metal blinds of the west side of the house. The temperature had dropped below freezing after a fairly nice day. The ground was bare, and had been for many days.)

DELETED SESSION
MARCH 4, 1981 9:18 PM WEDNESDAY

(Today I mentioned to Jane that I'd like Seth to go into some of the elements of question 17 on the list I've compiled so far—especially those parts of it pertaining to why didn't the overall personality know when it had gone far enough, or even too far, concerning the symptoms. I also was curious as to what he'd say about my speculation that the symptoms themselves might actually be one of her main challenges in this life.

(Following those items, I wanted Seth to comment on question 2, having to do with the good things *we've accomplished over the years.*

(Once more, Jane wasn't comfortable in her chair as she prepared for the session at 9 PM. "It's really weird to be so unambitious," she said as she tried to get settled. She'd done some excellent notes for her third essay for her book of poetry today, though she hadn't worked at it as much as in other recent days. She'd also slept several hours today, though as usual after laying down for a short time her arms and legs became very sore. She'd soon wakened from that first delicious snoring.

(As for myself, I've been trying to get in four hours of painting each day, without succeeding, by the way, but it's still a real treat. Last Saturday I bought over $30.00 worth of flower seeds, and I'm slowly trying them out in a variety of pots and containers to see which flowers do best under what circumstances—artificial light, natural light, etc. It's turning out to be quite an intriguing endeavor, and I plan to keep the house decorated with fresh flowers winter and summer.

(The index proofs for God of Jane *arrived day before yesterday, and Jane found them okay when she checked them today. Tam told her recently the book would be out in May. Mass Events was supposed to come out on March 13, but this date is evidently in error, since we've just learned we won't see front-matter proofs until next week. Jane thinks Tam meant the paperback edition of Volume 2 of "Unknown," since the week's sales figures, which arrived today, show sales of some*

3,000 copies of that edition. But we're still uneasy over the whole Mass Events *affair —the disclaimer question, Jane's reaction to the book itself since Seth started giving it, etc.—and any delay only serves to make us more suspicious, I'm afraid. I guess I never saw a book being looked forward to less than that one.*

(Jane began to feel Seth around by 9:15. Then:)

Now—

("Good evening.")

—a few comments.

Many difficulties arise when you compare yourselves to stylized or idealized versions of yourselves—to <u>composite</u> images of yourselves that you may have picked up along the way—a subject that we have mentioned earlier.

Such images have little to do with your own basic or natural personalities, or with your own individual backgrounds, but you apply such images upon yourselves like overlays. In such cases you are unable to really estimate your own progress of your own accomplishments, for you are not looking at them based upon your own capabilities and inclinations, but using the hypothetical idealized images instead.

For example: You were pleased, Joseph, with the portrait you did and showed Ruburt, remarking, however, that you wished you had done such work earlier, and on other occasions you have made similar remarks. You will compare your own life and work often in a critical fashion to artists who were obsessed with one art from the beginning of their lives, or who pursued what is really a kind of straight and undeviating course—a brave courageous one, perhaps, and highly focused, but one that must be <u>in certain respects</u> (underlined) limited in scope and complexity, not crossing any barriers except those that seem to occur strictly within painting's realm itself *(all intently.*

(I should add here that as Seth gave this material I found myself thinking that that wasn't too bad a way to go, after all. I do admire that intense focus, that whole-hearted commitment, and history offers plenty of examples—famous, too, if you will —of gifted individuals who lived their lives that way and made great contributions....

(Pause.) Now you have always from childhood drawn or painted, and in that regard there has been that constant interest. You looked out at the world through the eyes of a painter—but it was more than a painter's world you saw *(a great line, as Jane said).* You were also always interested in writing. At times you expect from yourself a kind of accomplishment that the first kind of artist might produce, without any due regard for the fact that you are your own person, that you possessed a love of words as well, that you had excellent <u>critical</u> capacities.

You also ignore the fact that even the kind of painting you do could not be done by anyone else, and contains within it the raw material of your own unique and natural experience with life, and no one else's.

That experience of that kind does not come at 20, or even at 30. Part of your accomplishment lies in our sessions and your own considerable work with the notes, and with the invisible aura contained in those notes, for there in a different way you are painting a portrait—a portrait of two lives from a highly individualistic standpoint, extremely unique—and that is the kind of experience that would be ripped out of your life's fabric, were you the hypothetical idealized version with whom you sometimes relate—a version highly romanticized, let me add.

(Pause at 9:35.) Such ideas, then, prevent you from enjoying your own accomplishments, as you should more properly do, and from enjoying their growth through time, from the background that was your own. The same applies to Ruburt.

He may think of some hypothetical literary writer—a composite image again, comfortable enough, slightly avant-garde, fashionably so, in contact with his peers, quite forgetting again that his—and his mind has always been far less conventional than that, far more probing and again, forgetting that he always enjoyed viewing society from a vantage point slightly outside of it.

As a rule, psychics are not particularly good writers. He tries to view his own work through some idealized image of a psyche who is as gifted as he is as a writer, and also highly gifted in meeting the public, putting on performances, acting as a healer, as a prophet, and as an expert therapist all at once, and in so doing his own characteristics and natural abilities and inclinations become lost along the way.

The books themselves show that he is <u>more</u> than fulfilling his promise as a writer, both in scope and artistry. They possess signs of greatness *(matter-of-factly.*

(I agree.)

Both of your minds are doing more than fulfilling <u>their</u> promises: they are being used to excellent capacity. Your emotional understanding has also deepened greatly through the years. This applies to both of you. Ruburt does beautifully with people, individually and with groups—particularly for someone who <u>is</u> (underlined) largely so given to solitary work.

All of these issues are important. You should always address yourself to the natural person, and when Ruburt becomes confused about images, it is because he is relating himself to other composite versions that he <u>thinks</u> he should live up to.

(Long pause at 9:48.) Give us a moment.... *(Long pause.)* The strain of try-ing to live up to such images causes tension, of course. It also causes feelings of self-disapproval, where a constant reminder of one's background puts current situations at least into perspective. Now Ruburt's body is trying to rid itself of those tensions, and he is learning to let go of them, and with your help, which lately has been considerable.

The relaxation will allow for the easy natural expression and the return of normal motion. It is important, however, that he remember what I said about inner motion in our last session: some return to light psychic experiences—the opportunity set aside for them.

(Pause.) Today's mail shows of course the better side of your readership, letters from people in many walks of life who are not fanatics, but who are nor-mal individuals who recognize quality and who are seeking it. You are changing their lives, or allowing them to do so, of course, helping them release their own abilities—accomplishments that should be considered in line, again, with your own backgrounds, and not compared with hypothetical ones.

This is all apart from the considerable accomplishment of holding your own in the society while doing your own things, and in achieving a good deal of freedom in that regard. Your psychological growth is not something you can look at in the mirror, yet it is that growth that is also responsible for your paint-ing and writing Ruburt's books and his connections with me. In a fashion Ruburt's symptoms are caused because he tries to understand his abilities and his life in a too-limited context, with definitions still too narrow. We are trying to broaden those definitions.

(Pause at 9:58.) There are considerable freedoms available to you that you ignore because your connections with those idealized images governs some of your joint reactions. I will discuss some of those at a later time.

Some of your psychological growth is obvious through the books, of course—obvious to others if often not to yourselves. The books make a psy-chological impact difficult to describe—one of course that overall presents a kind of multidimensional portrait, highly difficult to assess. *(Long pause.)* You lose contact with yourself to whatever extent as you compare yourself to others, and therefore your own work can escape you, again, and the contour of your own experience. You are planting seeds, and with the books you are planting seeds, only the results are not immediately before your eyes—a good point to remember.

This will be a brief session, and unless you have other comments I will try to answer two or three of your questions at a time in the sessions immediately following.

("Okay.")
Then I bid you a fond good evening.
("Thank you, Seth. The same to you."
(10:05 PM Jane was out of trance at once. and I could tell that she was pleased that she'd held the session. I told her it was excellent—that we ought to paste it on our foreheads and memorize it, along with last Monday's session.)

JANE'S NOTES
DREAM MARCH 5, TUESDAY

Nap. Background: Last PM Seth gave a session for me and this dream seems to be in direct response to it. During the night I was awakened several times, with that peculiar soreness in thighs and arms; at the same time my jaws dropped noticeably and I could feel motion going through my body. At breakfast when Rob read me the session I grew very relaxed and had to lie down. Then I had this dream:

Jack Gridley and a few others, Rob and I, were in a room. I was very relaxed. Jack was ready to leave, maybe for a trip. He asked me to vacuum his room, nonchalantly as if it were taken for granted that I perform the chore. I said, the vacuum (which was ours), was right there in plain sight. If he wanted his room vacuumed he should do it himself. Then I awakened.

Jack Gridley was a politician we knew in the 60's just about when the sessions started. In dream, he stands for authority; he was also quite a drunk. Anyhow the vacuum represents my work as a tool—I give the vacuum but people have to pick up their own dirt; I don't have to do it for them. I may have picked up a feeling of responsibility to do just that, back when we knew Gridley....

Later insights disconnected from dream come to me during the day:

1. I don't have to be embarrassed that Seth gives so many sessions for me; plenty of people go to doctors or therapists all their lives and this is at a much more complex level.

2. To consider: my feelings that people come here to see Seth, rather than me.

3. To consider: my worries when Seth was dictating Events *about the effect of his ideas on medicine and impulses on others.*

The question: Why am I afraid of my psychic abilities?

JANE'S NOTES
MARCH 8, 1981 SUNDAY MORNING

Part of me doesn't want to contend with this material at all but last night I had one of the strangest, quite frightening experiences—all the odder because there are so few real events to hang on to. Anyway early after we went to bed I realized I was in the middle of an odd nightmarish experience, one terribly vivid emotionally, yet with no real story line. I only know that the following were involved: a childhood nursery tale or/and a childhood toy like the cuddly cat doll I had as a child named Suzie that I thought the world of. Anyway, the point was that the story.... and there I lose it; I don't get the connections. All I know is that I awakened myself crying, my body very sore, sat on the side of the bed and made the following connections from my feelings at the time:

They were these; that the entire world and its organization was kept together by certain stories or one in particular—like the Catholic Church's; that it was dangerous beyond all knowing to look through the stories or examine them or to look for the truth and that all kinds of taboos existed to keep us from doing this, since.... since on the other side so to speak there was an incomprehensible frightening chaotic dimension, malevolent, powers beyond our imagining; and that to question the stories was to threaten survival not just personally but to threaten the fabric and organization of reality as we knew it. So excommunication was the punishment or damnation.... which meant more than mere ostracism but the complete isolation of a person from those belief systems, with nothing between him or her and those frightening realities.... without a framework in which to even organize meaning. This was what damnation really meant. To seek truth was the most dangerous of well intentioned behavior then.... and retribution had to be swift and sure.

At the same time I can't remember the events connected with the nightmare that gave rise to the feelings.... but I was being assaulted or attacked by.... A psychological force who wanted me to understand the danger of such a course, and when I went back to sleep somehow the entire thing would happen again.... once I think the title of the—(Jane left this blank)—or the children's tale appeared in the air in large block letters. The idea also being that outside of the known order provided by these stories, there were raging forces working against man's existence. (The old Pandora's Box idea comes to mind.)

I equate this with three events: a movie I saw on TV the night before last where Sean Connery sees through the god of his people after reading The Wizard of Oz; a Raggedy Ann doll Rob found in the yard and brought in that reminded me of my old Suzie; and a part of a review I read yesterday on a book about death.

The book was based on the idea that nature was against man; and that religion was man's attempt to operate within that unsafe context. The feelings I was getting went even further, that religion or science or whatever weren't attempts to discover truth—but to escape from doing so, to substitute some satisfying tale or story instead. And I suppose that if someone persisted long enough, he or she would find the holes in the stories.... and undo the whole works. The idea of the stories was to save each man from having to encounter reality in such a frightening fashion.... the characters in the stories did this for him in their own fashion.... and if you kept it up.... you threatened the fine framework of organization that alone made life possible....

DELETED SESSION
MARCH 11, 1981   8:58 PM WEDNESDAY

(See the attached copies of Jane's reincarnation and grandfather dreams of March 6, and her nightmarish experience of March 8. All of these are very important, I think, with the experience of March 8 taking precedence, I'd say. They're all classics. Jane woke me up often during the night while she was having the March 8 experience, and we think it contains many important clues to her hassles. She's reread all of the experiences several times so far, and has made a few additional notes about the March 8 event in particular.

(We'd thought that Seth might refer to them in the session for last Monday, but none was held because once again Jane was so relaxed on the couch after supper. She was also somewhat blue and discouraged. In fact, I hadn't expected a session tonight until she called me at 8:40, so relaxed was she. She's been sleeping much better generally, though, is still taking a nap in the late morning as well as our usual nap break just before supper. She's also been heading for bed a half hour earlier at night.

(She was very quiet as session time approached, but wasn't too comfortable in her chair. I was quiet too—we'd been more or less that way all day. "I think it'll be short," she finally said.)

Now.

("Good evening.")

Ruburt's nightmare experience *(of March 8)* is a beautiful example of the kind of explosive emotional content that many people carry, fairly hidden, representing certain taboos, translated of course in individualistic manners.

I do not want to go into a history of <u>culture</u> here, but your organizations historically have largely been built upon your religious concepts, which have indeed been extremely rigid. In the light of those concepts, artistic expression has been channeled, focused, directed along certain lines. It has been discouraged along other lines. The repressive nature of Christian thought in the Middle Ages, for example, is well known.

Expression itself was considered highly suspect if it traveled outside of the accepted precepts, and particularly of course if it led others to take action against those precepts. To some extent the same type of policy is still reflected in your current societies, though science or the state itself may serve instead of the church as the voice of authority.

Behind such ideas is of course the central point of Christianity, or one of the central points at least, that earthly man is a sinful creature. He is <u>given</u> to sin. In that regard his <u>natural expression</u> must be closely guarded. It must be directed toward officialdom, and outside of that boundary lay, particularly in the past, the very uncomfortable realm of the heretic.

In medieval times to be excommunicated was no trivial incident, but an event harkening severance that touched the soul, the body, and all political, religious and economic conditions by which the two were tied together.

Many people's economic well-being of course was dependent upon the church in one way or another, and in reincarnational terms many millions of people alive today were familiar then with such conditions. The nunneries and monasteries were long-time social and religious institutions, some extremely rigorous, while others were religiously oriented in name only. But there is a long history of the conflicts between creative thought, heresy, excommunication, or worse, death. All of those factors were involved in one way or another in the fabric of Ruburt's nightmare material.

(*Pause at 9:15.*) Again, many people carry the same kind of emotional charge. Ruburt's fears, as expressed in that material, can be encountered, of course. It is when they are <u>hidden</u> that difficulties arise, because their charge is then added to other issues.

There are, however, classic connections between creative thought and heresy, between established belief and the danger of revelatory material as being disruptive—first of church and then of state.

The church was quite real to Ruburt as a child, through the priests who came *[to the house]* regularly, through direct contact with the religious *[grade]* school, and the support offered to the family. Ruburt's very early poetry offended Father Boyle, who objected to its themes, and who burned his books on the fall of Rome, so he had more than a hypothetical feeling about such issues. Many of those fears originated long before the sessions, of course, and before he realized that there was any alternative at all between, say, conventional religious beliefs and complete disbelief in any nature of divinity.

In the time those fears originated, he shared the belief framework of Christianity, so that he believed that outside of that framework there could indeed be nothing but chaos, or the conventional atheism of science, in which the universe was at the mercy of meaningless mechanistic laws—laws, however, that operated without logic, but more importantly laws that operated without feeling.

He [Ruburt] was afraid that if he went too far he would discover that he had catapulted himself into a realm where both answers and questions were meaningless, and in which no sense was to be found. To do that is one thing, but to take others with you would be, he felt, unforgivable—and in the framework of those fears, as his work became better known he became even more cautious.

(9:28. A very significant sentence:) The entire structure of fears, of course, is based upon a belief in the sinful self and the sinful nature of the self's expression.

Outside of that context, none of those fears make any sense at all (equally important, of course). In a large regard the church through the centuries ruled through the use of fear far more than the use of love. It was precisely in the area of artistic expression, of course, that the inspirations might quickest leap through the applied dogmatic framework. The political nature of inspirational material of any kind was well understood by the church.

By such tactics the church managed to hold on to an entire civilization for centuries. (Long pause.) Ruburt well knew even as a child that such structures had served their time, and his poetry provided a channel through which he could express his own views as he matured. Later the old fears, if they surfaced, were not encountered. They seemed beneath him, unworthy or cowardly—but in any case their validity as feelings was not recognized or understood.

Ruburt did initiate a small religious order in the 16th Century, in France, and he was in love for many years with the man he met in his dream—a cleric. The love was not consummated, but it was passionate and enduring nonetheless on both of their parts.

(Long pause at 9:37.) Ruburt had considerable difficulty with church doctrine even then, and the rules of the order as actually carried out through practice were later considered to hold their own seeds of heresy. Ruburt was forced to leave the order that he had initiated, as an old woman. He left with a few female companions who were also ostracized, and died finally of starvation. It was a time when unconventional patterns of thought, of unconventional expression, could have dire consequences.

The name Normandy comes to mind, and the name Abelard. The dream came to remind Ruburt of those connections, but also to remind him that his life even then was enriched by a long-held love relationship. The two corresponded frequently, met often, and in their ways conspired to alter many of the practices that were abhorrent yet held as proper church policy.

Some of Ruburt's short notes, written after the nightmare experience *(and which I've asked Jane to copy for this record)*, show that he is beginning to put that material into its proper reference. Those fears, however, have been pertinent, since they <u>stood between</u> old beliefs and new ones—that is, they prevented him from taking full advantage of his newer knowledge, and of the abilities and good intent of the spontaneous self.

Both the nightmare experience and the dream were partially triggered by our last session *(on March 4)*, of course, and served to show Ruburt why he had begun to cut down on <u>some</u> (underlined) of his own psychic experience, inspiration, and expression—a policy reflected in the repressed nature of bodily expression.

The dream representing his grandfather symbolically allowed him to go back to the past in this life, to a time of severe shock—his grandfather's death—which occurred when he was beginning to substitute scientific belief for religious belief, wondering if his grandfather's consciousness then fell back into a mindless state of being, into chaos, as science would certainly seem to suggest.

In the dream his grandfather revives. His grandfather <u>survived</u> in a suit too large, which means that there was still room for him to grow *(as I'd suggested to Jane)*. He *[Ruburt]* had a small experience of hearing a voice speak in his mind *[yesterday]*—a voice of comfort, all he remembered of quite legitimate assistance he received from other personalities connected with the French life, that came as a result of the French dream.

He still needs your reassurances, and should tell you when he feels discouraged for his legs are further loosening, and all he needs is the revival of confidence. I bid you a fond good evening, and I have not forgotten your questions. My fondest regards—

("Thank you very much, Seth.")

—and to you and your flowers.

("Good night."

(9:55 PM. I smiled, thinking of the mixed results I'm having trying to get various flower seeds to germinate both in and outside of the planter Jane gave me for Christmas. The sweet peas and marigolds are doing great, the godetia and dianthus not so great, so far.

(Half joking, I said to Jane, "What did you think of <u>that</u>? Are you trying to

tell me religion has been in back of this all of the time? I thought you left the church. It appears you didn't leave it at all.... I'll have to arrange for an exorcism for you."

(Jane laughed, sort of. "Well, I'm glad I had it."

("So am I. It just might be invaluable. Actually, the material goes into a couple of the questions I've got listed about reincarnational connections with the symptoms."

("I thought it might," Jane said. "I'll have milk and a cookie to take my aspirin with, then I'll go in the bedroom at 10:30."

(Bill was still alternately sleeping and preening himself beside me on the couch, as he'd been doing all through the session. His coat is glossy and beautiful. I admired the tender loving care with which he addressed himself to each portion of his body.

(I suggested to Jane that she see what she might be able to pick up on her own about the French life. I mentioned that Normandy province is in the northwestern corner of France, some 20 miles across the channel from England. I've read that it's predominantly rural in character, and thought that it was probably even more so back in the 16th century. It could have been a grim, if beautiful, setting.

(We speculated that Abelard is a famous name, historically and in the arts, though we couldn't think of any specific connections. But like Normandy, it must apply to a number of people and topics.)

DELETED SESSION
MARCH 18, 1981 9:19 PM WEDNESDAY

(No session was held Monday night because Jane was so relaxed again—that is, I'd thought that was the reason, but more about that later. "When I sit on the couch and relax after supper, I don't want to do anything," she said. "I don't even want to have a session tonight. I don't feel him around at all." She'd called me at 8:45. She still sat in her usual place on the couch, and following a suggestion I'd made the other day she decided to try having the session from that position. It meant she'd be able to lean back, "taking the pressure off my ass," she laughed. "But I don't know how it'll work out."

(The result was that I sat in her chair, facing her across the inevitable coffee table. She didn't know whether to sit upright or lean back: "It feels odd already, and I haven't even started. So I'm just waiting."

(Actually, I learned as we talked, Jane had called me for a session Monday evening, but I hadn't heard her. I'd taken it for granted that she wanted the rest instead. But she said when I didn't answer she decided to let the session go.

(See the attached experiences of Jane's, of March 13 and 16. I showed them to

her to refresh her memory. As with her earlier experiences, these were excellent and quite to the point considering her hassles. It was easy to lose track of them, unfortunately. "I've completely forgotten your questions, too," she said. As I had, for the most part. Nor have I added to that list for a long time now. One thing that inhibited me is that I was aware, of course, of the predominantly negative context or tone of the whole idea of the list. It's a contradictory attitude, of course, since these private sessions are an effort to learn something about our hassles—not a self-congratulatory exercise.

(At 9:12 Jane reminded me that she'd been sleeping much better recently. "And my arms are definitely longer, and go out to the sides farther, and I think my legs are better too—they don't stick up so high under the covers when I lay on my back."

(Since Seth mentions such episodes tonight, I'll note here also that lately Jane has had a number of dreams involving television programs that we've seen—shows like Dallas, *TV movies, etc. Now as she prepared for Seth to come through she sat upright on the couch. Then:)*

Good evening.

("Good evening, Seth.")

Now: we have been having a rather concentrated group of sessions, and it is quite natural that Ruburt should want to take some time out as he has, so that he can assimilate the material.

He is having this evening's session at least partially out of his sense of responsibility—because he thinks he should, and because he thinks you think he should. He must, or should, feel free to have the sessions—to have the sessions.

He has used the materials of your culture—the television programs and so forth—to excellent advantage in the dream state and otherwise, so that messages of his own psyche come through. The TV programs become like dreams, and indeed they appear rewritten in the dream state also, as the psyche seizes upon different kinds of vehicles for its own therapeutic expression.

The Mafia dream *(of March 16)* based on the gangsters' series, for example, served to bring into conscious awareness not just the information, but Ruburt's feelings about the dominant male role in your present culture. It is the feelings that are so important. They should not be shunted aside, or treated as stepchildren, but compassionately understood. Then (underlined) they can change into something else. The same applies to Ruburt's feelings in the religious area. There is no need saying, "What a ridiculous way to feel" —not an attempt to disinherit the feelings, but to accept them as one's own, and compassionately explain the mitigating circumstances and new knowledge that alter the initial circumstances that stimulated the feelings to begin with.

Our late sessions helped bring about several important dreams that I have mentioned, and also activated other therapeutic layers, so that different kinds of messages have been received while Ruburt was in the sleep or dream state.

(Now Jane began to lean back on the couch; she looked to be much more comfortable.)

To that extent he has carried on the sessions, using them to good purpose. The natural person is of course the natural dreamer, and it is for that reason all the more unfortunate that psychology managed to divorce the world of dreaming from natural healthy psychology. In the natural person, dreams <u>always</u> serve a balancing function, leading toward self-illumination, self-instruction, self-help.

(9:32.) That process has been strengthened as far as Ruburt is concerned once again. The Stonehenge poem *(that Jane began writing earlier in March, when we received an English postcard from Michael Lorimer)* in a way is a case in point, since it shows the reawakening of a certain kind of creative and psychic activity. So does the bodily relaxation, however, and that steady reduction of tension is bound to show good results as he learns to trust himself further.

(A good point. I mentioned to Jane when I read the session to her from my notes this morning that it's one of those obvious things easy to overlook: Jane's steady relaxation is bound to help....)

He is beginning to identify better with his body—a very important point.

I want to give you all the pertinent information you require. I also want to see, however, that Ruburt's own rhythms are followed, so that you do not get an overconcentration of renewed worries or concerns. We are embarked upon a journey of expression, some of that expression will necessarily involve feelings that have been inhibited, of a stressful nature. The problem is not with the feelings, but with the fact that they have not previously been expressed or accepted.

There are other repressed <u>inspirations</u> and creative insights that will also come to the forefront. Unfortunately, it is amazingly difficult to verbally describe the connections between the dream state, health, cultural stimuli, and the way all of these are put together in the interrelationship of body and mind —but Ruburt's notes on his dreams and other experiences, being specific, can offer some excellent clues.

Your own interest in *(flower)* <u>seeds</u> right now presents you with an excellent example of the natural person's inclination to seek out fresh stimulation, and to ally itself, however innocently, with those forces of natural creativity. The exterior interest, the physical manipulations, also stand for, and reflect, inner manipulations with psychic growth, and serve as symbols of a united psychological approach.

There are other dream episodes that Ruburt has forgotten, and help that he has received, that does not need to become conscious. All that is primarily needed is trust in those healing processes, and particularly in the body's relaxation.

Natural therapeutics always operate, of course, but in your society at least there is considerable pressure put on the other side, for it is the natural person you are taught not to trust. *(Pause.)* The switch of course, again, can never become total, but science—and medical science in particular—almost managed to divorce man from his natural feeling of trust in his own capacities, so that it seems for example that medical science per se knows more about any given individual's body than the individual does himself. *(Pause.)* This is because of the projection of the entire idea of <u>body mechanisms</u>, per se, as opposed to inner spontaneous bodily workings.

Few people, then, have little experience with those interrelationships that connect dreams, daily events, and physical health.

I recommend again that Ruburt not forget to look into the library, to do some energy research on himself, and in whatever way possible try to encourage an atmosphere in which he is "less careful."

(Pause at 9:50.) I also want to stress the fact that the entire psychic area of expression belongs to the natural person. It is not some esoteric addition. Man, for example, exhibited natural psychic activity long before the birth of science —and for that matter before the initiation of formal religion. There is therefore a great connection between creativity—poetry in particular—dreams, and psychic exploration. If anything, these provide humanity with a great rich structure of psychological activity <u>from which</u> all of the later cultural, religious, or scientific elements emerge. So remind Ruburt that his psychic activity represents a most basic portion of his nature—and of <u>human</u> nature.

(Long pause at 9:56.) The entire dynamics of civilization to a large extent is related directly to man's individual and mass psychic experience, and he ever receives fresh information from those inner sources. Otherwise his physical dilemmas, individually and worldwide, would have ended in sure catastrophe centuries ago.

(Pause.) Our material was precisely the kind that would directly threaten old beliefs, so in that regard there were bound to be points of conflict. Ruburt would meet them fairly directly, since after all he was not some hypothetical person reading our books, but the person responsible for delivering them. In a fashion the material <u>returns him</u>, however, to a natural yet mystical inner knowledge of his childhood <u>before</u> (underlined) he cloaked it in the church's robes, and it would be good for him to remember that and perhaps try to recapture some of

those very early feelings that he has consciously forgotten.

In other words, the psychic development is a part of his natural growth *(long pause)*, a reaffirmation and <u>restructuring</u> of inner information that in one fashion or another was always available to him, but needed to find a conscious format, a conscious expression, a way to pierce the seemingly opaque habits of knowledge of the cultural world.

Such reassurances and reminders can help connect him with feelings from that earlier time. The early vivid feeling for reincarnation, when he knew Roberts was not his proper name *(as a youngster)*; the episode when he watched grade school children as no more than a toddler himself, and knew he had gone to school before; the flying out-of-body dreams; and the sense of identification with nature, and particularly with the night—those feelings waited for their vindication, for they did not fit into the world as he was told then. Period.

(10:08.) In other words, the entire psychic sequence only <u>seemed</u> to be thrust upon him in his thirties. *(Long pause.)* A reconciliation now can help revive those youthful feelings of support, however, and the enjoyment of natural knowledge and natural characteristics.

(Long pause.) I am trying to connect present and past here in a very important manner, so that Ruburt can understand his own psychic roots, for they are indeed the basic ones, and that understanding is as important to his development now as any other material that I might give. I will then end the session, unless you have a question that you particularly want answered this evening.

("No...." Actually I had many questions, but decided to forgo them since Seth had remarked earlier that Jane needed time to assimilate the material he's already given.)

Then I bid you a fond good evening *(smile.*

("The same to you. Good night."

(10:12 PM. Jane's delivery from her new position on the couch had been steady and emphatic until she slowed down noticeably toward the end of the session. I told Jane it was an excellent session and that she'd done well. She'd alternated while sitting between perching upright and leaning back.)

JANE'S NOTES
MARCH 13, 1981 FRIDAY

Last night in bed all through the night off and on I had the following hard-to-explain but welcome experience. First, after just half asleep I suddenly knew how to turn over in a particular easy way that didn't hurt nearly as much as usual. Then

*sometime later I realized I'd been very comfortable, sleeping great, but was now get-
ting sore again—hips in particular, and arms. Then I became disoriented, and
couldn't figure out if I was in bed or in my chair. Realized I was in bed, in a particular position and making certain motions that were self-conflicting, leading to the
discomfort; and that I was in this position because I thought I'd done something
wrong that somehow necessitated the position. Guilt was involved. At the same time
almost I realized quite clearly that I'd made a mistake; I hadn't done anything wrong
and the position was needless. And at once my physical discomfort vanished. This
same process—with different positions in bed—happened four or five times, each
time with the discomfort vanishing just about instantly. (AM. I'm quite uncomfortable though.)*

*The experience is hopeful though and taken along with my recent dreams seems
to indicate that my psychic abilities are warming up again at least....*

*The voice episode Seth mentioned in our last session was very brief, not too
vivid, but definite. During my nap a few days ago, as I wakened, a voice in my head
was saying.... "We're leaving now. We tried to take this terrible weight off you and
think we have, though you might not realize it quite yet...."*

*Called Tam yesterday, March 12; Events expected a month from today. (We
haven't seen front-matter proofs yet.)*

JANE'S NOTES
MARCH 16, 1981 MONDAY

*[I] am writing down two dream experiences, each with some nightmare ele-
ments, though not too intense.*

The first was Saturday night, March 14: We'd watched The Gangster
Chronicles *on TV that evening, about the Mafia. The experience seemed to last all
night gradually deepening in intensity, without overt dramatic story line — there
was material on the Mafia in its relationship to family and particularly in connection with women—this seemed to be the focus point. I guess the idea was that males
operate as a Mafia regardless of gangster connections.... there was a lot on this; I'd
half wake up, very sore; half crying.... Because I remember few details it's difficult to
explain the nightmarish quality this had. There was also some material on my mother....*

*Sunday night I slept very well until dawn arrived. Then again I went into a
nightmarish quality dream, with no story line. Or very little. I imagined the different ways magazines like* The National Enquirer *could trick someone into giving an
interview to start with, and turn people against each other, (Carol Burnett is suing*

that paper—the story was in the news lately.) From there some wild stuff that does-
n't make sense now, with strange things happening to my chair pillow as I sat on it....
not at all sure but the idea was that unpredictable unpleasant things could happen I
suppose to "knock you off your ass." Again I grew very sore—after being fairly com-
fortable for the night—half awakened crying as different things happened that I've
forgotten.... So all I have out of this I guess is released feelings that the world is at best
unpredictable and can hurt you at any time. I also half knew that the entire affair
was exaggerated.... the idea being to bring the feelings to the front of my mind.... The
affair reminded me of an incident when I was a kid, in science class, as a freshman
in high school. Another kid pulled my chair out from behind me so that when I went
to sit down I fell on the floor instead. This was the same class in which I took the
church's stand against evolution to my teacher's disgust....

DELETED SESSION
MARCH 25, 1981 9:19 PM WEDNESDAY

(Jane said she'd first called me for the session at 8:20, but I had been work-
ing in the studio closet and hadn't heard her. She called again at 8:40. It was 9:00
by the time I got settled—and she still didn't "feel him around"—meaning Seth,
of course. She added that she was having the session because she supposed she ought
to.

(No session was held last Monday night because Jane was so relaxed, just as she
was now. Her bodily changes continue, with some good news about improvements in
her legs contributed by Frank Longwell after an examination. So does her active
dream-experience nightlife, still based upon, often, television programs. Jane had a
"scary" dream episode last night, one that was quite unpleasant, she said, and
involved her seeing herself in different time frames and three different programs or
movies on TV at the same time. By now she can't say why the episode had been so
frightening.

(Jane had reread my list of questions for Seth, based on this last group of ses-
sions, and referred to often. After supper we'd talked about questions 2 and 13, the
same ones we'd asked that Seth discuss in another recent private session; he hadn't
done so yet, though. And, of course, his material throughout these sessions can't but
help touch upon various facets pertaining to the questions. So upon that premise, the
questions are being discussed all the time.)

Now.

("Good evening.")

I have told you that you are born into your times knowing in advance the problems, challenges, and potential developments that are possible.

This applies to everyone, of course. All of you have a hand in the formation of world events. Those connections are worked out at all levels of reality, in the waking state through your communication devices and culture, and through the far more complicated arena of the culture of dreams. Your dreams are your own, yet they interact with others, and the dreams of others are background issues in your own dream encounters.

Ruburt's symptoms are not his challenge this time, as you asked (*in question 13*), but the philosophical connotations behind his difficulties certainly do involve his challenges this time.

In one manner or another, each person mirrors the experience of the world, while also adding to that experience in an original way, impressing reality as no other individual could. It is true to say that reality as you understand it changes <u>as each individual changes</u>. Your thoughts then do change the world, whether you act upon your thoughts or not, they have their effect.

Ruburt's difficulties are based upon certain philosophical dilemmas, that are his own personally—dilemmas, however, that also belong to your time, and are therefore largely responsible for the difficulties in your historical period. To some extent or another, again, the entire affair is an endeavor in which all persons have their parts to play. The issues involved affect, for example, Ruburt's personal mobility. They also are connected with the much larger social issues, such as the uses to which your nuclear technology will be put.

You have been taught for centuries in one way or another that repression, generally speaking, now, was all in all a natural, good, social and moral requirement, that expression was dangerous and must be harnessed and channeled because it was believed so thoroughly that man's natural capacities led him toward destructive rather than positive behavior.

Energy was feared, expression suspicious unless it was directed and tempered in conventional fashions. Through all of man's religions and philosophies that line of thought has been most prominent; those who had the most energy suffered from it the most, of course. If you did not believe that energy was more naturally dangerous than beneficial, you would not have any difficulties at all concerning issues like nuclear bombs.

(*9:34.*) Instead, your natural creativity and your natural energies would some time ago have led you <u>naturally</u> (underlined) to a more productive use of nuclear force, to ways of rendering such use harmless in the short and long run, so that it could take its place in a loving technology. You take the opposite for granted, of course, and you consider psychological energy in the very same terms.

Ruburt has tried, as I said before, to use his abilities while being very cautious. He has tried expressing those abilities while feeling he needed all kinds of safeguards, both because he partially shared the belief that energy was dangerous, and because he also feared that other people would react to him in that fashion.

You are alive to express the individualistic life-force that is the source of your being. You have been taught not to trust that energy, however, and in one way or another your social programs and your governments themselves are based upon the proposition that man must be protected from his own nature —a nature seen as unsavory at best.

In your times the individual problems of masses of people are bound up with such issues, and as they work toward their own solutions, then in their own ways they help solve problems at the level of world action. You are quite correct: Ruburt spent many years "building up his defenses." Determined to use his abilities, while also determined to protect himself, and from *(pause)* any danger that those abilities <u>themselves</u> might carry with them.

One of the main issues is the recognition of the fact that energy is good, that its expression is to be naturally encouraged, and that through such encouragement each individual best fulfills his or her life, and also adds to the development and understanding of the species.

Your country, for all of its obvious errors, still is one in which such issues can best be worked out both philosophically and practically. Now in both of your lives, you have managed to express creative abilities to advantage, to draw upon these not only at isolated <u>periods </u>of your lives, or in partial form, but in such a fashion that they have provided you with continuing frameworks of self-discovery and creativity—so when you are counting accomplishments, remember that *(in reference to question 2.)*

(9:49.) There are qualitative leaps that exist impossible to bridge with the intellect alone that separate, say, well-meaning, adequate-enough attempts toward artistic achievement, and works that are of themselves naturally artistic exhibitions. A lifetime of concentrated effort and intellectual concern alone will not, for example, turn a poor poet into a good one. Techniques may improve, the work may become more polished, but the quality of the poetry itself is what is important.

You have both been able to count upon that quality.

It has provided you with an extra framework through which to view reality. Now yours is, say, the poetry of painting. Now in the philosophical area we are discussing, you are also dealing with imaginative leaps, with casts of mind and spirit that are as rare as true artistic ability is. In that area you are asked to merge philosophical insights with the practical, everyday nitty-gritty of life. You are asked to bring those delicate understandings to practical flowering—a considerable task, and doubly so when the philosophical issues involved go so against the established grain of historically accepted knowledge.

(Pause.) In one way or another, Ruburt always understood that his natural leanings led him in such directions. It is easy to say that he overdid his <u>defenses</u>. *(Pause.)* Those defenses also served, however, <u>to some degree</u> (underlined) as a part of a larger learning process, and as a way of containing knowledge that he wanted and felt he required.

Exactly what were the mechanisms of such defense systems, as individuals used them? Nations use them in the same way. All of this can be quite difficult to explain. It would be highly unusual for Ruburt to have been untouched by the belief systems of his times—particularly if he had set out <u>to change them</u>. *(Pause.)* You are not simply trying to look at the world differently, for example, or to change a hypothetical reality, but to creatively bring about some version of a creative and artistic vision that results not simply in greater poems or paintings, <u>but in greater renditions of reality</u> *(all very intently.*

(10:06. With a smile:) When you want to express darkness you might paint your canvas with black instead of your magic white *(a la William Alexander)*, so that then the use of lighter colors upon it will indicate more clearly the quality of light, at least for the painting's purposes. So to some extent or another, Ruburt's own adherence to past beliefs of a "negative" nature were also used in his life itself, appearing as symptoms that only the more pointed out the necessity for light, and the need for the greater understandings toward which he was searching.

This does not mean that he was <u>fated</u> to do any such thing, that it would not be done more easily in other fashions, but you can see some correspondence there by looking at <u>his</u> (underlined) paintings, and the vivid use of contrasting colors that are not subtle. This is of course one way of looking at the entire issue. The same philosophical dilemma, again, lies at a basis for your mass events. Ruburt has been using television programs and such cultural data as a basis for some of his own dreams. In such a way he sees his own personal situation more clearly—but he also sees the world situation as it reflects the same kind of philosophical questions.

In a manner of speaking you have your dream newscasters, of course, only these are both more extensive and more personal than your television equivalents. Your dream newscasts come down to the question of what actions are taken <u>by individuals</u> (underlined)—and individual actions, again, are as influenced by the knowledge received in dreams as they are from exterior activity.

Ruburt then has indeed been involved in working out his dilemmas, both in their private and public nature through the use of such dream techniques, the subsequent feelings aroused in the daytime, and the intuitive resolutions and insights that then occur. He has not "given up" the book sessions, by the way, but suspended them for these sessions, to give you more time, but they are merely in abeyance.

I am trying to insert answers to some of your questions in a way that also is in rhythm with both of your needs at each session—so I bid you a fond good evening.

("Thank you, Seth. Good night.")

(10:22 PM. Jane's delivery had been surprisingly good and emphatic, considering her relaxed state. "I just had the session because I felt so like not having it," she said. I told her it was a good one, as usual.

(We discussed Seth's reference on page 85 to Jane fearing that others might actually look upon her as dangerous because of her abilities. At first I'd thought this a new insight on Seth's part, but we decided that it wasn't, that he'd covered this ground in other material from a variety of viewpoints. There's something about his simple statement, though, that is intriguing—that others, in addition to considering that Jane was antireligious, say, would also think of her as dangerous.)

DELETED SESSION
APRIL 13, 1981 8:50 PM MONDAY

(We haven't had a session for three weeks now. To my mind, our situation has steadily deteriorated. I think it came to a head yesterday, when I finally realized that for the last few days Jane had cut down her visits to the bathroom to just two times a day—upon arising, and before going to bed. Her reason for this, when I questioned her, was that "it hurts to move. But I'm working on it."

(I did not understand what there was to work on about going to the john, since it was absolutely essential that one do so. I told her that as I understood such matters, her behavior could lead to uremic poisoning, or dehydration, should she compensate for "holding it" for such long periods by cutting down on her intake of liquids. I added that dehydration could be just as fatal as uremic poisoning. It was all too obvious that she had reacted to her problems about as far as she could go, at least in that direction.

(We've had several of our famous discussions since the last session on March 25. I feel caught in contradictions—for if Jane's new feelings in her hips and legs are signs

of new muscular activity, as she thinks, and as Frank Longwell agrees, that's good news; yet those same feelings, her acute and prolonged bodily discomfort, her aches and pains, have caused her to become almost totally inactive. As I wrote in question 13 some weeks ago now, she has surrendered just about all activity except that involved with getting up and lying down, eating, going to the bathroom on a very limited basis, and puttering about in her breezeway writing room for an hour or so on occasion. She's managed to get her poetry book out to Prentice, and now is not at work on any writing. She's even let go writing up her recent dream material, some of which has been excellent, with apparent precognitive information of a positive nature.

(She spends a good deal of her waking time on the couch watching TV, or sleeping away part of the day.

(A remark she made yesterday probably had helped crystallize my own new determination to do something about what seemed to be a badly eroding situation: She said that Tam had recently told her that Mass Events *was due to be published on the 13th—today—with* God of Jane *due out early in May. These two books are, I think we agree, the most recent triggers that she has responded to in a negative way, so yesterday I suddenly realized that Jane must be reacting presently to the imminent publication of those two works. It seemed obvious. I knew they were due out soon, but slipped up in my own awareness that their publication could—would cause her additional problems; my opinion was based on her paper of last December, in which she wrote that from its very inception she had been concerned about the reception* Mass Events *would be accorded by various elements of the public.*

(I still think that paper is a very revealing one, for it contains several important clues that we should keep always in mind, but often do not. Among them is Jane's fear of the controversial nature of Seth's medical material, which led to Prentice-Hall's installation of the hated disclaimer.

(Several times during recent weeks I've said that I wished we'd withdrawn Mass Events *from publication, using the disclaimer controversy as a ready-made excuse. The idea being that this would hopefully free Jane from worry on that score, at least. Yet working with the pendulum in the bedroom at 12:30 AM last night, she said she still wanted the book published—and therein lay at least one source of much trouble, I thought and said.*

(The pendulum session was not a success, in my opinion. I didn't think Jane asked specific-enough questions, that she was somehow reluctant to or unable to do so—even that she appeared to be somewhat ill at ease while using it. She was upset of course, and so was I. I went to bed very unhappy with our situation—and I suppose that that feeling helped lead me to the group of statements below the next morning, and this session.

(Jane didn't sleep very well, so I didn't call her this morning. Instead after breakfast I wrote down my list of points to discuss with her. I saw them as making a significant alteration—at least potentially—in our lives. But then, I thought, given our present situation our lives were going to change anyhow and perhaps drastically: her not going to the john properly wasn't a good sign.

(Jane did get up by 10:30. and an hour later I initiated our little discussion. I read to her, and explained, each of the points on my list:

(1. We are going to have sessions nightly, or at least several times a week, in a last-ditch effort to get to the bottom of the problem.

(2. She is to call Tam to verify that the two books in question are to be published as expected. Especially important here was Mass Events, *which I regard as the main trigger of the moment.*

(3. She is to start going to the john at least four times a day.

(4. She is to begin taking at least one step *a day with the help of the typing table.*

(5. The number of "crash" sessions held will depend on progress made, what help Seth can offer. I plan to try to objectively understand any beneficial effects there are. I don't think of such sessions running indefinitely—perhaps three weeks or a month at the most.

(6. The next step will be to seek medical help—namely, going to a hospital for tests, therapy, diagnosis, medication, whatever. I plan to ask Paul O'Neill about how to get her admitted, or at least examined. Or I'll go to a hospital myself and ask to talk to someone. The idea isn't that a stay in the hospital will work a miracle cure — though I'd be delighted if it did —but that some help or easing of Jane's symptoms might eventually be achieved through therapy or whatever. My personal opinion at the moment is that we should have taken this step a long time ago. Interesting, to speculate about why I've concurred in Jane's dogged avoidance in seeking establishment medical help.

(Jane didn't react as much to point 6 as I thought she might. The last time I'd suggested that she consider getting medical help had been at Christmas time, when I asked her to think it over and let me know. But I haven't heard a word on the subject from her.

(Jane has had several vivid dreams since we held the last session; they've been of the type described in recent private sessions—combinations of nightmarish events and characters, along with flashes of insight into the causes for the symptoms, and visions of herself walking normally, etc. But she's written very little on them. However, they've been valuable in showing that she is still contending with previously buried fears. We keep hoping these will play in important part in letting her achieve more physical release. But at the moment it seems that everything is difficult,

or worse, especially so when I worry about how far she has to go simply to get her legs to straighten out at least partially. I did feel, I told her, that a time of decision was very near.

(Jane sat on the couch in her usual position for the session, and I sat facing her across the coffee table while using her own chair. She spoke slowly much of the time, and often while sitting stiffly upright.)

Now—

("Good evening.")

—we will begin briefly and gently.

Ruburt's feelings of physical mobility are to some extent connected with his feelings of creative mobility—that is, the connections are strong.

As far as dilemmas go, he feels one as far as Prentice is concerned, since he sees Prentice as a <u>vehicle</u> (underlined) that moves his work out into the public arena, and he feels that that vehicle is at best presently stalled, while no other one is in immediate practical sight.

Both the change in Tam's position, and changes that take place in the company contributed, along with your own strong dissatisfactions with Prentice to begin with. Creatively, on that level alone, he also feels stalled, since he does not know whether or not to continue with my book, or whether or not to begin one of his own—so you have a stalled mobility, without any particular decisions being made of a clear-cut nature.

(As soon as I'd finished reading my list of points to her, this morning, Jane called Tam about the publication of Mass Events. *He told her the book hadn't arrived in the office yet, but that he expected it to, and that he would check to see if it was on schedule. He would then send us the usual first copy.)*

In that kind of period, he is more apt to be dissatisfied, brood about his physical condition, and therefore aggravate his symptoms. They are, however, the exterior picture of the inner one—to go ahead or to retreat. To go ahead in what direction? Instead the situation is a stalled one.

In the background there is of course his reaction to the two books. Some of that material I have given. *(Long pause.)* Some is difficult to explain clearly, because Ruburt wanted to make sure of the validity of the sessions from the start, and because of other material given in the past, he did not fully accept the sessions or his own psychic abilities as an <u>integral part</u> of his personality—since they <u>appeared</u> relatively late in life, where the poetry, for example, had always more or less been apparent.

(9:02.) He felt a strong commitment to poetry and writing. He could not early accept the idea of having a <u>mission</u> in life outside of the simple one to write, which always propelled him. He examined the sessions thoroughly then

for years, not feeling the same kind of self-assurance as he did, you see, with his "own" writing.

His own writing underwent its own kinds of transformation, however, and indeed it began those translations years ago, even before the sessions, so that for example even the science fiction could no longer contain or camouflage the larger intuitive framework that he was developing.

(*Long pause.*) I have remarked before that part of the problem lies in discrepancies of growth. You spoke (*today*) of some artists painting formula paintings. For Ruburt to try to publish usual novels, for example, would not work: he has outgrown the formulas. At the same time, for many reasons there has been a difficulty in accepting the natural patterns of his own individualistic growth—and that is partially because there were no neat categories in which they seemed to naturally fall. So in searching out new ways, personally and creatively, Ruburt felt himself on insecure ground.

That insecurity has largely prevented him from fully using his own abilities on his own behalf (*intently*). He is gifted precisely with the kind of abilities that can clear up all of his problems. Fears, however, have prevented him from fully trusting—or consistently trying—such avenues, not only fears, but the batteries of past beliefs, both on his part and yours, with their unfortunate patterns of behavior and conditioned responses. It is sometimes difficult for me to translate what I know about the situation into terms that you can accept jointly, because of the press of those beliefs and the accompanying habitual behavior and conditioning.

(*9:16.*) I am aware of the pressing nature of your concerns, and of the sharpness of the physical picture as you perceive it—yet I must continue (*almost with a smile*) to maintain the following points: a concentration upon a problem deepens it. An overly intense search for what is wrong is debilitating—particularly when you end up looking for events as scapegoats rather than for the beliefs with which certain events are perceived.

Your feelings presently that Ruburt is on the brink of being bedridden are —mainly now—the results of negative conditioning—they seem very realistic. Certainly the evidence seems (underlined) to give those feelings at least some support. They are the end result of a recent concentration upon the problem. And in this case you both fell into their sway at the same time.

All of this involves you in the private nitty-gritty of dealing with the ways of thinking and reasoning that are so characteristic in your society and in your time. In certain areas where the contrasts in the other direction are as startling, you have largely escaped such conditioned behavior. You have escaped it because you have learned and grown easier in those directions—or you both consciously and unconsciously applied new concepts to those other areas.

("Like what areas?" I asked Seth. When he stared at me, I repeated the question rather insistently.

(Almost with a laugh:) I was ready to tell you. Those areas include the psychic one, the creative one, the financial one, and the mental one. That is, there are areas of your lives that operate quite smoothly, yet in a fashion <u>almost</u> outside of your conscious direction. What I mean is that these areas bring you most fruitful rewards, so that to a degree you take them for granted, without being aware of the manipulations that occur to bring them about.

(This was one of the spots where I felt like interrupting Seth to protest that I for one—and Jane. too, I believe—do not take such benefits for granted. I try to be grateful each day for what we have, while still being aware that the mechanisms that deliver those benefits to us may operate largely on unconscious levels.)

Your minds become accustomed to a very high quality of conceptual thought, for example. *(Pause.)* Money comes to you in comfortable amounts. *(Long pause.)* Creatively you deal with events and episodes that are by contrast with most people's lives, most remarkable. In those areas you have grown beyond the negative conditioning of the society in large measure.

Ruburt's physical situation therefore seems even more apparent in the light of such contrasts. In the area of the symptoms, <u>comparatively</u> speaking, you have still more or less stayed in the same framework of behavior, relatively speaking, as others of your society, at least in many respects.

Even there you have learned, of course, and Ruburt's knowledge and yours has helped you both in your health in many ways—but you have not used your abilities in that direction <u>in the same fashion</u> that you have otherwise, and in the newest attempt to help set him free *(deeper)*, I hope to lean you in those directions.

We will be dealing with Ruburt's beliefs, of course, with the psyche and the books, and the other furniture of the mind that seems so obvious, but I hope to teach you to transform those issues into something else. I do not want to speak of <u>great missions</u>, yet it is also true that in its fashion each creature's life is a mission, with all of its characteristics and abilities uniquely suited.

<u>Ruburt's abilities carry along with them all of the support, protection and strength he needs to use them freely and creatively, but he has not understood that that was so.</u> That sentence should be completely underlined.

(Pause at 9:41.) You are conditioned to behave in certain fashions in times of stress, so it is indeed at such periods that old beliefs often seem to emerge with fresh force. I will deal with the situations involved, but I will also try to elicit the creative use of your own psychic and mental abilities, so that they can be <u>direct-</u>

ed specifically toward clearing up such issues—and I am of course willing to have daily sessions at your request.

That is enough for this evening's beginner—

("May I ask a question?")

You may.

(My questions are paraphrases of the ones I actually asked Seth, since I didn't take the time to write them down because of their length during the session itself. But much of the phrasing is almost verbatim, since I made notes after the session, besides remembering them clearly.

("Why has he responded to his feeling—how did you put it?" I asked as I rummaged through the session's earlier pages, which I'd thrown on the floor beside the chair—"stalled, by giving up his physical mobility even more so now? I'm terribly concerned about all of this. I don't understand why he can't walk inside his own house, at least, where it's safe. The whole thing has become very threatening."

(9:46.) The closest answer I can give you, I thought, was clear in tonight's session, but to clear it further: *(Long pause.)* He believed that his motion was blocked, that belief was physically expressed. It was to bring the situation out into the open, as indeed the feelings of panic also served to make him consciously aware of the difficulty—a difficulty that basically has to do with psychological motion and growth.

This subject is a part of one that I plan as an evening's discussion. Before, the feelings of panic remained largely hidden, and he has felt to some degree stalled of course for some time, apart from the two books involved.

(Pause.) Both physical stalling of late—and the dreams and occasional feelings of panic—have been incentives of a kind to deal with the deeper beliefs. Those beliefs involve the freedom to move and grow safely and fully to one's capacities within the framework of your current society.

(Seth paused, so I asked: "But what does he think he's doing? Why carry anything to such lengths? I'm not asking for a perfect performance, and I couldn't deliver one myself, but it's extreme behavior on his part when he can't walk across the goddam room—")

Each personality is in a state of his own growth and development, and you cannot impose any standard demands upon such a process, however tempting it is to do so.

("But I don't think asking him to be able to walk is a standard demand," I said. "What good does his giving up his physical mobility do? There must be many other ways of calling attention to any problems than doing that.")

(Seth replied patiently:) I am giving you the best information that I can,

and it would be better if you read the session thoroughly and understood it before forming new questions.

("All right, but nothing I've said here is new. I've had these questions for years.")

I am aware of that—

("Okay.")

—and I bid you a fond good evening.

("Good night.")

Have Ruburt make one simple request, and no other, before sleep: that he receive therapeutic healing experiences at all levels of his existence as he sleeps, beginning this evening. End of session.

("Okay. Thank you.")

(9:58 PM. Jane had done well. She was very quiet when she came out of trance. I felt that some sort of start had been made when I asked my questions and spoke my mind at the end of the session. As noted earlier, I'd wanted to interrupt a number of times while Seth was speaking.

(Jane remembered my talking to Seth—the longest exchange I'd had with him for years. She explained that in trance she was aware of my questions "in the back of her mind," and of Seth answering them, and that in a way the questions would get in the way of what Seth was trying to say; they could interrupt too deeply; I'd known this from a few infrequent, much earlier, experiences in the sessions, and had often thought that if too persistent the questions could bring her out of trance. But now I felt that we had to do something drastic to make a start, and that we had achieved something.

("We've got to get the information," I told Jane, and found myself repeating a lot of what I'd said to Seth; I felt the emotional charges behind the questions once again. Jane was very glum. "But I'm running into trouble coping with this thing," I told her, "and I need your help. I have to get it, too—otherwise there are going to be drastic changes in our lives."

("And what gets me in all of this," I said, "is that if I didn't raise hell about it nothing would be done. Do you agree with that?"

("I don't know." Jane said quietly, even glumly.

("Well, I know I'm right." I said. "I've seen the same situation come up many times in the past, and let it go, but we can't do that now...." And I didn't even get to mention the doctor-hospital option to Seth. I did tell Jane I understood what Frank Longwell was doing, and appreciated his efforts to help, so generously given. But I added that FL could massage her legs "till doomsday," and it would do little good until we came to terms with the basic causes behind the symptoms.

(Small wonder, I thought, that my stomach, back, and a tooth had bothered

me all day.

(See the attached dreams of Jane, for April 4, 6, and 12. The latter has a distinct bearing on the events of tomorrow morning, Tuesday the 14th.)

JANE'S DREAM
APRIL 4, 1981

Saturday PM. Healing dream. Long, involved though I missed lots. I was dancing with middle-aged man who had <u>some</u> limp or such. To a native rhythm. Anyhow, in a short matter of time I'm completely healed. Walking normally, delighted, telling R.

Also <u>very</u> vaguely recalled. Friday, Saturday, Sunday <u>nights</u>. Various confusing dreams.

JANE'S DREAM
APRIL 6, 1981 MONDAY PM

A good part of night or so it seems. Body very sore. Then my hip area turns into a hotel or old castle—like they show in horror movies. The soreness turns into the rocky walls that heave. The whole thing is <u>feeling</u>. Can't describe it—"Bad." A voice says, "May your womb shrivel and die!" A terrible thing to say, I think—separate enough to understand and comment. I realize these are feelings from childhood. Church—at a very creative level—or the feeling, use the creative ability to bring about punishment, illness or whatever. And that's how say "black" magic works. (Also I'd lately seen a show on Jack the Ripper and I think the women were so convinced of their "evil" ways at those levels that they broadcast their need for punishment.) Finally awaken—sleep off and on but sore. And as I waken, very sore, feelings of panic (or nearly). In past I wouldn't have granted those feelings that expression—

JANE'S NOTES
APRIL 6, 1981 MONDAY

Tam calls! He got poetry book okay and will read it at once! Really pleases me. Out Spring 1982.

JANE'S NOTES
APRIL 7, 1981 TUESDAY

*Off and on been doing Stonehenge poem—type up 6 new pages of it today....
Frank L. comes noon.*

JANE'S DREAM/NOTES
APRIL 12, 1981 SUNDAY

April 12 have a "dream" that a man is talking to me about Mass Events *primarily, saying that he's seen a copy and there is nothing about the disclaimer to anger me, that it's ok, and then mentioning* God of Jane. *There was stuff I've also forgotten though that made me waken at once, furious; some connection between the two books, also whole bunches of feelings rise to my mind about the disclaimer being like a sign or statement that I'm a liar or that my work isn't truthful or like, hell, the letter A for adulteress they used to pin on wicked women....*

JANE'S NOTES
APRIL 14, 1981 TUESDAY

April 14 Rob decides we really have to do something to tackle my difficulties which have been more than considerable lately, he suggests I call Tam to see when Events *is out; or if it is, since April 13 is date of arrival. Oh, wait; it was that same day, the 13th that I called. Tam said he'd call back; no books had come yet but should, as far as he knew. Then on April 14 Ethel Waters calls from Production at Tam's insistence saying that after* Events *was delayed till May 14 because of the disclaimer problems; so it would come out the same month as* God of Jane.... *but that there were 10,000 back orders for* Events, *so I'd say that my dream probably gave me that indication, that something was held up.*

DELETED SESSION
APRIL 14, 1981 9:42 PM TUESDAY

(Jane slept late this morning, and after she had breakfast I read her last night's session. We thought it excellent, of course. She now amazed me by saying that she now thought she understood that if she turned her focus away from her symptoms toward

Prentice, say, or any other "outside" entity or situation, that she could improve physically by giving her body the freedom to do so. She sounded like things I'd said—and Seth too—many, many times; I'd thought she understood this. The notion is an important breakthrough for her, and one that must be accomplished if she is to improve physically.

(In the notes preceding the last session I wrote that Jane was to call Tam about the date of publication for Mass Events and God of Jane. She'd called, and Tam was to call back yesterday or today with the information. The expected call came as I finished reading to Jane at breakfast time—but it wasn't from Tam: Ethel Waters apologized for the fact that now Mass Events has been delayed until May 19, or just possibly only May 4. Mass Events and God of Jane are now due to be published in the same month. The news tied in with Jane's upsetting dream of April 12—see the copy attached to the last session; this makes the dream precognitive in at least some sense.

(Ethel, incidentally, told Jane that she too has trouble communicating with Prentice's legal department, just as it seems everyone else does.

(At first we were unhappy with the delay, but then began to see it as probably a good thing. For it gave us the extra time to have these sessions before the book's publication. If we needed preparation for any reactions after publication, etc.

(I reread last night's session to Jane after supper, since today I didn't make even a start at getting it typed. I painted for an hour this morning while Jane slept, but felt a peculiar heaviness or loginess I was unaccustomed to. By noon I was having trouble keeping awake. A nervous physical reaction—including my stomach and back upsets—to yesterday's personal events, I thought. Jane also felt it. We went to bed at 2 PM and slept until supper time, after watching the perfect reentry and landing of Columbia, the country's first space shuttle.

(That event, as well as the launching of the shuttle Sunday morning, had been very emotional doings for me, somewhat to my surprise. "But what makes me so furious," I said to Jane Sunday, "is that the species has the ability to accomplish something like that, but then makes such a mess of things back home on the planet. I have the awful suspicion that if we had enough shuttle craft, and there was a habitable planet within range, that we'd move key members of the species there, start over and try to leave all of our troubles behind, instead of trying to solve them."

(Because of our changed schedule, Jane had gone to the john only twice by supper time, whereas I'd envisioned at least three visits to that abode for her by now. Nor have we done anything about trying for a step a day with the aid of the typing table. But I told her before the session that I wasn't yet going to dispense with the list I'd originated yesterday, including possible hospital treatment.

(I kept trying to verbalize a thought that had come to me after supper tonight, *but couldn't get it out. "It's got to do with understanding that one must protect or encourage personal integrity before anything else," I said, "even if it means projecting one's troubles out onto an entity like Prentice, the church, or whatever. Even though we can't blame those entities, really, for doing much that we hadn't <u>allowed</u> them to do...." But I knew I was trying to get at deeper approximations of some sort of truth, and so did Jane. As Seth says, we each do create our own reality.*

("I very vaguely feel him around," Jane said at 9:30, after we'd been sitting for the session since 9:10. I'd been busy with these notes while waiting. Earlier, she'd finished a small acrylic still life of flowers and fruit.)

("These must be hard for me to give, or something," Jane said at 9:40, "or I wouldn't be still sitting here waiting...." Then:)

Now. Good evening.

("Good evening, Seth.)

For Ruburt: you do not lead people anywhere. You cannot force them to change their beliefs. *(Long pause.)* No most hypnotic fanatic leads any group of people astray. You make your own reality. The people use the materials of the world as they come into contact with them, in their own ways and for their own reasons. To imagine that you or anyone else can lead large masses of persons astray is a highly erroneous conception.

In a larger sense, for example, the Catholic Church was originally formed as a psychic organization, on psychic levels, by <u>large</u> groups of individuals, as the mass psyche formed the basis of Christianity.

If you believe that your own great energy can lead others astray, you are actually saying that others have no power of their own. Ruburt has been extremely cautious in the past, wanting to make sure, as mentioned, that he was not leading others down the proverbial garden path. He did not feel the same way about his poetry, which largely in its way states the same messages that our own books do.

The books are different, however, while the poetry carries the more clearly recognizable stamp of his accepted identity, so he was afraid that <u>I</u> would lead people astray unwittingly perhaps, through the energy and power of our communications. That worry persisted, regardless of what kind of status he assigned to me. The relationship, of course, is unusual: very few people have such issues to contend with. Ruburt discovered how basically easy it was to have our sessions. But also how basically easy it was for his, say, *Cézanne* and *James* books also, for creatively he moved very quickly.

(Long pause at 9:54.) Ideas of using considerable caution have been with him for that matter before the sessions began, when he recognized his own energy, the ease with which he could encounter people. As for example when he

acted as a salesperson years ago, sometimes gathering small groups at the street corners in Florida. He learned to fear his own energy to some extent—or rather, he believed that he must be very cautious in its use. Those habits were there, again, before the sessions began, and they have their basis in the church's concepts of the <u>sinful</u> nature of the basic <u>self</u>.

Most people operate at one largely exclusive state of consciousness. Even most creative work is done at the recognized threshold of the normal waking consciousness. Ruburt was presented with—or presented himself with—a situation in which large portions of his creative life appeared in books that were written in another state of consciousness entirely. Little wonder, then, that he felt he must alert all natural and normal controls.

(Long pause.) In that regard his symptoms developed more along the lines of exerting caution rather than, say, seeking protection. *(Long pause.)* <u>It is as if</u> someone on his own developed a spectacular amazing fast craft, and built a secondary system—a backup system—that allowed for great braking power in case this was necessary to offset the craft's own speed.

(Long pause.) He felt it his duty to examine his psychic material with supercritical force, since it seemed to come from the other side of consciousness, so to speak, and since it presented such a different picture of all aspects of reality. *(Pause.)* His symptoms served other purposes as well, though, as has been given often. In a fashion they served as regulators that he felt at one time allowed him to live on an even course, tempering spontaneity or psychic exploration lest it progress too quickly for him to follow, yet also protecting him from other distractions so that he could continue his explorations.

(10:12.) In other words, he felt he needed a countering force for his own spontaneity. He received some ideas of that nature from you in the past. In a way the symptoms were almost a method of presentation that in another fashion completely paralleled your own notes *(an excellent point)*. In that regard they were meant to show that he was as reasonable, orderly, critical and responsible as your notes certainly showed you to be. The symptoms have fluctuated, serving sometimes one purpose more than the other—but what you have overall is a belief in a kind of braking power with which to handle spontaneous activity.

Again, that belief in the <u>need</u> for control is rooted in the earlier concepts of the <u>Sinful Self</u> *(long pause)*—concepts that have come to the fore in current contemporary world events with the new attention being given to religious cults and religions. Current events can trigger such reactions, therefore. Ruburt has told himself that such feelings were beneath him, but often the feelings themselves went underground. Those feelings were nearly incomprehensible to you, so that it was difficult for you to see how they could even be taken seriously.

(10:22.) It was in *Mass Events* and *God of Jane* that the usual concept of the Sinful Self was most directly and vigorously addressed, and in which the value of individual impulses was stressed with consistent vigor. Ruburt has been dealing with that material since then. *(Pause.)* Many people in your society and others are dealing precisely with the same issues, though in different contexts.

You are in the process of changing your definitions of yourselves as creatures, and each person is in one way or another involved. The idea of the Sinful Self has served as a large portion of that definition for centuries, bringing with it innumerable difficulties, of course. As Ruburt frees himself from that idea, as he *must* and can, the need for such unnecessary cautionary behavior will dissipate by itself.

It is no coincidence that you have been relatively free of that concept in its traditional religious connotation. You worked <u>that</u> out in your Nebene existence to a large extent, and because of your own preparations for a life in which you are now involved.

Again, the issue is not some hypothetical one, but one that directly affects people's most private actions. It must be swept aside, and recognized clearly as having no <u>natural</u> part to play, for it is an <u>anti</u>-natural concept, flying in the face of the good intent of each of nature's individuals of whatever species.

If you consider the self as good, you feel free to express it and its abilities. Some of Ruburt's ideas along those lines were highly reinforced by his mother as well as by the church, and later in its way by the very pronouncements of science.

Since Ruburt's work involved him most directly in an examination of the self and in the unknown reaches of the psyche, then his experiences led him into a conflict with the idea of the Sinful Self. One of the main points of his work, and mine, is the definition of the well-intentioned self, of course. Ruburt was to some extent afraid to accept that concept fully—therefore he has been unable to utilize it fully in his mistaken belief that he must maintain a largely critical stance.

That is enough for this evening.

("Can I ask just one question?)

You may.

("This morning Jane said she was beginning to understand that if she turned her focus away from her symptoms, toward some place outside of herself, that she might improve by giving her body the freedom to do so. I was surprised, because I thought she understood this.")

He has had such glimmerings briefly in the past, but was not able to separate himself far enough from his physical situation to understand that issue clearly.

The material I gave this evening should help him see the reason for the problems behind the symptoms. *(Pause.)* It is humiliating to realize that you consider yourself as a Sinful Self, potentially evil, and to encounter the feelings themselves *(intently)*—so Ruburt has shoved them underground.

In personal terms, he feared that his father abandoned him for that reason, that his mother disliked him for that reason, for each person will interpret the belief in his or her own life according to circumstances.

(Again I was surprised, and groped for words as Seth sat quietly waiting. "Wait a minute.... Are you actually saying that he feels that his mother and father both thought of him as _evil_—that now he thinks he's that evil?")

He thought that he was such a bad person that he drove his parents apart, perhaps caused his mother's illness, perhaps his grandmother's death—for which his mother did indeed several times blame him—and that the <u>classical</u> idea of the Sinful Self was individually interpreted in that manner in Ruburt's personal early life.

His mother told him he ruined everyone he touched. Those experiences were relatively unfortunate enough, but they were a part of the early life of someone who later finds themselves embarked upon in the study of the very nature of the self, so that they led him to believe that strong cautionary methods must be used. Period.

If Ruburt had been involved in other endeavors requiring unusual amounts of expression and creativity, however, the same cautionary methods would also have been activated to varying degrees.

I am not implying that he was so fated to behave. The prosaic reasons for the beliefs, however, do lie in his private background and to that extent in experiences humiliating for an adult to recall. Instead, Ruburt tells himself he should be above such feelings, or that they simply should no longer apply. They are not <u>destined</u> to apply, but there is a give-and-take between the future and the past. Understanding those issues can further help Ruburt give up the entire construct.

A good question and a good evening.

("Thank you.")

(10:58 P.M. I was glad I'd asked the second question in particular—at first I'd found it hard to believe that Jane thought of herself as evil for any reason, parents or whatever. Not that we hadn't known from earlier material and our own conscious experiences that her mother especially had often exerted an unhealthy pressure upon the daughter—but I'd been taken back to realize that Seth was actually saying that Jane had considered herself _evil_.

("This Sinful Self thing is liable to turn into the primary cause behind the whole business," I said to Jane. "Imagine—atonement, self-punishment for things learned more than 40 years ago. Incredible."

("How are you going to handle a session a night?" Jane asked.

("Do we need the material?"

("Yes...."

("That's your answer.")

DELETED SESSION
APRIL 15, 1981 9:14 PM WEDNESDAY

(After supper today Jane said that for the first time in some little while she went to the john without a feeling of panic. She did a little better. I'm just finishing typing last Monday's session, the first in our new series, but already I think the program has helped her.

(She's been sleeping in the mornings because I haven't called her at 6:15 when I get up, but starting tomorrow she plans to get up with me so we have enough time through the day to do more things. Jane still hasn't been going to the john more than three times a day, nor have we yet tried point 4 on my list: taking one step a day with the aid of the typing table. She slept well last night. I also feel better following my exhaustion of yesterday. Frank Longwell visited this noon.

(I was so absorbed typing that Jane had to call me three times for the session. Finally I heard her at 8:50. Once again we sat waiting, she on the couch as before. I mentioned what Seth had said about her father in the last session, and asked her if she thought material on her mother might help. To my surprise Jane agreed. But I didn't want such material to interrupt whatever Seth might be planning for tonight.)

Now:

("Good evening.")

Continuation, apropos of Ruburt and the Sinful Self.

Ruburt found great comfort in the church as a young person, for if it created within its members the image of a <u>Sinful Self</u>, it also of course provided a steady system of treatment—a series of rituals that gave the individual some sense of hope the Sinful Self could be redeemed, as in most of Christianity's framework through adherence to certain segments of Christian dogma.

When Ruburt left the Church, the concept of the Sinful Self was still there, but the methods that earlier served to relieve its pressures were no longer effectively present. The concept was shifted over to the flawed self of scientific vintage.

Science has no sacraments. Its only methods of dealing with such guilt involve standard psychoanalytic counseling—which itself deepens the dilemma, for counseling itself is based upon the idea that the inner self is a reservoir of savage impulses. Period.

(Long pause at 9:20.) Ruburt's creative nature early began to perceive at least that man's existence contained other realities that were deeper. *(Long pause.)* Some of this is difficult to separate. To leave the church, say, meant to carry still some of the old beliefs, but without the Band-Aids that earlier offered some protection.

He began to search actually from childhood in a natural fashion toward some larger framework that would offer an explanation for reality that bore at least some resemblance to the natural vision of his best <u>poetry</u>. I have said before that many creative people, highly gifted, have died young in one way or the other because their great gifts of creativity could find no clear room in which to grow. They became strangled by the beliefs of the cultural times.

In that regard, Ruburt's creativity kept struggling for its own growth and value fulfillment. His psychic recognition or initiation represented a remarkable breakthrough, meant to give him that additional psychic room that would insure the continued expansion of the abilities of the natural self. The Sinful Self concept is a personal one for each who holds it, but it is also projected outward onto the entire species, of course, until the whole world seems tainted.

At the time the sessions began *(pause)*, the world was beginning to seem senseless, truly incomprehensible, to anyone who held any sense of poetry or sanity. Your private lives were showing their own difficulties, and the national situation was horrendous. Ruburt's creativity broke through those frameworks to provide our sessions and to release the psychic abilities that had earlier been <u>nearly</u> but not completely repressed.

His poetry acted in some regards as a stimulator. That breakthrough, you might say, with perhaps some exaggeration, was a life saver, for without some such expansion Ruburt would have felt unable to continue the particular <u>brand</u> of his existence. It is not possible to say in words what one person or another <u>looks for</u> in life, or what unique features best promote his or her growth and development. Even two plants of the same kind sometimes require completely different treatments.

(9:37.) The sessions then opened the door to a particular kind of value fulfillment that was natural to Ruburt's being. Now to some extent it was that poor, unhappy Sinful Self, a psychological structure formed by beliefs and feelings, that was also seeking its own redemption, since even it had outgrown the framework that so defined it.

I have said that in almost every case of severe dissatisfaction or illness the underlying reasons will not so much be found in the discovery or expression of buried hate or aggression—though these may be present—but in the search for valued expression of value fulfillment that is for one reason or another being denied.

(Long pause.) Ruburt broke through both psychically and creatively—that is, the sessions almost immediately provided him with new creative inspiration and expression and with the expansions needed psychologically that would help fulfill his promise as a writer and as a mature personality. He was still left, however, with the beliefs in the Sinful Self, and carried within him many deep fears that told him that self-expression itself and spontaneity were highly dangerous.

In that regard, you have what amounts to a creative dilemma.

It is one thing to say that the dilemma is unfortunate, but it is also true to say that the dilemma existed because of a breakthrough that gave him what amounted to a new life at the time....

(Long pause at 9:48.) As he became better known, so it seemed greater demands were put upon him. Another image of the self comes into consideration, so that it seems to him that he is expected to be nearly a saintly self—or at least that he is regarded as someone who is expected to perform in an altogether superlative fashion. Almost a superself: Again, an excellent television personality, an accomplished healer and clairvoyant, and writer and teacher to boot.

In the light of this discussion, now, that self was as <u>unrealistic</u> at its end of the spectrum as the Sinful Self was at the other, for Ruburt felt that he was supposed to demonstrate a certain kind of superhuman feat, not only managing on occasion to uncover glimpses of man's greater abilities, but to demonstrate these competently at the drop of a hat, willingly at the request of others. At the same time he believed he was the Sinful Self, and that expression was highly dangerous—so between those two frameworks, the psychological organization, he operated as best he could, still seeking toward the natural value fulfillment that was his natural heritage.

(Long pause.) The superself image itself seemed to condemn him, of course, since he felt he could not live up to it—and therefore along the line somewhere both the superself and the Sinful Self became in their ways joined, or at least allied. Through all of that Ruburt of course looked for further creative developments and intuitive breakthroughs, for, again, he needed more room.

In the meantime, since he was older, and in the light of our sessions, it seemed to him that he must have outgrown many of the beliefs of early childhood, and that he must have enough perspective so that those earlier feelings and fears no longer applied. They were highly unpleasant.

With his mother dead it seemed highly unsporting to cast, for example, any aspersions or express fresh anger against injustice. In the meantime, his own understanding was growing, and his creative capacities. In my book we rather elegantly pinpointed those precise problems that have so tainted your world, and in *God of Jane* Ruburt made an excellent attempt to uncover the nature of the Sinful Self, and to outline the dilemma.

Now those books were the result of value fulfillment and creativity. They were necessary projections of understanding and growth. They were also bound to bring the entire concept into light, to bring the problem to the surface. Ruburt therefore encountered newer bouts of symptoms that effectively demonstrated and mirrored the feeling of lack of mobility. Again, he needed room to grow.

(10:08.) The psychic abilities and the creative abilities—nearly impossible to separate—themselves provide all of the help that he requires, but the concept of the Sinful Self prevented him from using those abilities sufficiently—for how can the expressions of the Sinful Self be trusted?

So we must now show Ruburt the source of the Sinful Self to begin with, and convince him that such is not his natural self at all and to do so we will to some extent at least go into his early background. The main thrust, however, will be the need for expression and value fulfillment that to one extent or another has always been impeded by the beliefs inherent in the entire Sinful-Self concept.

A point: the answer does not lie for example in deciding not to finish my book *(Dreams, "Evolution," and Value Fulfillment)*. You are free to finish my book or not as you prefer, but not to finish it thinking that such an action will help solve your difficulties would not work.

(I should note that Jane seems to misunderstand my attitude here: the aim is not to use halting work on Seth's latest book as a curative device, but to at least keep things from getting any worse. It came to seem to me that finishing this latest book would only be more of the same, with the same attitudes and beliefs behind it— hence, how could it help? I never told Jane, for example, to not finish the book. I did suggest that she hold off publication of it until we'd tried to learn something. Even so, it will be a long while before said volume is finished, let alone ready for the press. I devoutly hope we manage to learn something in the meantime. I only know, meanwhile, that what we have been doing so far has led to results that we fear. It will be interesting to see how this little dilemma is resolved, and what the long range results are, if any.)

For in that regard, you are simply deciding to cut down on value fulfillment further, and to limit expression, while the limitation of expression is a part of the problem. Expression is not the problem. A fear of expression is.

(Exactly, I might add. Therefore, how could publication of the next Seth book help?)

The creative abilities, again, can help provide the necessary psychological motion and direction—they have in a large regard in the past, but they have not gone far enough. They have not gone far enough because Ruburt did not come to terms with his private version of the Sinful Self, and therefore still kept himself open to all of the negative conditioning that is so involved there: a conditioning that views all creative expression with distrust.

(10:17.) Ruburt was not responsible for his mother's reality, for her characteristics, reactions, or beliefs. He was not responsible for her marriage, its breakup, for his mother's illness, again, or for the entire "tragedy" that he sees as his mother's life.

(Long pause.) He acted toward her according to his own understanding the best that he could. He does not need to punish himself in any way for any actions or any omissions in that relationship. This does not mean he could not have acted better in any particular instance, perhaps, for that can be said about almost anyone.

(A one-minute pause at 10:22.) Ruburt chose his environment. Ruburt chose his parents for his own lifetime: he was born in the right place at the right time. Now in that larger light, even the concept of the Sinful Self has its reasoning, for it is once again shared by millions of people for centuries. Ruburt set out to shoot it down.

(I grinned at Seth. "Isn't that a rather large undertaking?")

That concept will be changed because many people in your society and in your times were indeed born with the same intent, and in their private and public lives they are tackling that issue.

The mass reality is ready for such a change. *(Long pause.)* In the past the Sinful-Self idea was so a part of Ruburt's conditioning that it set up an entire framework of behavior. The need to justify life through writing, the exaggerated need for protection from the deceptive unconscious and the unsafe world, and the concept itself were so involved with his entire thinking patterns that he could not isolate it to see where and how it bore upon his activities. Now we can separate those strands.

(Long pause.) Those beliefs to some extent or another appear without their strong religious connotations in your own life and background also, and this will also be discussed in the series. The idea of Ruburt's book *(on rationalism)* is a good one because it represents creative impetus—undertaken, however, in the light of newer understanding, and I will have more to say concerning that issue.

End of session.

("One question?")

You may.

("What do you think about the idea of one step at a time with the typing table each day?")

An excellent suggestion.

("Can you give him a suggestion that would help him with the table, and going to the john?")

Leave things as they are for a day or so. Then i will have more to say in a day or so.

("Okay.")

A fond good evening.

("Thank you very much, Seth. Good night."

(10:33 PM. Jane had done very well. She remembered Seth mentioning her book idea—on rationalism—although she didn't have "any great feelings yet" about it—how to do it or start it. I was surprised that she was interested in a study of rationalism, since her own abilities would seriously question many of rationalism's tenets, at least in ordinary terms.

(But I stressed that no matter what she did about books, no matter what hassles we might get involved in about that activity, she just couldn't give up physical mobility in order to express any lack of _psychological_ mobility that we might become involved in. It was too high a price to pay, too unnecessary. "You just can't," I said, "no matter what happens, professionally...." She agreed.

(I added that I'd had no idea that the idea of the Sinful Self occupied that prominent and basic a position in her life. It was beginning to look as if the Sinful Self concept occupied the central position in her beliefs. It would make a lot of sense, I said, if it were true, and would account for things like an obsession with work, giving up other life activities, etc.—all done in a disguised attempt to appease that Sinful Self that merrily carried on year after year.... "But in a funny way that may be okay," I mused, "because if that's it, we now know where we can grab hold of the Sinful Self, once we know what we're doing, not groping around in a morass of suppositions and speculations.")

DELETED SESSION
APRIL 16, 1981 8:42 PM THURSDAY

(I've finished typing last Monday's session, and have 5 pages done on Tuesday's, so we're in good shape now with only Wednesday's to do. Each morning after break-

*fast I read a session to Jane. They're uniformly excellent. This morning she got up with
me, and has spent a relatively peaceful day, taking her usual morning and afternoon
naps.*

*(I felt a bit tired, but thought the malaise was more psychological than any-
thing else. Jane was also a bit depressed after reading my notes for Monday's and
Tuesday's sessions, although she already knew their contents.*

*(She called me for the session at about 8 PM, although it was later than that
before I was seated opposite her and starting on these notes. We were still waiting at
8:30.)*

Now: for all of its seeming sophistication, the self as generally seen by science is only science's interpretation of the Sinful Self in mechanistic terms.

(Long pause.) Both religion and science see the self as primarily heir to
flaws, decay. Only science's Sinful Self operates in a framework in which there is
no sacramental redemption. Science sees the world as rushing toward its own
dissolution, and the self as the mechanistic system running down from the
moment of its conception.

It seems under those conditions that only pessimism can be an adequate
response, so that any private or global condition of an adverse nature, left alone,
will further deteriorate. Remember, along with these passages, material I gave
recently on the uses of the rational mind, and its necessary dependence upon
intelligence that it cannot itself directly perceive.

The world in those terms *(pause)* is as much the result of unpredictable
behavior, unforeseen events, unexpected benefits, unforeseeable conditions, as it
is the result of predictable actions, usual cause-and-effect phenomena *(pause)*,
and a close inspection of public and private life would show quite clearly that
both are magnificently touched by significant coincidences. Unexpected events,
unpredictable actions of the most auspicious nature.

(Long pause at 8:53.) When it seems that left alone Ruburt's condition will
only worsen, you are following those old patterns of conditioned thought, projecting negative situations into the future, imagining the unfortunate outcome
or outcomes, and acting as if you operated within a closed system. You are concentrating upon the problem in order to solve it, often scaring yourselves into
further depressions.

That is the way you have been taught to solve problems.

The <u>Sinful-Self</u> concept causes you to expect the worst in any given situation. In that light, hopeful expectation seems quite out of place, and unwork-
able. Without the dictates of the Sinful Self, however, you can begin to sense the
contours of the natural self, or the natural person. You can begin to sense your
own good natures, in other words, and those basic natures are automatically

optimistic.

They automatically expect the best from any situation. They represent your natural persons. As Ruburt begins to understand the "artificial" characteristics of the Sinful-Self concept, then those natural characteristics of the natural person will more and more emerge. It will be, for example, less difficult to have pleasant expectations, for they will begin to bubble up by themselves into the mind.

It is true that the Sinful Self carries with it a group of patterns or reactions; methods of dealing with problems, and so Ruburt's beliefs along those lines have colored his reactions, his plans, his dealings with you through the years. In the past, however, those methods seemed to make sense: if you believe that the self is sinful or deceptive, then you must indeed set up barriers so that you allow expression while monitoring it very carefully at the same time.

The barriers become unnecessary when you realize that the <u>self</u> is not <u>sinful</u>. I use the word "sinful" in Ruburt's case because of the early church connections in particular. Science's flawed self still carries the same import, however, the idea being that while science does not deal with values, so its says, it misleads itself considerably in making such statements, for it projects the worst kind of values both upon mankind and the rest of nature—so even if you are not tainted from religion's old beliefs, it is difficult to escape such ideas.

(Pause at 9:10.) Many of Ruburt's beliefs have changed, <u>but the core belief in the Sinful Self has been very stubborn</u>. While you do not possess it in the same fashion, you are also tainted by it, picking up such beliefs from early background, and primarily from your father in that regard.

The natural person can be evoked, and its responses elicited, particularly through touching and through statements of love and affection. The Sinful Self feels it does not deserve such attention. Love is therefore surrounded very carefully by all kinds of barriers by both science and religion, and in your own lives you could now be much more demonstrative in those regards. For they offer a natural therapy.

(Long pause.) I do not want to give you too much charged material in a concentrated period of time. Therefore, remember during the days for example to allow yourselves some enjoyments, and to consider any feelings, even unpleasant ones, as valuable <u>expressions</u> of sensation or emotion.

Ruburt was not responsible for the housekeeper's death when he was in high school. He felt such accusations, however. Even those made him question the nature of reality. They were grist for the mill. They were the way the problem was stated.

An important point here: You use consciousness—what you think of as rational consciousness—in an unusual manner. Obviously other species use their consciousnesses differently. In a fashion their knowledge is immediately acted upon. This carries with it an exquisite sense of biological and spiritual security. Your kind of consciousness, relatively speaking, involves some intrinsic difficulties, along with spectacular potentials. You are learning how to form reality from your own beliefs. While having at the same time the freedom to <u>choose</u> those beliefs—to choose your mental state in a way that the animals for example do not.

<u>In that larger picture</u> (underlined) there are no errors, for each action, pleasant or not, <u>will</u> (underlined) in its fashion be redeemed, both in relationship to itself and in relationship to a larger picture that the conscious mind may not be able presently to perceive.

(Pause at 9:26.) This means that you deal, even consciously, with vast areas of probabilities, with various combinations, with ways in which identity itself will be defined and experienced. You will react to your definitions of yourselves. <u>In that regard</u> the Sinful-Self concept represents an exaggerated, distorted version of man's recognition that in certain ways he <u>seems</u> (underlined) less sure of himself than the other species, less at ease, for he has taken upon himself the creative recognition of uncertainties *(all intently.*

(Long pause.) He is learning to create whole private and public worlds that directly correspond to his own states of mind. The possible diversity and the vast <u>assortment</u> of the creative ventures possible mean that he had accepted certain measures of uncertainty. He hits snags.

Even these, however, act as automatic learning devices, and left alone they themselves <u>trigger</u> the necessary creative procedures that would begin corrective measures. When the belief in the Sinful Self is held, however, the very corrective measures themselves are often not trusted.

(Long pause at 9:37.) In Ruburt's case the core belief, again, in the Sinful Self was hard to differentiate, because it could appear in many other guises. It dropped its most obvious religious coloration for some time, and could simply appear as an unusually strong dedication to work and discipline. The Sinful Self has no use for play, because it believes so fervently that left alone it will indeed be lazy or childish, or fritter itself away—or, looking at it the other way, it fears that left alone it will <u>only</u> play, or will be slothful. You see this most clearly in Protestant theology.

These issues can all be encountered, however, and adequately encountered once they are clearly understood. It is not particularly necessary that Ruburt dig back into the past on purpose to discover those old feelings. Many will now surface most likely on their own in response to current events, as per this morning: the memories will not be <u>frozen</u>, but will move naturally into present experience, and take their natural place.

He should definitely express any feelings that come to mind in that fashion, and as he did with the flashing moment of anger at you *(this afternoon)*. Those feelings represent communication. They will work themselves out as long as they are expressed.

That will be all for this evening.

("Okay," I said. As Seth, Jane waited, staring at me, her eyes wide and dark, for some moments.)

No question from the gallery?

("Nope." Actually I had many questions, but wanted to give Jane a rest.)

Then I bid you a fond good evening.

("Thank you, Seth."

(9:49 PM. I told Jane the session was very good. At times during it I'd felt somewhat overwhelmed, thinking of what we still had to learn and accomplish, as well as about what we hadn't learned in the past: Why was it all taking so long? The thoughts stemmed from my rather somber mood before the session. But the session was very good, I saw, and at the same time I felt a renewed hope.)

DELETED SESSION
APRIL 20, 1981 8:46 PM MONDAY

(Yesterday was Easter, and a very quiet day in the neighborhood. We've been very busy. Jane called me at 8 PM for the session. We had lots to get information about.

(We didn't get to bed last night until 1 AM. By 3:30 Jane had had a series of three or four dreams—very pleasant in the main, containing "a prognosis, as though I'd made a good decision. The intent of one of them was pretty specific." She sat up in bed and wrote them down, which took her half an hour or so. Copies of them are attached to this session.

(When she tried to get back to sleep, however, she kept waking up very sore, and took aspirin at 5 AM. At the same time she "knew my body was trying out some new positions in bed, like it used to before all this happened. I also knew I was working out some conflicts, and I wasn't worried. But then after I decided to stay in bed when you got up, the panicky stuff started.... I tried to remember what Seth had said, and follow the feelings through so I wouldn't repress any of them...."

(True—for from my painting room I could hear her turning and tossing rest-

lessly in bed all morning.... "Panic and fear—fright—is the closest I can come to it all," she said. "Nothing evil, but certainly a fear of letting go, of expression, maybe abandonment." All of this was accompanied by strong physical sensations of her being sore.

(Then when I called her at noon, Jane cried for at least half an hour. It was hard for her to verbalize her feelings, to even tell me about them, but she felt waves of panic and fear sweep through her—not hidden or covered up now, but faced and admitted, although with much difficulty. These feelings lingered throughout the day, though they seemed to be about gone at session time. Perhaps it was just exhaustion, for she felt quite relaxed by now. We didn't discuss the dreams or the crying experience, or even read a session after breakfast. Nor have I read her notes on the dreams. "I'd decided I'd deal directly with the world again in the first dream," she said. She plans to type them for this session.

(The whole experience was obviously very therapeutic, and to me it seemed like an excellent sign of encountering beliefs that had helped create her Sinful Self. Truly, Jane has gone about as far physically as she can with her physical blockages: It was some little while before she could trust herself enough to get from her bed to the chair, and longer before she could move from her chair to the toilet seat.

(Watching her struggle to do this reminded me of the fix we both face, and that must be resolved. It was also a reminder of how far she had carried her resistance to change and confrontation with the Sinful Self—and often without my really understanding just how badly off she is. Once again in the bathroom I was amazed that any belief could have such a powerful effect upon a person that they would tolerate such physical limitations day after day, year after year, rather than to come to terms with them in an effort to obtain at least some relief. I'd still like some material from Seth on why the personality would choose to go to such lengths in the name of self-protection.... I didn't mention any of this to Jane, since she had done so well today, but do want to make note of my feelings here.

(It goes without saying that we hoped Seth would go into the whole experience of early this morning, since it represented such a good improvement in her effort toward self-understanding.

(I'm caught up typing last week's sessions. It seems hard to believe that only a week has passed since we asked Seth to begin this latest series.

(This afternoon I mowed grass for the first time, and trimmed a tree or two. After returning to the house, I felt a return of my own panicky feelings in my chest and throat as I made ready for a nap. After I got up, the pendulum told me the feelings came because I resented having to do the yard work without Jane being able to help me. The fact of doing the work itself was innocent, I learned. Nor do I have heart trouble. Once I obtained the necessary information the feelings disappeared,

and I was quite comfortable eating supper. And again, I did not discuss this situation with Jane.

(We were still waiting for the session at 8:30. I finished these notes. Finally:)

Now: even as a young person, Ruburt was the <u>type</u> of person who was considered out of place, rebellious, or even slightly dangerous in any Roman Catholic congregation—particularly in the time of his own youth.

(Pause.) He took the dictums of the church seriously, but questioned them with as much passion and enthusiasm as he overall used in his affiliation with the entire church organization. The church did not like that kind of questioning, and in a fashion it has always been highly suspicious of those who were too mystically inclined, for such people in their originality are not easy to lead.

(Leaning back on the couch, eyes closed:) When Ruburt was a church member, however, the church itself <u>was</u> there, easily identified. To some extent later, even when it was a worthy opponent, Ruburt could see where his own ideas fit in or did not. There was only so much leeway granted, so much questioning allowed—for beyond a certain point of course the entire dogmatic structure would fall apart.

Most people were too emotionally dependent upon the entire organization to let it go. *(Long pause.)* By the time Ruburt left the church, he thought that it had also lost its emotional pull upon him. He felt free, and he immediately leapt toward what you can generally think of as the scientific viewpoint.

(Long pause.) Many other people were making that same leap at that time in your society. He was far from any scientist, of course. He did poorly in science in college, for that matter, for if his mind was too scientific for religious dogma, it was too creative and emotional for conventional scientific thought.

Even later, as he began writing science fiction, that writing fell under the then less envious label of science <u>fantasy</u> (underlined), which was not considered as pure in science-fiction circles.

(Long pause at 9:02.) The <u>Sinful Self</u> shows itself in a period of transition from its religious to scientific format in science fiction or fantasy in particular, where you can almost trace the translation of religion's self, tainted by original sin, to the Darwinian and Freudian concepts of the flawed self, bound to destruction one way or another, propelled by the unbridled unconscious or evolutionary defect.

[Ray] Bradbury's stories, for example, are actually tales of a religious moralist. When you fear that man <u>will most certainly</u> destroy himself through his misuse of technologies, then you are expressing the same feeling in different form expressed by the religious attitude—only religion's devils are turned into technological devices. <u>So Ruburt's belief in the Sinful Self</u> went underground in those years.

The creative abilities must revolve largely about man's definition of himself, his source and purpose, and all of your Western literature and art has revolved about the concept of the Sinful Self in one way or another. The Shakespearean plays are an excellent case in point, even when they concern even older heritages, so the creative artist in any field has certain creative traditions that become classic models for his art and that of the world.

(Long pause at 9:13.) The use of the Frankenstein monster and so forth in television dramas, and the merging of strong destructive tendencies intermixed with the psychic abilities in current psychic horror stories, shows again the potent mixture of religion's Sinful Self and science's flawed self. To some extent, though in a different fashion, both fear the emergence of new knowledge, since new knowledge is apt to upset either framework entirely.

Science, of course, insists it searches for such knowledge, while at the same time narrowing its acceptable field of definitions so that it effectively blocks any information that does not agree with its own precepts. *(Pause.)* Both science and religion, generally speaking, provide certain services, which again generally speaking can be withheld to those who rebel against such authorities.

The church can excommunicate you. Science in its position of authority can mock those who disagree with it. Ruburt's basic beliefs of the Sinful Self were formed in childhood, individually <u>interpreted</u> through his own experience, given strong emotional validity in other words, and emotional charge.

(Long pause.) "The church" was not a hypothetical entity, but was encountered through Ruburt's experience with the priests who visited, their effect upon his life and his poetry, and with the entire fabric of a young intense daily life. If the church became upset with what Ruburt wrote or read, then Father Ryan burned one of his books, or argued with his poetry, for example, so all of that was living emotional content.

Ruburt's creative abilities still had those classical models, yet because of his mind's originality and his natural intuitive nature; those creative abilities were also fueled by <u>unofficial</u> information: he was always to some extent in strong connection with the knowledge possessed by his natural person—and that knowledge kept seeking expression. Its expression directly contradicted first religious then scientific precepts. It kept seeking a larger framework for its own fulfillment and expression, of course, and at the same time it seemed to Ruburt it brought about further dissension. It made him more of a rebel.

It took some time before such a framework began to develop—a kind of double one—represented by my work and by his own—an excellent accomplishment, of course. Also an accomplishment that clearly stood out as a direct challenge to religion and science, that not only contradicted their theories but offered an alternate framework through which reality could be experienced.

(9:34.) Through the last few years religious fundamentalism has begun to grow, bringing to the forefront in exaggerated form many of the old beliefs with which Ruburt thought he had dispensed so neatly. Science, if it bothered, might label him a fool, but fundamental religion could label him as evil, or claim his work was inspired by the devil in Christian terms, and so the old beliefs in the Sinful Self or evil self were activated.

(Long pause.) They had always been present, of course. He did not admit those feelings, however. They were pushed back further and further. They seemed especially humiliating in the light of what he thought his public position should be. They inspired all the doubts. I want it understood that those feelings nevertheless <u>were</u> often used as creative propellants. The other material recently given on the Sinful Self should be kept in mind along with this session.

The term "morality" is a poor one, yet in the simplest of terms men are born with the knowledge of their own basic goodness—so in the simplest of terms they seek good actions. It is when dogmas distort the natural goodness that trouble develops. It is not <u>natural</u> to feel you exist in a sinful state.

Religion, having in certain terms created the entire concept, had then to create the idea of redemption to rectify it. Ruburt has not been able to utilize the natural grace of the basic self because of those beliefs in their sinful nature. Those feelings were the ones that he experienced this morning—the fear that the self's very expression was somehow wrong, since the self <u>itself</u> was intrinsically flawed. Your own lovemaking the other evening, and your renewed expressions of affection, helped initiate the entire experience, by letting Ruburt feel safe enough to be aware of and experience those sensations. Of course they reflect upon the body. They seek expression. It is not that they are so fearful in themselves, but the effort to repress them gives them additional charge.

Of course, the experience represents an important point of progress, as do the dream intentions. The release of those feelings will clear the air in all areas, allowing the insights of the natural person new freedom so that new needed information at all levels can flow into his experience.

I want to emphasize again the poor reputation held by both science and religion concerning unofficial knowledge, an attitude clearly put forth in many tales and legends, from Adam and Eve to Pandora's box to the Frankenstein monster. Ruburt felt he was someone who was bound to have access to such information. You did extremely well in helping him with the day's events. End of session, unless you have a question.

("Nope.")

Then I bid you a fond good evening.

("Good night, Seth. Thank you." 9:55 PM. Once again, I told Jane the session was excellent—especially the material on this page.)

DELETED SESSION
APRIL 21, 1981 8:39 PM TUESDAY

(Jane slept well last night, got up with me this morning, and has had a relatively peaceful day. She said that "stuff's been going on in the right side of my body all day. I don't know what it is, so I've tried to ignore it."

(She hasn't typed her dreams of yesterday yet for the last session. Today, however, she did get several more notebook pages on a "Speaker's manuscript"—an idea she began to receive material on last Thursday, she thinks it was. She usually takes down that material while sitting on the bed. Today, as she has often lately, she worked on painting a small acrylic landscape.

(She didn't have any questions for Seth. "I think he's going to go into some of that stuff I got last night about true and false, so I just thought I'd let him go.

(She sat in her usual place on the couch, and I faced her in her chair across the coffee table. Behind me in the fireplace we heard once again the mysterious scratching or chucking or chirruping sounds we've become aware of lately, as though a family of animals or birds has young hatching our or growing in a nest on the other side of the closed damper. I'd heard the same sound a few days ago, but since it had been a windy day I'd thought the noise was caused by branches rubbing against the house or fireplace outside. We don't know exactly what should be done about the situation, if anything. My present concern is that if there are young birds in the fireplace they may be trapped, not having room enough to learn to fly. But why would birds build a nest in such a place, assuming they could get to it to begin with? It didn't seem natural for any creature to do that. We've also been under the impression since we moved in here that the fireplace had a screen sealing off the chimney from such possibilities.)

Good evening.

("Good evening.")

Now: all in all, the overall systems of conventional belief are relatively simple, and serve to define reality by numbering as truths or facts certain kinds of events, therefore accepting them as legitimate furniture for the mind.

You have a true or false world in that regard, and a relatively very flat psychological view of identity. Within that framework, however, you do have the creative abilities, and these stand out in their own fashions, since they "play with the facts." They often do not honor conceptual conventions. They do not fit the true-or-false category. The imagination can of course conceive of many events, whether or not those events actually exist.

Straight-laced people have often frowned upon the use of the imagination, considering it most disruptive. *(Pause.)* From the beginning Ruburt has questioned whether or not our material gave a <u>true</u> explanation of reality—or at least presented one that was as <u>approximately</u> true as possible. Or were only creative hypotheses being offered? Was the material true or false?

The idea of the <u>Sinful Self</u> came into play here, for if the material was not true, then in that framework it must necessarily be false—or at the least very misleading. This led to many questions. Is creativity itself involved in a kind of mischievous lying? All of those questions make sense in a framework in which the dictums of one belief system—Christianity—are accepted as true, and everything that does not agree with them is accepted as falsehood.

In that same framework then the nature of my own reality also of course comes into question. Am I an independent personality, who has indeed survived not one but many deaths? *(Pause.)* Inside of that framework you have very few alternatives to deal with. In the first place, as you are learning, your world accepts as valid that <u>portion</u> of an event that can show itself within your recognized time and space coordinates.

This applies not only to seemingly "pure" objective events, but to the more complicated event of an individual psychological being. Indeed, the entirety of your own identities does not usually appear to you in your lifetimes, because that reality is too complicated, too multidimensional, to fit into your accepted picture of personhood. In that regard the larger facts would not show themselves. There would be no way for you to perceive them from <u>within</u> (underlined) your system of reality.

(9:01.) When you are dealing with that kind of philosophical investigation, you are more or less forced to look for other definitions. *(The noise from the fireplace was now quite loud.)* Your very ideas of the nature of reality change. You are still to some extent forced to recognize conventional structures and organizations, including psychological ones. At the same time you search for greater evidence of a vastly different kind of reality. *(Long pause.)* The larger facts about psychological reality, for example, cannot be fitted to the world's definitions. You can only get versions and interpretations. Translations and dramatizations that serve to give you glimpses of psychological structures whose very natures do not fit the facts of the world *(all intently.*

(Pause.) Creative abilities are most helpful in that regard, for they are able to stretch recognizable concepts to their uttermost, allowing you some glimpses of organizations too vast for your own world's dimensionalities.

Those structures include the unexperienced portions <u>of your own</u> identities. All of your concepts of gods and goddesses are basically creative attempts to portray psychological dramatizations of other portions of the psyche that do not appear in the flesh. To hint of other abilities and dimensions of being that cannot of themselves be <u>squeezed</u> into your own smaller definitions. So when Ruburt asks such questions from the framework of old beliefs, with their old meanings, then he can find no adequate answers.

(9:14.) The yes-or-no, true-or-false categories simply do not work when you are dealing with such issues. *(Long pause.)* In that regard it is important that he realize this. The entire concept of the Sinful Self can only exist at certain levels of experience. It can only seem to make sense in a very limited context. *(Pause.)* The creative abilities most often serve as psychological bridges, enabling man to conceive of the existence of realities outside of his own particular point of reference. They can hint at the greater diversity of being, the larger dimension of events. They can present dramatizations. They can serve as thresholds *(long pause)*, but they cannot contain direct experience themselves with events that are intrinsically beyond those reaches.

(Long pause.) In that regard, the attempt to be too literal is of no benefit. Religions have gone astray, of course, by insisting upon the literal interpretation of symbolic material. I am not saying that there are no greater facts, but that those greater facts cannot be contained within your system as themselves.

(Long pause.) Basic reality deals with far more than any true or false category, and the deeper dimensions of actuality contain the source material from which, indeed, your true or false world emerges—so it does Ruburt no particular good to <u>over</u>concern himself. Our material is the best approximation, the best approximate model you can perceive of a vaster psychological field of existence.

(Long pause.) You are in the position of living in the ordinary world, while sensing those other fields of actuality in which that world has its existence. The Sinful Self idea can be detrimental in particular when it is faced by experience that <u>must necessarily fall</u> outside of its realm of reference. Both church and science, again, possess a deep suspicion of unofficial or revelatory knowledge, for this must necessarily involve the insertion of new information into a system unable to explain any facts but its own.

(9:34.) The same kind of recognizable standards that are normally applied to the true-or-false category do not work for such knowledge, since that knowledge is basically, automatically large enough to contain the entire true-or-false realm itself—that is, revelatory information puts true and false designations side by side, and ends up with a system large enough to contain both, in which each

are seen as valid constructs that are only part of a larger view of psychological events.

I recognize the difficulties, for example, that you encounter quite personally as you struggle with Ruburt's physical condition, or those you experience, say, watching television news as you see spread before your vision unfortunate events that seem to portray most clearly evidence of man's flawed nature. It is impossible for you to perceive in the same direct fashion the majestic, almost unimaginable field of creative action in which any of those events occur, however, in which each act, however seemingly destructive, has vital creative purposes that may or may not appear within the limited references of your conventional dimensions.

(Pause.) In that regard, the questions of Ruburt's "Sinful Self" must indeed seem <u>to it</u> most alarming, for it possesses no frame of reference in which its own questions can be answered. These very passages are meant to help open the door of understanding, so that the Sinful Self itself can understand why it feels as it does, so that it can also realize that there are other systems in which its questions can at least be considered.

When Ruburt closes his mind to the <u>feelings</u> of the Sinful Self, he locks it up within a prison as if it could receive no new information, but must always operate with the distorted beliefs of its birth. It cannot get feedback.

(Long pause.) Its fears of such feelings, rather than the feelings themselves, cause difficulties, for the repression keeps the Sinful Self forever locked in the past, uneducated, panicky. The release of such feelings allows the Sinful Self some expression, and gives it a sense of communication so that it can indeed be reached by the understanding gained by other portions of the self—a highly important point.

The feelings involve the fear of being abandoned and alone, outcast. The Sinful Self believes it is unloved and unlovable by nature. You talk to it as you would comfort a child. You tell it that it is loved, and will not be abandoned. That it is good and that those who told it anything else <u>were in grave error</u>. No portion of the self is beyond reach in <u>that</u> (underlined) regard, or unteachable. When Ruburt feels that kind of panic it is indeed the small child's fear of abandonment for being bad *(emphatically)*, and feelings of powerlessness because of the child's relative lack of power in reference to the adult world.

Those feelings, again, can be accepted as <u>belated expressions</u>. In that way, Ruburt's own current experience can reach back to comfort the child in the present. Such a process is relatively simple rather than complex, and can be most beneficial. The Sinful Self can be told it is a good self, it is loved, it is safe to express itself, it is free to follow its own motion and curiosity.

End of session. A fond good evening.

(*10:03. "The same to you, Seth. What's this he's playing with about the Speaker's manuscripts?"*)

Ruburt knows and does not know he is onto something. We will see how far he carries it. It can be highly important, of course, but it and he should be left in that regard to their own paths right now, so I will let the matter rest.

(*I nodded good night.*

(*10:06 PM. "It's me," Jane said. "I knew you asked the question. I guess I don't want to know about it either, so that I'm not under any pressure." I agreed.*

(*The animal/bird noises continued in the fireplace chimney behind me. Mitzi had strolled in during the session and had listened briefly and intently to them, but made no startled response. Right now the noises seemed to have receded somewhat.*)

DELETED SESSION
APRIL 22, 1981 8:31 PM WEDNESDAY

(*This morning Jane slept until noon again, as she'd done last Monday. She slept well until 2:30 AM, but had a rough night from then on, often sore, and tossing and turning.*

(*After I got up and started painting, she began to experience another series of very uncomfortable waves of panic in her sleep, combined with her aching body. They were "somewhat less" than those of last Monday, but still powerful. I often debated about waking her when she began to cry or whimper in her sleep. These were because of her physical discomfort, she said later.*

(*At the same time, on the occasions when she'd come half awake, Jane told herself that she remembered Seth's material on expressing previously buried fears, and made strong efforts to go along with it by letting the feelings surface where she could encounter them. So I think that my not calling her—out of sympathy, say—had been the right course to follow.*

(*Jane had no questions for Seth. I told her I had lots of them, but had been refraining from asking them for the most part until we see what we can learn from the material. Some are personal, some more theoretical and/or general. I haven't written down any of them.*

(*Now I did mention to Jane perhaps the overriding question I have, and have often puzzled about: the intensity of her personality's response to the idea of the Sinful Self. Though, as I said, I didn't think of her Sinful Self as something entirely separate from other portions of her personality, but as a part of them. Why didn't the "Sinful Self" get the message that it's gone too far, and back off at least somewhat so that the whole personality had room to breathe—to begin physical recovery, in other words? Its actions, as they are, are clearly self-defeating. There are many fascinating but serious questions here. Jane agreed.*

(I said that I was quite aware that Seth had recently said that all actions are eventually redeemed—but what about in the meantime? How does one live until that happens? As I discussed the question Jane said she began to feel Seth around. I certainly hadn't expected him to go into the question tonight; in fact, I'd come very close to not mentioning it at all at this time.)

Good evening.

("Good evening, Seth.")

A very difficult question to answer.

I will try a comprehensible response, however. The child or infant is highly suggestible to parental belief systems, so that it can early be provided with a conceptual framework that is complementary to its surroundings, to the group or environment.

The child at such a time for one thing is not in the situation to do conflict with belief systems—it is too young and dependent. The belief systems can be like blocks, which are used and then later changed or replaced, but there is a kind of (underlined) bonding of the childhood self with those ideas it takes from its parents.

There is great leeway here. Some people, remember, are only peripherally involved with concepts or ideas. Ruburt has always been highly fascinated by both. Children want to "be good." They look for approval. It is quite true that later they seek independence also. And shrug aside many early beliefs. The Sinful Self identification is a particularly unfortunate one, for to "be good" means that the child must consider itself bad or sinful.

Right there, the child is presented with a quandary, of course. *(Pause.)* Children and adults also need self-respect. The church itself, again, had an elaborate system within which the Sinful Self could be at least momentarily redeemed, sins confessed and so forth—so within that system the pressures set up by the entire concept were at least momentarily lessened through such releases.

The Sinful Self was given some hope, then.

There were all kinds of aids available: indulgences, litanies, rosaries and so forth. When Ruburt left that system intellectually some of the old bonding power remained, the emotional glue, but he no longer believed in the indulgences, the sacraments and so forth, so the Sinful Self was left fairly isolated, still believing to some extent that to "be good" it must be bad, but without the releases of guilt once provided by churchly help and belief.

(Long pause at 8:46.) Give us a moment.... Science provided no such releases, of course, for it looked upon all such values to begin with as meaningless, including the entire concept of the soul. For some time there was no direct <u>challenge</u>, however, made to the Sinful Self once Ruburt left the church. His creative abilities were growing and developing, his concepts enlarging, but he was for some time so convinced of science's viewpoint that the ideas of the Sinful Self were looked upon as unworthy and superstitious. He was allied with rationalism instead. Many issues therefore remained unresolved, lying there unchallenged. When his creative abilities found contemporary scientific thought also too narrow, however, and his natural intuitions had led him toward a new framework—one that, again, introduced values having to do with the nature of consciousness, or soul—then the new ideas began to conflict directly with the old buried ones, particularly those that had to do with the conflicts between creative expression, the church, and "forbidden knowledge." To go ahead creatively, forming new versions of a <u>spiritual</u> reality, to state that man and his impulses were good, brought him finally into direct conflict with the old beliefs of the Sinful Self, whose value system was based upon the idea that the self was indeed sinful, not to be trusted.

(And here we have an excellent capsule answer as to why Jane has grown progressively worse since beginning Mass Events—*see her paper of last December about her unease over that book and* God of Jane—*and why her symptoms have become even worse as the publication date of* Mass Events *draws near. Now it's supposed to be in May.)*

Beside this, people were reading our books, so to the Sinful Self Ruburt was leading those people astray *(deliberately).* Here you have a rather intense situation. *(A one-minute pause.)* Give us a moment.... The natural self operates within a state of grace, by whatever name, a state that allows for spontaneity, and implies self-trust. Most religious concepts, unfortunately, regardless of the original intentions behind them, end up by dividing man from his own sense of grace—his sense of <u>rightness</u> within the universe, and the individual will do almost anything to gain back that sense, for it is highly vital.

(9:00.) His Sinful Self therefore tried to restate its position in order to right the situation, but its reasoning, again, was that a sense of grace was dependent upon the prior admission of a sinful reality. You have a divided self, of course, in that regard, operationally speaking, and this happens often in your society. The result is repression of one kind or another. The material I gave last night gives valuable information as to how to communicate with that portion of the personality, and bring it up to date, for example.

(Long pause.) That is at least a partial answer to your question. Ruburt

began at once, you see, and has done well. Your help has also been of great value, for it showed of course that he was not being abandoned, for one thing. I am going to keep our session brief for this evening, however.

Give us a moment.... *(Long pause.)....* Once such material is out in the open all of the portions of the personality can work together. Until then you have parts operating at the very least without a sense of unity. *(Long pause.)* The Sinful Self was, again, formed in childhood. It <u>can</u> be comforted. It can be told now what it yearned to be told then—that it was indeed good, and not bad or evil, that it could indeed use its curiosity without the threat of abandonment, and that it could trust its own creativity and love of play.

The Sinful Self is "an <u>artificial</u> psychological construct"—thrust upon the natural self to some degree, and at one time it objected thoroughly against such conditioning, so with communication it will be glad to let those old beliefs go —as long as the entire affair is not allowed to go underground, of course.

The creative abilities will instantly begin a new attempt to reconcile the entire affair, given a freer hand than before.

("Have we reached that point yet?")

You are beginning to approach it. The Sinful Self does not identify as well with the creative abilities, <u>for it does not trust them</u>. In that regard a light hand is the best policy, but the changeover is approaching.

(9:16.) Watch your television, or otherwise divert your minds for the rest of the evening, and when you have another question I will end the session.

("I do have another one, but you can discuss it later. It concerns Ruburt's mother, and her own intensity of reaction.")

We will save that for another time. That will take some time.

A fond good evening.

("Thank you, Seth. Same to you.")

(9:18 PM. Jane's delivery had been much faster than on other occasions lately. Note that she also needed much less time to go into the session. My question turned her on, she said. I think it may turn out to be a key question in our search.)

DELETED SESSION
APRIL 23, 1981 8:43 PM THURSDAY

(After supper Venice McCullough [Palmer] visited us. She and her husband are staying overnight at Bumbalo's before she goes upstate to help her daughter while the granddaughter has an operation for a cleft palate. Venice seemed good, yet was

heavier than ever. She dwarfed Jane as the two sat side by side on the couch. "Now there's something she could do, something about by making a decision," I said later, meaning her weight. I thought such a decision would be simple compared to the ones Jane is trying to cope with.

(Jane slept well last night and got up with me this morning. When she went into the bedroom for her 11 AM nap she ended up getting some forgotten memories about the dishonest treatment she'd received from her mother. Quite a bit of emotion was attached to the memories. "My mother assaulted me psychologically in front of others," she said. "She was, what do you call it, a pathological liar...." Jane described several humiliating incidents her mother had perpetrated upon her. At the same time, it seemed obvious that these memories surfacing represented a therapeutic instance of what Seth had said would happen: memories bubbling to the surface where they could be examined and defused, instead of being kept repressed in the past. Very good, I told Jane.

(It was 8:20 when Venice left, and we sat for the session. The noises from the fireplace had been quite loud earlier, but now all was quiet. "They're squirrels," Frank Longwell had stated this noon. He promised to bring a ladder to the house next week so we could inspect the flue from the roof. I felt better: Squirrels at least would have a chance to get out—but fledgling birds?

(I had 2 pages typed on last night's session, and gave Jane page 1 so she could refresh herself on my question, the one that Seth had begun discussing, about the intensity of her reactions. "Well, I almost feel him around now," Jane said at 8:42.)

Now: Ruburt made an excellent connection today.

His overconscientiousness as a young person, and his intense concern— overconcern—at times with the literal "truth" of any given situation, is and was largely his reaction to his mother's habitual, often mischievous lying pattern. He had not realized that earlier.

His mother's pathological lying meant that Ruburt had to assess and reassess any given situation as a child. He determined not to be malicious as his mother was. His anxiousness led to the most severe examinations of conscience, such examinations being a recommended Catholic practice.

It was also excellent that one such memory carried with it a direct emotional response. That kind of response means that there is communication between, say, the present and past areas of the psyche.

The information came in a natural manner—which is, again, excellent. I do not want to rehash his entire early background, but it is important that he become aware of its emotional content. I wanted to make a few additional points. Ruburt became aware of non-Catholic Christianity to any degree only after our sessions began. The <u>Sinful Self</u> is quite as evident there as it is in the

Catholic Church. The Protestant version is often intermixed, however, with psychic organizations. In that light, as in the Catholic one, the female's guilt is seen as even larger than the male's. So that additional pressure is cast upon the women, who are indeed seen as spiritually inferior—or (underlined) on the other hand painted as pure, pedestal-like individuals in the manner of the Blessed Virgin. That particular subject matter can be discussed at another time. Ruburt has often wondered at the poor quality of most intuitional material, particularly since it is supposed to be so important. The truth of course is not intrinsically in the nature of the material itself, but in the very fact that it is almost exclusively translated in terms of Christian thought, however bizarre that interpretation might be. For that matter, such material often simply restates the entire concept of the Sinful Self in different form. Often that form is highly inflammatory. The main point is a good one to remember, however.

(9:01.) Ruburt's intuitions, his nature, his creative abilities, and his intellect, have led him into a study of the nature of reality, as, again, he sought to find a larger framework of reference. And he has pursued that course vigorously even when he did not consciously see the continuity of such a project at any given time.

The Sinful Self was highly suspicious of any such activity. I believe we have begun an excellent natural therapy in that regard. Ruburt is working at all angles of the problem at other levels of consciousness now, and the Sinful Self is beginning to feel a new sense of give-and-take. (Pause.) Other portions of Ruburt's personality do utilize our material also, of course, and we deal with a certain kind of natural pacing. It is an excellent idea to go over these sessions one at a time and keep the material in the forefront of consciousness for a while.

When memories come concerning his background, then these can be used to provide a necessary feedback system. Ruburt's feelings of panic can then be understood as originating in response to a highly complicated, intense early life, and in concrete situations. There is no doubt that he was mistreated. Ruburt's mind was concerned with the larger framework, however, in which his mother's life existed. He could not be satisfied with an answer like, "That is what life is," or with a simplistic denouncement of man's basic nature.

Again, material I gave last evening fits well with this material. There will be specific references that come to Ruburt, as today's emotional connection did, which will again not only lessen what panic remains, but show that the panic itself has a more or less reasonable basis—not in some formless fear but in specific events. (A very good point.)

The Sinful Self itself can also make such realizations once the door to communication is opened. You are bringing contemporary information into the past, freeing blockages and clearing the way for natural healing. Again, there will be a natural pacing, and on the part of the entire personality additional motion as the information is assimilated and adjustments made to a greater accommodation.

The sessions themselves work to activate many different levels of activity, and to provide source material. Many of Ruburt's current attitudes, for example, will at least make more sense to him as he sees that they originated in response to situations against which a child had no recourse. Ruburt did not tell anyone about his mother's lying, for example, not until he was in his teens, and he was too ashamed of how his mother often treated him to tell anyone.

(9:21.) That treatment reinforced his beliefs that he must indeed be a wicked or sinful person. Remember all of this material, again, in the light of what was said about his public image. Where he felt he was expected to behave in an almost <u>supersaintly</u> fashion—for you have of course two completely different versions of the self there, each unreasonable.

(Pause.) With the God of Jane Ruburt beautifully and expertly described his own experiences with beliefs, and at least hinted of his background. At the same time he felt that he should be offering more: the public image, the saintly understanding, and so forth.

Do you have a question?

("No, I guess not, except to continue with the one from last session.")

I am pacing these sessions now, granting the four or so a week, according to his own experiences, so that the material can also be assimilated along the way. The last few sessions are highly important. (Long pause.) Some of that material is now being used by the so-called Sinful Self itself—which is now open to new information. It is quite earnest in its own desire to "be good," or to feel a sense of grace in its being, so it does understand that kind of purpose.

("Does it have any conception of the physical results that have come about in Ruburt?")

All in all, those results are considered by the Sinful Self, now, as regrettable but necessary, as perhaps the use of overly severe discipline, or the use of punishment "for the personality's own good"—all of which makes perfect sense within the <u>belief structure</u> of the Sinful Self and the larger philosophical structure of Christianity itself.

(A most revealing and damaging answer. "Does the Sinful Self have any conception that its policies have now become self-defeating?"

(Pause.) Another difficult question. (Long pause.) I would have to give a "no" answer in the light in which you asked the question.

In the framework of the Sinful Self's points of reference and in the

Catholic philosophy in which it is based, suffering for a good purpose, toward
a good end, toward a good goal for the sake of the soul, is a virtue. *(Pause.)* The
entire Catholic dogma is built about Christ's agony and death. Now to a portion of the personality believing in that system, Ruburt's position makes hardly
a ripple. That system regards the body as highly distracting, disruptive, heir to
the lusts of the flesh, and so forth. Its discipline through suffering is one of
Christianity's most appalling effects.

(*9:38.*) The ideas of the flesh itself being graced also seemed quite blas-
phemous then to the Sinful Self. It is quite ready to reorganize its reasoning,
however, once it is reached. In the past it has been ignored—another good question. Incidentally, it has been unaware of Ruburt's own knowledge of the close
connection between inspiration, for example, and the body's comfort and relaxation. *(Pause.)* It approves of inspiration, but it is the part of the personality that
is also afraid of unofficial information because of the very belief system that gave
it birth.

Again, it is capable of such understanding, however, and it can change. Its
motivation is to feel at one with a state of grace, at one with its place in the universe. That purpose is the same as Ruburt's own, but its methods and understanding are still at a certain level, a level that can indeed be changed and reed-
ucated.

(*"Is the Sinful Self that closely connected with the physical self, then, or did
other parts of Ruburt's personality bring about the symptoms because they knew of the
beliefs of the Sinful Self?"*)

(*Long pause. Seth stared at me for a good moment.*)

I cannot answer the question as you gave it.

(*"Did the Sinful Self have help in creating the symptoms, in other words?"*)

Give us a moment.... Save the question. I will restate it for you and answer
it at another session.

(*"Okay."*)

End of session and a fond good evening.

(*"Thank you. The same to you."*)

(*9:47 PM. "I feel you did it again," Jane said as soon as she was out of trance,
"hit on some real good stuff."*)

(*I thought so too. The first question automatically led to the following ones.
There were many more to be asked, too. I was appalled, while thinking at the same
time that perhaps at last we've finally reached the core of the problem, and can take
steps to do something about it. The Sinful Self.... What a concept, I thought, specu-
lating briefly about the untold damage it must have done to millions of people over
the centuries. My first thought after the first question's answer had been that it must*)

be excised from Ruburt's character, or at least that its beliefs must be changed so much that it becomes unrecognizable compared to what it is now.

(Jane turned on the television after a very brief discussion. I wanted badly to study this session with the idea of basing future questions upon it. I wanted to know how suffering could be good for the soul, among other questions, since from its supposedly exalted position one would hardly think the soul needed suffering to improve its position or understanding. My feelings toward the Sinful Self were certainly not charitable, nor was I about to concede it a state of grace in view of its damaging actions, even if Jane has ignored it and shut off communication. There is much to be learned here. Perhaps we've finally got a good hold on what needs to be done.)

DELETED SESSION
APRIL 24, 1981 8:17 PM FRIDAY

(Jane spent one of her worst nights yet last evening: "It was pretty shitty." She slept very poorly and was continuously restless. She took aspirin, sat up often, and even called me to rub her legs and backside when those areas bothered her much more than usual. Nothing helped much. She slept until 11 AM, then spent a very silent and depressed day moodwise. Her legs especially bothered her.

(We were fairly sure her reactions stemmed from the barrage of material Seth has given us since we began this series of "crash" sessions last week, but that knowledge didn't help her much today. Particularly apparent, I thought, would be effects from last night's session, which I regard as excellent. This morning in bed Jane had thrashed and whimpered almost constantly while both sleeping and waking, unable to get comfortable. The panicky feelings wouldn't allow that, though—they expressed themselves in waves just as they had last Monday and Wednesday mornings. I took this to mean that communication continued between her Sinful Self and other levels of her personality.

("Bob, all I want to do is get better." she said in the bathroom, half crying, after another struggle to get back into her chair from the john.

("Maybe you'd better have a session tonight," I said. I didn't really mean it, since we'd thought sessions were over for the week on Thursday.

("I don't want another session," Jane said. "I just want to watch some dumb old thing on television tonight and forget it all."

("Incredible," I said to myself, thinking about the daily struggle she now had to contend with just to do a few basic things like using the bathroom. Last night's session was in my mind, of course. And I thought that years ago, [and with my own unwitting cooperation] Jane had given over control of her life in certain large ways

to the <u>Sinful Self</u> through the symptoms—and yes, abjectly allowed it to exert such power and influence that now she finally found herself in the grip of a strong force, or set of beliefs. Why such a course of action, such a surrender, as I saw it? A little suffering in life—okay, I thought, considering the session last night—but this? She'd reached her limit in some areas, such as the bathroom.

(At noon, as we ate, I asked her what she thought the Sinful Self might make of the Speaker manuscript material she'd been getting in recent days. Jane said she'd been wondering also.

(She was very glum and silent as she spent much time on the couch this afternoon and after supper. "Something's got to be done," she said. "I can't take much more of this." She herself suggested the session, then, and of course I agreed. I also told her I hadn't forgotten about the list of 6 points I'd made for the deleted session of April 13, 1981. That seemed like ages ago now. The last of those points described our seeking medical help for her. To my mind at the moment, that course of action would be the "something to be done" if we failed to get enough help from these late sessions.

(Seth started right off tonight with a rather surprising statement and a hopeful one too. Jane began speaking for him with unexpected vigor:)

Good evening.

("Good evening, Seth.")

Now: One point I wanted to make for the record. The Sinful Self, however, no longer identifies with the Roman Catholic Church, as once it did, and in years past it also became dissatisfied with that framework. It represents <u>what is left over</u> of Ruburt's questioning and doubts, those unresolved areas that were emotionally charged not only because of, say, Church doctrine, but intensified because of emotional episodes with his mother, or other such issues. In that regard the Sinful Self, then, is not pleased with its situation.

(Long pause.) It did not feel it was being given any satisfactory recognition, however. The main issues are the ones already given. You should discuss them together in the light of the sessions, and with understanding. They are involved with the importance and the nature and reliability of revelationary material and as it is related to a literal true-and-false interpretation.

The <u>Sinful Self</u> wants to be sure it is not lying, because it <u>feels</u> that according to its definitions it is naturally given to such behavior—being bad, sinful, et cetera. The entire false-prophet syndrome comes from those feelings.

To a lesser degree the same question applies to any highly inspirational creativity—which, again, has always been questioned by the church organization, which has been firmly against even, say, individual interpretation of the Bible itself.

The idea that our work might set up a new church, therefore, is a very touchy one. These are all matters to be satisfactorily discussed and explained and understood, however, once it is understood that such questions are legitimate ones, and not foolish worries to be just thrust aside.

(8:30.) They actually represent very complex matters, and complex ones to explain, for in themselves they contain the seeds of material necessary for any <u>understanding</u> of the nature of reality and beliefs. Religion itself, of course, would hardly stand the test.

Many issues once connected to that Sinful-Self core of belief have long ago either been satisfied, reconciled, or otherwise changed. *(Long pause.)* The feelings of panic represent any child's fear of being abandoned by its parents or community if it is too rebellious. *(Long pause.)* Those feelings of panic are the ones that he has repressed, of course. They often represent humiliations, most often at his mother's hands—humiliations that convinced him that he was indeed unlovable and bound for trouble.

The feelings themselves are hardly unmanageable, however, and can be coped with. While we are dealing with such material you should definitely try to be a bit more indulgent with yourselves, generally speaking—Ruburt in particular. Make love more if the opportunity arises. See occasional visitors or whatever. *(Long pause, then intently but with a touch of humor:)* I know you know this, but do not concentrate upon the problem. You undo half of your good work when you do. You narrow your scope of interest.

("Can I say something?")

You may.

("It seems Jane can do little else." I was thinking of her depressed response today to her symptoms. "She certainly wasn't up to anything else, it seemed. She felt very bad.")

Today was a day in which feelings became conscious and pervaded the emotional air, as if the mustiness from a suddenly opened closet door spread out into the living room. That kind of situation will soon be over, for it is a reaction —quite natural—on the first reopening of that door into past feelings.

Before, the feelings were present but completely camouflaged into the bodily symptoms. For a short period of time, it may seem <u>that on occasion</u> (underlined) both symptoms and mood are intensified. That will also vanish, and be of brief duration.

In the last period of time Ruburt has also produced his material on Speaker manuscripts, for example, when his mood has been on an entirely different nature, when he was immersed in creativity, and he felt a sense of accomplishment. The same applies to the half-dozen or so small paintings.

("We were wondering what the Sinful Self might think about work on those

Speaker manuscripts.

(Seth either didn't hear me, or chose to ignore the question.)

Old habits are involved, of course. The part about not concentrating upon the problem, however, is still paramount, and so is the necessity of seeing the situation in its larger framework. I mean that literally. In the face of Ruburt's background he has managed as well as he has, and that in the other areas of life you are doing far better than you habitually give yourselves credit for.

(9:49.) Those areas have a tendency to be neglected in your minds, as if next to Ruburt's problems they are relatively insignificant—but you would not find them so insignificant if they represented their own vital problem areas.

Give us a moment.... *(Long pause.)....* I realize that you can only do so much, Joseph, but on a particularly troublesome night, if you would sit up, talk with Ruburt for perhaps 10 or 15 minutes, you could both shorten troublesome episodes to a considerable degree. This last period was intensified also since both of you were in the same mood at the same time. You must remember that the entire problem does indeed exist in a larger personal framework in which life and energy are abundantly and freely given.

All parts of Ruburt's personality are indeed working with the material, and working toward reconciliations. I will on another evening reply to your troublesome question *(which I mentioned a couple of days ago, I believe)* concerning those issues where my interpretation of Ruburt's situation certainly often does not correlate with your own.

I must add most probably still another such instance *(almost with humor)*, by telling you that the condition of Ruburt's legs is indeed therapeutic. It is also true that he is frightened that that is not so, and that the fear itself makes the situation more unpleasant than otherwise need be.

Under certain conditions even pleasant so-called body experiences can be experienced as painful—and indeed vice versa *(intently)*.

Ruburt's situation is not fated to get worse. *(Long pause.)* He is not temperamentally <u>trapped</u>. *(Long pause.)* You have each of late allowed yourselves to see the situation in its poorest light—and that of course is part of the problem. I realize this is easy to say from my viewpoint, and that your expectations must certainly be based somewhat upon current experience, yet you have far more leeway there than you use.

End of session.

("Question?"

(Seth nodded assent. I repeated my question about the Sinful Self's opinion of Jane working on Speaker manuscripts.)

I am letting that go for this evening.

("Okay.")
The situation can easily begin to improve, whether or not I know consciously how this is being done. Use that suggestion in the meantime—<u>with</u> a light hand.
("Okay.")
A fond good evening.
("Thank you, Seth. Good night.")
(9:05 PM.)

DELETED SESSION
APRIL 27, 1981 8:24 PM MONDAY

(We really wanted this session, although at 7:30 PM Jane was so far out of it that I didn't know whether she'd make it or not. She said she'd try, and I hoped the session would come about.

(For last night had been one of her most uncomfortable yet. She woke me up crying at 4 AM, with flashing, shooting sensations in her right leg, from the hip all the way down to the foot. "By the time it reaches the foot, it almost feels good," she said. She'd taken Bufferin but it hadn't seemed to help much. She has had similar sensations in recent days—see the chronology for the weekend as listed below—but last night they were steadier and more intense. Jane also had another series of dreams, but unfortunately could remember hardly anything of them. I rubbed her legs for half an hour, then she fell asleep. In fact, she was snoring before I could get back to sleep myself.

(Jane slept until noon, and again during the morning thrashed about often in her sleep, and sometimes whimpered or cried out, presumably because of a dream. Yet when I called her she said she'd slept well. The hot, shooting sensations continued in her right leg, though to a lesser degree. Frank Longwell visited this noon, and massaged her legs also. He said the sensations were a positive, therapeutic sign of "nerve activity." Yet Jane was back in bed by 3 PM, and slept until suppertime.

(Frank, incidentally, had brought a ladder so he could get upon the roof to look down our chimney in an effort to see what creatures were causing the rumpus in the fireplace above the damper. With my flashlight, he glimpsed a medium-sized <u>coon</u>, but couldn't tell if it was male or female, or whether it had young. He returned at 5 PM to drop a heavy rope down the chimney in the hope the raccoon might climb out. But then, I thought, it must be getting in and out by itself all along, for at least three weeks now, and I was sure that late at night I could hear more than one voice chattering above the damper. It certainly seemed that parents were feeding the young.)

(*Frank, also, has never come across another case like Jane's, from the days he was a chiropractor until now. He said that doctors would have trouble diagnosing her symptoms. If memory serves, Seth said a long time ago that Jane did not have arthritis, but for her own reasons was mimicking her mother's disease. Jane is really bothered, though, and we trust that Seth was correct in the last session when he said this phase of Jane's symptoms would soon pass.*

(*I showed Jane a copy again of my dream of April 23, and asked that Seth discuss it this evening, since I was sure it contained at least some positive omens for her.*

(*Now here is a brief chronology pertaining to Jane's symptoms from last Saturday, the day after the last session was held:*

(*Saturday morning, April 25: When we went to bed, Jane dreamed about her mother and about writing about her life with Walt. She has an unpleasant experience involving her mother as we got into bed, but I reassured her and she slept well. She had a good day after I suggested she try not to concentrate upon her symptoms.*

(*Then before supper on Saturday she began to feel new, very strange sensations: painful in the hip, but much more pleasant by the time they reached the foot. Sometimes she made nearly involuntary quick movements of the leg or foot. We thought this added feeling of sensation might be the result of the last couple of sessions especially. Walter Zeh was her first husband.*

(*Sunday, April 26: After breakfast at 11:30—for Jane—I found her sitting with her legs propped up on a chair. The same sensations were running painfully down her right leg from the hip—but again, "they feel good by the time they reach my toes."*

(*"Well, I still feel far from up to doing much," Jane said as we waited tonight at 8:15, "but there's no doubt about it, things are still going on. That sensation is now right here"—she pointed to the top of her right knee—"and goes on down into the ankle." She'd also noticed new sensation on the top of her right foot, an area she'd been quite unaware of for a long time.*

(*"I assume I can have a session, but beyond a certain point it's too hard." she said—and winced as another shooting sensation "got me right in the knee. But I vaguely feel him around...."*

(*Once again she sat on the couch, and I sat in her chair facing her across the coffee table—with behind me, the closed-off fireplace. Up beyond the damper, I could easily hear our raccoon guests busily chattering away: perhaps it was feeding time, their noise was loud, now—a sure sign of growing things, I thought. I thought the racket might disturb Jane going into trance, but such wasn't the case.*

Now (*leaning back on the couch, eyes closed*): First, we will begin with Ruburt's physical sensations.

He is dealing with what is a kind of nervous generation—regeneration —

reawakening the activity and function of the nerves involved in normal walking —a reeducation process in which nervous sensations are reintroduced.

The intensification has a purpose in bringing those nervous connections to conscious attention, and in *(long pause)* reasserting those connections to the proper physical connections to the brain. In a manner of speaking those sensations had been played down, muffled. Now they are, say, amplified temporarily. They do of course signify motion and impetus, and they serve also to activate all other portions that are involved with walking's activity.

To a lesser extent they affect the whole body, of course. The sensations are "leader sensations" meant to initiate cycles of other activity.

(Pause at 8:33.) Now give us a moment.... The sensations do portray beneficial change, and are <u>stimulators</u>. Now. A small segment this evening on television gave you a picture of the confused activity that can take place in exaggerated situations—the segment dealing with the abused children, for there you have parents reacting in the worst possible way to the religious dictums as interpreted by "<u>Sinful Selves</u>." *(I'd thought of that at the time. but didn't mention it to Jane.)*

All sense of proportion nearly vanishes. On a larger social scale the same thing applies in your wars *(pause)*, in which the most drastic measures are considered as sane enough and reasonable if only the goal is "a good one." Ruburt's dreams have been helping him identify his own personal experience as he interpreted such beliefs in early life. *(Long pause.)* He has been bringing a combination of physical and mental events together, so that they can be encountered <u>in the present</u> and in the light of his new information.

(Long pause at 8:42.) The <u>Sinful Self</u> is of course <u>put upon</u>, turned into what it is. It is not a natural psychological construct, so when it is allowed to it naturally seeks its own release also, when it is denied communication that is most difficult. Some of last night's dream material dealt with the ideas, again, of creativity—sometimes seen as harmless enough for children, as in the play Ruburt remembered taking part in his Catholic public school. In larger measure, however, creativity was considered something that adults grew out of, a mark of a prolonged adolescence, particularly unsuited for the woman whose thoughts were meant to turn toward husband and child.

(All of a sudden the noises from the fireplace were so loud and intimate that I thought that somehow the raccoons had managed to get past the closed damper and were behind the screen in the fireplace itself, but Jane continued as usual in trance.)

The creativity for which Ruburt was praised as a child—the writing of his poetry, for example, became more and more frowned upon by the church as he became older, and in particular when the poetry contained concepts that did not fit Christian dogma.

(Now the noise in the fireplace was fluctuating.) There you run into problems involved with Catholic or Christian devotion, the natural feedback needed in the development of creative work, and the striking originality of creative ventures that strike out on their own, forming their own paths.

(Pause.) The creative self is made to feel guilty for its own originality and productivity. *(Long pause.)* Added to all of this, you have varying social climates throughout a life. So the individual will also respond according to the cultural situation. If Ruburt understands these issues the entire affair will resolve itself, for he will feel at one with himself. *(Pause.)* He is getting rid of feelings and sensations however that have blocked his progress in the past. Again, the material should be read and discussed now, and let him mention specifically any events that come to mind naturally as you read or discuss the sessions.

(Jane discussed such an incident the next day, Tuesday, at noon, even before I began typing this session. It involved the death of her mother's housekeeper, Mary, and the blame Jane's mother placed for this upon the daughter.)

(Pause at 8:56.) The intensity of the hip and leg sensations has already reached a peak, and will be subsiding—and your own assistance last evening was invaluable. The main issue, again, is to reassure that one important portion of Ruburt's personality that the self is not sinful, not bad or evil, and to show it the limited nature of the framework that so defined it.

I would prefer to let your dream go for now. Its hopeful aspects are obviously apparent. Ruburt should be experiencing some fresh periods of refreshment and relaxation, both mentally and physically, and I will end the session unless you have a specific question that you consider important.

("Nope." I had lots of questions, but thought Jane needed rest.)

I would like the material assimilated and read.

("Okay.")

Try to arrange your time. You can take two or three nights without sessions to read the material, or find other time during the day or whatever, making your own decisions, and a fond good evening.

("Thank you, Seth. The same to you.")

(9:00 PM. Jane's delivery had been good. I mentioned in a fairly mild way some of the questions I had for Seth, saying I didn't want to pass judgment too quickly on a given concept or idea like the Sinful Self. "My feelings toward the Sinful Self aren't very friendly," I said, "but I don't want to be too hostile or I might create other problems...." I also wanted time to reread the most recent sessions particularly, for I think they contain the best material for us at this time. And again, I said to Jane, why had it taken us so long to get to this point? The years pass.

(And Jane's leg sensations had returned to a degree. There was no doubt that

she was uncomfortable as she sat on the couch. She didn't know whether to watch television or have a cookie and milk, or go sit on the bed and make a few notes. As it turned out, we did go to bed perhaps half an hour early.)

DELETED SESSION
APRIL 28, 1981 8:44 PM TUESDAY

(We'd wanted to read over some of the late sessions today, but didn't do it. The time seemed to fly by. Jane slept until about 10:30. She hadn't done badly, and I'd rubbed her legs before we slept. She had some right leg sensations—strong enough to notice but not nearly as strong as before, and she's had them "off and on all day, particularly in the knee and lower leg. I haven't had any feeling there for I don't know how long." She'd maneuvered somewhat better in the bathroom this morning, and said her right hip worked well.

(All of these signs are good ones, of course, and we hope they continue. These sessions have surely helped, as I've been hoping they would.

(Frank Longwell visited today. He came to get his rope out of the fireplace chimney—our family of raccoons is still there, evidently immune to the temptations offered by the rope. They are chattering mildly behind me now as I work on these notes.

(This afternoon I mowed some grass out front as soon as it stopped raining, then typed last night's session, almost finishing it. I did complete it after supper. Jane didn't feel like reading and discussing sessions, though, so we decided to have one tonight and perhaps do some reading tomorrow.)

Now: a few instructions.

As you read this group of sessions, the idea is in no way to accuse the Sinful Self. It is instead to understand it, its needs and motives, and to communicate the idea that it was sold a bad bill of goods in childhood—scared out of its wits, maligned.

The idea is to show it that those beliefs no longer apply, that the framework in which they were learned was highly faulty. Instead, itself—the self—is indeed good, as it supposed before it took on such nonsense. Treat it in a way like a frightened child who can be comforted, and who can understand.

(Long pause.) It should be made a party to the process, then, very definitely, for it is its transformation and understanding that you seek. I will shortly give you a very, very brief collection of suggestions that you can read following each reading session of your own, to clear the air.

Ruburt is doing very well under the situation. The feelings in the leg and the knee do indeed signify new motion, and the willingness to move. Again, the feelings of panic will naturally subside, but they are important for they are in their way the signs of the child crying—and earlier, <u>Ruburt as the adult would not listen.</u>

Ruburt's entire group of symptoms do not follow any established pattern. They are the result of applied stress, exaggerated finally by feelings of hopelessness, and by some relative feelings of isolation.

(Long pause at 8:58.) The Sinful Self obviously is not a burden that Ruburt carries alone, but one inherent in your civilization. Unfortunately its <u>values</u> have in their way appeared throughout your culture. *(Long pause.)* In terms of goodness, you can certainly tell the <u>Sinful Self</u> that health and vitality are indeed not only good, but in their way they represent the spiritual attributes. No self really needs a baptism. It is already blessed by All That Is before its birth, and its desires, impulses, and characteristics are also inherently good, meant to insure its own fulfillment, to bring out its best characteristics, and to help the rest of the world as well—all very important issues.

(Pause.) Ruburt might have one or two imaginary conversations with the Sinful Self. This can be quite advantageous, and will certainly speed up communications. Ruburt will probably begin to experience the refreshment I mentioned, and relaxation, more and more, but it was also important that he be aware of the subjective state that had been causing the difficulty. That state can then dissipate through expression.

This will indeed be a brief session, but I did want to give it to you before you seriously began studying this group. Do you want to ask a question?

("I've been wondering lately about how much of a role his psychic abilities have to do with the intensity of his reactions to his childhood experience. I know you've gone into aspects of that before, but—")

The creative abilities after a while were themselves suspect. The Sinful Self was taught to distrust its own nature and expression, believing that that nature, by virtue of original sin, was flawed—but in a tragic fashion—literally damned by God, of course, because of the sins of the forefathers.

(9:10.) Psychic abilities, as such, were relatively unimportant to Ruburt when the Sinful Self was receiving all of this instruction, so in that regard they, taken alone, were simply seen in a somewhat worse light than the creative abilities. The problem came with the insertion of questions of good or bad, truth or falsehood, and certainly with any possibility of, say, setting up a new religion.

I made those points clear in a recent session, and they are important.

End of session.

("Thank you.")

A fond good evening—

("The same to you.")

—and you have done well also, handling the entire situation. *(Long pause.)* One small note: again, the Sinful Self should be assured it is good, it is not sinful. It is safe to express itself, it is safe to move, and it was produced by All That Is out of the great energy of universal love.

(9:15 PM. "Well. I'm glad I had it," Jane said. Note that Seth began commenting right away on the notes I'd written at the end of the last [yesterday's] session, about my unfriendly feelings toward the Sinful Self at this time. In the session he also touched upon several other points I'd raised very recently, including the nature of Jane's symptoms.

(It had rained hard after supper, but slackened as session time drew close. As I turned on a couple of additional lights in the living room, to see to write by, our friends in the fireplace began to sound off—adding a new sort of whistling or crying sound—and Jane made what may be a good point: light may leak past the closed damper enough that the raccoons respond to that stimulus. But they became much more quiet as the session progressed.)

DELETED SESSION
APRIL 30, 1981 8:27 PM THURSDAY

(Jane had a pretty good day today—until we read over some of the late sessions this afternoon, those having to do with her relationship with her mother. Then she became "irritated and edgy" as she lay down for her nap. And last night, as usual, she'd had some dreams bearing upon our currents efforts to help her. They hadn't been nightmarish, though. Actually, she'd slept well, and got up to have breakfast with me. This morning she did an acrylic of the mums Frank Longwell had given her for her coming birthday.

(When I joined her for the session I found her sitting on the couch with her eyes drooping, half-closed in relaxation. Yet she wasn't sleepy—"I've slept enough today," she said, referring to her morning and afternoon naps. She didn't have any questions in particular, though, even considering her upset over the session material. We'd also reread a group of sessions last night instead of having a session, but I didn't want to pass up the opportunity for a session tonight, since it was getting later in the week.

("See, I got scared then," Jane said at 8:17, coming awake and sitting up straight on the couch. She wasn't sure whether the momentary fright came from the sleeping or the fear of relaxation, though my feeling was that it was the latter. "I don't

*know whether you should ask any questions about my mother," she said, "that's
charged material...."*

*(This afternoon I'd suggested that she might like a word from Seth on her
mother's* <u>present</u> *situation—meaning that if her mother now had more insight as to
her treatment of her daughter, this knowledge might help Jane feel better about her
own reactions to her mother. Yet Jane wasn't sure. When I repeated the suggestion now
she said it regenerated those feelings of panic and/or unease, "but we haven't time to
go into them now, with the session due and all."*

*(I attempted to reassure her, and added that we dared not let those feelings "go
hide" again, underground in the psyche. Jane agreed. This afternoon I'd also said that
I wouldn't let her do that any more.*

*(And by 8:22 she was feeling Seth around. Her whole body was still changing.
"The legs have been changing completely—I guess I didn't tell you—both knees have
sensations," she said. "I can feel them when I walk, and that scares me. My hips and
shoulders, and the feeling of moving in the right hip, on top...." But she hasn't had
the shooting sensations to any degree like she had since I rubbed her legs in the middle of the night two nights ago. She's been much more comfortable.*

*(Our raccoon friends were stirring in the fireplace behind me. They'd been
pretty quiet most of the day—so much so that we had wondered if mama and papa
had evacuated their family from that cozy spot.)*

Good evening.

("Good evening, Seth.")

Now: we will take this gently.

Ruburt's mother often told him she wished the birth had not taken place,
and that Ruburt had not been born. She let Ruburt know that she wanted a boy
—a son—rather than a daughter to begin with. So Ruburt felt that he was certainly a disappointment to say the least.

He was made to feel often that he was at least strongly responsible for his
mother's illness. It was also true that on other occasions his mother apologized
for such statements—but the statements of course were highly charged and
emotional, while the apologies were relatively prosaic.

(Slowly:) Ruburt's mother chose her own life. She did then obviously
decide to have a child, abortions or no, for in this case they did not work. *(Long
pause, eyes closed.)* She and Ruburt chose a relationship that would terminate, so
the two would go their separate ways. *(Long pause.)* His mother actually found
in the nursing homes a certain kind of comradeship. She was always involved in
the politics of such institutions.

(Long pause, one of many, at 9:36.) Ruburt's background formed its own
<u>relative</u> uniqueness—<u>the household was charged</u>. Give us a moment.... Ruburt

picked that background because it afforded certain opportunities. Those opportunities involved emotional understanding, a very close and emotional contact
with a particular belief system, and a firsthand view of a certain kind of reality
structure.

*(Long pause at 9:41, eyes closed leaning back on the couch, the 'coons chatter-
ing away in the fireplace.)*

It also allowed for the emergence of creativity. In a fashion it presented a
kind of concentrated learning course. Ruburt has changed in many ways, but
throughout Marie's life, Marie changed relatively little—that is, any change was
well with a certain recognizable scale.

Why should anyone choose that kind of a lifetime? That was one of many,
many questions *(pause)* that Ruburt had slated for himself. Where did that kind
of belief system end up? How could it be altered or adjusted or rearranged to
suit the needs of his own generation—or had it served all of its purposes? What
were its benefits as well as its unfortunate aspects? How did creativity operate
under such conditions?

Now to some extent each person tests the nature of reality in each life for
himself or herself, and also for the entire generation. How can life be made better? So all of that was a portion of Ruburt's challenge. Marie's purposes were her
own, but the two obviously embarked on a relationship together, knowing that
it would go so far and be relatively unsatisfactory.

As I stated before, Ruburt was not responsible for his mother's illness, the
break-up of her marriage, the deaths of his grandmother and housekeeper *(long
pause)*, and had he had brothers or sisters, for example, they would have reacted in their own fashions to Marie's behavior. Ruburt had been put in the
Protestant day camp for an unfortunate short summer following the grandmother's death, and later into the Catholic home for a more protracted period
of time. To some extent he thought of that as punishment, of course, of being
abandoned, forced to take charity as well, and the home reinforced all of the
Catholic beliefs, particularly stressing the sinfulness of the body. Remember for
example the bathing episodes. There was no distinction made: to be sinful was
of course to be a sinner, and in that home there was no time to foster any kind
of independence—the children had to follow strict schedules, toe the mark.

(Long pause at 9:56.) He spent a good deal of time on his knees, then,
doing penance when he did not fit into that structure. If he looked into a mirror and was caught at it, he was then caught in the sin of pride. When he wet
the bed in the fourth grade night after night, the act was characterized as dirty.

(Long pause at 9:58.) When he wrote the letters to his mother they were
censored. The nuns told him that he must say he was happy, whether or not he

was. By the time he returned home he was quite rigid and moralistic. On the other hand, for the time being he had a very secure belief system against which for quite a full number of years he could test his own mental, emotional and spiritual vigor.

(Long pause.) He used dogma in a mystical manner, only to discover, however, that the church's mysticism had no place to go: it was in its fashion dead-ended. It squashed creativity unless that creativity cowed under dogma.

(Long pause.) In that background Ruburt saw firsthand an example of many of the most unfortunate issues with which we have been presently concerned, to at least some extent, as he followed his mother's adventures through the medical system, for example, through the welfare process. Marie was also a woman living without a man for many years. She was a strong personality. She lived in a relatively tumultuous emotional climate, provided with one kind of emotional excitement or another all the while.

(Long pause at 9:10.) In a large manner, however, Marie's daughter was always—somewhat, now—on the periphery of Marie's life, and not at its center. To whatever degree anyone ever was at its center, Del was, even though they had not seen each other for years. *(Delmer Roberts, Marie's husband.)*

Marie did not hate Ruburt, though at times she could be quite hateful in her expressions. She was primarily bitter, and that bitterness lashed out at anyone, with Ruburt the nearest target. *(Long pause.)* Her last illness, while painful, was not a long lingering one. Ruburt need not blame himself for not attending Marie's death.

(Long pause at 9:17.) The emotional situation did not lean in that direction: they had parted too many years before. It was as if Marie were saying, "This is the kind of a life those beliefs can create. Now you go out and see what you can do to change it." Those events also added high drama, rich content, and provided unique creative material. Even in that background and with Marie's behavior, Ruburt received a grounding in poetry, you see. His mother tried her writing. It would never have occurred to your mother to try short stories.

The priests introduced "good" music, poetry, and a high educational background, even if it was a limited distorted framework. Father Traynor provided some kindliness, compassion and good will as he tried to translate Catholic dogma to Ruburt's rebellious mind. He tried to restrain Marie in her expressions of bitterness.

Marie also found peripheral relationships throughout later life, with nurses or attendants who turned into friends—and while her life certainly was not a happy one, it was not as tragic as it now seems to Ruburt to have been, so that the beneficial elements of that early background were used without quarreling, of course. The unbeneficial elements were also used, many with quite creative results.

Some of those unfortunate conditions, however, or questions, remained unresolved, and it is with those you are contending. They end up neatly summarized in the concept of the Sinful Self—a self so sinful that its own body had to be hidden from itself while it washed *(all intently)*.

Ruburt's grandmother taught him to sleep with his hands above the coverlets, so that the child would not even begin subconsciously to feel its own parts while it slept *(again intently)*. The Sinful Self then became very alert: how could it trust its own works, if it were so indelibly tainted?

(Long pause at 9:32.) Worse, its questions were largely ignored, so that its panic grew. Another portion of the self seemed to be initiating an entirely different system of reality, in complete opposition to that early background, and the <u>Sinful Self</u> was bound to react with some alarm. It is already beginning to change its views. It wanted the communication to begin with. In the meantime Ruburt felt—<u>because</u> of those beliefs—to some extent now, I am simplifying — that he could not do enough, produce enough, help himself or others enough, that he could not satisfy you enough in many areas, because he felt he was so flawed to begin with, therefore he did not deserve love, and would have to work for it, or plead for it.

So such attitudes were reflected, and kept him from even appreciating his own work. All such matters will be covered.

That is enough for this evening, since you read sessions today also. You should be quite encouraged, however, by Ruburt's responses of late—

("Yes.")

—and I bid you a fond good evening.

("Thank you very much, Seth.")

(9:38 PM. Jane said as she came out of trance: "That was hard for me to get into. Just as I stopped I remembered something: When I lay down after we got through reading the sessions, I had another one of those sorts of half-conscious out-of-bodies, I guess you'd call it. One thing that happened was that I was standing an inch or so higher, and I was walking pretty fast—but I was still bent way over, like I was still <u>in</u> my body like that first time this happened. I was real pleased, though."

("And now I feel real funny—funny, ha-ha," she said with little humor.)

DELETED SESSION
MAY 5, 1981 9:35 PM TUESDAY

(Jane didn't feel particularly like having a session last night, and the time just passed without our holding one.

(See the attached notes of Jane's, concerning her experiences of April 30 and May 2. Actually, much else has taken place also, but I didn't keep daily records and feel somewhat lost in trying to reconstruct events. This morning, for example, Jane slept until noon, and after I got up at 6:30 she had a number of recurrences of her "panic attacks." Last night she'd slept fairly well, although at one time she sat up and wrote some notes on the Speakers' manuscripts. The night before, she'd come up with good material about how to conclude her third Seven novel. I should add that she stayed up all day yesterday, for the first time in many days. She did take a nap late in the afternoon at the same time I lay down.

(Jane began crying after I called her this noon, as she felt the waves of panic sweep through her, and she continued to cry for some little while. She said the feelings didn't seem to be related to any specific events that she could remember. They were very unpleasant—frightening—and we thought that they were supposed to be therapeutic in nature, in line with Seth's recent material. Had she succeeded in repressing them, as she had done in the past, more trouble would have presumably erupted at a later time.

(Jane felt recurrences of the panicky feelings to a lesser degree through the day, and occasionally she cried or whimpered a bit. "All I want is to be loved and cuddled," she said upon getting up, and I tried to offer what help I could—very inadequately, I'm afraid. She did make out fairly well in the bathroom, however.

(Frank Longwell visited yesterday noon. During one of our discussions yesterday, also, I mentioned to Jane some of my own ideas about the power of the Sinful Self, according to Seth's material. For even though it was seemingly somewhat isolated or cut off from the personality's creative processes, as well as from many current events and ideas, still it had that power to so drastically influence the physical body. This of course implied strong connections with the body as it operated in daily physical reality. The two states almost seemed contradictory, I said to Jane, and hoped that Seth would go into that matter eventually.

(Debbie Janney visited unannounced for an hour after supper—all the time Jane would give her—hence the later start for the session. She also missed a chance to meet the Weissenbuehlers from Big Flats, whom we saw last Friday night, since DJ was in Washington, DC over the weekend.

(Today Jane called John Nelson and Tam, and learned where I am to sign the Seven contract, and that Prentice-Hall would be receptive to her third Seven novel.

She was also reminded by Tam that Pocket Books has bought the paperback rights to the second Seven, *which we had quite forgotten about. The advance was cut considerably from that given for the first* Seven *also. Pocket Books hasn't scheduled* Seven *#2 for publication yet, as far as we know.*

(Jane wanted Seth to discuss her panic feelings tonight, although she didn't seem overly enthusiastic about a session either. When Debbie showed up and the time approached 9 PM, I thought Jane might choose to pass up the session after all. "It's important, though," I said to her when Debbie was out of the room for a moment. Jane agreed, saying DJ was ready to leave, and we held the session after all.)

Now: it is sometimes difficult to explain certain issues so that you do not end up with a simple black-or-white explanation.

Everything I have said about the Sinful Self applies. The <u>Sinful Self</u> is not the "villain". It is not a case of one portion of the personality inflicting difficulties on other portions so much as you have a <u>pattern</u> of reactions to various forces in the personality—which to some extent end up serving certain purposes. There may be very unpleasant side effects.

Illnesses are in their way inadequate methods of solving problems. Ruburt had strong elements of personality still caught up in the beliefs of what I have called the Sinful Self. At the same time, for many reasons, he had the idea that he was expected to be not merely a well-adapted natural person, but a kind of superself, solving other people's problems, being a public personality, a psychic performer, and so forth. There was a vast gulf between those two extremes—one that was bound to cause strain and effort and misunderstandings.

The entire Sinful-Self syndrome should remind him of his own personal background, so that he can see the growth of his personality, for in the large he has of course grown out of that framework. If he had not, he would not have done any of his creative work, and in the light of his background his achievements become even more outstanding. The symptoms are the result of the strain between the still-lingering beliefs from childhood, clashing with the unrealistic goals of being a kind of superself, for in the light of that kind of superself image so much is expected that almost any achievement is taken for granted.

(Long pause at 9:48, one of many.) It almost dissolves in the imagined light of super-expected performance. This generates a sense of disapproval, of course. It also tends to being about a bigger division between those two images of the self. *(A one-minute pause.)* We want to speak more of reactions between elements of the personality, so I do not want you to settle upon one portion as the villain. At the same time, I do not want to play down the unfortunate aspects of the beliefs connected with the Sinful Self. Those aspects are at the psychological core of your civilization, and at the very heart of your organizations, whatever they

are.

To some extent Ruburt's panic is also the result of trying to live up to an impossible image, while forgetting his own personal background, and by expecting himself to behave as if that background was unimportant. *(Long pause.)* He <u>was</u> a person taught to believe that expression was somehow wrong. Despite that he became an excellent writer. He uses expression constantly. He expected himself to be a public personality—that is, he felt the responsibility to be one, as if that had always been a goal, when of course it had not been.

(Long pause at 9:58.) He had been shy with people, shy about reading his own poetry, though determined to do so, yet he felt that he should become this public personality, or to perform. I keep trying to think of examples so that you know what I mean. The entire idea of responsibility has been over-stressed. The creative work was expected not only to be creative, imaginative, intuitive, to contain the highest elements of conceptual thought, but must also be capable of solving the most concrete physical problem, tuned with some magical tuning fork so that it could serve almost any purpose required of it.

The symptoms were the result of strain placed upon the personality by the <u>conflicting pulls</u> of various beliefs—beliefs that did not fit the basic natural makeup of his personality or temperament.

(Long pause.) He was also expected to be an excellent businesswoman, a fine artist, an extrovertish personality, to shine in any company, an introvert capable of greater spiritual exertion. He expected too much of himself. At the same time, of course, to some extent he blocked his own <u>natural</u> motion (underlined), which followed directly from his own motivations and abilities, his own desires and instincts.

He may not want to be a public personality, but he does enjoy expression. He does enjoy his own brand of teaching. Part of all this is due to the original aspect of your work itself, which does not have any well-defined definitions.

(A one-minute pause at 10:11.) You have always been do-it-yourselfers, so your strengths and weaknesses become quite noticeable. *(Long pause.)* Who can say when determination ends up in stubbornness? *(Something I've wondered about at times.)* Ruburt has been facing the feelings of panic, however, that he had buried. They may not be pleasant, but they are <u>expressions</u>, often enough of valid-enough questions and fears that were overlooked or pooh-poohed as insignificant or foolish in the light of this superself image, who was expected to have no doubts, no fears, only flawless performance.

(Long pause at 10:18.) Ruburt felt that fears were beneath him—or <u>should</u> be beneath him. He felt that you also expected him to cast aside such feelings, particularly if they did not correspond with your own. This is a time of clearing

the board. You live physically in present time, so it is the body that takes the brunt of such difficulty. *(Long pause.)* It always tries to right itself, but it must also work within the effective overall pattern of beliefs and expectations.

The panic is <u>dissipating</u> through varying stages of expression. Expressions of love and support on your part are invaluable. So that Ruburt understands that you love him for the person that he is—not for some better self that he should be. He is beginning to move ahead again creatively, which will also be physically reflected. The two are related.

The present situation has been bound to result in more concentration upon the problem than usual, but in this particular instance the overall results become constructive, because they result in the psychological motion of the released feelings of panic. The experiences he had, of better imagined walking, for example, are important indications of inner resolutions, and that the body is making progress. *(Long pause.)* The panic kept him from trusting his body, and as that dissipates his innate trust in his body and in his own capacities will improve, and his performance, of course. The suggestion I gave about his situation is important in that regard. *(See session of April 24, 1981.)*

That is enough for this evening. Generally speaking, however, both the physical discomfort and the panic have passed their intense periods. The idea of responsibility has hampered him. The panic-in-the-morning episodes will also begin to pass, but—they are also caused by the feeling of not being able to measure up, no matter what one does.

End of session. He has begun, generally now, to feel more energy, and that will continue. End of session unless you have an important question *(elaborately.*

("Only about that discussion we had yesterday, about the power of the Sinful Self to cause such physical reactions—")

I tried to answer that question this evening.

("Okay." I knew it, but asked anyhow in case Seth wanted to add to his material.)

A fond good evening.

("Thank you."

(10:36.) A note to Frank Longwell, by the way—that all in all he is handling the events of his life well at this time. It will help if he trusts that such is the case, so that self-doubts are minimized. It will also help if he remembers what he likes to do and enjoys doing, as opposed to what he thinks he should do in the line of business.

End of session.

("Good night.")

You are being carried through this period, by the way. You are being protected for this period. It will help the two of you to remember that.

(10:38 PM. "Well, I guess I feel somewhat better," Jane said, "even though I can't remember too much...." Her delivery had been punctuated by many long pauses.

(Frank Longwell visited this noon, and I read him Seth's material from my notes. I'll type a copy for him.)

JANE'S NIGHTMARE
APRIL 30, 1981

Awaken from this, shouting for help. Forget start. On a nighttime street in a city, maybe New York, a shot rings out. I may possibly be a policeman but am myself too. I run into a nearby store where a very young man is shooting —robbery in progress maybe. I lunge for him, chase him to street. He keeps shooting. I lunge again, grab his arm. He begins to disintegrate until he's just a hulk of a hand, shooting the gun at me, which now I'm holding—since his body is gone. I know this refers to the belief in man's sinful nature or deadly intent; when you believe that you end up with the assailant's hand your own. You shoot yourself down....

JANE'S NOTES
MAY 2, 1981

Nightly adventure: Last PM we ask German couple from Big Flats over, the woman mentioned in God of Jane, *decide we should change the pace from intense sessions, etc. Anyhow, I liked them both very much. Played old Safe Universe Seth tape for them, was struck by Seth's discussion strongly and saw how back in '75 he had the issues already organized for the future.... anyhow, he did a terrific session then on the Sinful Self.... When we went to bed I was restless. Body really wanted to move all around, hips stretching, legs, and so forth. At the start, I went along.*

Then suddenly—I felt myself on bedroom floor, again not normally stretched but higher than in previous 2 episodes, trying to talk; felt support on floor. Checked it, so delighted I wanted to be sure. Call R. who I believe to be in writing room. He doesn't answer. I don't shout, don't want to startle myself, but determined to show R—and to walk, maybe half across room. His voice says he's busy.... and just then, as I'm irritably aware of his reply, I realize I'm in bed and so is he. Snap to; awaken; have cigarette and aspirin.

Sleep great rest of night till near morning when I believe I had a session last night for the couple who visited and I am aware of some feelings about the sessions that have angered me since the beginning. I know what they are but lose them when I awaken, left with feeling of anger (and energy) that I try to actively pursue.

Do realize I'd like small twice a week contained class, though....

DELETED SESSION
MAY 7, 1981 8:53 PM THURSDAY

(Yesterday morning I read Jane Tuesday's session, concerning her exaggerated sense of responsibility, and so forth, and it seemed to have an almost immediate effect upon her: She became very relaxed. We had a discussion about ways to minimize that feeling of responsibility, should it persist to any degree. One of the topics was the mail. I thought of Jane confining her replies to correspondents via postcard only, or at least only rarely sending out the letters with a longer reply to someone truly in need.

(However, I told her we might have to dispense with answering the mail if no other relief is obtained—anything to cut down on the feeling of responsibility. I did mention one good point, I thought: If she must be involved with ideas of responsibility, then let her think that she has already fulfilled her responsibility to help others, through the work/books she's already done. No need then to carry it further. She did have feelings of panic to a milder degree at times throughout the day.

(This morning she got up with me, after sleeping well, and again feeling traces of panic. Frank Longwell visited later this afternoon, and applied to Jane's legs and back a heating device he'd lent us some time ago. It furnishes moist heat, and Jane found it quite effective; she ended up quite relaxed.

(Jane did decide to have a session tonight, though, since we'd missed last night's, and we had company—Rhoads and Gallaghers—scheduled for Friday night. We waited a long time for the session to begin. I was tired and discouraged. Behind me in the fireplace our raccoon friends were mildly active. Otherwise the evening was quite cool and very quiet.)

Now: when you write a book, you see it through to completion.

It should leave you with a sense of accomplishment. The ideas in the books go out into the world, where they will be worked upon, worked with, in numberless fashions, in ways that you may never know. You do know where the book begins or ends, more or less, in your creative lives, however, and you have the satisfaction of that creative activity.

(Pause.) Your mail presents you with glimpses of the people who read our books, from all walks of life, in all circumstances. You cannot follow their lives through from beginning to ending as you can in a book. You cannot write their "books" of life for them. You can comment very briefly on the small glimpses you have been given of another's reality. The true interchange comes as those people themselves read our books, of course, and where our ideas intersect with their lives.

(I could add that yesterday and today especially the mail had embodied the extremes of response Jane often gets to her work—from the incoherent to the very complimentary, from people literally begging for relief from possession, say, to inquisitive, thoughtful letters from psychologists and other professional people. But I caught both of us talking about the "negative" letters rather than the positive ones.

(Long pause.) Ruburt has at times gone overboard in a feeling of responsibility toward those who write in need. The Sinful Self, so-called, now, is only too willing to accept such responsibility, for it believes to some extent that such responsibility is a kind of penance for its own shortcomings. *(Long pause.)* Ruburt is <u>not</u> responsible at all in such areas to hold sessions for others, or to provide that particular kind of individual help.

(With emphasis at 9:04:) I have never proclaimed myself to be a healer—nor for that matter a <u>specialist</u>. Our work should end up to some extent illuminating many fields of knowledge and interest, because it is not directed to one or another subject matter, and certainly not <u>restricted</u> to information that must be immediately utilitarian. The natural flow of the sessions has never run in that direction, nor has Ruburt's own natural inclinations.

(Pause.) The feeling of responsibility to help those in desperate need is but one facet, however, for he has felt a <u>responsibility</u> (underlined) to get our material to the people as soon as possible—a responsibility to appear on television or otherwise, to promote our ideas, or to present them to the world—a responsibility that I have <u>not</u> encouraged.

(Long pause.) He grew up of course with many responsibilities in connection with the care of his mother. Again, there were no known <u>rules of procedure</u> *(long pause)* to follow as far as his own career was concerned. The idea of responsibility, however, began to overweigh the joy of creativity. So it seemed to Ruburt that the books were not considered to be enough: he was expected to do all of those other things beside. *(Long pause.)* That kind of responsibility runs directly <u>counter</u> to creativity. You understand that I must simplify that to some extent, but generally speaking creativity does not deal with questions so much like "this is true, or this is false," <u>it</u> says this <u>is</u>, period.

Creativity often deals with material that is not known, not cut-and-dried, not even immediately useful, perhaps—so Ruburt would feel, for example, sometimes at least, that poetry was not responsible, or even that his own spontaneous activities were not responsible unless they were immediately useful in practical terms. At one time or another, the idea of responsibility was overlaid upon his ideas of work. All of this made him feel that he was not living up to expectations, that he was to some extent a failure for not doing all of those things.

(*Long pause at 9:22.*) Now nothing is all that simple, so there would be changes in his attitudes: He would tell himself, for example, that television or whatever would fritter away his time, or at other occasions other fears would rise so that the Sinful Self would think "Suppose such activity succeeded only too well, leading whole groups of people away from established systems of belief?" (*Long pause.*) There seemed to be little resolution. The only resolution of course is the realization that no such responsibilities actually exist. If he must think in terms of responsibility, then the only responsibility he has is to express the spirit of life as it is most naturally felt in his experience, through the development of his abilities in their natural flow (underlined).

He naturally knows what fits his temperament, abilities, and disposition. (*It might help if Jane did a little writing on those topics, I thought.*)

(*Very long pause.*) People often react to their beliefs about the kinds of persons they should be, and to imagined events. In such a way that the imagined ones are as real in their effect upon their lives as physical events are. In some cases the imagined events never do show. A person may see himself or herself, say, as a daring explorer, an inventor, an opera star or whatever, and react against such images. They may be perfectly normal people—even gifted in other fields rather than in the specific field of their dreams. However accomplished they might be, however, some consider themselves failures because they have not lived up to those ghost images. Now there are reasons for such behavior. In Ruburt's case, however, he felt that he should (underlined) act on all the other ways I specified, though he did not want to. Again, on occasion he promised himself that if he walked normally he would be only too glad to perform in such ways. This simply added to the threatening picture. He was also afraid that spontaneously he might want to do such things after all, as if his spontaneous self would work against his better interests.

Actually, of course, the creative abilities follow a larger vein of knowledge, and are responsible to themselves. They also adhere to a greater order that is far superior to ideas of responsibility as they are usually interpreted at normal levels.

(*9:42.*) All of this finally led Ruburt to feel that he had little room to move in. The feeling of gloom deepened. The release of those panicky feelings has been important. He has been doing well in that regard. You were of course of great help to him this morning. And talking out his feelings allowed for the release of <u>energy</u>, physically speaking. Frank's gadget can now serve as an excellent natural physical therapy, particularly useful at this stage, sending the message also that Ruburt is willing to let such relaxation occur.

It shows a change of belief —being willing to bring the body physical pleasure instead of the Sinful Self's idea of, say, penance or atonement. Pleasure is good for the body and the soul. Religions have been denying the right of the body to pleasure for centuries, so changes in those attitudes are significant. I'll bring the session to a close. It is enough to digest at one time, unless you have a question you particularly want answered this evening.

("No, I guess not.")

Then I bid you both a fond and somewhat pleasurable good evening.

("Thank you." 9:52 PM.)

DELETED SESSION
JUNE 1, 1981 8:08 PM MONDAY

(So much has happened since the last private session was held a month ago [on May 7] that I told Jane tonight that I'd make no attempt to summarize it all here. Suffice it to note that, as I also told her as we sat for this session, that these last few sessions may be "the last gasp" before we seek outside help, or are forced to. Indeed, that process has probably already begun. Events began to come to a head last week with the professional visit of "our" optometrist, Jim Adams, to check Jane's double vision problems.

(Jane's symptoms, especially her walking ability, have become much worse since the last private session was held—so much so that all of a sudden it seems to be a question of how much longer she can continue to make it to the john here in the house. It can hardly be a coincidence that last week, too, we received our copies of Mass Events *from Prentice-Hall, along with word from Tam that the controversial book is now being shipped nationwide. I'm positive, I said, that she became worse because of that book's publication, along with the forthcoming publication of* God of Jane, *probably later this week. I for one am holding my breath in the hope and trust that* God of Jane's *issuance doesn't also contribute to a worsening of her symptoms. Her feet are more swollen and slow-moving now than I've seen them be in a number of years.*

(Jane now spends much time afraid that she won't be able to manipulate in the john, so it seems that now is the time to go on to other modes of help than our

own and Seth's, I said—unless these last few sessions can help, unless they can add an understanding and/or stimulus that will bring her some relief. I'm quite distraught and beside myself, personally, and so is she. "What's the matter," I asked her after supper tonight, "do you feel guilty because you think you deserted your mother?" I explained that I felt self-punishment, a feeling of unworthiness, self-doubt and mistrust must lie at the root of her symptoms—that she felt she must pay a price for each success, like the publishing of a book. Why else would a person put up with what she has for well over a decade, without asking others for help? Incredible, I said, and added that I must have contributed mightily to her behavior. What has happened to my lovely wife, I wondered, sitting beside her on the couch as we ate supper of bacon and waffles? What could possibly be so bad in life that we had to pay such a price?

(Perhaps it was no coincidence that before supper tonight Jack Joyce visited to discuss how much we should pay quarterly on our estimated NY State tax for 1981 — another success story that must be paid for?

(Jim Adams also called just before supper, and I relayed the substance of his call to Jane. Last week he'd said himself that Jane's eyes were good, that she had no eye disease, or glaucoma, etc. —worries Jane has fretted over for years. Jim agreed with us—and Seth, incidentally—that Jane's trouble with double vision was muscular in nature. He decided against using prisms to unify her visions because of frequent problems people had with nausea, etc. Instead he measured her for new reading glasses, and these alone evoked an enthusiastic response from Jane, since she could see to read much better with the test lenses.

(Jim Adams also suggested that Jane see a medical internist to get at the root of the muscular difficulty, and gave us the names of three local doctors he recommended highly. He also promised to call an ophthalmologist friend of his, to explain Jane's case to him and hear what this individual—a Dr. Werner—had to say about Jane's double vision. Thus, tonight in his call Jim told me that Dr. Werner had said that Jane's double vision was "the end result" of something muscular in nature. Dr. Werner recommended that she be tested to discover the causes, and asked Jim if Jane had ever had any "mini-strokes," since such unsuspected and even unfelt attacks could have muscular repercussions. Dr. Werner added that he felt Jane should get attention, since help could lengthen her life span through muscular relaxation. Jim Adams is to see us later this week to check on black frames for Jane's new glasses, and she can question him on Werner's responses then.

(I might add that Frank Longwell has suggested that Jane's extreme slowness of movement currently stems from healing changes taking place in her muscles, and that such movement is protective in nature. Perhaps, I said, but the slower motion doesn't appear to be leading anywhere, as one might expect it to. We gather that Frank isn't particularly in favor of contacting the medical establishment, but what is one to

do, I asked Jane, if one cannot bring oneself out of his or her difficulties unaided?
Jane has been having steadily increasing difficulties in the bathroom ever since the
last private session was held—and, of course, even before that. Seth has said often
that just because one has physical difficulties does not mean those problems are fated
to get endlessly and progressively worse, but this hasn't been born out in Jane's case —
so far. How much longer dare we wait? Jane herself said during Jim Adams's first visit
that "I don't want to go to any hospital for tests."

(Jane had thought she might not be able to have a session tonight, but she
began to feel Seth around soon after I began writing these notes, at about 7:30. She
did well in the session, if rather slowly, but at the same time I became more upset and
frustrated as Seth spoke.)

Now—

("Good evening.")

—good evening. You wanted to create a point of crisis, believing to some
extent that this would help solve Ruburt's difficulties.

To a large extent you ended up concentrating upon the problem, so that
it loomed ever larger in your minds, and therefore in your experience. Regardless
of everything that you have been taught, and your own beliefs to the contrary,
I still tell you that to mentally minimize a problem is to minimize it—to minimize it in fact. I realize, however, that this is extremely difficult to do in your situation.

Ruburt is not in a life-threatening situation. There is nothing wrong, say,
with his blood, though circulation is impaired. Your optometrist told you more
or less what I told you about Ruburt's eyes. In that no eye disease as such was
responsible. Ruburt has not had a series of strokes—or any strokes.

The physical condition itself, on that level *(pause)*, is caused *(long pause)*
by "improper" relationships—that is, things not working together well, though
the parts themselves are not diseased, per se—and that is the result of stress,
habitually applied, of bodily habits. Ruburt's reaction to the books is partially
responsible for the latest difficulties, but so is the creation of the crisis situation
itself.

Because of the Prentice situation, and because of the decision not to work
on our book for a while, he felt blocked, not knowing how or when to <u>move</u>
ahead (underlined). For all of your own regrets and recriminations about
Prentice, for example, he was himself pleased by Tam's letter today, that that
bridge toward motion had not been severed.

(For the record: Seth referred to Tam's letter in which he informed Jane that
Prentice-Hall had granted her a continuation of the old contract terms and royalty
rates. The new organization at Prentice-Hall, the General Publishing Division, has

announced a new, reduced system of royalties, but Jane continues as she has been. Tam also sent Jane a copy of the new Prentice-Hall contract form, but informed her that she can continue to use the old one she's accustomed to, if she wants to.)

He is waiting for reactions to my book *(Mass Events)*, of course—and they will serve to mollify him when they begin to arrive. The book will help people, and as they write about that to him some of his old fears will be allayed.

The crisis situation led him to concentrate upon his difficulties, which aggravated his stress, of course. The discomfort and concentration cut down on his creative abilities, which added to the problem. The books were held up, mine being only recently released, and as yet he has had no reader response, which does provide him with a kind of feedback.

At the same time he was trying to uncover the basic reasons for his difficulties, so that all in all a good deal of loaded material of one kind or another was being encountered, some discussed in these sessions.

(Pause at 8:30.) His fears have to a strong extent come out into the open: the fear that he will not be able to go ahead or of blockage, that fear being physically translated—but again, it stands for an inner fear that he has creatively blocked, or psychically blocked, that he has learned—that his own fears stand in his own way and cannot be resolved, or that he is at an impasse.

· The physical condition is the mirror of that attitude. The material on the Sinful Self and so forth gives some insight into the nature of the problem. That is, it gives expression to the portion of the self that holds attitudes that are behind the difficulty.

All of the material I have given about attitudes toward revelationary material are important in that context, and please realize that I am categorizing. To that degree and in the light of this discussion, you end up with <u>what I will call</u> —and have in the past called—the overly conscientious self, which attempts to deal with the attitudes of the Sinful Self by checking and double-checking all the time, by being, in other words, overly conscientious: is Ruburt dealing with "the truth," and so forth? That kind of question is endlessly considered by the conscientious self. You are taught as children to be honest in very literal terms, and often children's natural imaginative abilities and creativity get them in a good deal of trouble.

When our material began to deal directly with the world, then, Ruburt's questioning intensified. At the same time, however, the self will not be denied its creativity, and it will most stubbornly seek out those areas of its own expression, so not working on my book will not help solve Ruburt's difficulties, and may indeed aggravate them, simply because of the further inhibition of expression.

Ruburt's nature leads him toward the kind of creativity he is naturally embarked upon. It represents his true nature. The fears and difficulties may be deeply ingrained, but they are largely learned. To cut down on creative activity will not alleviate the situation. An <u>overconcern</u> (underlined) about the mechanics of publication, or the necessity of publication, or the wheres and hows of publication, or a sense of responsibility about the work, can indeed cause difficulty, but the basic creative expression—which has been impeded in the past by fears—should still be encouraged.

The fear of relaxation is still there, so that mentally and physically it still impedes progress. In all of this, however, thoughts of self-accusation simply must be avoided as much as possible, for to a good degree in one way or another such activities and misunderstandings are behind any illness, and Ruburt is hardly to single himself out in any one area as being more stupid than anyone else. All of these issues are responsible for the bathroom difficulty, and once again I maintain the steady attempts of the body to recuperate. Your reassurances, when you are able to give them, are invaluable.

(8:54.) Ruburt always wanted to help his mother, and felt largely powerless to do so. His mother's condition made him ask questions, of course, concerning man's condition, at a very early age. To some extent trying to help the world is a larger, expanded attempt to address such situations. Again, he was in no way responsible for his mother's condition, however, or for her unhappiness, nor is he in those terms responsible for the unhappy situations of other people.

Our material does not work by providing bandages, but by providing an overall aura of creativity that in itself <u>generates</u> self-healing and self-understanding—and that is how other people are helped.

(Long pause.) He can help himself beside the sessions by encouraging the use of his own abilities directed toward self-understanding and healing. Once a day an exercise in the utilization of healing energy should be used. This can be of some value, particularly when done with some regularity. In their way library exercises are also helpful, as is the forgotten point-of-power exercise—all practical techniques that have not been put to any concerted use.

Ruburt's body has been given an enlarged dose of stress lately, for the reasons mentioned here. The philosophical issues, involving truth or nontruth, and so forth, are highly important in practical terms, and should be discussed freely.

That is quite enough for this evening. I sympathize with the situation, and expect that the session will be of some help in that regard. A fond good evening.

("Good night.")

(9:07 PM.)

DELETED SESSION
JUNE 2, 1981 7:50 PM TUESDAY

(Jane said she'd like a session as soon as we'd finished a late supper—by 7:20 PM—and expressed the hope that Seth would deal with her immediate situation— sort of an emergency treatment.

(After last night's session I was so upset I couldn't talk about it, nor did Jane ask me anything about the contents of the session. I was upset because I felt it was all true, and because I'd felt like interrupting constantly as Seth was giving his materi- al. I wanted to protest, to agree, and to disagree most vehemently. I also couldn't see how we were going to get through these difficult moments.

(Our difficulties made themselves known with a vengeance when I pushed Jane into the bathroom in her chair after 10:30 PM: because <u>for the first time, she failed to be able to get up from her seat on the john, and back to her chair as I stood waiting</u>. She tried twice, but her feet and legs just wouldn't support her, much less navigate well enough for her to walk. She said several times that she was frightened. I couldn't reach her to help from the other side of the chair, because of our bathroom's architecture. The ultimate fear had manifested itself, then: Jane was no longer able to maneuver in the bathroom. What now?

(I stood waiting many minutes while Jane struggled to get up. I was speechless once again, hardly able to sort out the thoughts and feelings churning in my head. When Jane finally admitted she couldn't make it, I went back out to the kitchen to do the dishes and close up the house for the night. The wait hadn't helped; she still sat waiting on the toilet. I lost my patience and my temper as I stood beside her, threatening to leave her sitting there all night while I went to bed. My own fears left me seeing visions of a drastically changed relationship between us, and a different life-style, one probably considerably less private if she needed nursing care, say, "What are you trying to do to me?" I demanded, and so forth. "Please don't holler at me now," Jane said. "Do it later...."

(Eventually, and very reluctantly, since I considered it a sign of a major fail- ure, I ended up carrying her physically from the john to her chair—rather awk- wardly but not with as much trouble as I'd anticipated, yet also feeling a bit of a strain in my lower back. I am still aware of a muscular sensation there, although I slept well. Jane was much relieved that I could move her, and surprised, but I had my doubts about being able to do that on a longer-term basis: I dared not endanger my own physical condition lest I be unable to take care of her otherwise, regardless of how poorly or with what ill grace I might do that.

(So this morning, Tuesday, I also carried her to the toilet seat, and once more she was quite relieved. She'd also slept well. We spent most of the morning working

with the pendulum, and this seemed to help, and brought us some fresh information. A few of the answers were surprising. We have started a notebook for the pendulum material. I should add that Monday night's session had actually begun to give us glimmers of hope, and that this buoyed-up feeling had begun to manifest itself this morning, whereas yesterday we'd felt pretty hopeless about the situation. This morning Jane also mentioned that she had the idea of trying to walk with the typing table —something she hasn't done since last November 16, 1980, by the way—so I got it out. She tried several times to get to her feet; she almost made it, but couldn't quite. She wants me to get the table for her each day now until she is able to walk with it in the old way. An excellent idea.

(We haven't yet made any firm decision about seeking medical help, but are obviously very close to doing just that.)

Now....

(I nodded good evening to Seth. Jane leaned back on the couch.)

What you want is not a crisis situation, but a therapeutic situation—so change the statements of your thoughts. Your intent now is to create a therapeutic situation. Otherwise, your concentration is upon crisis.

What elements help bring about such a situation? They are elements that do not seem perhaps to have anything at all to do with the matter at hand. *(Long pause.)* Love-making is extremely important in that regard, for of itself it brings about an overall betterment in body and mind. It helps bring about the kind of mental atmosphere that is conducive to healing at all levels, and it involves you both at the same time. It should have a much higher position in your priorities.

Your love is large enough for each other to withstand any natural expression of aggression or resentment on either of your parts, as mentioned earlier. Because of Ruburt's background *(long pause)*, he feared abandonment often. It seemed to him that he did not offer what most men expected of women, so that if he wanted a good lifelong companion he had to tread lightly. He felt that many of his own characteristics were considered disadvantageous in a man-woman relationship.

(I should take a moment here to note that Seth has said this before, and that Jane has referred to it also. I for one haven't had any such feelings, since from the very beginning of our relationship I've always felt certain that in Jane I'd found the ideal mate—an achievement I've considered most fortunate, one I'd hardly dared dream I'd manage to do. Looking back, our meeting and getting together seemed the most natural and inevitable things in the world; how could I improve upon that? I've always been intensely proud of Jane's achievements and abilities, and glad to be able to participate in them to whatever degree. The thing that has left me distraught, nearly broken-hearted, is to see her in such a progressively poor physical situation as

the years have passed. Especially devastating is this when the material explains very clearly that things don't have to be that way. No wonder I say to her that we've paid too high a price for our achievements. I want to see her able to manipulate like other people, of course, and to have her achievements also; that things haven't worked out that way so far can't but help have a profound effect upon my feelings, hers, and our relationship, which I've always taken absolutely as being as solid and enduring as the elements.)

At the same time, he does indeed need the expressions of love on your part, as you need his. He identifies strongly with his work, so that there is often, however, a misunderstanding on his part, so that if you criticize, say, any portion of the work, or his handling of it with Prentice or whatever, he often takes that as a criticism of himself.

(8:03.) Your joint love for each other is highly important precisely because you do work in such solitary fashions, and because the bent of your minds does not lead to a natural give-and-take with an emotionally friendly group of nearby colleagues.

Love-making makes your situation safer, so that it encourages expression and automatically comforts <u>all</u> portions of the self. That comforting agent is highly vital. *(Long pause.)*

Ruburt has been afraid of your reactions as *Events* and *God of Jane* meet the public world. I do not want to hurt either of your feelings *(pause)*, but in your cases the creation of a crisis period is not beneficial. This does not mean there cannot be discussion, or decisions made about seeking help from others, or whatever, but that <u>the idea</u> of a crisis situation aggravates the very natural feelings *(long pause)* that are present and unfortunately exaggerated in the entire situation.

Now some people deal with critical situations, and it is in the nature of their temperament. This would involve many in various categories: they run from one crisis situation to another, using such crises as impetuses. These people often relax completely in between, however. In chronic situations you often have a steady drainage, say, of energy. There are little reserves, in usual terms, now, for such crises.

In your cases, you both began to concentrate upon the negative elements. It is not merely that you brought some elements, say, to consciousness, but that they led the field of your attention. This applies to you, Joseph, as well as Ruburt: what would happen if Ruburt got worse? How would you protect yourself, or your time? Any anger that you felt toward Ruburt in the present was then exaggerated by this negatively imagined future, so that you became angrier.

Ruburt at his end performed in the same manner: how would he react to your reaction?—and again, regardless of what either of you may think at certain times. That kind of behavior will not give you therapeutic results.

(8:19.) You have both tried to handle the situation by yourselves, and that statement applies to you both. The approach is quite characteristic of you both, all in all. It can be seen in other forms *(pause)*—in your interest for example years ago in situations like survival, using the land's resources; in your imagined dealings with a possible nuclear war in the past, when you saw yourselves relying upon yourselves; in your behavior during the flood; in your determination to seek yourselves for the meaning of life rather than look to the authorities— and indeed in your own dealings with your own health when such issues arise. There are lines drawn: you see dentists, for example, but the overall pattern is a pattern highly characteristic.

I simply want to make this understandable. That pattern often means that both your strengths and your weaknesses appear in exaggerated form. I am not suggesting that you become <u>inflexible</u> in that regard, but that you understand your individual and joint reactions more clearly.

Ruburt's condition does not just have a physical significance, then, for either of you, but becomes intrinsically tied up with your personal philosophies, your values about creativity and self-reliance. Those values on Ruburt's part in particular have been contaminated, so to speak, by the fears and issues we have earlier spoken of. We therefore want the concentration upon, again, a therapeutic situation. This automatically should bring about a change of focus. You can still leave open your decision about medical help, or make it, or whatever, but you will not use fear as an impetus.

(Long pause.) Expression should be encouraged on both of your parts, so that that nonspecific directive is freer to find its own specific utterance. The first thing is to get Ruburt calmed down again. *(Long pause.)* Your conflict personally about doing the lawn, or having it done for you, is by the way a minor example of your do-it-yourself tendencies coming in conflict with other ideas—a point I wanted to mention.

Ruburt should definitely begin some kind of energy exercises, as I suggested last evening, and take other creative approaches toward the setting-up of the therapeutic situation—some painting or poetry or writing or whatever should be reinstigated. This is highly important.

(8:38.) You were quite correct, of course, in reminding him that his eyes themselves were healthy. Planning for a small group is (underlined) constructive, and should be encouraged. The planning alone has some beneficial result, since in his mind he already sees himself with some considerable improvement.

The idea of the ramp falls in the same category.

Adams mentioned that actually Ruburt's eyes responded rather quickly to the various lenses. He also mentioned that when prisms were used the resulting activity on the muscles often led people to complain about dizziness, nausea, and so forth. That entire muscular group has been trying to improve itself of late, and at such times Ruburt does feel disoriented with changes in head pressure, balance, depth perception. Those sensations frighten him. The body understands those situations, while in a state of fear they can arouse new distrust.

There is a relaxation going on, and a loosening between the hips and the legs, that causes other large muscles to hold back to maintain balance temporarily, to move more slowly to compensate for the unaccustomed looseness of other portions. That loosening also frightens Ruburt because of the resulting disorientation—but the disorientation represents a breaking-down of old patterns.

(8:52.) Now that situation, plus the mental strains of the crisis condition, brought about the present situation. The physical situation will change in any case, and for the better *(long pause)*, but the crisis situation itself helped rearouse Ruburt's lack of trust. It has often been thought that love-making in some way impairs creativity; in fact, it is highly conducive to all kinds of creative endeavor—a point I want to emphasize.

End of session, unless you have a question.

("Can you offer a few words of encouragement about his movements in the bathroom? I carried him last night and this morning, and I can feel a strain in my back.")

The strain is a result of your own attitudes, of course—of a burden being applied that should or need not be. It seems there is nothing wrong with your back. It is your attitude that hurts. And that also speaks to Ruburt to express your own feelings: you cannot depend on me to do this all the time. The same statement was made when you carried Ruburt to the car. In exaggerated form, Ruburt makes the same statement of his own with his own symptoms—that is, they also express attitudes. Theoretically, your love alone could sweep the discomfort away, so that Ruburt felt as light as a feather. They express your reluctance, of course, and outrage against the situation.

If you follow the suggestions in last night's session and tonight's, the situation itself will automatically change. Ruburt will find himself dependable enough to walk in the bathroom again, and within a relatively short period.

(Long pause at 9:04.) You must each try to encourage your feelings of optimism. They are not unrealistic. They are highly pertinent, and they are more realistically a part of your biological behavior than your patterns of pessimism

are.

Again, help Ruburt trust his feelings of relaxation, and trust your own. End of session. A fond good evening.

("Thank you, Seth.")

(9:06 PM. Jane had done well. The family of raccoons in the fireplace behind me had been quite active and sometimes noisy during the session. I told Jane the session was very good, and she sighed with relief. I said it gave me a surge of hope, and that I hoped it would affect her the same way when I read it to her this evening, which I now proceeded to do. She agreed when she'd heard it, though it was more difficult to listen to the session than to read it at leisure.

(It's the next day as I finish typing the session. The hope continues to manifest itself, and both of us feel much better. I carried Jane in the bathroom last night before bed, and this morning when she got up after 10 AM. Both times worked well. Although I feel a minimal sensation in the back, it has lessened considerably since Seth's comments about its true origins. Now when I think about the back I remind myself that I can find Jane "as light as a feather." I anticipate no more problems in that area.

(Frank Longwell visited, and also offered Jane a lot of encouragement as he explained the functions of different muscle groups to her. Seth's material, and Frank's, goes a long way toward easing her feelings of fright, for now we see that those feelings represented her—and my—misunderstanding of her own bodily functions as the body ceaselessly tries to right itself.)

DELETED SESSION
JUNE 3, 1981   8:53 PM WEDNESDAY

(I've finished typing the sessions for Monday and Tuesday evenings, and Jane has read and reread them. So have I. She was much affected by my note on page 156 of last night's session, just as I was while writing it.

(She slept well last night, and got up at about 10 AM. She's felt somewhat better today. I had a snack with her while she ate breakfast, and tearfully she said she couldn't blame me if I felt I could only stand so much, and wanted to go my own way. She said, as she has before recently, that she would try to get along on her own, and hire someone to take care of her. I've thought of trying to find another place to paint, especially for the larger works I plan to do, but not of leaving her. It's true that my patience has been sorely tested of late, and, as I told her, I feel that I've done a lot during our relationship to help her and go along with her ideas.

(Jim Adams visited today with some sample black frames for her reading glass-

es, and repeated to Jane what I'd quoted him as saying his friend Dr. Werner had said about Jim's description of Jane's condition. Interesting, for I think Jim phrased some of his quotes somewhat differently to Jane than he had to me earlier this week —although I think the gist of the remarks is pretty much the same. But Jane and I have trained ourselves to try to recall accurately what others say, and we are aware of how information can be distorted as it's passed on. We told Jim we haven't made any firm decision about seeking medical help, but will when the glasses situation is taken care of. In the meantime, Jane is getting used to the idea, should we do anything about it.

(Frank Longwell also visited today—before Jim did, as a matter of fact —and helped Jane experiment with certain exercises for her legs in the bathroom. He explained the procedure if Jane goes to the hospital in Sayre. Jim, on the other hand, is in favor of Jane seeking local treatment. This would be easiest, of course, providing the treatment is equal. Frank thinks the clinic in Sayre could offer more services at once. He said Jane doesn't have rheumatoid arthritis or thyroid trouble. Jim said he couldn't comment on Jane's situation from a medical standpoint, except to say her eyes per se are okay.

(Jane also tried walking with the table with Frank's help, as she had with me the day before, but once again couldn't quite get up on her feet. She did better, though. She also tried the library today, as Seth had suggested, but with "nil" results, but didn't try the energy-healing exercise yet. She plans to keep at both. She did have an unclear image while trying for the library, and discovered it was a bit scary. Yet while trying the library she felt "relaxed and panicky at the same time."

(Incidentally, Jane today received her first letter—from a lady who has written her before—about Mass Events. *So the book is getting around. The person was connected with Robert Monroe's institute in Charlottesville, Va. [Incidentally again, it is Thursday afternoon as I type, and in an hour one of the Ryall boys from the Handi Book Center in Elmira will be at the house to have Jane autograph 20 or so copies of* Mass Events; *the store received them today, and has a number of orders for copies.*

(I'm still carrying Jane in the bathroom, and making out with a minimum of discomfort. "Light as a feather....")

Good evening *(whispering.*

("Good evening," whispering.)

Now: within a fairly regular *(pause)* framework of habits and range of activity, you have both actually chosen a course that is in many ways uncertain, irregular, unpredictable.

You are free-lancers, so that you do not deal with a regular, specified financial state, of course. To that degree your livelihood depends upon many elements. You are never certain of your income's exact amount per month, say, as you would be if you had salaries. The very nature of the work that you are involved in implies uncertainty—and this aside from psychic activity. That is, writing and painting themselves embark you upon uncertain routes. Again, they are not products with known specifications and measurements. The psychic work brings in a further extension, both of a do-it-yourself element, and the creative uncertainty.

(*Pause.*) You value rather "set" habits that serve as more or less steady platforms for the pursuit of the uncertain nature of both your arts and psychic activity.

(*Long pause, one of many.*) You are after the answers to many questions. In the meantime you have no guarantee that the answers will be found, for the questions themselves constantly evolve, and yet you are of course always in the process of examining the material that you have, and seeing how it applies or does not apply to the world as you know it.

The official world has its answers, methods, philosophy, standards, all set. The civilization is built around them. You are looking for better ways to live your lives, seeking a larger framework of existence. This is not some dry academic undertaking, but a matter of intense personal activities on both of your parts.

(*Long pause.*) To some extent it means that you try to live your lives in accord with a philosophy not yet completed, methods not yet completely achieved or stated, and this of course involves you with uncertainty. Ruburt for example feels obligated to tell correspondents with health difficulties to see the established authorities, certainly those with serious illnesses. (*Long pause.*) He suggests that others follow their own intuitional material, while at the same time holding on to the established frameworks upon which most people depend.

(*Long pause.*) He has also tried to follow our material, to trust it to the best of his ability. In important ways at certain levels, while the proof may be in the pudding, the dish of pudding is not nearly filled (*with some humor*).

All of the material is not in yet. Now in matters of personal health, this is bound to add to the uncertainty: you are trying to live your lives according to new rules that are as yet not completely given, so to that extent it is somewhat natural that Ruburt and you become at times uneasy, wonder at times about the personal material, wonder if it is distorted in those areas, or whatever—and there are no known ways to check such material—the material itself is that original.

(*9:17.*) It was therefore beneficial when Adams gave the "diagnosis" on Ruburt's eyes. Now because of these uncertainties—financial, creative, and psychic—other certainties become highly important, as a framework for such seeming unpredictability. You value therefore the certainty of your love for each other. The certainty of a more or less dependable environment, and Ruburt therefore valued, and values, the certainty that existed for many years with the Prentice connection.

The paragraph he read concerning your enduring love for him this evening struck him deeply. *(Long pause.)* There is no doubt that for many reasons given he feared the dependability of your love *(long pause, eyes closed)*, if his actions did not please you. That fear had its roots in his childhood, and of course in the male-oriented culture. To some extent then he felt even the safety of your relationship threatened when you became irritated, say, with Prentice. He became frightened in particular when he feared that his relationship with Prentice might make you ill.

People react differently to stress. Ruburt's reaction to stressful situations was a repressive one: he did indeed often feel in a steady state of some alarm. Because of other beliefs it seemed that it was not safe to relax. The applied tension itself in that framework came to imply a kind of support. It seemed to offer a dependable framework to keep him from going too far in one direction or the other *(intently)*, and was used as a cushion against the other uncertainties in your lives. The panic he feels in some particular kind of relaxation episodes does indeed involve the psychological feelings that were buried within that releasing tension.

(9:33.) Initially, as the tension releases it releases along with it the buried panic about which it was formed *(long pause)*. It is important that Ruburt realize that. He, again, also learned to identify with tension, so there can be some alarm as he lets it dissolve. This only applies to certain periods of relaxation, however, that are connected with the eventual freedom of the most vital motions of the body.

All of the issues I have mentioned—love-making, the energy exercises, poetry and so forth—lead toward a therapeutic situation *(pause)*, toward the realization that expression itself is safe, and serve to remind him that creativity's uncertainty is itself highly creative, providing its own safety within a context of exuberant expression. It is important then that he begin using his psychic abilities to help heal his own body, and he will begin doing that as he understands that it is indeed safer to let that tension go, and to free his psychic and physical motion.

(Long pause.) Now, regardless of many objections to the contrary, Ruburt's condition still has served your own ends as well as his—and into the present. To an extent they have served as their own stabilizers, giving you both excuses and

protections from events of perhaps an intrusive fashion, such as the interviews or guests, or even strangers at the door. *(Long pause.)* <u>In a fashion</u> they produced their own kind of certainty. They also reflected—to some degree, now—<u>your own</u> perhaps more subsidiary beliefs that it was not safe to relax, or that spontaneity might lead to further uncertainties. It is not necessary that you learn to gush endlessly about your love for Ruburt, but it is important that you do express it, and you have indeed been better in that area. Your joint acknowledgement of your love, however, vastly increases the feelings of safety in your lives, and the love-making involving touch is very reminiscent of the childhood state involving freedom, when children rejoice in touching themselves and other objects and so forth.

End of session and a fond good evening.

("Thank you very much, Seth. Good night.")

I hope that what I said involving relaxation and panic is understood, and that you help Ruburt understand himself in those circumstances.

("Yes.")

(9:55 PM. "I thought there was something involving you toward the end that I didn't get," Jane said. When I answered that the material seemed clear enough, she said that it concerned something that didn't come out in the session. She was also genuinely surprised at the time, it being much later than she thought it was: "I can't get over it.")

DELETED SESSION
JUNE 4, 1981 9:13 PM THURSDAY

(Jane was in a low mood for part of the day, but perked up before I took my nap. She wrote one verse of a poem this morning, but isn't very pleased with it. We didn't try the table today, but she did do the healing energy thing, and evidently with some success: She's to write a description of it to insert in the pendulum notebook. I'm still carrying her in the john, but with increasing difficulty, I'm afraid. Frank Longwell visited today.

(Today I picked up from Mr. Steiner the life-size enlargements of my parents; they're remarkably good, and I plan to paint portraits of the folks from them. I also plan to do the same procedure with Jane and perhaps others.

(Today we had the lawn mowed by Bill Tolbert and Jeff Colucci, who were recruited for the steady job by Frank. It's the first time this year that the grass has all been cut at once.

(Many changes continue to take place in Jane's body. As we sat for the session she reported extra movement in her right eye—increased muscular activity that she

could feel even in her throat. "I'm just waiting," she said at 8:56. We'd had a late
supper. The day had been beautiful if cool much of the time.

(Whispering:) Now—good evening.

("Good evening.")

(Pause.) Ruburt's depression-part of today represented, again, his recognition and expression of feelings that before were to a large degree buried in the symptoms, or translated into them.

Such expressions do not mean backsliding on his part. They should be recognized for what they are, and he should (underlined) definitely express them to you when he feels that way. They are momentary—or at least having expressed themselves in a certain rhythm they then give way to other positive experience. This does not mean that he should concentrate upon them, of course. This period of time is leading you both away from black or white patterns of thought to some degree, so that you can consider the aspects of your lives, bothered less by absolutes. It is certainly time to look at your prerogatives, as I have stressed. Love-making, expressions of loving support and encouragement should come higher up on your lists on both of your parts than before.

It may seem that the question of services (like the lawn) is a mundane one, yet it is connected of course with your attitudes toward work and daily life. Your writing and painting provide "services" of a different order. You should make no absolute decisions in the latter, say, of other services. Some can be enjoyable adjuncts, and serve as relaxation. In other words, avoid black or white thinking. Take advantage of having services occasionally performed by others, and be more flexible in that regard.

Ruburt receives esthetic pleasure from looking at the clean rugs or windows—a pleasure which actually encourages his creativity. The same applies of course to you and the yard.

(Pause.) Art provides its own services to the individual, whether or not it appears to be utilitarian. Ruburt's own inspiration operates with its own rhythms: his Stonehenge poem, or whatever. In between, while it may seem he is not being as creative, inner work is being done that will later appear in a new burst of creativity. This applies to long or short projects.

(9:28.) It is very important that he understand that. His creativity, in other words, is renewing itself now. (Long pause.) An animal in Ruburt's physical condition would simply be resting, perceiving body alterations and odd states with patient acquiescence, doing what it could physically and forgetting about the rest, trustful in the body's capacities to heal itself. The more Ruburt relaxes the quicker his body will show the improvements that are now developing. Certain attitudes should be clearly expressed. There is no need condemning the attitudes he will be inspired by on both the long and short projects. He will receive new insights and inspirations. Now he becomes frightened that he will not. You can help him there as he discusses his feelings. He depends upon creativity, for example, as you do, to provide a more or less steady source of enjoyment, excitement, personal accomplishment—not to mention livelihood —and as per last evening's session, creativity operates in ways that may appear uncertain.

(Long pause.) Tonight's assurances in that area should themselves encourage him. Absolute thinking can often lead to dead-ended thoughts or plans. His attitudes toward the medical profession (pause) are indeed changing—not that he sees medical practices in any more favorable and overall light, but that he recognizes that absolutism is no answer either. Nor should such decisions be made through the auspices of personal fear. There are degrees of participation, for example. You should be free to make your decisions with a fairly clear mind.

The same applies in a fashion to services, or even to your physical establishment. There are various organizations possible in your house, for example, if you forget absolute thinking, and if you forget conventional thinking in general when you apply it to creative benefits.

I am merely citing examples. Your house is perfectly set up, however, so that if you wanted to it can be expanded to suit further needs: the large center portion (gesturing) serving as your communal living quarters—this area—and with some creative extensions you could have quite appropriate separate working wings at either end, providing you both with more work space, feelings of privacy, and esthetic pleasure.

(Pause at 9:42.) I want you to see that in many of your situations there are creative possibilities that can be flexibly considered, for these will also be reflected in life's daily enjoyments, in creative satisfaction that literally cannot be measured in terms, say, of how much money is expended, and with the proper attitude the money simply will not matter, it will be so easily replenished.

Ruburt thinks that way fairly easily, so let him use the same kind of thought with his physical and psychic mobility, mentally imagining that he is opening inner rooms, discovering inner territory that has remained unclaimed or going back into delightful rooms, filled with motion that he had momentarily forgotten.

Such a mental exercise, done in a light manner, can be highly beneficial, and serve as excellent impetus.

This will give you your fourth session in sequence again. Read the four sessions, and discuss them. Have Ruburt make sure he begins to follow all of the suggestions given therein. (Long pause.) The changing of priorities should become more or less second nature, and not forgotten after a week or so. Again, Ruburt's body is changing, and for the better.

(Long pause.) The momentary feelings of hopelessness, then, should be recognized, because again they clear the way for further motion, expression, and relaxation.

End of session, unless you have a particular question.

("Nope.")

Then I bid you as always a fond good evening.

("Thank you very much, Seth.")

(9:56 PM. Jane's delivery had been good. "The thought of adding rooms makes me shudder," I laughed—"not that we might not do it...." Jane laughed too, while agreeing she's thought of alterations often. Right now, though, she's much more interested in once again feeling well enough to start doing some typing, writing, or whatever. Her double vision continues to plague her.

(It's Sunday night, June 7, as I type this session. On Friday noon Frank Longwell visited. Jane told him that that morning I'd had considerable difficulty lifting her in the bathroom. In fact, my back was bothering me considerably, whether the cause was physical, psychological, or both.

(Frank had an idea about placing one of our old chairs on rollers so Jane could be wheeled right beside the john to slide over onto it while she was having walking difficulties. He went for his tools and supplies, returned in an hour, and the two of us spent much of the afternoon making such a vehicle. It worked—but barely, for it was too high for the john, and had no cushion for Jane's backside comfort.

(I decided to rebuild it, so Saturday morning I went to the lumber yard for the supplies, and spent the day doing the work, including cutting down the chair even more. The larger rollers especially helped. [I'd changed the original, fancy rollers Frank had used, but the replacements were also too small.]. The new chair worked much better, but Jane had trouble keeping the cushion in place. My back bothered me considerably Friday and Saturday.

(We had company Saturday night. I let Jane sleep Sunday morning while I spent a couple of hours fastening the cushion in place and covering it with linoleum tablecloth material so that she could slide more easily on it. We tried the new contraption at noon when Jane got up, and it now works fairly well, well enough to be of consistent use. I may try a slicker covering for the cushion if one can be found.

(I didn't feel well Saturday night after company left, and not much better Sunday. The back continued to act up, to a slightly lesser degree, however. I slept for a couple of hours in the afternoon. I was exhausted.)

DELETED SESSION
JUNE 8, 1981 8:14 PM MONDAY

(Last Saturday, the 6th, was not only "chair day," as I told Jane, but seemingly synchronicity day also. Four little events took place, or culminated on that day, that certainly seemed to be more than mundane "coincidence."

(A week or so ago Jane had invited the Lords, Cec and Jim, to the house for last Saturday evening. Saturday morning, then, as I was in Robinson's lumber for parts for Jane's chair, I met Curt Kent, who used to work with Cec and myself at Artistic; I haven't seen Curt for perhaps two years, Cec since last Christmas. Jane also invited the Weissenbuehlers Saturday evening. When Jane called, Ellspeth told her she'd been working at fixing up or restoring an old chair—as I was working with an old chair for Jane. When they arrived Saturday night, Ellspeth and Heinz brought with them some homemade cheesecake. It happened that Saturday afternoon I'd taken a package of frozen cheesecake out of the freezer and thawed it out with the intention of serving it Saturday evening. It was still sitting on our kitchen counter when Ellspeth and Heinz carried their cheesecake in. Then when Debbie Janney arrived Saturday evening, she told me that she had just missed meeting me at Steiner's photo studio earlier that week; going there to have a portrait taken, she'd seen by accident the enlargements of my parents that Mr. Steiner was making for me. I was due to pick them up the next day, and she asked Mr. S. to tell me she'd been there, but he forgot to mention it.

(Jane was quite relaxed as she told me she wanted a session at about 8 PM. Both of us had slept for better than two hours this afternoon, and felt that we could sleep even more. The evening was beautiful. Frank Longwell had visited at noon, and I'd showed him the new chair I'd made for Jane, based on his design. She is doing much better with the chair, by the way. My back still bothers, but perhaps to a slightly lesser degree. I haven't been getting in much painting time for the past week.

(Jane had no questions for Seth: "I'm just hoping he'll go on as usual." I replied that I could have many questions, but since I hadn't studied the material or written any down, I too had to say I had no questions.)

Good evening.

("Good evening, Seth.")

Now: there are obviously beneath the psychological areas that you recognize many other deeper layers of action and interaction. It is actually at those levels that the world of material activity is ordered and supported. It is beneath the usual cause-and-effect area that the true "causes and effects" lie. You have, again, perceived some small clues as to such inner behavior. These clues are seemingly oddly assorted ones involving such issues as cheesecake, the repair of an old chair, old photographs and a photography shop, and the meeting of an old acquaintance after some period of time.

(I should add that we never did see Cec and Jim Lord last Saturday night. I'd planned to tell Cec about meeting Curt. But they didn't show up due to a misunderstanding re dates: Cec thought they were to visit next Saturday evening—the 13th. Jim kept asking her if she had the date right, incidentally.)

(I should also note that when I met Curt at the lumberyard I never really got to talk much with him, because I was so busy running down parts and asking clerks for help. Perhaps Curt didn't have much time to spare either, for when I did get a minute to talk, I saw him going out the front door. There is a sort of similarity here, then, beside the ordinary synchronicity: for if we didn't get to see the Lords at all, I didn't get to talk to Curt much beyond saying hello and shaking hands. I may have appeared somewhat rude to him, and plan to phone him.)

These are all quite mundane events, of course, yet they show over a period of a few days glimpses of the inner order of activity, similarities and coincidences that actually lie at the heart of events, and serve as their true organization.

As far as you are personally concerned, Joseph, you became alarmed by what seemed to you to be certain implications when you carried Ruburt in the bathroom. You feared this made it too easy for him. You were afraid that then he would not try to resume making it on his own. And you also did not trust your own body to perform adequately under such a situation—hence your own personal discomfort.

The chair made it easier for Ruburt than it had been earlier. It made him more a part of the process. You both understood that situation rather clearly at certain levels. As far as his condition is concerned, its most pivotal aspects are being dealt with: the mechanics of walking and motion. Again, the body knows what it is doing. It is as if the springs or inner mechanics of motion had been tightly held back, so that as they are being relieved there is considerable inequality, unpredictable springing motion—a loosening here and a tightening there momentarily, as if before he had been too tightly wound *(deliberately)*.

(Long pause, one of several, at 8:31.) This is particularly pertinent in his feelings concerning the jaw and neck, and the eye connection and his sense of balance *(all items Jane has mentioned often recently)*. It is also responsible of course for the frequent alterations in depth perception, and all of that to some extent helps explain his frequent uncertainty about getting on the couch *(from the chair)* and so forth.

It is highly important, however, that you read those sessions over together, and discuss them, even if only one session at a time. All of the relationships in his bodily behavior are changing for the better, but reading those sessions will make sure that the old beliefs <u>are not buried</u> again, and hence allow the process to continue, and <u>more smoothly</u> accelerate.

Your person-to-person encounters with reality have been unusually supportive of late: Adams, Frank, your new friends the Germans, and even your encounter with the photographer. These encounters in their own ways are meant to show you that other people do indeed mean well, that they send good wishes in your directions *(long pause)*, and the small clues mentioned earlier are meant, again, to remind you of the inner unity and correspondences beneath events.

Your love-making has been of benefit, and your continued attempts to jointly express love and affection verbally and physically is important —and to both of you particularly at this time.

(Long pause.) At deeper levels you are being sent support and energy from all of those people, known and unknown, who have your best interests at heart.

This session will be brief, because I would like you to use the rest of the session time to read from the latest material, and discuss it. I want that material assimilated before I pile new material on top of it *(humorously)*. Do you have a question?

("No.")

Tell your body that you do indeed want it to feel comfortable now. Before, you did not know whether or not you wanted it capable enough to lift Ruburt, for you were afraid of setting up an unfortunate pattern of behavior. This should take care of your own difficulties.

End of session and a fond good evening.

("Thank you, Seth. The same to you."

(8:46 PM. "I know what he said," Jane laughed, "but I don't know whether I can concentrate upon doing it." I felt the same way: "I could go right back to bed."

(The evening seemed to be quite warm and humid. It wasn't quite dark yet. "Just for kicks," I told Jane, "I almost asked Seth to say something about Israel and Iraq, but I didn't...." We'd read late this afternoon, then saw on the TV news as we ate supper, that on Sunday Israeli warplanes had destroyed the almost-completed nuclear reactor at Baghdad, Iraq. "The Iranians must be jumping for joy," I said to Jane when I first saw the headlines in the newspaper. Iran is at war with Iraq. "You've got to give the Jews credit," I added. "When they see what they regard as a true danger to their homeland, they do something about it, no matter what others may think." I thought of their daring raid to free their countrymen and women held hostage at Entebbe, Uganda, a few years ago; that event was also mentioned in tonight's newscasts.

(After this session was over we did settle down to read over this month's previous four private sessions, and talk about a few points as a result. But we were both tired, and made ready for bed earlier than usual.)

DELETED SESSION
JUNE 9, 1981 8:47 PM TUESDAY

(Jane has had a relatively good day, and has done much better with the new chair for the bathroom. She even used it to go to the john an extra time this afternoon—a heartening sign. She had no questions for the session this evening, "But I had a feeling he might say something about that Kubler-Ross thing, and that there might be some charged material in it about me—that's the feeling I get, so I'm just waiting...."

(The article in question is a Playboy *interview with Elizabeth Kubler-Ross. Leonard Yaudes left the May, 1981 issue recently, and Jane has been reading the interview therein once I noticed it and suggested that she review it. Kubler-Ross's hassles —at least some of them—remind us of our own. I'll note briefly that late last year, in November-December, Jane attempted to get in touch with Kubler-Ross at the behest of a friend of KR's who had attended Sheri Perl's classes. Jane was to call KR at a conference in Wappinger's Falls, NY; she tried a number of times, always to be put off by a rather unpleasant and officious woman who was always saying that KR was "in conference" and couldn't be disturbed. Jane wouldn't leave our private number. KR, we were told, knew that Jane would be calling—indeed, had requested that she do so. The two never did make contact, so we figured it was for the best, for whatever reasons. According to our phone bill, Jane's last attempt at contact was on December 5, 1980. "Well," I said, "presumably KR knew you tried to reach her, so since you never got a letter or note later, forget it. That is, if that secretary, or whatever she was, was relaying your messages...."*

(I spent part of the afternoon and evening writing to Tam, asking him to defend us from the well-meaning but evidently inept efforts of various people in Canada and Switzerland to arrange for translations of Jane's work in French, Italian, and Spanish—and I'd sworn off writing such letters following the fiasco with Ariston....

(Our family of raccoons was stirring a bit in the fireplace behind my chair as I sat facing Jane on the couch. My back felt a little better, although not clear. "If it works out and you have a minute tonight, and if you're in the mood to say something about Israel and Iraq, it would be interesting," I told Jane. She nodded. She was very relaxed.

(We waited. Jane became even more relaxed. "I think I'll start in half a minute or so," she said, "but how far I'll get, I don't know," she said. She lit a cigarette.)

Now.

(I nodded.)

There are vibrant redistributions of energy going on within Ruburt's body, reorganizations in which energy patterns are realized. Highly important.

This does indeed mean change at other levels of activity, the Sinful Self not only loosening its hold, but relinquishing some of the energy that it had withheld and repressed, so that the energy becomes available practically speaking for the body's use once again. This does occur in rhythms, periods of assimilation being usually though not inevitably necessary.

(One-minute pause at 8:52.) I did want to make some comments about the Sinful Self in general, and how it is perceived and assimilated in say, Castaneda's work and in the belief structure of Kubler-Ross.

Both represent systems of belief quite different from our own material in many respects. It is important to realize that in usual terms even great visions need not agree with each other. For they are each viewing experience from a highly concentrated yet uniquely individual standpoint. They each see "reality" from a different angle, and thus create a different view.

It is of vital importance, however, for overall clarification that a belief system recognizes itself as such. Otherwise it becomes another closed system of thought, bathed in absolutism, and doomed to the weightiness of dogma.

The Castaneda system accepts the power of evil, for example *(long pause)*, presenting a framework in which those people who do accept such power can confront it, along with a system of exercises and beliefs meant to minimize evil's effects. In a fashion that particular approach, for all of its reliance upon "sorcery," is not actually true to the magical approach at all, because it insists so fervently upon the impediments that stand in man's way, and stresses the importance of rituals and methods, and the almost superhuman effort that is required *(pause)* in order to meet the "magical ends."

(Long pause.) Spontaneity is not trusted, and left alone the spontaneous self is seen as slothful, given to the pursuit of meaningless pleasure. To some extent the spontaneous self and the Sinful Self wear the same mask or bear the same face. It goes without saying that the framework is male-oriented —but even then the male is really no adequate male unless he becomes a warrior, and pushes himself to perform against the powers of darkness, on the one hand, and against sloth on the other.

The system does not practically approach any lively sympathy for the masses of mankind, or any particular understanding of the more mundane events that mark man's daily ways.

(*9:13.*) Kubler-Ross does not believe as deeply in the existence of evil forces, but is convinced of the importance and necessity of suffering in one way or another as an important means of achieving a good end. (*Long pause.*) Because your world is built around a certain charged acceptance of beliefs so thoroughly, it usually seems as if reality as you perceive it is the one that must be inevitably perceived, while all others have the status of hallucinatory visions at the very best.

As I have tried to explain, however, your assumptions about reality do indeed form it. You may literally perceive certain elements of consciousness in a personified form, as spirit guides, angels, or even as gods and goddesses. You may perceive them instead merely as undefined and undefinable veiled qualities of thought, ever-elusive and unformed, or as sacred physical portions of the earth, or as charged physical objects.

Overall, it is short-sighted to say that one kind of such perception is truer than the other or more or less factual than the other. The existence of physical objects could be a highly debatable subject in other realities than your own, for example.

The spirit guides are perceptions of other kinds of psychological and psychic activity. In some cases your station of reality automatically transforms them to fit the patterns of your beliefs. They can be dealt with at that level, but that level is <u>to some extent now</u> a superficial one relatively speaking. Kubler-Ross's system is still highly tinged by beliefs in the prominent necessity not just in the existence of suffering, but that it must for all of its stress upon hope (*long pause*) end up to a large degree in stressing <u>certain</u> aspects of suffering and martyrdom.

(*9:27.*) Visions of an entirely different nature, seemingly saying different things, can still be highly legitimate visions, leading in fact by different routes toward other larger reconciliations. (*Long pause.*) It will be useful if Ruburt remembers this when he views other systems of reality. You make your own reality in "a thousand times." You put together psychological events in various ways. You merge what is seemingly fiction or fantasy with what is seemingly factual. From those elements you form your picture of the world.

Now, in politics and religion, (*Prime Minister*) Begin believes it much more practical to deal with the Sinful Self and its "evil prerogatives" than he does with the better self that may indeed represent "the Son of God in man." He is not waiting around, therefore, by relying upon or overrelying upon, in his view, man's good intent. The Sinful Self is convinced of its own evil, and the evil intent of others, and so it is driven to protect itself ahead of time.

Like most of your allies, it is taken for granted that nuclear plants will ultimately be used in the manufacture of bombs that will ultimately certainly be used in a destructive fashion. At that level, therefore, Begin destroys a nuclear faculty before its damage can be done. *(Long pause.)* God helps those who help themselves, may I say sardonically, is the belief behind such actions.

Now Ruburt's body is responding very well, and the material we have given on the Sinful Self—and other subjects—is being assimilated. Your lives of course reflect redistributions of energy constantly. That is apparent in your activities at all levels. At such times hints and clues from Framework 2 often become more than usually available, so keep your eyes open for them.

End of session unless you have a particular question.

(I hesitated. "I wasn't going to ask this tonight, but earlier today I found myself wondering how much of Jane's symptoms result from my own attitudes and statements about Prentice. I guess I now think she reacted to my ideas there more than I realized.")

The subject matter is too large to begin with this evening. Bring it to my attention by stating the question before our next session. Now I bid you a fine and hearty good evening.

("Thank you. Good night."

(9:47 PM. Jane had done well. As we had last night, both of us felt out of it after the session.

(I thought Seth's brief answer to my question merely reinforced my suspicion that my attitudes toward Prentice had *unduly influenced Jane. He's dealt with the question a bit in past sessions, of course, but evidently not in the required depth. I couldn't help but think his material wouldn't be exactly flattering to me. I didn't know whether I looked forward to it or not, but felt it essential that we get it. There must have been a reason, I thought, that I asked the question at this time.*

(Yet, I noticed, Jane didn't seem all that bothered by its implications....)

DELETED SESSION
JUNE 11, 1981 8:52 PM THURSDAY

(We haven't held a session since last Tuesday evening. We've been very tired, even exhausted; I've been sleeping in the afternoons with Jane. She's been doing very well with the new chair in the bathroom, and is now going to the john three times a day. [When I remarked that I'd like to see her up her trips to four times a day, she at once became defensive, so I cooled it.] I followed her advice and sprayed the linoleum-covered chair seat with furniture polish to make it more slippery, so that she can more easily slide sideways from the chair onto the couch or john. "A great idea,"

I told Frank Longwell yesterday noon.

(I've reread the last session to Jane from my notes each morning since it was held. The question I asked at its end—about what effects my opinions of Prentice-Hall might have had on Jane over the years—has been on my mind ever since I asked it, and Seth replied that it was "too big a subject" to go into at once. Tonight I explained to Jane after supper that I now believed many of my opinions were taken by her as negative personal opinions about her work and efforts—which meant, I added, that they must have contributed at least substantially to her symptoms over the years.

(Jane tried to half-heartedly deny this, without really considering the question, I thought—not that I wanted her to to any great degree before Seth got into it. He's mentioned the subject occasionally, of course. But I told Jane that now I'd need advice on how to handle my reactions to Prentice-Hall so as not to alarm her further.

(Speaking of Prentice-Hall, today Jane received her first copy of God of Jane—*a handsome-looking volume that I hope does well as the years pass. We'd been wondering if Prentice-Hall was going to stick to its schedule in bringing the book out early in June, and lo the book arrived without any fanfare at all. I told Jane I think it's her best book yet.*

(This afternoon, when I returned from running errands—paying state and federal taxes, etc.—Jane told me that she was having all kinds of "weird things" happening in her back and legs, as though various portions of her anatomy were loosening at uneven rates. Her balance and double vision were affected too. We slept together during a nap. I woke up with my stomach bothering me, and Jane, half crying, with a continuing of the strange, intensified feelings of uncontrolled motion/extra-slow motion combined and manifested in her back and legs. She worried about not being able to get from the bed to the chair to the john, but did well nevertheless.

(Yet she found the changes frightening, although she kept in mind Seth's material that the fright was not to be feared but understood as expressing buried fears, to put it simply. When she called me for the session at 8:30, she showed me how she has picked up unaccustomed movement in her legs: She could raise her legs several inches higher—the right one the easiest—than she'd been able to do this morning; obvious signs that the changes were beneficial. Yet she couldn't move her right leg to the side at all—"There's no action there at all," she said, "as though something's blocking it." I said it meant other groups of big muscles were tightened in order to help support her while the first groups were rejuvenating themselves in safety. I also said that I thought the publication of God of Jane *at last had served as a stimulus for the changes. I looked forward to more physical improvements for her.*

(Now I explained to Jane what I considered to be "a gorgeous little illustration" of how unconscious hassles can go on in the psyche quite unsuspected by the conscious

mind as the cause for physical difficulties: As stated, when I woke up this afternoon my stomach hurt. It's been bothering me for the last few days, for no apparent reason; looking back, probably since Jack Joyce visited a few days ago about our making estimated tax payments to NY State. Interestingly enough, though, I made no such conscious connection until I began writing these notes. Then it came to consciousness: of course. Today I paid estimated federal and NYS taxes, and had planned to do so since seeing Jack. At once I checked with the pendulum—and got a great big yes — that was why my stomach had been acting up. My old bugaboo had returned, but very craftily so that I hadn't been aware of it. I'd thought I'd managed to dismiss concerns about taxes, and actually have succeeded in doing so to a large degree—witness my physical well-being when paying taxes last April 15, for example. "Yet," I said to Jane, "it shows how conflicts can keep going underground if you don't watch it, and can be very damaging in the long run...."

(So as we waited for the session I told Jane that I didn't know which to ask Seth to talk about—my question from last session, or the arrival of God *of Jane and her new physical changes.)*

Now.

("Good evening.")

Ruburt's body is now <u>addressing</u> itself to those areas that deal primarily with motion and locomotion, and in righting the body's balance.

(Long pause, eyes closed, leaning back.) Ruburt cannot understand all of the processes that are involved, but the body knows what is to be done, and is working with its own rhythms. This may cause temporary disorientation, but that will also pass, as you can see. Certain portions of the body were released this evening. By all means let Ruburt continue to express his feelings to you about the situation, however, and reassure him of his body's competence.

Work is being done that will vastly improve the double-vision condition also.

Now: about Prentice. I do not want to lay stress upon any negative effects, but to explain differences of opinion and behavior. The initial relationship began some time ago, of course, and in a fashion had its own background as far as Ruburt was concerned. When he wrote short stories, for example, he was forced to search for a publisher for each one—a magazine. He learned to deal with the various editors by mail. He sold most of his stories to *Fantasy & Science Fiction Magazine* when Boucher was the editor.

Later editors did not see eye to eye with him about his work. He learned that his work must be sold in the marketplace if he wanted to continue writing. He tried unsuccessfully to publish several novels. *(Long pause.)* When Frederick Fell took the ESP book he was delighted. In a fashion Fell represented the next step upward from, say, pulp magazines. On the other hand, Fell did not go for the next projects that he either offered or had in mind—nor did Ace Books, who fell into the same category.

He considered Prentice-Hall a further excellent step upward, a reputable-enough publisher. Tam as editor did not go for his first—or that is, Ruburt's first presentation, however, but suggested the book that ended up as *The Seth Material*.

(Long pause at 9:07.) In many ways Tam and Ruburt got along quite well, even though Tam was a good deal younger, where before Ruburt's editors had been people a good deal older than he. When the book was done Ruburt began another, along with several different attempts. *Dreams, Astral Projection and ESP,* I believe was to be the title. Ruburt signed for the book but had difficulty with his presentation, and it represented his indecisions, so Tam respectfully at first suggested large alterations.

Ruburt himself recognized the book's deficiencies, and he and Tam together hit upon the idea of switching my book, *Seth Speaks*, which was not yet contracted for, instead of *Dreams. (Long pause.)* Ruburt was therefore impressed to the ears with the necessity of getting a book to market, and of the importance of a decent working relationship with an editor, particularly in the uncertainties of even usual free-lancing writing were taken into consideration.

Ruburt's subject matter, however, was not routine, particularly back in those times. He felt that its unique nature meant that it could be quite difficult to sell. When he and Tam began to reach a relatively workable relationship, therefore, he began to value this more and more. He felt that in the beginning Tam stood up for him at Prentice several times. And Tam, it seemed, kept his hands away from the manuscript itself in the one way that Ruburt clearly understood: he did not generally change the copy. As the years went by Tam and Ruburt arrived at certain methods of operation that suited Ruburt <u>personally</u>, and that were understood by both of them.

(Long pause at 9:19.) These methods of operation involved certain evidences of play, some social chatter, mutual trust, and left open the doors to a certain kind of unpredictable pattern of development—a pattern in which, for example, Tam could recognize the latent book in the Emir dream, and help fire Ruburt to write it, even though eventually Prentice was not the publisher.

These were not elements of behavior that seem particularly businesslike, however. Overall Ruburt felt quite competent, however, even in battling away at his advances two-thousand dollars at a time. He valued the relative permanency of the association, judging it in his mind against other situations in which time might otherwise be necessary to find a different publisher for each book, or an agent with whom Ruburt might feel rapport. Period.

The national economic situation led him to value that relationship still further. He made comparisons, of course, between that relationship and what he knew of other publishers through reading or through direct dealings, such as with Eleanor, for example. He valued the more or less clear channel of operation from the completion of a book by himself to its publication.

Now overall he wanted an attractive package, of course, yet to him the book was in the <u>copy</u> mainly. *(Long pause.)* The Bantam photograph covers did displease him, but in a fashion he did not expect any more from the mass paperback situation. For some time he felt competent then in those business dealings. He felt loyalty to Tam, who he felt was loyal to him. At the same time he did not idealize Tam, and was well aware of some of his natural failings.

Many of the typos, for example, did not exist for Ruburt. He valued the good feelings that existed between himself and Tam, and quite preferred for example not to deal with too many other people at Prentice, but to keep the situation as simple as possible. They settled many matters by hastily scribbled notes *(pause)*, and by other methods that sometimes did not even seem to deal with the matter at hand.

He trusted you in the manuscript itself of a Seth book to provide the accuracy of record, in which he felt he was himself relatively deficient, and also to contribute the background material he felt so necessary, yet which he found difficult himself, and he valued of course your loyalty, support, and inspiration.

(9:38.) He therefore became upset whenever there were difficulties in which you and Prentice disagreed, or you and he disagreed, and he became highly uneasy if you and Tam seemed to disagree. He began to feel less competent in his dealings. He began to feel somewhat humiliated that as a woman he needed his husband to take care of such matters, and he felt threatened not only by such circumstances, but of course by the changes going on at Prentice itself and by Tam's own growing restlessness.

He realized that at another house he might receive more money or more publicity, or possibly another more esthetically-presented package, yet against the other uncertainties and vicissitudes he felt he had an acceptable framework of operation. Whose difficulties were <u>minimal enough</u> under the circumstances —one that provided creative freedom since, until *Emir*, Prentice had published his world-view books, poetry and novels, as well as my work. He made the *Emir* decision regretfully but very clearly.

(Long pause.) The problem with the contracts and the entire translation affair bothered you both deeply. Ruburt felt at times that you were too severe <u>on occasion</u> in your dealings with Tam for a while. *(Long pause.)* The entire situa-

tion bothered him deeply. He valued the relationship with Prentice *(long pause)*, and he valued the idea of distributing the books in foreign lands, even if that venture meant misunderstandings or quite deliberate translations such as the shortening of one book, feeling that Prentice, while negligent, was not <u>deliberately</u> negligent, and that the situation would be righted and the material restored.

That involved the deletion of copy, you see. He agreed with you thoroughly there. Though he did not agree about your opinion of Prentice per se, involving the difficulty, he blamed the foreign publisher. He felt, however, that some of your own anger against the foreign publisher was directed at Tam. Much of this involves simple differences in temperament. He did not deny the fact of your own visually acute behavior. He felt stupid when you became annoyed at typos or misspellings or whatever that he did not even perceive until you mentioned them. He felt between you and Prentice and Tam at various stages, of course, and did not feel certain of his old capacity to set the relationship right. He also began to distrust his own earlier methods of dealing with the situation.

He is pleased now that both books are on the market. He is pleased with their appearance. There are a few other issues I will add, including his changing attitudes and yours toward the disclaimer—but that is for another evening.

I bid you a fond good evening.

("Thank you.")

(10:01 PM. Jane's delivery had marched right along....)

DELETED SESSION
JUNE 15, 1981 8:44 PM MONDAY

(Today had been very hot and humid—close to 90 degrees—following heavy rains yesterday and last night. The temperature was still high at session time; even hotter weather was predicted for tomorrow. We were aware of many of the noises in the neighborhood that we didn't hear in the wintertime. Jane had slept till noon, following her very restless night, and she also took a nap when I did this afternoon. She had bouts of panicky feelings, and I tried to reassure her. Sometimes her feelings resulted in a few tears.

(We've begun getting letters mentioning Mass Events—*all laudatory—and these have helped, as Seth mentioned they would.*

(Jane expected Seth to continue with his Prentice-Hall material tonight, when I asked if she had any questions. These quotes are from her paper of last Friday, 6/12:

("I slept late, till 10:30, after a poor night.... Think that Rob's and my relationship might now achieve new highlights, when suddenly I feel like crying."

("Realize that since '79 at least I've felt to some degree that I had to protect my work *even* against Rob, whose ill feeling at Prentice might.... make that situation worse. Make Rob ill, or contaminate his feelings towards Mass Events and Seth's latest book: [See last PM Seth session, which Rob is typing as I write this.]"

("With this I feel I'm at the bottom of the panic—that this material represents the last involved elements. I feel myself letting go, yet still sense that escaping panic, so that I'm afraid to step on my feet, to turn and get on bed; like it's the last of the panic."

("Also—Tam's....esthetic integrity slips in my estimation in what I understand as his own writing intents."

(I'm doing my best to stay out of interfering with Jane's dealings with Tam and Prentice-Hall. Tam has requested that we send him a letter outlining our position re a competent professional translator of the French Seth Speaks. I was going to do the letter this weekend, but didn't. I asked Jane if *she* would write the letter, and she agreed to. I felt better about that.

(After supper Debbie Janney visited without seeing Jane. Her cat, Kitty Cat, has been missing since 8 AM, and Debbie fears for its safety and/or life. She gave me a color photo of the cat to show Jane. The incident upset Jane, signifying as it did people's urges to ask her all kinds of questions for all kinds of psychic help—taking it for granted that she was able and willing to offer that help. Jane said it made her feel "incompetent" that she couldn't, or didn't, pinpoint what had happened to the cat. She didn't want to do such psychic detective work, she said, because it reminded her of her own difficulties—an obvious point we both mentioned. Yet there's no controlling other people's reactions to a given body of work, from which among other things such possibilities as finding lost animals—or people—could be deduced. Jane recalled her successes in helping to reassure the parents of two lost girls some years ago [in separate incidents] in the Midwest. I'd forgotten about these events, which contained some striking "hits" on her part. Neither girl was dead, by the way.

("But I don't want to be in the position of finding out that that cat's dead," she said. "That's really the rock-bottom thing in stuff like that...." And now she recalled a third incident she'd helped in, involving a young man in Florida who'd attended her class just once. She'd been correct in this case also, saying the person was not dead; he returned within the time she specified, also, namely one dating several months after his disappearance. She was eventually brought up to date on the situation by letter.

(So we know she has the ability to do that sort of psychic sleuthing, but it turns her off. I'd say that it would do so even if she had no hassles of her own.

(Before the session I mentioned the question I kept in mind for Seth, concerning what the Sinful Self may have learned since this last series of sessions was started. I said it was essential that we communicate to that personification [named by Seth for convenience's sake only] that its performance was quite destructive to Jane, and that it must release its hold. I wanted to know the Sinful Self's attitudes toward the fact that it had rendered Jane literally helpless as far as her survival was concerned; she couldn't take care of herself physically without the aid of others, I said, so this obviously implied that the Sinful Self was creating its own demise also. I wanted to know what it "thought" about such a contradictory situation, whether it understood the implications, and so forth. No matter how it must reason or react, it had to be concerned about its own survival—but in what ways, and based upon what knowledge and/or reasons? All of these points could be subsumed under the one broad question that I wanted Seth to go into when he'd finished with the Prentice-Hall material.)

Now—good evening.

("Good evening,")

Comments. Most jobs, or even vocations, carry along with them implied guidelines, specifications, and definite requirements that serve to define the work involved. Within those specifications certain actions are performed. Within those specifications certain standards are met or not met. There are pats on the back for achievement or whatever. There are certain methods involved as a rule, and perhaps time requirements. Very often specific meanings are given to certain words, so that you have what amounts to a professional vocabulary. Often specific mediums of expression are concerned. The professional violinist, while involved with music, is not necessarily expected to be a great vocalist: he may sing raspy notes indeed *(with humor)*, without any aspersions being cast upon his playing of the violin.

Ruburt is operating in an area in which there are few such specifications, simply because no one knows what can or cannot be done, practically speaking, at psychic levels. Some people highly gifted with psychic abilities gravitate toward various activities. They find themselves acting more naturally, creatively and efficiently following their own natural bents. They are naturally devoted to healing, whether or not for example they may be highly proficient. That is the field of their interest, intent and ability. Then within the realms of your practical reality they learn to utilize that ability.

Others for their own reasons—as numerous as there are individuals—are interested in pursuing the "wicked," finding the lost, teaching creativity, seeing into the future or past or whatever. The psychic abilities operate along with your other characteristics.

The person interested in the psychic pursuit of the wicked, for example, certainly has as much in common basically with the policeman or detective as he or she has with other psychics, regardless of the differences that seem to exist. Psychic musicians or artists are highly interested in music, using their psychic abilities in that direction.

In those situations natural leanings and intents help specify what is expected and not expected. Now in those terms, Ruburt has often expected too much from himself. Part of the reason lies in the pervading popular misconceptions about psychic ability. Part lies in the very fact of the unknown elements that are involved. He does possess natural desires, characteristics and intents that help focus his own activity. And he also feels strong disinclinations in some other areas. Those disinclinations are quite healthy indicators that in those cases he is straying away from the strong areas of his own proficiency and interest.

(9:00.) When he demands too much of himself, there is nowhere along the line where he can securely rest, pat himself on the back, and say "You have done a good job," because what he has <u>performed</u> seems so inadequate in the light of what he feels is <u>expected</u>.

It would be most handy for him after some thinking to draw up his own statements of the areas of his main concentrations. Generally speaking, anything outside of that area is not to be expected from him: he need not concern himself there. He can quite honestly state that such and such is outside of the area of his concentration, at the far periphery of his "field." People will understand if he is clear in his own mind. The same applies of course to healing. Regardless of the differences with which the public considers exists between the medical profession and psychic healing, psychic healers have very much in common with doctors or nurses, and use their psychic abilities in a way that follows those characteristics and leanings.

Basically, Ruburt does not have those characteristics. Everyone has healing abilities *(long pause)*, but Ruburt, basically speaking, is interested in the theoretical and philosophical concerns that underlie the condition of health. He would not on his own be a doctor or a nurse or whatever, so his psychic abilities are not naturally enthusiastically expanded in those directions in terms of a vocation, or the requirements of a profession *(all very intently)*.

This does not mean that at times he may not help others generate healing abilities within themselves, since he is indeed involved in those other <u>patterns</u> of action that interweave with all of life's activities. He should not expect himself to perform as a professional healer, or be disappointed with himself if he does not.

The term "psychic" is ill-defined, so he must define for himself the field of his activity, specify clearly for both of your sakes where his own strengths lie, and his intents, and what is to be expected of him and what is not. Even within that statement there must be room for growth and accomplishment, "to explore the nature of reality."

(Long pause at 9:14.) Now how do you practically interpret such an intention? Where does such an exploration begin or end? Ruburt's natural psychic abilities follow his other abilities, again, and characteristics. They cannot be patterned upon other people's. *(Long pause.)* He has his own way of dealing with details—an instinctive manner. They all go into the creative mill, for example, where they are in their ways uniquely sorted, transformed into patterns, emerging into creative illuminations. He may on the other hand appear to normally ignore details.

I suggest that such a statement be drawn up, for it would certainly help clarify many situations, and show Ruburt that he was performing very well indeed. The nebulous nature of the "psychic" has served to help build up a picture of an unrealistic superself *(long pause)*, mentioned earlier, that is supposed to perform a dazzling array of activities, solving everyone's problems, displaying all of the psychic abilities at once, from healing to finding a lost kitten.

It is in the light of <u>that</u> image that Ruburt feels incompetent—a highly important point. He feels caught between that image of expected super-competence and the image of the Sinful Self, which feels competent of doing <u>very little. The Sinful Self</u> and the superself are alike unrealistic.

(Long pause.) Ruburt's material about Prentice-Hall was quite correct. He is not a businesswoman in the terms that a person is who is primarily devoted to business. He does, however, possess excellent instincts in certain directions that automatically bring money to you and insures the publication of his books and so forth. These operate quite naturally in your lives.

He felt that he was at certain times caught between you and Prentice: more worried about dealing with your attitudes toward Prentice than he was about dealing with the situation itself, with Prentice. As he tried to comprehend it, he also felt that certain attitudes of yours toward the marketplace would spill over and threaten the unimpeded clear channel that he felt has been formed to convey his writing to the public realm.

(With humor:) He realized that the channel had some muddy spots in it, some impediments, that it ran more clearly in some areas than others. He did not idealize the situation, in other words. The entire situation, however, bothered him deeply, since he felt of course a great sense of loyalty to you even when he did not share a your particular beliefs at any given point. *(Long pause.)* He also, as he stated, was afraid that your attitudes would splash over to color your

feelings toward future Seth books, and toward your future contribution toward them.

All of this existed, of course, in a situation in which the aspects of Tam's position and the Prentice situation were themselves changing and uncertain.

(Long pause at 9:38.) All of this should be considered along with the natural uncertainties that exist in creative ventures—his desire for inspiration and so forth. He needs to clarify the circle of his expectations, as earlier suggested this evening. All of these issues added to increased tension, so that he did not know what direction to move in (underlined), and felt his motion blocked.

(Long pause.) Added to this, the two of you had a tendency to concentrate upon the problems, which contributed in a large manner to the entire situation. It is important that Ruburt define what is expected of the practical self, and what falls outside of its realm.

The Sinful Self in the past has felt even more sinful, or example, in comparison to the unrealistic expectations set upon the self by the super-images. Ruburt expected to be the super healer, super clairvoyant, and so forth. Ruburt is *(pause)* a natural receiver of psychic information, of knowledge from another level of activity, a natural receiver of deep insights that are a part of your spiritual and biological heritage, and a natural translator of such material *(all with emphasis)*. That is his primary, most proficient area of exploration and accomplishment.

His body is indeed releasing tensions, adjusting at the most profound levels of motion, and the process involves, as stated, the release of old panics. Additional vigor can be expected as the energy that had been used by the panic is now made practically available to the body. He is supported by his own nature, and by the source of his own nature.

End of session and a fond good evening.

("Thank you. Good night."

(9:51 PM. Jane's delivery had been faster than it has been of late, although she began to slow down a bit toward its end. She remembered Seth's material about her statement of ability and intent. "I have to admit it's something I haven't thought of myself," she said—nor have I. Once mentioned, though, it becomes one of those obvious things to do.)

DELETED SESSION
JUNE 18, 1981 8:40 PM THURSDAY

("I almost have the feeling that you're not supposed to have a session tonight,"

Jane said at 8:19. "It's one of those things where you're so relaxed you shouldn't inter-rupt it—but if I don't have a session then I'm afraid it'll be a cop-out. You can't win...."

(She was indeed very relaxed, sitting as she was with her head bowed, leaning forward on the couch. Leonard Yaudes had just left. Today Jane had worked a little on page 6 of her "Manifesto from the Sinful Self"—a long dissertation from that entity that she'd started to get yesterday afternoon. [She'd slept 'till noon.] The mate-rial had begun to flow quite effortlessly because of her concern over what I'd written in my notes for Monday's session, about her being unable to take care of herself phys-ically any longer. As soon as she'd read that passage on Tuesday, she'd begun to talk about it, to question me, so I knew it had struck a sticky point.

(I hadn't deliberately planned that those notes would do that, yet in retrospect I was glad they had—especially in the unprecedented response Jane was getting from her Sinful Self. Her paper was very well done, and would make fascinating materi-al in an autobiography, for instance. The Sinful Self's material is too long and com-plicated to describe here, except to say that it contains the Sinful Self's own view of reality and its relationship to Jane's background and work, it's regrets, its defensive attitudes, its questions, and its genuine puzzlement that man has for so long —per-haps for most of history, indeed—persisted in the creation of and reliance upon such entities as the Sinful Self.

(Nor was Jane finished with her dissertation. A unique situation. I told her, feeling that only good could come out of such a dialogue between parts of the overall self or personality. It will be very interesting to see the results. I wondered how often such a clear-cut dialogue or exchange was on record as having taken place between such various portions of the self. A search of the psychological literature would be very interesting.

(Jane has also had some very vivid dreams in connection with this material, although she hasn't written them down and actually cannot recall much about any of them. They've involved healing, however, and in one of them she even expected to wake up healed—but found herself moving slowly on the bed as usual. I'll attach a copy of the Sinful Self's material to this session if Jane ever types it in duplicate. She's done practically no typing for days now because her arms have been very sore.

(The day before yesterday we received the first copy from Prentice-Hall of God of Jane. Today I picked up at the office for her the new reading glasses Jim Adams prescribed for her. [He's out of town.] They seem to work well for her. Although she can read much more comfortably now, she still has the double vision. A note: It appears that the family of raccoons inhabiting our fireplace chimney may have left— or so it seems.

(I told Jane at 8:39 that I didn't know whether or not Seth was through with his Prentice-Hall material, and she said that we'd gotten to the heart of it. In answer

to my question about material in the last session, she said that yes, she still felt to some degree that she had to protect her work from me and my feelings about Prentice-Hall. She continued that she felt that my feelings about Prentice-Hall had influenced my own feelings about Mass Events, *and so they have. She then said that she also thought my feelings about Prentice-Hall had influenced my feelings about Seth's next book more than my feelings about* her *did.*

("You've got it backwards." I said. I said that I reacted much more deeply to my feelings about her than any I have about Prentice-Hall; I was much more concerned about her own condition. "Prentice-Hall is a faceless entity out there that we come into contact with once in a while," I said, "but I see and live with you every day. Your situation is much more important to me than anything Prentice may do or not do.")

Now: there are session-related events that do not necessarily appear within the sessions themselves, except as they are related through your own notes.

These often involve responses to session material. Ruburt's message from "The Sinful Self" is a case in point, for it represents a response both to my material and to a question of your own. It gives a clear declaration of the Sinful Self's attitudes in the past, and its new growing recognition that those attitudes have been unfortunate. The Sinful Self has also raised some questions that are pertinent, and with which we will shortly deal.

It is important that its questions and attitudes be taken seriously. Ruburt's forgotten dream was a clear psychological statement in which all of the elements in his personality momentarily joined not only for a discussion, so to speak, but blended their forces, exerted their energies, and set up a firm intent to clarify the entire situation, and to exert all of their energies in a successful healing venture.

The advice of the Sinful Self should also be followed as given in the last paragraphs of that material. The statement that I suggested should also be written, along with those procedures; the plans for the front porch *(via Frank Longwell)* and for the small *(class)* group should be further considered, for they also represent motion on other levels.

(Pause.) I understand Ruburt's distress at times with the odd feelings of balance, but remember that these represent multitudinous changes and motions within the body, new positions requiring minute alterations of muscular tension that are actually highly beneficial. There is a certain rhythm to these sessions — that is, to this particular group—so that certain elements are strongly presented for his consideration. They serve as focal points of his interest, of course, and initiate various physical and psychological responses. They elicit responses on your part, of course, as well—responses that further help form your questions or note material.

Then there are quite necessary resting periods in between, in which <u>theoretically</u> (underlined) the matters would be best dropped from conscious concentration. Such a period is then followed again by perhaps more pointed activity. It is necessary that assimilation take place, of course. It is also necessary that there is room for certain psychological actions and motions to change from one pattern to another. The message of the Sinful Self shows excellent psychological mobility. *(Pause.)* That material can quite legitimately "take the place of" a regular session for the week. It was of great value in the fact that the Sinful Self was able, finally, to express itself <u>that clearly</u>—and I do not believe that the document is as yet completed.

(A one-minute pause at 9:00. It wasn't quite dark yet.)

The main issues with which the Sinful Self was concerned were focused most clearly in *Mass Events* and *God of Jane*, since more than the other books they represent a direct confrontation "attacking" the very legitimacy of the entire concept of sin and evil, insisting more dramatically on the good intent of man's basic impulses.

(Long pause.) Ruburt felt those issues could not be buried under the rug, but he did not realize the extent to which some of those old beliefs still lingered. *(Long pause.)* The Sinful Self's explanation represents a fascinating psychological document in that regard, and also shows the self's mobility and willingness to learn and change—once the intent is made <u>to take a stand</u> *(intently)*.

It might be of value to have Ruburt mentally ask the Sinful Self for a few comments on how its beliefs about the female sex were connected with its concepts of sin, and if those attitudes are changing. That material, plus my comments in this session, will set off further psychological mobility, of course, clarifying various positions more clearly.

The Prentice material will most likely return with somewhat of another slant. My own prognosis is quite favorable with the probabilities as they stand. This will be a brief session, unless again you have specific questions.

("No. I guess not," I said after some thought. I finally decided Jane wanted the rest, since she/Seth was calling for a short session.)

Then I bid you a fond, and to Ruburt a therapeutic good night.

("Thank you, Seth.")

My heartiest regards—and again, many session-related events are happening at other levels of activity. I wish you a fond good evening, again, and through Ruburt's experience enjoy your summertime.

("Good night.")

(9:14 PM. It's Friday evening as I type this. Seth's suggestion that Jane ask the Sinful Self for its comments of the female sex and sin were very acute—for today Jane

has received several pages of material from the Sinful Self on that subject. Again, well done, and not finished yet. Right now she's watching a disaster movie—The Poseidon Adventure—as I finish work.)

DELETED SESSION
JUNE 24, 1981 8:33 PM WEDNESDAY

(After the last session, which was held six days ago now, I realized I'd forgotten to ask Seth a question that had been on my mind for some weeks: I wanted his comments on Jane's swollen feet. Her right foot is especially swollen, including the instep and the ankle. I hoped that what he might have to say would ease my concern —although I haven't heard Jane mention the condition at all.

(Obviously, no sessions were held last Monday or Tuesday evenings. Instead, Jane has been working steadily on her "Manifesto from the Sinful Self" that she began just a week ago. It's a very remarkable document; she's now on page 26, and feels there's more to come. "It would make a great chapter in a book," I said yesterday. "Or maybe it'll turn out to be a project in itself." Jane said she'd see. I wondered if perhaps she'd already begun her next big endeavor without even being concerned about what she might do next. Certainly her paper is extremely creative, including insights also as it does about her relationship with Seth.

(Jane has gotten up with me the last two mornings, and has taken naps when I do. She is doing well in the bathroom with the new chair, but still feels momentary panic when she has to move from her chair onto the bed; I help her do this.

(I've picked up her new reading glasses at Jim Adams's office, but she hasn't been wearing them because they need adjusting. JA was out of town, due back last Monday. Jane left a message that he should call her, but she hasn't heard. I suggested she call again tomorrow.

("I don't feel I need a session tonight," she said, "or that I have an obligation to have one. I just want to check in and see what's been going on since Monday"— and she was quite surprised when I told her she hadn't had a session since last Thursday.)

Now, good evening.

("Good evening, Seth.")

Deeply *(pause)* therapeutic elements are operating at all levels of Ruburt's experience.

The material he is receiving is excellent, and later I will of course comment on it most thoroughly. I do not want to affect its <u>development</u> now, however, in an overt fashion by comments, and I prefer that many of the insights are directly expressed in that manner, rather say than by my own interpretation of them.

The physical situation is highly active: ligaments and joints in particular being released in the hip and leg area. This also applies to beneficial alterations in the ankles and toes, where additional fluids resulting in the swelling effect help cushion the new motion in particular of some joints, so there is no grating.

(Pause). Again, many events are <u>gathering</u> as the result of our sessions, and certain activities taking place at other levels of activity during what you might think of as our usual session times. I am overseeing some of those activities. *(Long pause.)* In a way the material that Ruburt is receiving will also open new doorways even as far as our sessions are concerned.

(Long pause—one minute finally—at 8:42. Jane leaned back on the couch with her eyes almost closed; it seemed they were turned up so I could see the whites.)

Ruburt is embarking upon a different kind of relaxation—highly important, so in that regard these times are extremely creative, and that creativity will indeed be reflected in bodily releases and what you might call <u>body inspirations</u>. Therefore the session is extremely brief—but the energy within and behind it is also being used on your behalves at levels that may not at this point be presently apparent to you. I give you then my fondest regards, and please note that I answered your question. A fond good evening.

("Thank you, Seth."

(8:47 PM. This, then, must be the shortest session Jane has held in years. "I told him that he could have the session be as long as he wanted," Jane said as soon as she was out of trance. "But I do feel like things are going on.... Strange.")

DELETED SESSION
JUNE 29, 1981 8:35 PM MONDAY

(The day after the last session I wrote down a question for Seth. I've thought about it often since last Thursday, then: Is Jane going to have to make known to herself consciously every bit of information about her symptoms before she recovers? I had the question partly because of something she'd said herself before the last session—and which I've now forgotten—and partly because I didn't believe that most people were able to deal with such procedures in their daily lives. Indeed, they wouldn't have the time or the <u>talent</u> to make consciously known to themselves all the details of their challenges that had made them ill to begin with. As a society we're generally not organized that way to begin with.

(I thought, then, that much of the time most people simply get well through an unwitting trust in their bodies to heal themselves. Obviously this didn't always apply,

since some people became chronically ill, or died, or suffered devastating illnesses —
but for the most part whatever helpings they managed to achieve came about through
subconscious mental and bodily processes. If and when they worked out solutions to
their problems, they did so quite unknowingly. In retrospect I believe this question
was triggered by remarks Jane made about insights she'd achieved through her man-
ifesto from the Sinful Self.

(For the last two days Jane hasn't worked on her paper from the Sinful Self—
the first break she's taken from it since she began to receive it 13 days ago, on June
17. She'd read me Friday's work that same evening, and I had some questions about
it, although it's very difficult to formulate questions while listening to something the
first time, and without having a written version to refer to. Yet as I listened to her I
felt that at times the Sinful Self seemed to almost be trying to put the blame for her
symptoms off on other portions of the personality—or let's say that that was one of the
feelings I had.

(We had a discussion about my questions, and I expressed pretty definitely the
emotional charge I've accumulated over the years about the whole affair. Jane said
several times that she understood my feelings, but that at the same time I was mis-
understanding what she'd written that day [Friday]. I could see that she was disap-
pointed in my reactions to her day's work, and she said as much.

(My viewpoint was that it was impossible for me not *to have strong feelings*
about the situation, even though—as I said—I agreed that her paper was a highly
creative piece of work, that it augured well for the future, and that it was so far eas-
ily the best material we'd gotten on the symptom affair. Yet I still felt questions and
statements going around in my head as we retired—and as is often the case in such
situations I wondered if I'd gone too far in my reactions, and needlessly interfered
with Jane's attempts to probe into and understand a most difficult challenge. My
question, above, was an outgrowth of my own feelings and questionings. I read it to
her as we sat for tonight's session, and she agreed it was a good one.)

("I don't really feel like a session," she said at 8:20. "So much is going on in
my body I don't know what's going on...."

(The swollen condition of her feet still concerned me, although I've kept in
mind Seth's material on that situation and feel better about it. I've managed to turn
my thoughts away from such worries rather successfully lately, yet when they do return
they can't but help cause concern, so conditioned are we toward anything unusual
about the body's behavior representing a state of illness or unease. I only hoped Seth
was correct about her feet, for indeed they're more enlarged than ever, especially the
right foot.

(Today I did order 8 oz. of DMSO gel, responding to an ad in the local paper
Saturday. We'd expected to see a long article on DMSO in the paper, written by Peggy

Gallagher, but it wasn't printed: Over the phone today Peg told Jane the article was put off until next weekend because of space limitations. Peg has interviewed many local doctors—and others—about the analgesic properties of DMSO, and we want to read the article before trying the product ourselves. But in the meantime the order is going through, so we'll be prepared. Much caution will be necessary, I told Jane.

(Jane had no direct questions for Seth, as usual, she said, unless he wanted to comment upon the DMSO question. She has been sleeping pretty well for the most part these days, but has had a great deal of soreness in her arms [and some spontaneous jerking movements accompanied by shooting pains; it seems the arms are lengthening somewhat]. The arm discomfort makes it quite difficult for her to move from either of her chairs to the bed and/or couch, however.

(Yesterday and today she did paintings of a bouquet of daisies and sweet peas that the Bumbalos brought back from their lakeside cottage. Both turned out rather well, as she agreed, finally, after at first proclaiming both of them to be failures.

(The evening was quite warm and very pleasant. The back porch door was wide open in the gathering dusk; even though we've passed the longest day of the year now, it was still not dark.)

Now—good evening.

("Good evening.")

You do not need to be consciously familiar with all the details connected with Ruburt's condition in order for him to heal himself.

He does need to be <u>generally</u> aware of his own beliefs, however. The so-called <u>Sinful Self</u> is actually giving him a more or less handy list of stubborn older beliefs that clash with his new ones—beliefs that often go underground — and the "Sinful Self" is giving the <u>rationale</u> behind such beliefs. The entire edifice appears.

Generally speaking, the best policy to pursue is to concentrate not upon the problem but upon its <u>possible solutions</u>, and this process can be a rather intense one. Then, <u>as much as possible</u> (underlined), the situation should be dropped for a period, concentration purposely directed as much as possible elsewhere. Thus giving the creative inner self the time and opportunity to let the entire physical system accelerate its own healing processes, and to begin again with the initiation of impulses, dreams, and so forth that will help bring a physical improvement about.

Again, it is important that you not <u>accuse</u> the Sinful Self *(which I took to be a reference to our discussion last Friday).* To do so is not advantageous. *(Pause.)* It deepens the Sinful Self's sense of isolation. That portion of the personality operated with its own good intent, and for some number of years other portions of the personality went along. The Sinful Self did not have a free hand, for example, bringing about physical difficulties all by itself. And it is the entire system that will clear itself. The Sinful Self is not the "villain." It is the personified holder of many of the beliefs that brought the physical condition into existence.

(Pause at 8:48.) Then a lack of communication developed, so that various portions of the personality "hardened" their own positions, sometimes holding quite different sets of beliefs. The <u>communication</u> of the Sinful Self's document is almost one of its most important values. Its beliefs may be exaggerated, but at one time or another various other portions of the personality at least weakly entertained a portion of them. They are also held together by a sense of earnestness and duty *(with a mock-severe frown)*—quite misapplied, but still characteristics hardly foreign to the personality as a whole—so these are misunderstandings to be addressed and understood, and the main issue <u>should</u> be an understanding of those issues specifically mentioned, so that the issues are met in the open and aired on the part of the entire personality *(all often with emphasis).*

It is important that the creative self understands what has been going on also. In such a way the various portions of the personality can reinforce and help each other, and the Sinful Self can see that the creative elements are not blind to its worries, but will <u>also</u> use its abilities to help discover explanations and answers to the questions of the so-called Sinful Self.

(Pause.) As that happens, the Sinful Self will also be able to take greater benefit from <u>our</u> sessions. You can see the Sinful Self's connection with creativity easily, as it communicated through its document, which is for example very well written, carrying its own flavor. You can also see where it is lacking: it has displayed little sense of playfulness, for example, or of expansion. It is overly serious, overly conscientious, and its thinking is largely in black-and-white terms. For all of that, it shares philosophic concerns that deeply interest the entire personality, so there is plenty of ground for a give-and-take.

There have been several signs of excellent cooperation between portions of the self—as when issues raised or discussed by the Sinful Self then initiated dreams or other psychic behavior in response. The concentration should not be, again then, on the problems. It should not be on any accusations, but on the recognition of the communication itself, and to those specific issues mentioned. These should be given direct consideration.

The <u>nature</u> of that consideration will show itself as a natural result of the psychological events now occurring. There may be a communication of one kind or another directly from the creative self to the Sinful Self, for example, in which those issues are sympathetically addressed. There certainly will be dreams and other such events that serve as communications from one portion of the self to another—and these may be initiated from <u>any</u> portion.

Some may even be initiated from the sessions. It is important that such portions of the self speak for themselves right now. I do not want to anticipate such communications, because Ruburt needs the <u>direct encounter</u>, so to speak.

(9:10.) A concentration upon painting, or developments about the home, with as many diversions as possible will also help, again, so that the entire personality can activate the entire system for healing processes.

Such events will follow their own rhythms if you allow them to. Your own love-making and communications of love in different ways is of continuing importance. Right now I act more as a monitor. *(Long pause.)* Remember that all portions of the personality are <u>conscious</u>. Everything does not have to be translated into your terms of consciousness, however. Quite creative solutions of course happen at other levels, arising into your usual consciousness sometimes by very diverse routes.

It is important to remember the benign unpredictability of Framework 2 in that regard, so that you leave the doors open for desired results in whatever way they might occur.

(Long pause.) Enjoyment by itself, regardless of the activity enjoyed, is on its own therapeutic. Anything that increases your joy or peace of mind will help in Ruburt's recovery, regardless of how divorced it might seem from what you want. In fact, sometimes the further divorced the better.

(Long pause.) The more stimuli, thoughts, desires and material of a diverse nature brought <u>into</u> the system—within reason—the greater the amount of material the inner self has to work with and put together in its own creative fashions—but do remember those sessions given that remind Ruburt that his body can indeed recover, that he can indeed trust his body's processes, and that he should not compare his life with anyone else's, but trust in the entire fabric of his existence, and you indeed should trust the entire fabric of your own.

End of session. I bid you a fond good evening—and again, remind you that session events are also taking place at other levels of activity. *(Pause.)* A fond good evening.

("Thank you. The same to you.")
(9:23 PM.)

DELETED SESSION
JULY 4, 1981 8:05 PM SATURDAY

(Jane surprised me at supper time by saying she felt Seth around and wanted to have a session. "Sometimes when we're <u>supposed</u> to have a session I don't feel him

at all," she said. "Other times, like now, I do, so...."

(We thought her desire has been triggered by a book a reader had mailed so that we received it yesterday—Magical Child, *by Joseph Chilton Pierce, copyright 1977. Jane has scanned portions of it and found it excellent; we're surprised that we haven't heard of it before, especially in light of Pierce's two bestsellers on* The Crack in the Cosmic Egg. *Jane said she thought* Magical Child *contained ideas reminiscent of her own and Seth's ideas, and was also remindful of a book idea she's considering at the moment, on the magical self. She had me dig out her notes for this idea yesterday —I believe before the mail, but am not sure.*

(The same reader also sent us a copy of a chapter out of a book by a Dr. Ariola, who I think writes for New Realities *magazine also on health foods and related topics. The chapter deals with the negative effects and aspects of inoculations, and certainly reinforces Seth's own material in* Mass Events *on the harmful effects of many inoculations. Again, we hadn't heard of Dr. Ariola's book either. I am filing all of the information discussed here. Jane feels good that "independent sources" have verified Seth's own material. Indeed, the reader response to* Mass Events *has been excellent, and possibly already heavier than on any of her previous books.*

(Jane has felt fairly well today. She still sleeps pretty good most of the time. We had the Weissenbuehlers visit last night; this afternoon Eve Longwell and daughter Jeanie visited, and we played on the VTR quite a bit of footage from the tapes we've made. Jane still has walking difficulties getting from her chairs to the john or bed, and her arms continue to be very uncomfortable.)

Good evening.

("Good evening, Seth.")

Now, we will begin with some material with a slightly new slant or cast this evening.

First of all, some of the ideas in the *Magical Child* book are excellent, and though he has not read the book thoroughly by any means, some new understandings have been reached through the use of those ideas and his own recent experiences by Ruburt.

(Here Seth referred to several examples of "synchronicity," involving especially a dream of Ellspeth Weissenbuehler's, and several events involving herself, Jane. She intends to write up this material for possible future use. "It's not all that great," she said, "but that Ellspeth seems able to tune in on us.")

I now want to put the <u>Sinful Self</u> material in a larger spectrum. Ideally, infants "bond" with their parents, particularly with the mother but with the father also—and then they "bond" with the general ideas of their society. This offers the sense of safety and security in which the youngster can then feel free and curious enough to explore its world and the nature of reality.

You are social creatures. You fear abandonment for that reason, since you are meant to develop individually while also interacting with others, that interaction giving you the peculiar quality of established civilizations.

Now Ruburt had only one parent available most of the time *(long pause)*, and he did not feel secure in that relationship—a situation <u>chosen</u> ahead of time, now. There is greater leeway in the nature of such bondings. There are also periods in people's lives, rhythmic times, when the self seeks to cast off certain such bindings for the pursuit and acceptance of still further data and knowledge.

(Long pause at 8:15.) With some people *(long pause)*, such bindings are so secure that in one way or another they provide an overall, fairly permanent inner and outer framework. The people within that framework will stray only so far from conventional beliefs. *(Long pause.)* They still enjoy—relatively—a good deal of freedom, however, of a sideways extension, so to speak, or in a horizontal manner, as excellent athletes, perhaps. Ruburt's relationship with his mother left much to be desired. The bonding did not secure him that important and vital sense of safety, and to some extent or another he felt at least threatened by abandonment. The bonding to cultural beliefs of religion *(long pause)* was very strong to make up for that initial lack. The strength of such binding elements, again, varies through a lifetime, and the binding to the parents' beliefs of course helps strengthen social structure. In a curious fashion, however, that circle of safety provides each individual with the freedom and curiosity to go ahead and test independent theories and situations—so it also serves the purposes of creativity and knowledge, and even allows for the acquisition of new knowledge that was not in the original belief structures.

The Sinful Self material represents those ideas that were strong element in the original belief structural of a cultural nature, to which Ruburt was "bonded." There were other ideas and concepts joined with these that he has successfully grown away from, so that they became less important.

In any case the "troublesome" material remained *(long pause)*, relatively <u>inactive</u> more or less—unless and until certain situations arose, unless and until his curiosity and ability led him to actively <u>challenge</u> those ideas while also in a situation where the natural fear of abandonment might be implied or suggested. The individual's impetus is toward growth, development and understanding. These, again, these seemed to imply a matrix for some kind of safety. At certain points, then, the assimilation of new information is so qualifiedly different from the original belief structure that in order to assimilate it the personality is left for a time between belief systems.

(A one-minute pause at 8:38. Jane had been speaking quite emphatically between long pauses. Seth's use of "matrix" above reminded me that before the session

Jane had mentioned that he wanted to discuss her Sinful Self material in a new sort of matrix.)

The point at which such a situation <u>happens</u> is of course internal, and it may or may not have anything to do with the quality of material, but with its nature. Each society—or each system of knowledge, for that matter—has its own taboos built in, and most of these imply abandonment by the community. A firm bonding with the parent ideally implies however that the child will not be abandoned, despite for example parental anger at any given time. Now remember that Ruburt's mother used words like "I hereby disown you," or "You are hereby disinherited," or "I consider you no longer my daughter." Such a situation increased Ruburt's sense of <u>not</u> being safe, of course, and yet also reinforced feelings of independence, for he did not have to feel as dependent upon Marie as he might otherwise.

In a fashion therefore he possessed a greater leeway of mental activity *(long pause)*. Our material, and his own abilities, represented various kinds of trials, development and growth, and also implied various kinds of threats of different strengths throughout the years. He could assimilate much new knowledge by means of the creative mechanisms, which could not transform troublesome ideas into other symptoms that could become quite acceptable.

The time would come, however, when the old bondings had to be encountered, for they simply could not hold the <u>newer frameworks</u> of understanding which were larger than they were. The ideas presented by the so-called Sinful Self represent several layers of activity, then, that should be understood as represented. Some of the most troublesome aspects of one's belief structures are shared by millions in your society, and by certain levels of Ruburt's own personality, where they exist with varying strengths. The personality is now trying to assimilate a greater framework to become bonded to a higher sequence of knowledge.

Once those old beliefs are understood for what they are, they will no longer be considered as shameful in themselves, nor humiliating, or as attitudes to be accused of *(long pause, one of many)*, but as a personality's way of still preserving old beliefs, whatever their nature, for the feeling of safety that they still implied. When that is understood you are already on the way to a new, more expansive creative path *(all emphatically)*.

The old attitude kept reinforcing the idea of self-disapproval, accusation, period. What is wanted is another matrix or support from which the personality can assimilate still newer knowledge, and continue to develop—generally speaking—with a sense of relative freedom.

An understanding of the issues as I just explained them automatically alters the nature of what is left of those old bondings, thereby releasing the natural, magical properties of the child or natural person within, who possesses its own built-in matrix of safety and trust.

(9:01.) This is like a kind of backup system, biologically pertinent, that always operates of course to an important degree, but that can now come more to the forefront of Ruburt's experience. It is very important that you understand what I am saying in this session. For it puts Ruburt <u>on top of</u> those old bondings, while still giving them their recognition as issues that can indeed be creatively reconciled.

<u>His idea of a project on the magical approach now is excellent,</u> for it suggests a new concentration or focus in which the natural and magical aspects of existence <u>are</u> courted, and the characteristics of the natural magical person encouraged to show themselves. In such a way the old fears do not go underground and are not concentrated upon either—but they <u>are</u> taken into consideration and acknowledged, let out into the open daylight, so to speak, where they can also benefit from the personality's newer knowledge.

Emotional support, such as that almost nonchalant (long pause) yet commonplace kind that happened this afternoon, is important. Such encounters provide an emotional support that cements feelings with your fellow beings, and that in a fashion helps minimize in the present some of the defects of Ruburt's childhood relationship with his mother. This also applies to your small group of friends and students, where the idea is one of friendly support and understanding. There are indeed clues in the seemingly innocuous material that Ruburt intends to note down, involving the soda, the cookies, and so forth.

The so-called doubting elements of the self have every right to sit in the council of the personality, rather than to be shunted aside, for they are themselves quite curious, and they have already of course been weakened. It is only when they are denied, accused of sabotage, that the situation becomes one in which positions are hardened at both ends, so to speak.

Now the body has suffered its difficulties, and there is no way out of it except to understand that there are difficulties of growth, regrettable at certain levels in particular—but growing pains nevertheless, extending over a period of time, tensions resulting over a person's natural tendencies toward value fulfillment and knowledge.

Many illnesses of a chronic nature exist in the same fashion, and the answers are philosophical ones and subjective illuminations.

There will be a good response to both Ruburt's book and mine, which will also serve in a supportive way. End of session. I will have more remarks in the same general framework shortly—and a fond good evening.

("Thank you very much. Good night."

(9:20 PM. Jane had done well. It was almost dark. From the valley south of our hill house intermittent barrages of fireworks had sounded during the session, and even now crackled anew. The situation was reminiscent, I thought, of other sessions we'd held on warm summer nights with the doors and windows open, and listened to the distant sound of fireworks....)

DELETED SESSION
JULY 8, 1981 8:29 PM WEDNESDAY

(The regularly scheduled session for last Monday was not held.

(Late yesterday afternoon we received our order of DMSO. We have hopes for good results, without hoping too much. I've started a detailed account of its use, including times of application, body parts treated, etc. Yesterday evening we checked to see if Jane would have any negative reactions. She evidently doesn't. So far we've tried it tentatively on various portions of her body, with what appear to be some promising results. Anything will help, of course, so we'll see. See my records for a complete account of our efforts with DMSO.

(We sat for the session at 8:10. We wanted Seth to comment on the DMSO, and on Jane's very swollen right foot. [The left foot has lost some of its original swelling, and now appears much better by contrast.] I told Jane I thought Seth was correct in the deleted session for June 24, 1981, in which he said the swelling effect helps cushion the new motion of some joints, so there is no grating. I also told her I thought another reason applied, however, one that led to the swelling to begin with. She is waiting apprehensively to see what the public's reaction to God of Jane *is. Although a few hundred copies of this book may have been shipped, it hasn't really come out yet. The idea had come to me some days ago that Jane's foot troubles were directly related to her fears of being accepted in a controversial role. "I thought you knew something like that was going on." I said. She shook her head: "I don't know what I think. I'd like him to say something about the DMSO, and that material I got this afternoon, and maybe the foot....")*

(Her material this afternoon concerned "the reconciliation of the Sinful Self and its transformation into the innocent self that it was before it was undermined —indoctrinated—with negative beliefs." I think it's excellent material, and designed to lead to fuller understandings of the whole symptom situation, and perhaps some sort of resolution. I said that even if the new innocence was achieved by the Sinful Self, it would be a different kind of innocence because it would contain all of the "Sinful Self's earlier convolutions" as it went through its stages, striving toward that

renewed innocence. Memory of that struggle would linger, I thought.

(An interesting debate emerged between us as we waited for the session to begin. When Jane read her material of this afternoon to me, I thought she likened the Sinful Self's renewal to reincarnation, meaning that she thought this renewal might account for many of our overt ideas of reincarnation—that at least some of our ideas about reincarnation were based upon our intuitive knowledge of the return of portions of one's self to that earlier state of innocence—a rebirth, in other words, that we might translate into the idea of physical incarnation. So when I agreed with Jane this afternoon, it was partly for that reason.

(But tonight she maintained that she'd never mentioned the subject of reincarnation in her paper, and that she hadn't meant reincarnation in that sense at all. So I was left frustrated, wondering what she'd said that I had mistranslated into that word. After being initially upset, I rather humorously thought that my idea wasn't a bad one anyhow.

(At 8:25 her right knee "doesn't hurt at all at this point," but she repeated that it took a while for the DMSO to really start to work. We'd applied it to her knee at 7:30 PM.)

Good evening.

("Good evening.")

Now: Ruburt's paper was well done, and is important to an understanding of what has been happening in his own life, as well as indicating the larger social framework.

Briefly—as mentioned—the child has a great sense of curiosity and wonder. That <u>field</u> of exploration is so vast, however, that it needs boundaries and determinations also. *(Pause.)* Although Ruburt did not mention this in his paper, reincarnation does have a part to play, for child's curiosity must somehow be fitted into a new social structure, generally speaking, from other reincarnational ones. Therefore it becomes "bonded" to the parents in a given life, and then bonded to the beliefs shared by the family group.

Such bonding provides a sense of safety and focus. The belief system may in fact be negatively attuned while still providing that overall <u>value</u>. The bonding is not meant to be <u>permanent</u>, however, and after a while the child begins to question its affiliations, the ways and means vary according to cultures. Some cultures provide symbols, or symbolic steps within the system itself, that allow for a steady "progression," in which a young person's curiosity and accelerated adolescent rebellion is subtly directed from within the society itself.

(Long pause.) All societies basically need the insertion of fresh challenge and knowledge, however, or they stagnate. At the same time, of course, the society wants to maintain its familiar stance. For centuries Christianity served to

preserve old frameworks while still allowing for transforming elements and symbolic activities that allowed individuals to assert some independence and originality by moving from one religious symbol, say, to another—still, however, within that larger framework.

(8:44.) In terms of reincarnation, Christianity in numberless cases even served as a uniting framework connecting lives: you could for example theoretically move from one century to another, and while there were social and political changes, the overall cultural framework might well be the same.

(Long pause.) The original ideas connected with the Sinful Self's beliefs were at one time, for example, not as obviously unfortunate, since the system itself also provided for salvation, methods of appeasement and so forth—all of which were thoroughly accepted through many centuries.

One of the church's most powerful allies was to that extent its understanding of human psychology, for if you left the church or its system, it knew that you still carried many of its beliefs nevertheless—only now you had something like an itch that you could not scratch. Finally, however, Christianity's structure became too limited.

I am speaking in your terms of time, now. Individuals born into your time do not feel, say, the same sense of familiarity with the religious belief systems of past lives. *(Pause.)* Your age requires a greater sense of freedom and curiosity. In any case, the original innocent self is bonded to the parents, and to the parents' beliefs for a time. This provides the necessary sense of safety and the sense of definition in which the child can safely use its explorative abilities.

When the person is a child no longer that need no longer exists in the same fashion. People often throw off their childhood beliefs then and begin to look for their own view of reality, once again. They may then count the more negative aspects of their backgrounds in a rather concentrated manner, for the system no longer serves to provide its psychological support. The person is forced to find fresh, more original solutions.

(8:57.) In Ruburt's case, the Sinful Self was the remnant, psychologically speaking, and the same applies to many within your society.

Now each individual is also given ways and means of a highly personal nature, characteristics or abilities that automatically begin to lead it out of such old belief systems, when those characteristics are allowed their freedom. They will lead the individual toward their own built-in feelings of support and safety.

(Long pause.) Those creative elements of personality must then to some extent or another finally communicate with the "Sinful Self" directly—sympathetically embrace that self *(pause)* as the part of personality that first accepted cultural and religious beliefs with all of their negative and positive influences.

The more creative portion of personality must then realize <u>that in a fashion it exists</u> because the Sinful Self did. Those negative beliefs then no longer seem so frightening. The taboos within lose their power, and the Sinful Self is seen as *(long pause)* <u>representing the stage of growth through which the self is passing</u> *(intently).*

It is then transformed into what it was before such indoctrination by the culture. Then it was the <u>innocent</u> self, of course. This understanding helps release that energy for the use of the entire personality, as Ruburt's paper correctly states. The personality is then free to explore and assimilate greater areas of original knowledge. You actually have the innocent self in a kind of second stage, for now it has the experience of the Sinful Self behind it.

The errors and discrepancies of the culture are apparent, and that information can then be used in highly creative ways. Solutions can then be sought for the problems of the culture as well. In such a fashion new data <u>may</u> (underlined) be inserted, changing the entire scope and shape of social consciousness.

Religion still serves within your time as such a uniting and also "disruptive" framework. It has so many variations now in the world culture that it allows many individuals to move from one belief system to another while still safely <u>cloaked</u> in religious garb. If you move from sinner to saint or saint to sinner, from Buddhism to fundamentalism of the Christian kind, or from one sect to another, seemingly with a diverse belief system, your growth and transformations are still being provided for by a religious structure.

Many people go through several such transformations, using symbolic transformations then that still serve to focus wonder and curiosity while keeping them well within the accepted picture.

(9:19. Long pause.) Ruburt is trying to move outside of the picture entirely. Only by so doing, of course, can the larger avenues of knowledge be opened and made available to the society—or to the self. For many centuries creativity itself was firmly directed by Christianity, <u>and to some extent</u> (underlined) Christianity brings with it an air of uneasiness for society—to the extent that any original thought or insight must indeed imply an intrusive force to a world that must exist in a rare balance that is the result of preserving old values and obtaining new knowledge.

More and more people are exploring revelatory information. It is only natural that most of it will simply help channel their own self-transformations by appearing garbed in one way or another in standard religious terms, however <u>exotic</u> that garb *(with humor).*

There are archaeological ages given to man's physical history, or the history of the earth, or to the coming or going of the physical events of nature. There are also reincarnational <u>themes</u> that have united people from various centuries. *(Pause.)* Even though many of the negative aspects of those themes may now be highly apparent—as with the Jews and the Christians, the Arabs or whatever— this is because actually those patterns are breaking up in your time. The origi- nal benefits are no longer as readily <u>available</u> as once they were. The itch is still there, but it is harder to scratch.

(9:33.) The strong bonding elements that were once of importance have served their purposes, and no longer soften the more unfortunate beliefs con- nected with such systems' beliefs. They may appear in frenzied outbursts—all the more frenzied—because the original purpose of the culture has deserted it. Its integrity has been undermined. Its reconciling forces no longer really oper- ate, and only its rough edges show.

(Long pause.) Now: the substance *(DMSO)*, used as you are using it, will not do Ruburt any harm, and can be of great value, as it introduces more equi- table bodily motions and sensations that now, with Ruburt's greater under- standing, he can accept, appreciate, and put to fullest benefit.

The short paper he wrote today, and my last session, should help here, for we are speaking of the transformation of the Sinful Self, sympathetically, as it is seen as a psychological structure of growth and change—a stage through which the self traveled—one that is no longer necessary and can now instead turn to a new state of innocence.

You should be able to apply my comments about religion—the Jews and Arabs and so forth—easily to many of your own questions involving contem- porary world behavior.

End of session. Have Ruburt translate your dream *(of July 7)* for you, and then I will comment. I wish you a fond good evening, and an acceleration of dreaming activity. You remember dreams when you are ready to assimilate new knowledge at conscious levels.

End of session once more.

("Thank you. Good night."

(9:43 PM. "Well," Jane laughed, "that's the most comfortable I've been today" —meaning in trance, of course. She's been having trouble lately getting comfortably situated on her end of the couch. She wasn't aware of her right knee, she said, mean- ing that it wasn't bothering her; we'd applied the DMSO to it at 7:30 PM, over two hours ago. I could tell that it had been absorbed, since her skin looked dry now.

(A note: Yesterday Jane had written a complete book outline on The Magical Approach.

(I was pleased by Seth's comments on the DMSO. I'd been thinking that it could hardly be a coincidence that Jane has been getting the Sinful Self material, that

Peggy G. wrote the article about the DMSO in the paper, that the paper carried the ad where we could order it, and that we'd decided to try it at this time....)

DELETED SESSION
JULY 13, 1981 8:33 PM MONDAY

(Jane called me for the session at about 8:10. She was very relaxed—very — but felt Seth around and decided to have a session, or at least try to. She thought Seth might talk about some of the letters she'd answered today, as well as some ideas of her own. During the past week she must have dealt with over 80 letters—with another group answered just before that batch bringing the total to well over 100. The mail appears to have increased in volume, at least for this time of year. It's difficult to tell —although if she takes a couple of weeks off from answering mail, as she had done, then the amount we do get quickly becomes apparent in a new way: sheer bulk.

(Jane's reported what seems to be a general improvement in relaxation since we began using the DMSO a couple of times a day. Today, however, we'd used it but once, on her knees and lower legs. See my separate detailed records. She's had no side effects, yet does have "an increased awareness" of her stomach. This feeling is mostly pleasant, she said, as if she's been holding it tense for some time. Yet I added that we didn't want her developing any internal reactions because of the DMSO, so we decided to keep watch very carefully. I ordered more of the product today, in case we do decide to give it a longer trial.

(8:29: "Boy, I don't know when I've been this relaxed.... I feel that he's ready —all he has to do is get me in shape for the session...." Jane burped loudly for the second time. "You don't have to put that in."

(Once again it was a very warm evening —about 80 degrees, and we had the fan on. Actually it was very pleasant in the house, with all the windows and doors wide open. The evening paper had noted that thundershowers were a possibility.)

Now. Good evening *(whispering.*

("Good evening"—whispering in return.)

I would like to explain more clearly a few ideas that came to Ruburt concerning certain kinds of correspondents, and to explain more clearly some important issues regarding his own situation that also began to come into his mind.

First of all, many of your correspondents' "predicaments" appear particularly disheartening, upsetting, or otherwise psychologically incomprehensible because your general (underlined) belief systems are not flexible enough, and do not reflect many important issues concerning human behavior, motivation, emotion or feeling.

Their definitions in fact squeeze human motivation into an impossibly small tube of action. *(Long pause.)* When that tube of motivation is all squeezed out, the tube is supposed to then become empty. The wide range of actual human experience is far too great for such small packaging. The belief in the struggle for survival so super-pervades that anything but the most competitive, determined, super-valiant, compulsive desire to hold onto life appears to be cowardly, a cop-out, at best an unexplainable, erratic, unnatural response to life's conditions.

(8:43.) In that framework it almost seems as if the most natural wish would be the wish to live one life for some kind of eternal duration. In that framework it seems as if people are cut down in their primes often, despite their own wishes, desires or intents, and it is taken for granted that death is the unde-sired, unwanted, <u>unsought</u> victor over creatures whose natural desires lead them to fight for natural survival at all costs. Certainly this suggests an almost unbear-able cruelty, thrust upon nature's framework. *(Long pause.)* The impulse toward life is indeed strong, brilliant and enduring. Each individual knows, however, that more than one lifetime is involved, and carries within it—as indeed the ani-mals do—the knowledge that earth's existence is in time and space, meaning that a certain turnover is necessarily implied.

Each person experiences time differently. It is not simply that for some time seems to go faster or slower than for others, but that time is <u>used</u> in differ-ent fashions according to the value fulfillment issues with which each individ-ual is concerned and with those of the species as well.

It is not either simply a matter of biological clocks, with some people using their available energies faster. Value fulfillment deals with certain kinds of qualities that must appear in time.

(Long pause.) The purposes and value fulfillment intents of some people are often reached in your terms at a young age. They give to life and receive from life more or less what they intended to, and are quite prepared to die and start anew. In a <u>manner of speaking</u>, now, illnesses also serve as gateways to death in that regard—which may or may not be chosen at any specific time. That is, they are available. No one is forced to <u>enter</u> those gateways. Some people *(pause)* know very well that they have decided to die—or do not care (colon): they may "come down" with severe illnesses and then change their minds because for other reasons the very crises revive them.

They may even seek the experience in order to put their own lives in a dif-ferent, larger perspective, many such people are not fully aware of such deci-sions, and so many face-saving psychological devices are used by the individual, and certainly by society, to smother the recognition of such unofficial motivation. It may then indeed seem to the individual himself or herself that the health crisis is being thrust upon them, unwanted, despite their own wishes or intents.

(Long pause at 9:02.) When people finally want to die they will pursue that intent, because each physical death does indeed come—despite your beliefs—as the final framing or finishing touches or culmination of a given existence.

In those terms it is like a creative venture, finished to the best of one's ability in the given medium, and leaves one with a sense of satisfaction, fulfillment, and completion. *(Long pause.)* One woman wrote Ruburt about the definite healing of her mother from cancer. There were many details given—but overall the woman felt that she herself had made a bargain with God, offering her own life instead of her mother's. The mother recovered under the most unexpected circumstances, and a short time later the daughter came down with the same symptoms.

She seemed to acquiesce to them. She did not feel alarmed. Ruburt wrote that one did not have to bargain with God for one's life—an excellent point. One had only to accept one's life—a second excellent point. Still, Ruburt was uneasy that the woman would accept the situation so calmly. Such recognition seemed almost unnatural: where was her will to live?

(Long pause at 9:12.) Many people, wanting to die, do not seek out illnesses, of course. They may die in their sleep of unexplained heart failure or whatever, or in accidents. They may seek death out in dangerous pursuits. In the framework of general beliefs, however, the natural desire for death is not included in the list of human motivations. Often such a desire comes naturally and passes naturally several times in a lifetime. The clear recognition of such a psychological feeling alone helps such individuals understand their own positions and intents, but usually the feeling itself is forced to go underground because people are so afraid of it. Such a feeling, recognized, can also serve—as it did serve the woman's mother—as a critical point of recognition that the desire to die was triggered not so much *(long pause)* by the feeling of life's completion as by the fact that the individual had set up too many restrictions in life itself—restrictions that were severely cutting back its own possibilities of value fulfillment, or future effective action. In that kind of a case, the situation can serve to reverse the conditions. The person recognizes the restrictions and changes his or her ways accordingly, opening the doorway not into death but to further life and action in this space and time.

(Long pause.) Overall, the psychology of death of course then involves the psychology of life, for people are seeking for a value fulfillment that connects each of their lives—that is, in reincarnational terms.

Following brief insights concerning these ideas, Ruburt found himself mentally making this kind of statement to himself (colon): I accept my natural agility wholeheartedly. I accept my ability to walk normally wholeheartedly. I accept my creative abilities wholeheartedly. I accept my psychic abilities wholeheartedly. I accept the natural ability to relax normally, wholeheartedly. I accept my characteristics wholeheartedly.

Now these are powerful and "magical" statements, and as Ruburt made them mentally he could psychologically feel his agreement with any given one, and also the degree with which in the past he had <u>not</u> wholeheartedly accepted those abilities, but had set up certain restrictions about them—so a new flash in communication was set up, and new recognition came into his conscious mind. Those statements can be used now to full advantage.

Children accept life wholeheartedly. They do not qualify it. The woman who had cancer and was cured gave up the restrictions she had placed about her life. Nothing in nature is wasted. There is no such thing as a wasted life, no matter how it might appear, and while the desire for death is a natural one, it can also serve at various stages as one that <u>extends</u> any given life for a while by clearing away old debris. The desire actually works for the purpose of value fulfillment, whether it can be pursued more fully in this life, or whether it is time to begin a new one.

Such a desire may come in cycles, just as the desire for action and excitement may come in cycles. Ruburt is at an excellent point now to use those statements, for they will act as magical learning devices.

End of session, and a <u>fond</u> good evening.

("Thank you very much. Good night.")

(9:36—Jane, coming out of trance, put her glasses on—then took them off.)

One small note: the same kind of statements can now be used to advantage as far as you are concerned, involving any particular symptom at any given time.

You might say, for example: "I accept the beautiful steadiness of my hand," then see what feelings you have.

Good evening.

("Thank you.")

(9:38 PM. Jane said that after she did the mail today she got a few quick insights that Seth went into much more. "Then I gave myself those statements as I went to bed for my nap. I could feel a certain amount of resistance, to varying degrees, to some of the statements. You can't verbalize it, but it was illuminating and helpful. I suppose because you thought you could overcome it, and it was afterward that I got so relaxed. But in this case I felt that Seth could lay it out for me better than I

could. I'm glad I held the session after all.")

SESSION 931 (DELETED PORTION)
JULY 15, 1981   8:37 PM WEDNESDAY

(The following material is from the 931st session.

(Today, for the first time since we received it on July 7, we didn't apply DMSO to any portion of Jane's anatomy. I thought it a good idea, myself, so when she slept until 10:30, and then became busy talking to Frank Longwell about the conversion of our front porch to a glassed-in affair, I didn't ask that she try any. Her stomach was okay except for a couple of brief episodes of that strange feeling mentioned in my own DMSO notes, so we don't know really whether or not the drug has any connection with the stomach sensations after all. Jane did experience feelings of panic when she moved from her chair to the bed, and on another occasion. She hadn't wanted to try getting on the bed from her chair, but I talked her into making the effort, and she did very well. She was quite relieved.

(9:57.) Ruburt's paper *(of today)* can be of great value to him. The statements of the Sinful Self show him clearly the reasons <u>why</u> he was afraid of pursuing the unknown, and afraid therefore of using his own natural abilities freely and safely.

Those statements should not go underground, again, but he should sympathetically address his doubts and the various points of their contentions can then be quite adequately settled—or at least resolved, reconciled.

Now I bid you a fond good evening—and all of these affairs will end up with noted physical improvements. End of session, and—the dream *(of mine)* will not go by the board, either.

("Okay. Good night."

(10:00 PM.)

DELETED SESSION
JULY 17, 1981 8:47 PM FRIDAY

(This session came about because of a phone call I took today from the publicity department at Prentice-Hall. The young girl made an innocent-enough request about Jane doing a radio-phone interview with a station in Houston, Texas. A few weeks earlier Jane had tentatively okayed with publicity the idea of doing an occasional radio-phone interview, based on the condition that first she obtain one of those

*desk microphones/telephones so that she **didn't** have to hold the phone for an hour or more. She's tried once to locate the equipment, but failed.*

(She's received several recent requests for such interviews from or through Prentice-Hall, and the call this morning brought the matter to a head. When I called Jane at 10:30 and told her about the proposal, I could see that the idea of it made her uneasy. I finally realized that she didn't really want to do such shows anymore, no matter whether the Sinful Self was involved or not. It came to me that this dilemma was the reason for her much worse hand and arm discomfort: She can barely hold the telephone now, and has much trouble typing. [I've also noticed that she keeps such requests lying around on her desk for days before answering them in the negative. I've seen her carry such envelopes from room to room with her work, even.]

(I did want the situation resolved, however, because I could see it drifting toward a larger hassle with Tam and publicity at Prentice-Hall. Prentice-Hall was bound to be confused about our motives and intents, and also there was the latest evidence that the uncertainty or resistance would lead to aggravated symptoms on Jane's part.

(What particularly upset me about the flap over publicity was that I saw in it a repetition of past ways of refusing to meet challenges head on involved with the psychic work. I finally understood that Jane didn't want to do any work involving publicity or interviews, and that for years now she's bitterly—if unwittingly —resisted such demands, and that these unresolved pressures were having a devastating effect upon her physically. This was all behavior I still could not really comprehend.

(For several days now I'd been thinking about a remark of Seth's in one of the earliest of this group of sessions, to the effect that Jane's symptoms would get worse before they got better as we tried to cope with them. I've wished, often that I'd asked him to elaborate at the time—or at least marked the session so that I could find the remark later. Well, now Jane's symptoms are worse. Before the session began I tried to locate the remark, but couldn't. I felt considerable frustration, and finally laid the book aside. "Well, I hope I don't ever have to find a specific remark in these sessions any more, "because it's becoming impossible."

(Meaning, of course, that the sessions have grown so extensive that they've become a closed system in themselves; without an index it's now very difficult to track down specific material. I gave up my few attempts at indexing years ago, and now don't even make notes on the index pages any more.

("But it's the same old story," I told Jane when I asked that she have a session tonight, to deal with her hands and arms, and Seth's remark. "I'm the one who's asking for it, not you." What I wondered, of course, was why she wasn't the one who demanded the help.

(One of the obvious reasons, I thought, was that the portions of the personali-

ty that were acting up became so powerful that they prevented or subverted a simple thing like asking for help to deal with a problem or challenge. Whatever struggles lay behind the hand and arm symptoms, for example, adopted their own protective armor, resistant to change....)

Good evening.

("Good evening.")

Now. I will answer your main question this evening—but I will approach that material of course in my own way, and I will begin by reminding you of some important issues mentioned before.

First of all, children seek enjoyment. They recognize that enjoyment and self-satisfaction are important gateways to the development of their abilities. You drew because drawing gave you pleasure. Ruburt wrote for the same reason. You did not draw or paint because you felt a responsibility to do so.

That kind of enjoyment provides the child with a feeling for its own center. The child becomes self-directed as it learns to follow those pursuits that particularly increase its own individual sense of enjoyment and satisfaction. It might be important that the child learn to put off enjoyment for a period of time, to extend the period between desire and gratification *(long pause)*. Such a period might include a training period, for example, where piano lessons might have to be taken before a concerto can be played.

Even then, however, the enjoyment of the act—in that case playing the piano—is paramount. The sense of enjoyment however does increase and extend individual abilities, and those impulses leading toward enjoyment are meant to serve each individual with a private inbuilt avenue of expression that will help center the person within himself, and within the world—and again, in such a way that both the self and the society are benefited.

(Long pause.) These issues are extremely vital in cases of creativity also, although they operate in all areas. The good parent, for example, is motivated by a sense of enjoyment and fulfillment, in which case his or her "responsibilities" are almost automatically reinforced and performed. People usually talk about what they should do only because they have forgotten how to remember what they want to do.

For some years, to varying extents, Ruburt and you also to a lesser degree became motivated by ideas of who you should (underlined) be, what you should (underlined) be doing, and what your responsibilities were. That tendency became stronger as our "work" became better known. To some extent—with some important variances, having to do with quite legitimate ideas of art—such feelings have also been behind many of your own responses to, say, the appearance of the books, as public packages in the world *(intently)*. In Ruburt's case the idea of responsibility became far more pervasive, resulting in what I have referred to as being almost a <u>superself image</u>—an image composed of his ideas of the kind of person he <u>should</u> (underlined) be in his position. That image largely at least ignored his own likes or dislikes. He felt he should do many things, for example, that he did not really like to do at all. Small doses of such attitudes can be handled, of course: people do not have to be entirely satisfied with their own performances in order to be reasonably happy and healthy. Remember that you react to interior events, not just to physical ones.

(9:08.) In the main you do what you want to do. Your idea of responsibility may give you a very poor rating, however, in your own eyes for your practical performance in life. The idea of responsibility, <u>as it is understood</u> (underlined), is at its heart other-directed. It may even lead to the idea that the enjoyment of the self alone is wrong. Often chronic physical problems are the end result of such dilemmas. Ruburt felt for years <u>that he should</u> (underlined) become a more public person, do workshops, television shows, radio tours or whatever—<u>that he should </u>(underlined) nearly perform miracles in the psychic arena, that he should have a large class, that he should hold as many sessions for others as possible. Those ideas come to him constantly, of course, or those suggestions, through the mail, the expectations of others, or his observation.

He feels somewhat guilty because he stopped holding his large class at 458 West Water Street, thinking that such a change represented a retreat from an action he should have continued. He stopped when the class became too public, too large—and therefore out-of-keeping with the requirements of his own nature *(intently.*

(Long pause.) As creative people, and as certain kinds of creative people — not being audience performers as musicians, for example—you deal with the creative construction of artistic worlds in which as your friend *(painter)* William Alexander would say, you are the master magician perhaps—but it is your world primarily, created according to your vision. All of the activities that bring you the largest pleasure in life generally are of that nature. This does not mean that you do not enjoy companionship, or that you do not have a give-and-take with society.

Ruburt began to feel a pressure as the books became better known to carry out a kind of responsibility, not simply to sell books, for example, but to get the message out into the world, to help others—all considerations that seemed to be—he thought—the acceptance of adult behavior on his part: actions that would be more or less expected of him. Again, they were actions that to a large degree went against the grain. They could be <u>performed</u>, however, to some extent, at least some of them, and he could on occasion enjoy them, and he did well enough, for example, with public speaking or the few shows that you did.

I gave you a session not too long ago dealing with the natural person, and specifically with Ruburt's natural characteristics. I outlined the ways in which he naturally behaved. This other-directed superself image, however, largely of social construction, superimposes the idea of responsibility over the idea of enjoyment, and in many cases is in direct contradiction as far as Ruburt's natural tendencies are concerned.

He writes because he wants to create a unique world, one in which during the act of creation as a creator he is in charge, and yet while he is in charge he is in contact with a certain magic of creativity that gives him experience with greater realms of being. People of that nature have very private ways, and to some extent now those ways involve a deliberate *(long pause)* repudiation of the ordinary world—not that they need to stop relating to it, but that they must momentarily forget it in light of another vision. This applies to you as well as to Ruburt. *(All very intently.)* You do not feel the need to go on tours, for example.

(9:38.) In a way, Ruburt's symptoms ended up as providing a system of controls, serving in several rather than one area, but areas that he is now exploring in rather concentrated form. The symptoms did serve partially as face-saving devices, and for both of you to some extent, to explain behavior of your own that perhaps you did not understand—though this largely involves Ruburt's behavior, of course.

Why didn't he go on television like other psychics, or have an organization, or at least have workshops, or seek out learned men and women "in the field," when it seemed that the dictates of normal behavior would suggest such activity?

No conscious decisions were ever really clearly made, because Ruburt felt that ideally (underlined), if he were giving himself true freedom and being true to all his abilities, he would and should be performing in such a manner. He would naturally want to be at least on the most intelligent of television shows, for example, or speak to those groups for which he had some respect.

The fact is, however, that he is himself a different kind of person. The radio shows were the least bothersome. He at least could do those at home. He did not want (underlined) particularly to do any of them, though he enjoyed most of them once he began. What he enjoyed, however, was the radio's fairly secret quality—the fact that he was hidden, and yet his voice went out into the world.

As he began to understand to some degree that he need not be expected to do tours and so forth, he thought of the radio shows as alternate ways of fulfilling his responsibility. The information I gave about his arms in the past was correct. It is also true, however, that his hands and arms became more aggravated in their condition precisely because <u>he did not want to be able to hold the phone</u> to do an hour show. In response, he thought about a gadget that would automatically allow him to speak without holding the phone for so long—this in response to Prentice's latest project. Tam hinted some time ago that additional ads and advertising to that effect would probably take place. Chronic physical disabilities and problems drag on in a certain fashion because they serve many purposes, and the last groups of sessions show the interior and exterior kinds of <u>controls</u> that those symptoms have provided.

Ruburt has been working with them on a much more conscious level. The stability of the system of course is threatened. The difficulty with Ruburt's arms and hands bother his typing now, showing him finally <u>in no uncertain terms</u> that the system has served its purpose long ago, and that his creativity is dependent upon psychological and physical mobility. The symptoms have been aggravated to some extent, then, bringing to the forefront of his mind the very problems that require his attention.

I do not mean to make derogatory statements concerning your social world. Generally speaking, however, the kind of person who performs as a public figure is not the kind of person who could produce highly creative material of an <u>original</u> nature. The public format requires a kind of social shorthand that does not allow for the development or expansion of ideas or creativity, so that the attempt to explain anything like "our work" would be extremely difficult in that regard. We are not speaking to the mass world, and television is set up for the mass audience, for the other-directed part of people.

Ruburt did well today, and made the proper decisions finally, being much more aware of his own psychological mobility as his moods and his <u>body statements</u> changed. The idea of the letter was excellent, and represented your contribution *(to Prentice-Hall)*. Your own difficulty with notes on our books or whatever comes mainly when you forget your own self-directedness and sense of enjoyment, and replace those with a sense of responsibility.

In Ruburt's case throughout these years, the <u>idea</u> of responsibility took over too much prominence. *(Long pause.)* His difficulties with inspiration arise when he forgets his ideas of natural enjoyment and replaces those with the idea that "he has a responsibility to use his abilities"—as if he would not fulfill them motivated by his own enjoyment and love.

The overdone sense of responsibility can erode love and satisfaction. Ruburt "loved" to do housework at one time. Later his ideas of responsibility told him he should be working—not because he <u>wanted</u> to be working, but because he <u>should</u> be. At the same time those same worldly concerns led him to wonder about the validity of his own "messages"—and how responsible he was to the world for them—so the symptoms also served to give him a greater sense of caution, to <u>temper</u> creativity, for all the reasons stated in the Sinful-Self material.

(10:13.) Your joint decision to tackle the entire situation shook the status quo, of course. It does also represent the highest therapeutic value, however, as such issues are brought out into the open. Ruburt is learning to understand that it is safe to be himself; he must learn to rediscover the sources of his own pleasure, for these provide the most dependable indications by which actions and decisions can be taken.

Have I answered your questions for you?

("You did on the hands and arms, but how about more on the remark you made in that past session, about Jane's symptoms getting worse before they get better?")

I did believe that I had answered that question this evening, specifically concerning the radio interviews, but also pertaining to the entire matter of Prentice publicity for the books just published.

("Okay.")

End of session. You will find there is more in it than perhaps you see presently, and my heartiest wishes to you both.

Ruburt is just about over those intensifications of symptoms, however, they could be expected simply because the old ideas were being consistently threatened, which added some additional stress. Overall, however, he did not back down, but has persevered.

End of session.

(10:20 PM. The session had been excellent—so excellent that I'd felt like interjecting many questions as Seth preceded along: one of those times when I had a hard time not injecting myself, with my own impatience, into the session. I did explode at its end briefly, however, and Jane sat silently while I ranted and raved.

(Upon thinking it over—it's now Sunday afternoon as I finish typing the session—I now believe that I should have said little or nothing, and I became concerned lest I undid, or tried to, what progress Jane has managed to achieve lately. I was angry at session's end, however, with the fact that she had responded to the publicity dilemma with aggravated hand and arm symptoms, and that it had taken me so long myself to realize what was going on. It made me question what we were doing generally, that such an obvious response should escape our notice. All of this is based on my deep concern for what has befallen Jane—or, more truthfully, what she has created for herself with my cooperation.

(I do think that it will all serve a valuable purpose, however, if we clear up the one major stumbling block over publicity—whether to do or not to do it. If we have *solved that dilemma, well and good. Earlier I asked Jane if she was willing to stick by her decision to forgo public life, as stated in the letter she wrote Prentice today, and she said yes. I certainly am, let the chips fall where they may. I for one have no real idea of how Prentice-Hall may react, although Jane told me today that she's picked up that Prentice-Hall plans to be much more aggressive on questions concerning publicity. I don't think there will be any hassle, for surely the people at Prentice-Hall know enough about Jane's abilities and sales and productive talents to know a good thing when they have one, whether or not publicity is involved.*

(A note: Jane did tell me Saturday that she's noticed an improvement in her hands and arms, and also in her ability to get onto the bed from her chair, since we made the decision to not do publicity.)

DELETED SESSION
JULY 20, 1981   9:16 PM MONDAY

(See the enclosed four pages Jane wrote covering her activities for the last weekend. Although she says it's incomplete, it still summarizes her activities better than I can do second-handedly. I can add to Jane's paper that we went over last Friday's session together Saturday night after I'd finished typing it, and discussed a number of points rather specifically. Jane ended up somewhat upset, and so did I in a way. But also that discussion resulted in some later insights on Jane's part, and I believe turned up in some of her poetry, which has been excellent lately.

(At 8:30 I asked Jane what her plans for the evening were. She said she'd have a session, after I explained that I was interested in Seth giving some information on her hearing, swollen feet, and what seemed to be some reactions she was having to our use of the DMSO. We've more or less decided to forgo the use of the drug temporarily because of those reactions, which aren't serious but which leave her feeling somewhat disoriented, with a strange feeling in her stomach, and lower back discomfort.

(Jane didn't particularly look like she wanted to hold a session, though, and said she felt some resistance to the idea. I went into the writing room to do some filing. Eventually she called me, saying she would have the session. When I went back into the living room I told her that we must be doing something wrong, or that we'd have achieved much better results over the years regarding her symptoms. "I think it's something we're blind to, that's right in front of us all the time, but we can't see it," I said. I reminded her of the stories one hears about the chronically ill, who run from doctor to doctor with no intention of getting well, because their illness serves purposes in the present. "Something like that," I said. "I never could believe that the first

few years of a person's life could have that much of an effect upon the rest of the person's life. It doesn't seem right, or natural, that an individual might have to spend say fifty years suffering in life for things that happened to him when he was a child, say; I don't think nature would arrange things that way—it's too self-defeating...." These are points we've discussed before, of course.

(I began to get a fresh insight to the symptom situation as we talked, hardly realizing that I was doing so. "It's just that the symptoms show that you're a human being like everyone else," I speculated. "They show that you're not ensconced on high, telling everyone else what to do through Seth, telling <u>them</u> how to handle all of their problems while you live a life of wealth, talent, and happiness, free of all worldly cares and responsibilities," I added.

(Now that idea, I thought as I went into the kitchen to get Jane some wine for the session, made sense—it could account for the perpetuation of her symptoms on a daily, present-life basis, and made a lot more sense than thinking she was suffering now because of something that happened to her when she was perhaps eight years old or whatever. In other words, I said, we'd been approaching the problem backwards: Jane wasn't sick so much because of her past as she was because of what we were doing every day in present reality—reinforcing and/or perpetuating the symptoms because they served a number of beliefs about present-day reality. I included myself in these speculations, of course. I thought I was onto something from a fresh viewpoint, and at the same time was afraid that we'd heard it all before and that the idea meant little. It was also difficult to visualize clearly enough so that it was not merely a repetition of old ideas, but a new slant on those old ideas.

("So you're in trouble," I said, "because that situation makes the Seth material legitimate. How could you possibly understand people's troubles unless you had pretty severe ones yourself—with my cooperation? No one can ever accuse you of handing down great insights from a position of being above it all.... You can say, 'Look, folks. I have my hassles too.'"

(Obviously, many facets of these ideas have been discussed many times. There was something new here, though, I thought, when one postulated that Seth as we knew him was acceptable <u>because</u> of the symptoms. Acceptable <u>and</u> accessible. Dealing with our personal situations was taking up more and more of our time. Strange, I thought, if it turned out that personal work would be one of the most creative of all the uses to which the Seth material could be put, rather than grandiose pronouncements coming down from on high, dispensed by one who was in a position of superiority.

(Jane surprised me after I said most of what I had to say by adding that she thought our attitudes about <u>children</u> also had something to do with the symptoms — a connection that I could say had never occurred to me. It seemed like a strange idea

to me, but I didn't have time to think about it at the moment. I didn't have time to really think about what I'd been saying myself, but I hoped there was something to it, and that discussing it would offer her some help in the form of improved health. For some time now I'd thought, often, that it could be that she wanted to be sick — that that was the role she'd chosen for this life, that in many ways all of our efforts to get out from under the symptoms were really beside the point. My latest insight, that the symptoms offered legitimacy to the Seth material, was, I hoped, itself legitimate.

(Jane said she thought Seth might discuss our discussion, as well as the three other questions I'd mentioned about her feet, and so forth. I also had questions about some of my recent dreams, including the one of July 7 that Seth had promised to comment upon, but I had little hope that he'd get into that material tonight.)

(Slowly, with many pauses at times:)

Now: I will answer your questions this evening—but rather than begin with them I would like to make some general comments about your own observation immediately before the session, and in a fairly neutral manner.

Even before our sessions began, you both knew that generally speaking, now, you were quite different from other people, highly gifted creatively and intellectually. You suspected that you were not as "mired" *(long pause)* as other people were, and also that in some fashion you were not as committed to usual (underlined) physical experience. You felt sometimes as if you wanted to spy upon life, observe it rather than live it directly. This was not because you were afraid of life *(as I often wondered when I was younger)*, but because your purposes and intents were different.

The usual framework of married life with children was not to be a part of your experience this time, and both of you took pains to see that you did not have children—or mates that wanted them. To some extent you both felt guilty that a certain kind of clear knowledge seemed so naturally and clearly available. Your own physical attributes and sports proficiency saw that kind of extension physically translated. To a lesser degree, Ruburt's agility, his performance as a dancer and so forth, gave him the feeling that even physical achievements carried an ease that many did not possess. You did not feel, however, as if you particularly related well with other people, and as you grew older it seemed that any changes would have to come from you *(not others.*

(Long pause at 9:30.) It might be fairly easy, Ruburt suspected, to become even contemptuous of others. You both felt, again to some degree, that people could not understand your particular kinds of creativity. They could easily become jealous. They could also highly resent your abilities. You both felt an honest and deep compassion for other people, however: even winning in a sports event, you felt sorry for the loser.

(Very slowly:) For a while you (underlined) considered the possibility of adopting a "handicap," such as one might in sports. You tried the role on for size, deciding finally that you could not accept it *(my back trouble at 458, etc.)*.

Ruburt picked up the idea instead, and toyed with it. When the sessions started you were both amazed at the ease with which the material was received, struck by its quality, aware at certain levels of its challenge. Ruburt was astonished, and became more so at the spontaneous nature of his own and my creativity. *(Long pause.)* There were certain deep questions about life, certain pressing problems about man's condition, with which you felt you had little experience, since your primary goals had been to examine life, to stand apart from it to study it, And therefore you both felt that you had few of the same concerns as those that led other people *(quietly intent)*.

You did not have the family concerns of children, as Ruburt mentioned. Without such concerns, you began to feel that you had an even more unfair advantage. *(Long pause.)* In the meantime, all of the issues we have mentioned as being connected with Ruburt's symptoms of course were present to one extent or another, in abeyance. You wanted to ask the kind of questions that were important to other people, beside questions of your own, because the meaning of life itself lay also in other areas than your own. You also wanted a bridge and protective coloration.

Ruburt received certain kinds of knowledge by taking various jobs throughout his early adulthood, including factory work or whatever. That knowledge was used in all of his writing. On a certain level he took those jobs because he needed money, not because he needed experience in other lines of work or with other kinds of people. When he sold Avon he was hearing the questions that his own work would later try to answer. He could not have faked pretending to need the jobs, or it would not have worked, so neither of you could pretend to have physical difficulties so that you could, for example, put yourselves in other peoples' shoes.

(9:51.) Yet, so it seemed to you, one of you would have to make such an effort. You needed extra impetus—again so it seemed—lest your relative nonattachment to life's conditions kept you from a sympathetic understanding of your fellow man.

These involved large vital issues regarding the nature of suffering. Neither of you had been vitally (underlined) touched by war. You experienced certain portions of it. You have that in common with your generation, but you had not been severely injured, or even—if the truth had been known—severely put out. Ruburt had been touched hardly at all. You were not to share the experience of violence.

(Long pause.) Your purposes meant that you required a certain amount of isolation from the world—so any handicap that was accepted would also be one that fit into those other purposes.

(Long pause.) All of the ideas of the Sinful Self had been in abeyance— *(10:00. The telephone rang, and at Seth's urging I answered it. Margaret Bumbalo told me she and her husband were going up to their cottage on the lake; they asked that I take in their mail.)*

—They were simply brushed up and renewed. They represented a kind of <u>psychological</u> handicap. The situation also helped serve to explain, you felt particularly in the beginning, oddities of your own behaviors in regard to society. When you gave up your job you did not have to explain why you did not have to find another as "any normal red-blooded male should do," but stayed at home devoted to a time of painting and philosophy. You also had a wife to look after who had physical difficulties.

If you wanted to monitor the number of people who came to the house, or the publicity involved, the symptoms provided a built-in framework. If you wanted deeply wrought psychological statements, the symptoms also provided a framework around which they could occur—an <u>inner</u> framework of personal sessions devoted to the workings of personality, an inner library beside the books themselves, that perhaps you would not otherwise think of without such an impetus.

(Long pause.) <u>In a way</u>, to a degree—the qualifications are necessary—you provided yourselves an extra kind of commitment that would keep your observations of life from becoming too surface, or so it seemed. When your parents were alive, <u>their</u> problems could be used somewhat in a second-handed fashion for the same purposes. Before that, jobs for both of you served to make you rub elbows, so to speak, with others, and to equalize your paths and theirs. As you became better off financially you felt the need again for that kind of equalization, or handicap.

(10:12.) Now: Ruburt's hearing is not impeded *(long pause)*, meaning that he is not losing his hearing. That condition was also related to the telephone one, adding the extra difficulty of clearly hearing a television—or rather radio— program, and the hearing difficulty was aggravated along with the hands.

Both of you—to some extent, now, following this evening's discussion — felt that with two books and perhaps even the poetry book coming out in one year, people would think it was easy enough for you to write your pronouncements from the hilltop, even though in those books you made certain that you mentioned any and all difficulties that came your way, collected your stories of hassles with scientists or publishers, and so forth.

The substance you are using *(DMSO)* acts <u>in its way</u>, now, almost like a shock treatment, introducing certain parts of the body to a relaxation that <u>feels</u> unnatural because it is not gradual. The body does not feel stable, for example. *(Long pause.)* That effect is somewhat aggravated by hot weather, by Ruburt's way of using energy, and because he is physically a small person. A larger person with more body area and weight would be less affected, for example, as say with alcohol.

(10:23.) End of session.

("Can you say something about the feet?")

I will indeed. Give us a moment.

(Long pause.) The feet are connected with the overall situation itself. In that they want greater activity and circulation. <u>More</u> exercising of the feet will be of benefit. On a physical level alone the heat is also somewhat connected. You used this <u>period</u>, however, yourselves, as a time to critically aggravate the symptoms *(long pause)*, almost as if you were looking over a body of work to see what you thought of it, and what you wanted to do next.

It is no coincidence that you examine the nature of our books or your notes on the one hand, and Ruburt's symptoms on the other.

End of session.

("Okay."

(10:30 PM. Jane had done well. I was encouraged that Seth too found something to talk about in my insight of just before the session. Later, I supposed that Jane's recovery—even if only to a degree—could <u>also</u> be taken as a sign of the legitimacy of the Seth material, since she'd be using it to see her way clear to bring about that recovery. That's the way I for one would like to see things work out.

(A note added Wednesday evening, as I finish typing the session:

(A situation developed Tuesday evening—last night—as I planned to begin typing this session. The event reinforced much of the material in the session itself, and my idea that had brought it about: As Jane and I were finishing supper last night Tom D'Orio from Binghamton visited us with two of his friends [they had a small Seth group going at home]. Tom is an "old" ESP class member. Jane evidently enjoyed talking to the three of them, and before we knew it over an hour had passed, whereas I'd originally asked Tom and company not to stay long because we were busy. It was around 9 PM when they finally left, and although I was getting tired I stuck to it and typed the first two pages of notes for this session while I kept in mind what I wanted to put down. Jane then read them and agreed with them.

(As we made ready for bed at the usual time, Jane said she "wanted to talk." She revealed that she'd thought of having a session for the three visitors. This surprised me. [She'd also thought of having a session before their arrival, so that Seth could con-

tinue the material he'd started Monday; she hadn't told me this.]

(Jane said that the reasons she didn't have a session for Tom and friends were that her own feelings were against her doing so even though she'd had the spontaneous urge, and that she was also tired because of her symptoms and sitting on the couch for so long. She also was afraid I'd get mad if she did such a thing. She very accurately pointed out that she'd used the symptoms, then, to keep the gathering under control according to our everyday ideas. It had never occurred to me, for example, that she'd consider such a spontaneous session these days—nor had she for years. She said she was also afraid that she'd keep the group here at the house for hours if she let herself go and did what she wanted to do, on the spur of the moment.

(So it seems that we do use the symptoms to serve our own ends, according to our current beliefs. Yet now there's been a change, or at least a thought about a change: "But I don't think having a spontaneous session would be all that bad," she said, "if by being spontaneous I got set free." Indeed. In the immediate past I would have automatically been against—or at least not in favor of—such a session for relative strangers on short notice. I would have been tonight, also, had I even thought of it—that is, I would have negated such a performance until I had the chance to study the implications of my reactions, in the light of my insight of Monday night, and Seth's excellent session following that insight.

("Now, I wouldn't care if you walked on the ceiling, if it did any good," I said. We talked about the fun we used to have on Friday nights at 458, years ago, when the sessions had just gotten underway, and Jane often spontaneously let Seth come through. Those times had had an innocence that we'd lost along the way. [Earlier Monday night, before the session, I'd asked Jane how one could "be a child again," while retaining the valuable elements from the subsequent events in life, but keeping that original clarity and simplicity of vision.] I'd been thinking primarily of painting.

(We did take Tom's address and phone number, Jane telling him that she might invite him and friends to the house some Friday night, with others. I explained to her in the bedroom that part of my initial resistance to Tom staying so long was my desire to start typing this session, which I consider very useful.

(I added another thought—that often lately I've reminded myself that I'm 10 years older than she is; at 62 I've managed during the last decade to say "the hell with it" to a lot of things that I used to pay a lot of attention to when I was 52, Jane's present age. I'd had that extra time to work some things out. Jane said she knew this. It seems that in recent years one of my main goals in life has been to pare down—or eliminate outright—a number of ideas and obligations and hassles that I'd finally realized weren't worth the time to retain. Each time I manage to dispense of something that way, I regard it as an achievement. Now, I told her, I want to spend my

time on the few things I consider important in life.)

JANE'S NOTES
JULY 17-19, 1981 "THE WEEKEND"

These particular events began Friday though now Monday afternoon I've nearly forgotten what Friday was really like. I do recall being awakened by Rob later Friday than usual. He told me that Prentice had called about a radio-phone show and that I was to return the call. I was aware of some dismay. I didn't want to be bothered; now that I'd recently agreed to do some such shows, everyone it seemed would start calling. Resolutely I replaced the issue in my mind by trying to compose a limerick....

I think it was that late morning that Margaret, our neighbor, dropped in late morning to tell us she and Joe would be heading for their cottage, but somewhere I got it in my head that it would be one of those summer weekends when people prowled around—found excuses to go to malls or visit strange towns or just wander the streets or through public buildings—or visit here, if there were any fans in the nearby locality.

I hemmed and hawed, decided after talking with Rob that I really didn't want to do any shows at all, so I wrote one letter so informing Prentice. In the meantime I was impatiently waiting Frank Longwell who promised the Tuesday earlier that he'd be here before Sunday with the final plans for extending the living room. He never came.

The phone rang, though. Peg G. from the Star Gazette called; there was a fan from South Africa, just in town from NYC to see me. He was right there waiting, would I talk to him at least—on the phone? My whole arm hurt as I picked up the receiver.... I'd been right about people prowling around all right!

Peg told me he was in his forties; he told her he'd written me but probably left before I could answer the letter. I felt defensive and guilty; he was trying emotional blackmail, and I didn't want to see him. But I thought of him, a stranger, in the newspaper office of a strange town....

"Hello," I said when he came to the phone, and <u>his</u> voice was dull and flat, full of self pity; he was sure I wouldn't see him. And instead of rousing sympathy in me his downcast mood had the opposite effect; I don't care if you came from Timbuktu by refugee ship, I thought. His call reminded me finally of his letter and my response that I wouldn't be able to see him during his trip. I said some usual polite things in a usual polite voice and that was that. The next day I learned from Peg that he'd come by bus, had to stay the night, didn't have much money—his reality, I

reminded myself firmly, not mine. Still, vaguely uneasy I called off a half-planned evening of company with friends—luckily before I'd actually invited them, and we had a Seth session instead, still another in an effort to get me out of my own physical problems. This one was at Rob's suggestion.

Most of the material disappeared instantly, like some dreams, but I did remember that Seth told me to stress pleasure over responsibility and that thought was in my mind as I fell to sleep Friday PM.

Enjoyment instead of responsibility: I determined to try that out Saturday, and I did enjoy myself writing a new poem; the theme—pleasure! I also typed up a few pages of material (on the Sinful Self.) Still, no Frank Longwell.

While Rob went shopping, I did some mail and on his return we fixed a roast chicken dinner, put it in the oven and took a nap. We hardly tasted the dinner because two "fans" came just as Rob set the chicken on the table. They were nice young men though; we liked then and they stayed perhaps an hour. No sooner did they leave, and we began dessert, though, than Debbie arrived at the door to tell us about a pretty nutty character who had just called her, looking for our address. She stayed for about an hour....

Sunday AM it was nearly raining. Rob fixed my hair. Still no Frank Longwell, but that afternoon I suddenly wrote one poem and began another that fascinated me. Was it somehow already translated Sumari? Connected with the Speakers Manuscript, maybe with some other material I'd been getting lately? And I kept scribbling The Pleasure Principle in my small notebook. What did that mean? In the bedroom for a nap I did another verse of the poem and suddenly understood that physically I'd gotten in the habit of identifying myself with pain instead of pleasure. So obvious once I realized it, but the insight made several issues clear at once.

I put the statement together with the little I recalled from Seth's session and then spent a few minutes feeling my body sensations: right knee—sore; arms—sore. My neck and certain parts of my back felt satiny and relaxed though and I'd ignored those feelings concentrating on the knee in particular.... and now even that sensation felt like an exaggerated or aggravated.... block of energy.

I thought of the many other people who must do the same thing if not with body sensations perhaps with events of other kinds. And I remembered things I'd written in old Contents of the Mind *notes about how we form focuses through which we then experience reality....*

In the meantime another excellent verse for my poem came to mind plus the phrase, the body of pleasure and the magical impetus....

Monday AM, July 20. I call Tam, saying I won't do any shows. He says that's okay! Tells me a big shot at Bantam called liking God of Jane *and inquiring about paperback rights, assures me our paperbacks are selling okay.*

DELETED SESSION
JULY 23, 1981 8:18 PM THURSDAY

(No session was held last night: Jane wanted to rest and also watch a 3 hour synopsis of the TV show Dynasty *while she caught up on the mail.*

(This afternoon while I was out doing errands, Jane had a rather strong if not lengthy experience that seemed to encompass an emotional understanding of Seth's material in the last session [for Monday]. She's already reread that session three times, and so have I. This time she got the emotional content of it, though, and scribbled a few lines while it lasted, perhaps 10 minutes. Tears were involved, or nearly so. She was coming out of it as I came back into the house. As we talked about it, each from a somewhat different angle, Jane ended up saying the experience seemed pretty "prosaic" after all in retrospect—yet at the time it had been pretty powerful.

(Both of us have been curious as to how the material in Monday night's session fits in with that on the Sinful Self, which Jane still hasn't typed except for the first five pages. I'm somewhat handicapped because I don't have the Sinful Self material to compare anything to, but I'm sure there are many connections between the two. I'd planned to write down some questions for tonight, based on Monday's session, but had so many actually that I decided to let that project go, trusting that Seth will cover them in his own way.

(One of the questions concerned Seth's material on page 218 of the last session, when he referred to the feeling that Jane and I have, that we had "an even more unfair advantage" without children—this, as he'd stated earlier, on top of our already being set apart from others because of our creative gifts. "It's like you've got to atone for being "better" or different than others, according to that kind of thinking," I said at 8:10. "It's the sort of thing I think is rooted in Sinful-Self stuff, on both of our parts—you're not going to feel guilty about the gifts of nature unless those feelings have a pretty strong base in the psyche, somewhere.... Why can't we feel glad *about being gifted instead?" I added that as I'd said this afternoon, guilt about superiority would make a lot of gifted people miserable if they paid attention to such thinking. And I'm afraid that history contains numerous examples wherein that very reaction has taken place. I realize that the very handicaps adopted could also be part of the given personality's overall plan for life—contending with* that *as well as the gifts.*

(Tonight as we waited for the session to begin I showed Jane my three recent dreams that I was interested in having Seth comment upon: July 7 [Sayre], 17 [reincarnation and Debbie Janney], and 19 [Jane recovering overnight]. Jane looked them over again, although she'd read them this afternoon. I've started a small oil painting based on the "chute" portion of the dream for July 7. I've also done a pencil sketch of one of the heads in the photos of myself in the reincarnational dream of

July 17, in case I don't get to paint it.

("All right," Jane finally said as she took off her glasses and began speaking for Seth with many long pauses:)

Now: I would like to recall some of your earlier history.

(Long pause.) Your mother believed that a man should work so many hours a day in conventional ways, whether he owned his own business or worked for others—and also of course that he should have a family. At certain levels (underlined), your brother Loren once compared your art to his love of trains—an enjoyable hobby, but not something to which a man devoted his life.

Even your father's originality was of the most practical variety. You had that kind of background to work with and against, then, and this well before the sessions started. They did add an important new link, though. The framework was loosely set up back in that time, however, when for a while, again, you toyed with the idea, for such symptoms would "justify" your staying home even part-time to paint.

Ruburt took on the bargain later, where the symptoms could be used as a backup system, preventing him from going out and working, so adjustments were made along the way. Later they prevented TV tours and so forth, keeping you both oriented at your joint works. This is apart from Ruburt's worries about revelatory material. The entire framework is indeed based upon a distorted idea of the nature of true responsibility.

(8:32; eventually a one-minute pause.) The symptoms have served to "allow you" a certain privacy, A certain detachment from the world, while at the same time providing a way of relating to others, of sharing life's misfortunes so that it might not be said, for example, that as artists or people you lived in an ivory tower, untouched by life's usual dilemmas. Again, there were twists and turns through the years as the symptoms might serve one purpose more than another at any given time, but falling within the general category.

Your idea of looking at events as you did the other evening *(re Tom D'Orio)* is excellent, and can be most illuminating. There will also be days when it is quite obvious that the framework provides only for your own inconvenience and discomfort—but the fact that it is a framework, created and maintained, is important.

(Long pause.) I do not want you to concentrate upon the situation any more, certainly, than you are doing, however. The idea is to keep the material as much as you can at a conscious level, then more or less drop it before picking it up again—without the steady bombardment. I mention this periodically. The idea of identifying with your pleasure, identifying yourselves with your pleasurable feelings and emotions, is highly vital. Small changes in your lives or habits

can also be extremely helpful, because small as they are they break down habit-ual habits.

Making a portion of the nighttime hours available in one way or another at least occasionally is also another way of breaking up habitual reactions, and of assuring a certain kind of privacy, using a completely different method entire-ly. Again, the material on responsibility is important to your understanding.

Your natural sense of enjoyment and pleasure will lead you back to your "work" naturally and easily.

(8:47.) Ruburt interpreted one dream in particular for you. I have little to add. He was correct *(about the dream of July 7, involving my return to Sayre).* The dream in which he was healed *(of July 19)* was to remind you that that proba-bility is still highly active. The dream involving the old granary is of the same nature as the bookstore *(Sayre)* dream *(as Jane said tonight)*—another version of it, reminding you of the kind of nourishment generations of the past received. As there were no real books in your bookstore, there was no available food in the granary. In the bookstore you felt that in a way the store was bigger than life, however, and in the granary dream Debbie's drawings of you are idealistically bigger than life. They represent her version of your life and work. If the granaries are gone, and if they provide no nourishment, then she looks to work like ours instead to provide a kind of idealized picture of human psychology.

(Long pause.) The desk is also another symbol for man's knowledge of the past. I do want to stress the advantage of examining such events as your visit of the other evening, and the ways in which either or both of you use the frame-work of Ruburt's symptoms, while urging you again not to overly concentrate upon such matters. Again, any changes you insert help break up old reactions. Your conscious awareness of the situation, however, will to some extent auto-matically alter the situation, for you are working with it at another level.

If you could manage it, working nights for a temporary period will also have the same kind of value, again, while automatically adding its own elements —that is, of providing relative isolation in a different way. I realize the difficul-ty that involves both because of practical living, and the question of light for painting. The focus upon the idea of pleasure will further alter the situation for the better, however, for again it inserts a different kind of focus.

The last group of sessions should be read over. The idea of continuing with my book at your own pace is also excellent *(as Jane suggested)*, so that it is kept current, even if we also have many sessions on other matters.

Ruburt's insights this afternoon are quite legitimate. Your notes were a way of presenting the material. The symptoms were a way of presenting the material. That is the connection Ruburt was trying to make. This will be a relatively brief session, and again other psychological events connect the session material with your private experience as you make certain translations that are necessary quite for yourselves.

Do you have a question?

("Only that in the dream involving Debbie and me and the photos: Jane said the dream was reincarnational.")

Give us a moment please.... *(a one minute pause at 9:06.)* There is some reincarnational influence, in that you and she were acquaintances *(long pause)*, of a minor variety, however—once in your Roman soldier existence, and I believe in the Denmark one. *(Long pause.)* You were on the periphery of each other's attention. Perhaps for that reason Debbie herself was not present *(in the dream)*. Ruburt was not involved with Debbie in the past, however.

I bid you then a fond good evening. Read this session with the last one—but read the last group together so you can see the development of ideas.

("Okay.")

A <u>fond</u> good evening, again, and creative dreaming.

("Thank you."

(9:13 PM. Jane knew it had been a shorter session. Seth had confirmed her reincarnational insight into my dream of July 17, but hadn't given much data. Nor did I ask him to. Note that originally Seth didn't mention the reincarnational connections in his interpretation of the dream. I do think Jane is still somewhat reluctant to deal with reincarnation. There could, of course, be almost endless questions about such reincarnational dream clues. Interesting, though.

(Note: Lately I've been thinking I would like to do some new reading and study of the first century A.D. in the Middle East and Europe, particularly Italy. This time and area still fascinate me. I would like to have a history that deals with that time and area specifically, but don't know of any such work. [Perhaps my desire will help make one available to me.] Interesting, then, that I subsequently have the dream involving Debbie, with the Roman captain connections.)

DELETED SESSION
JULY 26, 1981   3:14 PM SUNDAY

(See the copy attached of my dream of this morning. To my surprise the dream led to this session. I typed it as soon as I got up, and Jane read it at the breakfast table. As we discussed the dream I began to make connections on my own about my early days in NY City with Ralph Ramstad, as well as about commercial art, my parents, doing illustration, and so forth. I explained these items to Jane in some detail.

(All of that naturally led Jane and me into talking about our own experiences in NYC after our marriage. We went over a lot of ground, and it seemed to have very beneficial, even therapeutic effects for Jane. I kept recalling things about those times, and so did she as the morning passed.

("Synchronicity" also seemed to be involved with the dream, for in today's paper I found myself reading a column in the sports section, concerning knee injuries —and this in turn triggered my remembering that Ralph Ramstad had a "trick knee," as he used to call it, the result I believe of a childhood accident. And following those two connections, I speculated with Jane about a third: my hurting the lower left ribs about a week ago during the visit of Tom D'Orio and friends. Frank Longwell told me I'd strained the ligaments helping to support the ribs, and that "they don't like that." Most uncomfortable, even at times in bed. The seemingly innocuous injury, which hasn't even left a black-and-blue sign, is quite painful at times and most inconvenient in regards to various bodily functions involving any sudden movements, as in sneezing, etc.

(The pendulum told me I hurt the rib cage over my frustration at the visit of Tom and friends, although I wasn't conscious of any such feelings. Jane also enjoyed it, and we took Tom's address with a view to inviting he and wife Becky some Friday evening.

(But the dream, innocuous as it seemed to be, carried a big charge. I was amazed that Jane picked up so well on it, and that her insights extended to herself and the symptoms in ways that hadn't occurred to me. I'd even thought of not bothering to write down the dream in the first place.

("I don't know whether you're going to get it from me or Seth," Jane said at 3:05 PM. "Earlier I felt the stuff around from Seth, but also from me too," she said. "But I don't know. I'll let you know...." Then at 3:10: "I guess you're gonna get a session after all. I feel him around, but it won't be too long." I made her coffee, and she sipped at it as we waited. The afternoon was dark, wet, and quiet. I was all for anything that could help her.

(Amused:) Good afternoon.

("Good afternoon.")

Now: the dream is a continuation and a clarification of issues discussed in your own two previous dreams—the one about the magazine stores, and the one about the granary.

It goes into such issues in greater depth, however, in another way.

The service station and entire setup was chosen because it represented excellent symbolism, and unconsciously referred you back to the time when your father made his batteries, and owned <u>that</u> business.

The service station is significant on many levels, being used here as a particularly American symbol of the mechanical age, and also one that refers to a pursuit that is utilitarian and also provides service *(as Jane said this morning):* You deal directly with the public. There are two main areas and issues that wind in and out of this dream, as in the other two: the idea of work and service in relation to the idea of art and creativity.

In the first scene of this dream you see a probable self, who could reasonably be expected to be the kind of son your father might have, gifted with his hands mechanically, assertive enough to own his own business, however—after all, a part of the American dream, embarked upon employment that he enjoyed, and yet one that provided a service, hence physically seen between the ice *(and roller-skating)* rink, representing pleasure or fun, and the grocery store, representing service or nourishment. So you might have been that kind of person, with the belief system of your times, and with your background. A man if possible should own his own business, provide a service for the community—and, again, inventiveness or creativity were to be wedded to those pursuits. Your father's inventiveness, again, dealt often with mechanics.

In the next scene, you have the introduction of the artistic ability, however, personified by your friend of your younger New York artistic past. He represents someone highly gifted artistically, and therefore stands for your artistic self as you might have idealized it when you knew that young man. When he tries to put on ordinary working clothes, however, something happens: the shorts keep changing into a Turkish towel, and harder he tries to pull the pants on the more and more they change, until there is no mistaking that the shorts simply will not do.

The Turkish towel represents the private nature of the self—private attire that you might use in the bath, of intimate nature that comes into contact with the body not so much to hide it as to dry it, give it pleasure, or what have you.

(3:33.) The harder you try, therefore, to force your artistic nature into the public system of beliefs, to teach it how to service cars, for example *(intently)*, or to apply itself to the mechanical world, the more it resists, refuses the suitable apparel or turns it into private apparel—that is, it asserts its private self.

(Long pause.) The more you try to live "a life of service," or to concentrate primarily upon providing such a service, the more then your artistic self displays its private nature.

Now that material lay in your dream, a part of its message. You showed the dream to Ruburt after typing it up. The very fact that you remembered it, of course, meant that you were willing to become consciously aware of its message. The meanings began to come to Ruburt, and the dream itself stirred your own waking associations, so that the two of you discussed those days and the early days of your marriage.

(Long pause.) Ruburt made certain correlations. He thought, for example, of his own pajamas that he wears now instead of the jeans he wore before, and it seemed to him that in all his strivings he had in one way or another also acted like your friend whose jeans kept turning into the Turkish towel: he had been trying to protect an important way of relating to the world, or to protect a way of life.

Some of this has to do with the complicated nature of creativity itself, and with the contradictions that seem to exist at certain levels. Your kind of creativity has always been together and jointly of a private nature—so much so that you do not even like to work in rooms too close to each other. You have often thought of living under more isolated surroundings. Ruburt has been fascinated at times by the idea of working nights, his ways of assuring such isolation. You began to accumulate some ideas of a different nature, wondering more about your responsibilities to the world as adults, wondering how "useful" art should be in the world.

(3:49.) Ruburt began to wonder about television and so forth for publicity. He wondered if he did not have the responsibility, again, to spread the psychic message outward. Many different pressures operated there. In later years, as books were finished, the matter of publicity would rise anew, but his relative success meant that the issues stayed in the air, so to speak. Your discussion reminded him of how he used to be *(pause)*, and also brought up in his mind the seeming contradictions of creativity, in that it is private, but usually ends up as some kind of public expression.

(Long pause.) You kept your own studio apart, say, from the house's living areas. The whole nature of your independent and joint creativity involved a retreat from the world that you both enjoyed, followed by, in the case of books, an expression in the world—in which, however, the books appeared in your stead: a way of life that involved usual publicity—lectures and so forth—seemed to threaten that kind of existence to Ruburt, in which he feared expression itself would be diverted, simplified, so that the message that finally did get through would not be the same message at all as the original one. Yet still, because of misunderstandings and old beliefs, he still felt a responsibility to act otherwise, a social pressure to do so. *(All intently.)*

The symptoms became the sign of reluctance. They helped take the place of the isolated mountain cabin, perhaps. To a large degree they were largely the result of a lack of understanding of himself, brought on by his old religious beliefs of responsibility, then applied to his own creativity. So your dream sparked the discussion that sparked these later emotional realizations on

Ruburt's part—realizations that should go a long way toward <u>removing</u> such feelings of responsibility, and hence relieving the situation considerably.

(Long pause at 4:02.) To some extent at times you each dream dreams that can be used by the other one, and this is a case in point. Ruburt felt that a public career threatened his own, and to some extent your characteristic, natural and absolutely necessary ways of relating with the world.

(Long pause.) End of session, except to remind you that the dream message also reflects material that I have been giving you concerning creativity and the stressing of pleasure above responsibility. You paint because it gives you pleasure initially. You have the sessions together and you do the notes primarily because these endeavors bring you pleasure. They exercise your curiosity, creativity, and sense of exploration.

When you overwork the idea of responsibility—or service to the world—you erode that pleasure. All in all an excellent session, of course.

("Can I ask a question?" I made the request even though I could see that Jane was ready to call it an evening.)

You may.

("You don't have to go into it now, but will you discuss the mail situation and the idea of responsibility?")

I will certainly. Overall, I do agree, however, that our sessions <u>ideally</u> should not be tied to utility as a <u>primary</u> consideration, but should be freed of such considerations, at least generally speaking, so that their full potential can be expressed. A potential that belongs to all of art, whatever its nature, since it is daring enough, free enough to fly ahead of man's needs at any given time, and to create a new <u>atmosphere</u> that transforms the nature of being itself.

(Pause.) If you want the mail material now, then give me a brief moment.
("Okay.")

Rest your hand.

(4:12. Jane paused, lit a cigarette. It was still raining. The afternoon was quite dark and gloomy, the neighborhood very quiet.)

The mail represents the voice of the world, the needs of its people. It also represents the simple thanks of readers. Ruburt has indeed felt a strong responsibility regarding the predicament of some correspondents—again, because he was not certain as to which purposes his psychic abilities should be <u>put</u>.

If those abilities did lie in other directions, he would have felt strong impulses to hold sessions on the behalf of others, and would long ago have taken that course, so here again there are misunderstandings.

Our art can help alter people's views of themselves, change the mental conditions and the psychic atmosphere of our readers. To that extent they activate, say, the entire body defense mechanism, and this is much more likely to happen than it would be if we addressed ourselves to each isolated symptom or individual problem.

I may indeed dictate a new letter to you *(as Jane said recently)*, to make our position clear, but Ruburt's main position is not one of service: it must be one of pleasure and creativity. Pleasure and creativity <u>automatically and spontaneously</u> alter the world for the better, without methods and even without effort.

End of that material for now, and I bid you a fond good afternoon.

("Thank you, and the same to you."

(4:23 PM. "That was very good," I told Jane as she came out of trance. "I can't wait to go over it because it seems to contain stuff that will be helpful to you."

("What about you?" she asked.

("The same thing," I said. "It all basically has to do with this idea of responsibility. If you can get rid of that you might be home free. If it was up to me, I'd throw the idea of responsibility down the hillside and into the river."

("Yes, and then maybe I wouldn't answer any of the mail."

("You'd be free to do anything you want to," I said. "The idea is you'd be free to do as you please. You could answer it, or any part of it, as you wanted to.... Wouldn't it be a scream if a relatively innocuous-seeming dream like that one marked the turning point in this thing?" Indeed.

("Maybe. I started getting stuff on it right away this morning."

(I added that I thought I was already doing, at least to some extent, what Seth advocated in the session—throwing away any sense of responsibility or financial reward in painting, at this time at least. I trusted that whatever might result from the painting would be beneficial in various ways, possibly including the financial if the need arose. I explained to Jane that I'd reached the point in the last year where I just couldn't let anything interfere with the act of painting itself—and that I thought she needed an attitude like that in regard to her own work very badly. I could have said [in retrospect] that my attitude stemmed at least to a large degree from my watching her struggle with her own hang-ups. Not that I didn't think I'd reach it on my own anyhow.

("I'd sacrifice every cent we've got if it would get us that," I said, "because then we'd both be free. I'd sacrifice this house and live in a cheap apartment on Water Street again, if it would help, and we just had royalty money to live on." The other day I'd told her we had enough money to live for at least five years—and more— without earning anything, and I said it again now. "The funny thing is, if we were that free yet committed, we wouldn't have to worry about money because we'd automatically do the right things that would get us more whenever we needed it, just by doing the things we love to do...."

(Jane agreed.)

ROB'S DREAM
JULY 26, 1981 SUNDAY MORNING

In color as usual: Another return-to-Sayre dream. Jane wasn't involved. The dream was quite long and involved but I can describe here only one small portion. I was the proprietor of a gas station on Keystone Avenue, up near the skating-rink section, and on the other side of the highway from the Acme Market location. I seemed to be taller and thinner than I am in this life. I not only owned the station which serviced cars, but did the actual work; my clothes were worn and greasy. It was summertime and I wore shorts, cut-off blue denim jeans.

Now an old friend of mine from days at Pratt came to either work with me or visit. I believe the former. His name is Ralph Ramstad and we haven't heard from him in any manner for many years. I went through Pratt with him, and Jane met he and his wife once after we were married and were still living in the NY metropolitan area. In the dream Ralph, who is quite tall (6'4") and thin and wiry, needed some shorts to wear for work. He had none and I offered him a pair of mine, saying I thought they'd fit well enough. But when he pulled the shorts up around his waist the blue denim kept turning into a blue Turkish towel type of fabric that he tried to pin together so they'd cover him and wouldn't fall down. He kept trying to make something useful out this affair, and the more he tried the more obvious it became that he was trying to wrap himself in a blue-and-white Turkish towel in lieu of shorts. He didn't seem upset and wasn't as old in the dream as he would be now; still blonde.

(Note: Ralph had a "trick knee," also.)

DELETED SESSION
JULY 27, 1981 9:02 PM MONDAY

(See Jane's account of her dream of this rooming, attached to this session. She thinks it's very important, and Seth comments on it at the close of the session.

(At 8:20 PM Jane called and asked whether she should have a session—she couldn't make up her mind. I said I wanted more material on responsibility, that I wanted Seth to discuss it so it would help free her. "So I should have the session

because it's my responsibility to do it," she said. "No," I answered, "but it would be nice to have it in order to learn that your only responsibility is to get rid of the idea of responsibility. That's all I care about."

(I'm still typing yesterday afternoon's session. Things have been hectic here today, interfering with my painting: Frank Longwell and his brother started work today on the front porch, which is to be glassed in so that Jane can have more room. [In the meantime, she's moved into her writing room in back of the house.]

(Jane has felt somewhat better the last couple of days, and I've been hoping that what we're learning is "responsible" for that improvement. I told her as we waited for the session that I was all for more material on the responsibility question, for I see it as the key to setting her free. I said also that her decision to give up doing publicity, made just recently, might be helping her feel better.

("I guess I'm confused," Jane said at 8:55. "I feel responsible to get more on responsibility, I guess, where this afternoon I thought I'd like him to finish that chapter in his book and get started on another one. Then you came out and said you'd like more on responsibility, so...." I explained that my idea was only to get more material on what Seth had begun yesterday—but that didn't mean she couldn't do material on other things too.

(At 9 PM I was thinking of telling Jane to forget the session when she remarked, "I almost feel him around." I don't think we've ever "abandoned" a session once we sat for it, but was willing to do it if need be. Then:)

Now: comments.

Generally speaking, large segments of your official society do not regard the pursuit of art as responsible behavior.

(Pause.) For many years you both pursued your arts despite living amidst such cultural beliefs. The pursuit of art was considered egotistical in a negative meaning of the word—selfish, childish or adolescent, and indeed many psychologists of the recent past considered it in the light of prolonged adolescence, or saw it as a sign of the individuals' refusal to fully accept an adult role in life.

(Long pause.) In an industrialized society, people were trained to fit into assembly line productions. The imagination was itself considered suspect. It was felt that creativity served no responsible end in society. Again, you both pursued your own courses nevertheless. You did so, however, in the light of that psychological climate, so that while you went your own ways you also reacted to the social environment: you tried to show other people that you were indeed responsible—more, that you <u>worked</u> (underlined) not only as hard as others, but often <u>harder</u> (underlined).

To some extent you convinced yourselves that such creative activity was indeed in some respects more work certainly than play. In your own art you worked relatively slowly, <u>measured out your pleasure</u> in a fashion, even thinking sometimes in the past that your talent <u>required</u> (underlined) periods of indecision and difficulty. Often you emphasized impediments. It seemed almost sacrilegious to think that the production of excellent art could involve fun—or worse, an active sense of irresponsibility, a joyful sense of ease, so that if a painting came too quickly you could not trust it.

(Exactly, I'm afraid.)

Years ago, Ruburt picked up that idea of work, applying it to creativity in <u>his</u> (underlined) own ways. You made it clear to others that while they be free, free on weekends or holidays, you yourselves were still involved with <u>"work"</u> (underlined)—all of this to show that you were responsible persons.

(9:20.) In the world of official thought, work does indeed seem to imply responsibility. It seems to many that left alone people would not want to work at all, and that people's pleasures would lead them into frivolous behavior. In actuality, of course, people's pleasure, if it were understood and pursued, would lead to far more fulfilling and productive work, or working lives, since individuals would automatically know how to choose productive activities that brought them pleasure, and that were then pursued for their own sakes.

This artistic sense of responsibility was given a thicker coat by what seemed to be <u>psychic</u> responsibility: it seemed to Ruburt that he should use his abilities <u>primarily</u> to help others, or to help solve the world's problems, or to cast some light into man's condition. Certainly the attitude of some correspondents was involved there. Actually, however, it was the simple extension of such a feeling into the psychic realm, where it was further hardened by many religious views.

Now art itself functions in a different manner. First of all, the artist in whatever medium loves the activity for itself, and everything else is <u>basically</u> (underlined) secondary. You have a love of pleasure, focused into a certain magical kind of creativity. *(Long pause.)* This love and this pleasure automatically put the individual in harmony with the nature of existence itself, for existence operates in the same manner.

Animals care for their young out of natural pleasure and love, not out of a sense of responsibility. The word "responsibility" is often used precisely because people have forgotten how to feel natural pleasure with themselves, their activities or relationships.

Ruburt <u>saddled</u> himself with a feeling of responsibility, however. At the same time of course he naturally resented such dictates. They tempered his own inspiration, narrowed his spontaneity. The idea of that kind of responsibility is extremely persuasive, however, in your society. *(Long pause.)* Because women

were somehow regarded as less responsible than males, more easily given to friv-
olity, Ruburt also tried even harder to insure that he was acting in a responsible
way.

If creativity itself was sometimes considered irresponsible, or "feminine,"
or adolescent, then psychic activity, he discovered, <u>seemed</u> to be held in an even
murkier light, in which the abilities themselves were sometimes thought of not
as creative enhancements but as symptoms of feminine weakness and irresponsibility. He has recognized that, of course, to some degree, and written about it.

It added considerably, however, to the thick coat of responsibility that he
placed about his own shoulders. He is still harder on women than he is on men
in that regard. In that light then again, to stand somewhat apart from my material, to question it as a matter of principle, became a sign of responsibility. It
showed that he was not a frivolous female, fancifully following each stray imaginative trance image.

(9:46.) At the same time, he recognized the excellence of our joint creativity. When you overstress the idea of responsibility, pleasure largely goes out
the window, so he is now learning to redefine the term, "pleasure," and to experience it in its many forms. He is learning to identify himself with his pleasures
—a highly important point—one that, understood, can release triggers of healing energy and creative impetus.

The body itself is designed for pleasure. Value fulfillment seeks out pleasure. The entire idea of free will involves the making of choices between various
gradations of pleasurable behavior. Value fulfillment even with the animals
insists upon a <u>qualitative</u> enjoyment of life's existence—one that automatically
fosters a loving cooperation with the rest of nature as the individual follows
impulses toward various kinds of pleasures. But the word pleasure often has a
negative connotation to official morality. *(Long pause.)* If you follow the pursuit
of pleasure in this creative manner, then you will automatically begin to discard
faulty concepts of responsibility.

(Long pause.) Pleasure implies play as well, of course, and art involves a
kind of high free play—an extension of it that cannot be tied to personal or to
mass need. High play of that nature opens doors of excellence that responsibility alone can never touch, and results in far more valuable help to the world as
a natural by-product than any self-determined behavior can, so these are the
ideas that we want to stress, both in bodily terms and in psychic and creative
ones, and Ruburt is beginning to understand some of that now. The idea of creative play—and in those terms of a certain kind of abandonment—should be
encouraged; the kind of abandonment a child feels when playing a game, in
which it identifies with pleasurable activity. It therefore joins with its own

unconscious processes, and those processes are connected more intimately with the very source of its being.

Ruburt's interpretation of your dream is good, and his own dream *(attached)* is highly significant. As per his own interpretation, it clearly states a new frame of mind, and ensuing therapeutic adjustments.

End of session and a fond good evening.

("Thank you."

(10:05 PM. "I got something at the tail end of the session that he didn't say," Jane told me. *"I don't know whether it was right or not—it involved you. I don't know if you'll agree: You can check with the pendulum. The idea of the trouble you gave yourself with the rib was connected with the guys coming to work here, to give you an excuse to do your thing and be isolated so they wouldn't ask you to help, or strain yourself physically because you were already hurt. I got it at the very end. I don't know why he didn't say that. I waited to see if he was going to give it, and when he didn't, I did."*

(I told Jane that the other day the pendulum had told me I hurt the rib as self-punishment because of my resentment of the visit of Tom D'Orio and friends. Whatever—both cases would involve time and interruptions, a threat to what I see as my main course in life these days, painting. And that threat would be the main cause behind my self-injury: guilt at feeling that way. My own bout with using the pendulum had been very brief.

(Note that Seth didn't continue with his material on the mail, which he began in answer to my question on July 26. I also forgot to ask him to. In that last session I meant to add the thought that we may have to dispense with answering much of the mail. I'll gladly do this if I discover that it is behind any large-sized hassle Jane may be carrying around about public responsibility. The mail would have to go, at least until she'd resolved such an issue. It serves as a constant reminder of what many people regard as her responsibility, and could be more of an impediment or irritant than I had suspected, I told her the other day. People read the books, get something out of them—then want personal help that Jane can't give in any meaningful, long-term way. She's been very rigorous in answering the mail for a number of years, and my thought at the moment at least is that it—the mail—might be more of a time bomb than we realized in that respect.

(I would like to add that I found the session to be excellent as usual, but also found some of the material sad and depressing: It looked like we had a lot of wasted years involved in negative thinking, and that we were now struggling to get out of or rid of. At the moment I couldn't decide if everyone had such hassles in life, or if Jane and I had managed to create sets of beliefs that were indeed "beauts" and quite unusual. I was afraid our beliefs ruled our lives so completely, were so pervasive, that

we'd never get out of their mazes. As I asked Paul O'Neill last month: "How do you be objective about something when you're inside of it?")

JANE'S DREAM
JULY 27, 1981 MONDAY

Last PM I remembered the following dream that is very simple but, I feel, important. I think we were on a trip to England. Anyway a group of us were to be given a pill or some such that was actually a vaccine against some disease—perhaps polio. I was talking to doctor about this; I'm not sure if the people were even being told what this was, the idea being to slip the stuff as innocuously as possible. I refused in no uncertain terms to take it and gave my objections while also objecting to the secrecy in which the project was clothed. The doctor said OK I wouldn't have to take it of course.

In the AM the dream instantly reminded me of an almost completely different opposite dream, a nightmare that I had just about the time my eye troubles and other difficulties began in earnest: It was in the spring when I was doing James. *Frank was doing construction on the porches then, too, and I was worried about the Gallery-of-Silence people bugging Prentice and me. In the nightmare a doctor said I'd have to get a certain shot or vaccine as preventative medicine though he regretted having to do it. I was terrified and ran though he said it was for my own good. They caught me and gave me the shot, mentioning something about aftereffects. In last night's dream I wasn't frightened, just refused and gave my reasons. (I think the idea was that increased symptoms were "preventive" medicine against a greater feared event or condition....)*

This morning Frank's brother began work on new construction—enclosing the porch (the opposite too in a way from before). I felt somewhat better all over this AM....mentally more ambitious or something and moved to back patio studio.

SESSION 933 (DELETED PORTION)
AUGUST 7, 1981   8:22 PM FRIDAY

(The following Seth material is from the 933rd session.
(These notes for this deleted portion were begun on July 30, 1981.
(Two events transpired today [Thursday, July 30] that Jane handled very well. Both involved communication with the public—a sense of responsibility—which we

now know to be a source of constant tension for her. But when they were over I told her she responded well to them, and she seemed pleased that she'd taken positive actions re them through the telephone.

(One event concerned the telegram from attorney Thomas Bernier in Roseburg, Oregon. It arrived late this morning. When Jane called him the lawyer told Jane that his client was a 27-year-old schizophrenic who'd confessed to killing a certain woman he'd met in a Seth class both attended some years ago. He had confessed to her death several times, but no one believed him—until the last time, evidently. Now he was on trial. Jane didn't ask for details on the case, but instead explained to the lawyer something of Seth's ideas so that the attorney could use that material in his defense, making it clear that above all Seth was not for violence, even though the prosecuting attorney was evidently trying to make the defendant sound as though it was okay to kill because reincarnation was a fact: Since we all lived other lives, no one could really kill anyone. I sent Bernier a book list. Interestingly, in the small town of Roseburg he'd been able to buy James *and* Cézanne *and* ESP Power, *but no other Seth books.*

(The other event concerned a medium in Hollywood, California, who claims to be speaking for Seth, and who gave a well-advertised seminar at a Holiday Inn there. He's been doing such speaking in trance since the early 1970's. The literature a fan sent us last week made it seem that the medium claimed to be speaking for Jane's Seth. More arrived today from the same fan—and the quotes given seemed like copycat material of Seth's, down to calling himself an "energy-essence," and so forth.

(Jane was angered by this material [the second batch; I'd already sent Tam the first communication, asking for his help], and decided to call the medium, Thomas Massari, since a number was listed. She thought I didn't want her to call, but I told her to do as she pleased. Jane talked to Carole, the medium's wife who works with him, and stated clearly that she didn't want others claiming to speak for her Seth— who, incidentally, had told us years ago that he spoke through no one else but Jane. [It would be interesting to get material from you-know-who on this whole question of others claiming to speak for Seth.] No shouting or anger was involved in the call. I'd been concerned lest Jane become involved in an unpleasant situation that would have repercussions via symptoms —the idea of publicity, of public display, which she doesn't want—just when we were trying to learn more about the subject as she reacted to it.

(It turned out that the wife claimed her husband was not trying to capitalize on Seth, that they both respected highly the Seth material, and that as we had suspected he had written Jane several years ago telling her about his Seth. Jane had told him then that he wasn't speaking for her Seth. Jane told Carole that it was okay to

use the Seth name as long as claims weren't made that the two Seths were one and the same, especially the Seth who was producing the Seth books. Jane was reassured that no such claims were being made.

(Jane hung up seemingly satisfied, but I still wonder. We did agree that there must be a least unconscious cheating going on, on the medium's part, else why keep the Seth name all these years and speak so cleverly in imitation of Seth, who has garnered at least some sort of reputation, thus making the road easier for any other Seth? See the attached material. Jane plans to call Tam tomorrow to tell him what she's learned, and to ask him to return the first material concerning the Massaris. [She'd also called Tam today before contacting the lawyer and the medium's wife.]

(Sometimes I'm slow, and other times even slower. I discussed these notes with Jane when I wrote them—Thursday, July 30—and our individual attitudes toward the mail in general, which is steadily increasing in volume. Then it came to me: The two events described here certainly did speak well for some kind of accomplishment on Jane's part—and one greater than any she'd given herself credit for. For both events obviously involved effects her work was having in that outside world we shied away from: Seth, it seemed, had even managed to make his way into a court of law, the very fabric of our society; and regardless of whether he was praised or knocked, his ideas were "officially" discussed. And the medium, Thomas Massari, was basically spreading Seth's ideas among the so-called leaders of at least segments of our society: M.D.'s, psychotherapists, and others in the medical field. Even if, as we thought likely, all was not strictly honest on the medium's part.

(August 7, 1981. Last night Jane was faced with a little dilemma: She felt Seth around after supper, but also had the idea that we go to bed at 8:30 and get up at 4 AM to "work." I agreed. We started out with the best intentions, but ended up sidetracked—for Jane was so restless she couldn't sleep at all. I got her up at 11 PM, made her something to eat and drink, got her situated in the writing room, and went back to bed. She wheeled herself back into the bedroom at about 4 AM, and went to bed with my help. I got up at 7 to paint and she slept until 10:30. She'd enjoyed her nighttime hours alone, though.

(Then, not long before the session this evening, I mentioned to Jane my question about the Sinful Self's reaction to our latest efforts. We haven't seen the kind of physical response we want yet, and I wanted to know if our efforts were prompting the Sinful Self to step up its own protective behavior to keep Jane "under control." I explained to Jane that my own idea of why Seth's statements over the years, that she was on the way to recovery, were always negated was that these very statements alerted the Sinful Self to redouble its efforts to prevent Jane's recovery because of its own fears. I added that when I used the term Sinful Self, I only meant certain blocks of ideas that we've personified for convenience's sake.

(Jane's idea this evening was to have a session on book material, so I asked her for a few words on my question also. She said she didn't want more private material that would make her "feel more stupid." I'd mentioned a little earlier an idea for a book she could develop on Seth and the magical approach [she's had the magical-approach idea for some time], and she wanted material on that. See my notes on the book idea prefacing the regular portion of this session.

(9:06.)

Your earlier comments about Jane's Sinful Self is pertinent. *(Long pause.)* Remember, again, that the Sinful-Self designation is a method of identifying certain attitudes. Those attitudes are indeed changing.

In the case of our book *(Dreams)*, however, Ruburt himself was worried about your attitude. His overall concerns of course to some extent blocked his creative processes, which further alarmed him. The main issue here is that feeling of responsibility again, so that he writes or whatever because he loves to do it, not because he should or must, and that involves my books as well as his own.

He becomes overly serious, overstressing the entire picture, as you can at times, so that the affair seems hopeless: the evidence before your eyes, and so forth.

That kind of projection continues that kind of situation. You do get what you concentrate upon. I try to break up blocks of your concentration, and at various times have indeed succeeded, so that creative changes show in all areas, including Ruburt's condition.

Thus far, however, the old habits have returned, and for all of your joint good intents the idea of bringing things to a crisis point is still far less beneficial than it might appear This does not mean such a method cannot work at times. It does mean that on the whole it is a difficult method, and in utmost honesty and clarity in that regard, I can only tell you what I have said before: regardless of how ill-founded it may seem on certain occasions, that basically speaking the situation becomes less as you pare it down in your mind, rid it of significance in your mind, say things like "Well after all, it is not that bad yet," or in other ways turn your attention otherwise.

The main issue is of course not to project negatively into the future, for there you are borrowing trouble. With physical conditions already apparent in the present, you can at least realize that while these present you with a certain evidence, the evidence will indeed change—and can change, and is changing the minute that you realize that the evidence, while present, is not inevitably all the evidence available.

The body is at each and every stage also filled with health and vitality. Those rules do not change. Ruburt is safe and protected. Those reassurances are highly important here now.

End of session, end of lecture *(heartily)*—and a fond good evening.

("Thank you, Seth."

(9:25 PM. Jane had done well this evening, I told her. Seth's material above is certainly excellent—the latest version of what he's been telling us for years. I for one will try to reassure myself that "things aren't that bad yet." What can one lose? For little else seems to work.

(Lest some hypothetical readers of this material in the future regard Jane and me as idiots, incapable of learning, I'd like to note in our own defense that we've made many efforts to put the symptom situation out of mind as much as we're capable of, yet it doesn't leave us. My own idea about holding off on Seth's latest book, Dreams, is not that it will force any solution, but merely, hopefully, prevent things from getting worse. As I asked Jane the other day when she talked of resuming work on that project: "Can you stand any more complications?" I meant of course, that after 17 books, we're at our present situation, so I have difficulty understanding how doing another book will suddenly, magically, turn anything around for us as long as we stay on the same old course.

(My thought of course is that gritting one's teeth and plunging ahead with the new book in defiance of large portions of the personality may have unpleasant repercussions. I'm still shocked to realize that while I was laboring over Mass Events, *and Jane was doing* God of Jane, *that those two books had stirred up even more resistance on the part of that personified Sinful Self, and that when they were finished we were then confronted with a new barrage of symptoms that ended up restricting [and protecting?] Jane's physical manipulability even more. Not to say what's happened to her spontaneous creative drives. A strange way indeed to achieve one's goal, a strange bargain. Yet I try to accept Jane as she is and myself as well.)*

SESSION 934 (DELETED PORTION)
AUGUST 10, 1981 8:27 PM MONDAY

(The following material is from the 934th session.

(Long pause at 9:23.) I have said this before: the best way to solve a problem is to concentrate upon various solutions vigorously—and then to turn your minds to other subjects, divert yourselves while allowing the creative power some freedom. An overintentness, <u>prolonged</u>, is not of benefit.

(Long pause.) The entire idea of the magical approach is of itself sustaining.

(Long pause.) It should remind you of the true effortlessness that is in a

fashion responsible for your very existence. When you become overly concerned or worried in any area, remember that you are <u>thinking those thoughts</u> while the process of thinking is utterly effortless. That realization alone can further remind you that the conscious mind does not have to have <u>all</u> (underlined) the information required. It only needs to have the faith that means are <u>available</u>—even if those means are beyond its own scope of activity.

Ruburt's project—and this book *(Dreams)*—serve the same purpose to him, of course, as painting does for you, and such activity can in that light only benefit him. His attitudes <u>toward</u> such activities may indeed be something else again, but he is working those out, and needs some time to do so.

The realization that he need not be a public person, for example, is taking root, so keep this information at your fingertips. End of session. A fond good evening—and expect the new material on dreams in my book to further extend and illuminate your own dreaming activity. A fond good evening.

(9:35 PM. Note: The next afternoon Jane gave a telephone interview to a staff member of Frontiers of Science *magazine....)*

DELETED SESSION
NOVEMBER 9, 1981 9:00 PM MONDAY

(At about 8 PM Jane said she would like to try having a session this evening —whether private or regular she didn't know. She didn't feel Seth around, but lately has wanted to resume the sessions. She's been rereading a number of them lately.

(We sat for the session at 8:30. Jane was both nervous and impatient at the prospect of her first session since last August 13. 1981. Finally:)

Good evening.

("Good evening, Seth.")

Now: the session will be brief.

Ruburt is still dealing with spin-off material following or resulting from his Sinful-Self data, and this material generally follows the lines of development that are fairly obvious in the poems and notes that have followed since that time.

He knows what I am referring to. Some small portions are not as yet typed, and should be, for the typing alone of that material will act as an impetus. The entire Sinful Self material should be reviewed. He did indeed become afraid of faith itself.

(Long pause at 9:05.) He is presently encountering that kind of feeling, uncovering the reasons for it, and trying to recapture in a way the very young innocent self's sense of faith. That faith existed even before churchly doctrine

was imposed over it. He is trying to uncover his own natural faith. That attempt, of course, brings him into conflict with whatever doubts still stand in his way.

The body, again, does possess such a natural faith, and it has nothing to do with esoteric methods and so forth—but again deals with a kind of self-evident biological knowledge. There is a more emotional charge connected with those issues. Hence the temporary feelings of panic, for example. These should be discussed.

I will have further pertinent material myself to add to the overall category of Ruburt's situation, but I am simply making this evening's session to give him a sense of immediate direction, and in his case to break the ice, so to speak. That is, he should type up the small bit of material, and read over the Sinful Self's document.

(Long pause at 9:13.) I know how to quicken the impetus of the psyche. To give it a gentle nudge in the proper direction, to insert a hint of reassurance, and with this session that is my intent. (Pause.) The Sinful Self's material serves as a small psychic source at the moment: that is, he still reacts to it. And the same material may appear from different viewpoints. There are several lines of a poem and a few of the notes, untyped, that should be also typed at the same time—but he is pulling such issues together.

I will also have comments concerning your own reactions (to me), and I suggest—but only suggest—that again your usual two sessions a week be held, as a framework for the therapeutic endeavors.

I did briefly give him a message: attend to what is before you, for it is there for a reason. In each person's life, and in your own, at each and every point of your existence, the solutions to your problems, or the means of achieving those solutions, are always as apparent, or rather as present, within your days as is any given problem itself. What I mean is quite simple: the solutions already exist in your lives. You may not have put them together yet, or organized them in the necessary ways. The solutions lie in Ruburt's case in all of those areas with which you are normally concerned—the mail, the sessions, the psychic abilities. When you attend to what is there with the proper magical attitude of mind, then the altered organizations can take place.

(Long pause at 9:23.) A belief in a "God who provides," by whatever name, is indeed a psychological requirement for the good health of the body and mind. Ruburt did not want to face such issues. (Long pause.) He felt that they opened the door to all of organized religion's psychological quicksand of emotionalism. The Sinful Self material is doing its work, opening the necessary doorways of desire and intent. When Ruburt has typed those small later poems, the path will seem much clearer to him. (Long pause.) The innocent self is being uncovered.

I simply wanted to make these points, and look forward to another session this week, with your joint approval. I bid you then a fine and hearty good evening—

("May I ask a question?")

You may.

("Will you give us the entity names for Frank Longwell and his wife?")

You want to know Frank's entity name?

("And that of his wife, Eve.")

Give us a moment....

(Then spelled, but incompletely:) M-M-A-J-A is the current expression of Frank's entity name. and D-A-J-O-R-A-K-A is his wife's.

("Would you spell Frank's again?" I didn't think Seth had spelled it correctly —not the way he'd pronounced it.)

What do you have?

(I spelled it.)

You may add an H.

(I tried this, then said: "I can't get it right." Then Seth spelled the name again —this time as he'd first pronounced it:)

M-A-J-O-R-A-H.

("Okay.")

A note: the spelling of the names follows Sumari interpretation.

("Thank you.")

The clocks represent on Frank's part a creative interpretation.... There is an old saying: Time is money—and in his own way Frank would like to make that kind of a statement, clear, direct, and unambiguous: Turning clocks or time directly into good hard cash, a magic of a sort. This is also meant to make up for any "wasting of time" that he might otherwise be engaged in. In a fashion it is an attempt to deal more directly with beliefs regarding time, money, and creativity.

Ruburt is dealing with quite profound material involving the self's relationship with its own source—this material being worked out in your current situations. The solutions will automatically lead him not only to a solution in practical terms, but toward the areas of development that he has been seeking *(emphatically)* while being afraid of them at the same time. End of session and a fond good evening.

(9:50 PM. "Thank you," I said. Jane smiled, pleased that she'd had the session. "I still get scary after a layoff." She knew what material Seth wanted her to type.)

DELETED SESSION
NOVEMBER 12, 1981   8:46 PM THURSDAY

(Last night Jane decided to try holding the evening's regularly scheduled session tonight for a change. Slowly, after we'd waited half an hour for her to feel Seth around:)

Now: it is the effort<u>lessness</u>, the spontaneous relaxation, that worries Ruburt, in that it is not specifically decided upon at any given point, but seems to happen by itself.

Ruburt's body is allowing itself to relax, particularly on the couch when his back is supported. Tension is being relieved, and often this sudden lessening of tension also frightens him. It is excellent therapy on the part of the body, of a fairly temporary nature. Its breaks down, however, many strong elements of control after control continually being applied. These are of excellent benefit.

There is no doubt, however, that at times Ruburt becomes quite frightened, and the fear of course represents the fear that still lingers concerning the nature of spontaneous action. Rigidity is drained from the body by such methods. He is safe, supported and protected—that is, of course, the message that he is trying to get through his head at this time. You can be of help to him by reminding him of that support and protection. The body knows what it is doing *(emphatically)*.

It is embarked upon different processes now as it searches for the best conditions for self-healing procedures. His ideas as he tried to explain them to you earlier this evening <u>are</u> excellent. They remove him psychologically, particularly with your help, as he discusses them. The Sinful Self material is "timed" in its own fashion so that although there is a good deal of material already written, its effects are periodic—that is, they are clued to spring into even greater insight which may not be apparent at any one given time. The material acts like a time pill, for example.

He should keep in mind, say, to type several pages or so, put it with the other work, and let again several days pass. Some of that material will bring the reasons for his panic into clearer light, however, and so then will make even more sense than it might have a month ago. He is doing well dealing with that.

(Long pause at 9:04.) There is no doubt that differing portions of Ruburt's body are quite comfortable, and far more flexible, when he relaxes in such a fashion. He does well to move about in his chair, as he does often, exercising when he is alone. He can do more of that to his advantage. It is important that he tells you when he does feel panicky. However, the feeling itself does not last long.

(Pause.) Give us a moment.... *(Long pause, eyes closed.)* This advice, simple as it sounds, will lead toward further insights on his part. Relaxation, again, is a part of the creative process. It is the means whereby body and mind refresh themselves. Your talk this afternoon covered many excellent points. It is the nitty-gritty of his basic feelings that Ruburt has been encountering.

(Long pause.) I hope to finish our book regardless of your publishing plans and so forth, and at this general point that will be beneficial to our friend as he sees some daily accomplishment made in that area. *(Long pause.)* Your establishment, being cleared of working men, will also help clear the air.

This session will also be brief. I want Ruburt to see, however, that healing is taking place, that he can trust his own mind and body, and that all portions of the self are being dealt with, whether or not such is obvious at any given time. Our material on such points is not fiction.

I am still in the process of trying to reassure him, of course, but in a fashion we are indeed dealing with a kind of biological logic that will stand up in its own light—that will produce its own evidence as you learn to accept the rightness of your bodies *(pause)*, and their abilities, for they are natural healing mechanisms. The small panics themselves, for example, are meant to lead to psychological questioning and so forth in a give-and-take mental and therapeutic exchange of activity—an activity bound to release and activate the creative abilities also.

Unfortunately, in your society you need every good suggestion you can get, to offset fears and negative conditioning. Ruburt needs time to give himself a few suggestions in the morning, to start up his journal again, even to paint if he wants in a framework in which he allows himself that much freedom. Forget the rigors of publishing or whatever *(intently)*. He does not have to publish a book every year on the button. The creative material will flow. It flows as a result of his own characteristic nature. It is safe to express that nature. It is even safe to explore that nature, and it is safe to allow himself to take some comfort in the source of being.

(9:26.) The same advice, with suitable variations, could be given to anyone, of course, and be equally pertinent. His energy will flow through him easily and naturally and safely as he perceives that such is nature's way. *(Long pause.)* You have been of excellent support of late. Allow yourself at times to imagine, at least, an important portion of your own creative self as innocent, sweet *(gesture)*, and natural as that young Butts boy relative *(Steve)*. That is, think of that childish self as eagerly exploring the world, for that is certainly a part of man's heritage.

End of session and a fond good evening.

("Thank you."
(9:31 PM.)

SESSION 937 (DELETED PORTION)
NOVEMBER 19, 1981 8:30 PM THURSDAY

(The following material is from the 937th session.
(9:35.) Now: in a manner of speaking, of course, the same *(alteration of approach)* applies to Ruburt's condition.

What we want is an altered approach to life itself, to one that follows the kind of natural approach to living that children unerringly possess, but to one that is also enriched with experience that a child does not possess. Ruburt is in the process of gaining such an approach. This is perhaps no easy task in usual terms, yet he is indeed learning on his own part to use his consciousness in a different fashion than the one prescribed by man in one way or another for centuries.

Each person alive is embarked upon the same kind of adventure, dealing with it, however, according to his or her own characteristics and situation. What Ruburt has in mind—and generally—this includes the ideas that you have given, Joseph, in the taped material—those procedures are indeed paying off. Though the results are only showing here and there they are growing, and they will appear with greater and greater rapidity. They are building up momentum.

End of session and a fond good evening.

("The same to you."
(9:47 PM.)

SESSION 938 (DELETED PORTION)
NOVEMBER 24, 1981 9:07 PM TUESDAY

(The following material is from the 938th session.
(As I think the ideas in the session proper are among Jane's best, so do I think those in the material she delivered for herself equally good.
(10:27.) End of dictation. Now give us a moment. Rest your fingers....
(10:28.) You have been of excellent help to Ruburt lately. So far in our discussion of his own situation, we have not for good reason touched upon certain material because he was not ready for it.

(Very long pause.) As his abilities grew, however, of course he sensed the

outlines of other realities, the glimmerings of other worlds. He sensed these cousins of consciousness in one way or another—these environments that seemed real but not real, these further extensions of possible experience, and he decided that he must be very cautious: he must be prudent *(long pause)*, he must take his time, he must range but carefully—and certainly to some extent such feelings cut down upon his spontaneity.

The cautions are natural enough under the restrictions man usually places upon consciousness. Ruburt carries his protection and safety wherever he goes. It is a natural grace, characteristic of consciousness of any kind. Its protection and validity are always honored. Ruburt is safe wherever he goes. His psychological stance is honored wherever he goes.

I will have more to say on this subject in a personal context at our next session. These few statements, however, will help him, and help him enlarge on an inner circle of acquaintanceship with friendly colleagues that belong in those other categories, but are indeed friendly colleagues as well. End of session and a fond good evening.

(10:45 PM.)

DELETED SESSION
DECEMBER 1, 1981 9:45 PM TUESDAY

(I'm bypassing the lengthy notes I wrote prefacing this session in order to get the material typed up itself the next day so that Jane can begin studying it. The session itself indicates, of course, the nature of the notes. I'll add them to the end of the session.

(With a number of long pauses, and quite nasal in tone:)

Now: I have some comments to make on your discussion—rather brief for now.

Ruburt does not <u>owe</u> me anything. If he decided not to have sessions, or not to operate in the so-called psychic arena, this does not mean that he would be a <u>failure</u> in any way. He does not owe me a sense of commitment. The material I have given on his health, I will however stand behind, whether or not it is difficult for you to understand, or whether or not you can bring yourselves to accept it.

I <u>do</u> admit that from your standpoint—or viewpoint—that it may be very difficult to accept some of the statements that I make—that appear perhaps even to be directly contradictory to your observation of Ruburt on a daily basis, and to his own experience of himself.

It certainly does not seem to either of you that he is getting better. It often seems instead that the opposite is true. You may presently just find it too difficult to take the leap of faith required without more evidence to back it up—this despite the quite frequent feelings of release that Ruburt does experience along with the much more apparent disability. If those feelings go no further, then what good are they?—so you both are bound to wonder.

I know that they are indicators of the body's healing energies, and I also quite understand that in the overall you find such a statement unacceptable.

(*Very long pause—one of many such—at 9:59.*) I would never stand in the way, however, of Ruburt's recovery as you understood it. Nor would I feel that Ruburt has let me down, or that you had in any way. Ruburt does need a return to an earlier orientation. That sense of beauty, that reorientation, can relieve the feeling of responsibility that he has at times taken upon himself. He needs an orientation toward the simpler issues—those that carry within themselves a simpler childlike magic. He needs to turn away from an overconcern with life's more "weighty problems," to lose the feeling that it is up to him to solve those problems for himself and you and for the world.

(*More and more slowly:*) Most of that should be obvious to you. The stresses and strains are in a fashion not simply those of one person and that person's relationship with his own nature. Those (underlined) issues are compounded by Ruburt understanding as of now of other people's lives as they write to you. At the same time he does not deal directly with such people, so he cannot follow through, for example, as a therapist might. His class gave him some direct encounters through the years as he personally helped to direct others, and could watch the results through their achievement or behavior.

(*Very long pause at 10:14.*) He certainly expects more of himself than is required, and I have given a good deal of such material, several months back, I believe. I will, however, sort through his experience with your question in my mind, and see what other information I can give you.

(*Very long pause at 10:16.*) The other comments are simply handy Band-Aids, so to speak, but are extremely healthy along the way. When he feels panicky your loving touch—a light quick massage or embrace—acts as quickly on the nervous system as anything else, and far faster than any medicine. Animals even have long been aware of such immediate therapeutic action.

(*Very long pause at 10:21.*) The statements I have made regarding the innate nature of the spontaneous self can be of the greatest service if they are accepted. You are trying to redefine the very definitions of personal identity—no easy task. Not just Ruburt alone but the people of the world are, one way or another, now in the process of just such a redefinition. It is impossible to assign some time element to that (underlined) kind of assignment.

(*Very long pause at 10:27.*) In the meantime, Ruburt experiences the stress in a certain fashion.

There is little else this evening for me to say, but I will indeed make whatever further connections I might make, and I will add my own help and energy to him at whatever levels they can be most useful.

(*Now, in the midst of another long pause, her eyes closed, Jane began snoring: She was asleep—briefly. I couldn't remember her doing this in any of the more than one thousand other sessions we've held. She came back to her Seth consciousness with a start.*)

I will bring the session to a close then. I have ranged within it on several occasions this evening, to see what other glimmerings might have immediately come to my attention, and I wish you as always a fond good evening.

(*10:32 PM. Jane had no idea of how she could "wake up" in her trance state instead of her usual awake state of consciousness.*

(*I hurried to type the Seth portion of the session so that Jane could read it this evening—Wednesday—but from my writing room I can hear her snoring as she sleeps on the couch in the living room. So I'll begin my own notes…. They will be something of a hodgepodge, not always in chronological order, and are intended only to summarize our discussion before the session.*

(*We sat for the session at about 8:30.*

(*At about 8 PM this evening Jane fell asleep with a lighted cigarette in her hand as she sat leaning back on the couch. She'd told me a few minutes earlier that she wanted to have a session on herself tonight, and when I came out into the living room with my notebook I found her asleep for the second or third time since supper. The cigarette event was bad news, I saw at once, let alone Jane's sleeping after stating that she wanted the session. I stood watching her sleeping while the cigarette burned down toward her fingers. A long cone of ashes fell onto her lap while I wondered what to do about the session. When the smoke reached a certain point close to her fingers—I wouldn't have let her burn herself—she woke up with a start and stubbed the cigarette in the ashtray.*

(*She looked somewhat chagrined, while I explained what had happened. "I never, never do that when I'm here alone," she said in answer to my question about consequences. I could only hope she meant it.*

(*Yet even after this little confrontation, I found her asleep again when I returned from the bedroom with her office chair—the one I use now to take notes for sessions. Several ideas had come to me on my journey into the bedroom and back. I was about to leave Jane sleeping for the evening when she woke up. "I can tell you what I'm thinking," I said, "or write down my ideas and you can read them later…."*

We ended up with my explaining my thoughts now.

("It came to me rather clearly just now that you don't want to continue with the sessions anymore," I said. "I think we're surrounded by all kinds of evidence to that effect. Every delay or missed session is a clue, for you never offer to make them up, nor have you for a long time now said let's have a spontaneous session. You don't stick to any kind of a loose schedule. I think a strong part of you is now so against the whole psychic thing that you've ended up in an awful position physically because of the conflicts involved—pulling you this way and that. You're now about 90% helpless, so you're—we're—not solving the problems, are we? How far do you want to carry this business before we make some changes, like dispensing with the sessions and the psychic life?"

("And don't tell me you're present state means that you're getting better — like Seth does—because you're not. Don't have Seth tell me in the sessions that you're working out problems and that we'll soon see improvements, because it doesn't happen. It hasn't happened for years. I'm on the point—I'm very close—to telling you that I'll refuse to cooperate on the sessions any longer, meaning that I'll be trying once more to save you from disaster. You'll end up talking to the wall if you want to have a session, or into a recorder if you can learn to do it. I can't stop you from doing it by yourself, or with someone else, but I can refuse to encourage you myself."

("So if the next few sessions don't give some clues as to what's going on," I said, "it may mean the end of the sessions.... It may very well be time to do something else with the balance of our lives. What I think—and have, often lately—about illness is that we know so little about it that we're still literally in the dark ages in that respect. I've felt that way for some time, now—that our understanding of what human beings are is minute at best. I think it's very dangerous to take too hard a position at this time on anything we think we've learned, for I can't imagine that in future millennia we'll ever cling to very much of what we think is 'true' today—especially about things like illness. In the meantime we're groping around in the dark. To ask any one person to figure it all out now, and affect a cure on themselves, may simply be asking too much most of the time.... Learning about our abilities and capabilities is a social and cultural affair, and you—anyone—need help. Lots of it—only what does one do in the meantime while trying to learn a few things?"

("I'm not saying all of this to blackmail you into going into the hospital," I told Jane several times. "I gave up on that idea after Frank [Longwell] and I couldn't convince you to try that course last summer. And with Jim Adams, too...."

("I don't want to do that," Jane said about the hospital idea. "I wouldn't mind trying some things on my own, here at the house, like getting an eye, ear and nose doctor here, or an orthopedist—but no hospital. But I'm shocked at what you're saying."

("I didn't plan it all for tonight," I said. "It just came to me, so I'm saying it as the result of a lot of similar thoughts. I don't tell you everything, and I know you don't tell me. Would you rather I didn't say anything?"

("No, not at all." Jane had much more to say, of course, which can only be summarized here. I saw that our conversation was taking up much more time before the session than I wanted to spend—but then I'd known it would, I suppose. Her main concern at the moment was to express puzzlement that she could be so consciously unaware of what her real desires were, if I was right about her wanting to quit the sessions. I told her I thought we'd had plenty of clues as to her true resistance to them ever since the inception of Mass Events and the numerous delays involving that work. The delays had merely accelerated since then, so now it seemed to me that the real desire was pretty obvious, given the episodic method of holding sessions these days.

(Jane talked about writing poetry or novels instead, for example, and I replied that she would offer those products to herself and the public in an acceptable way to her own psyche. There'd be no conflict. "You haven't walked in 13 months now," I said, "so how can you say you're getting better? I'm aware that you may be coping with certain challenges through the psychic method, so the question becomes one of how far you want to carry the thing. I myself would put physical survival before anything else, obviously, at least in this probability. Would you? I'll have to admit that I wonder sometimes...."

("I've thought more and more lately about what happens when a person is born with very strong gifts—but can't stand to use them, or has to pay a very high price indeed if they do try to use them. At first glance it seems contradictory of nature to do that, or to make such a conflict possible, yet it must happen all the time. I used to think that if a person had a strong gift that nothing would stop the ability from showing itself in that certain way—but now I don't think so at all. Now I think things are far from that simple. I think a talent can be completely buried, or show up in probabilities, or be transformed or translated in a million different ways, as many ways as there are people. Or it can just be left alone during a life, for whatever reasons."

(Jane said that lately she'd "felt good" about getting back to work on Seth's Dreams and her own Magical Approach, although actually she hasn't done much on either of those projects for a very long time now. I also wanted to know what she meant about feeling good, when this noon she'd spent much time listing all the ways in which she didn't feel good, today. At lunchtime she said she felt panicky, and hadn't done anything that morning. After lunch we used the pendulum to try to find out something about the reasons for her panic, but had little success. As I told her today, and had a few days ago, it appeared that she was embarked on a long-range cam-

paign to eliminate her communication with the rest of the world, the environment she lives in. "And what's left of the psychic thing anyway except for an occasional session?" I asked. She's now developed difficulties with vision, hearing—especially in the left ear—walking, and practically all physical activities except sitting at her table or desk, or on the couch watching TV. The hearing trouble, a recent development comparatively, has already cut down on our mutual communication, for almost automatically I've stopped speaking to her unless we're facing one another; and then I often have to repeat myself, so that our conversation becomes more episodic and the easy exchange is lost. Jane has also cut her trips to the john to just three times a day —incredible! Her feet became badly swollen last summer, and stayed that way for many weeks. Very alarming, and now that the swelling has subsided to some extent she'd left with feet covered with a tough leathery skin that bears no detail and scales off in dead flakes.

(Actually, I said in conclusion, there wasn't too much left to sacrifice. She usually sits at her table in the morning and afternoons until going to the john around 4 PM; usually she doesn't do much in this period. Reading mail may take an hour of more of it in midday. She may make a few notes or try for a poem, or leaf through the manuscript for Magical Approach, or Dreams, or read a few later sessions for herself. When she sits on the couch at perhaps 4:30, that's it for the day: She'll seldom read while there, but naps or looks at TV.

("But that would be awful to give up the sessions," she exclaimed as I wheeled her on her chair into the bathroom after we'd had tonight's session.

("Don't worry, hon," I laughed. "I know none of it's going to happen. I fully expect that you're going to go right on working on those two books."

(And while she did so, what would happen? I wouldn't want to know in advance if I could. Where—how—does one find and/or make that leap of faith Seth talked about in the session? I fully agree that that leap of faith could be the key to solving the predicament we're in. I'll suggest to Jane that we try to cultivate such a state by starting—again—a daily program of reading the material together, probably after breakfast. It's not that I even disagree with Seth in his material, or find it unacceptable. It is that it doesn't work for us the way we want it to. It's also that I think many things are left unsaid or unexplored in the sessions, probably because they are sensitive to Jane or she may block them on unconscious levels. Tonight, I told her, Seth said nothing at all about what I regard as the central point of conflict—the conflict between her Sinful Self, so-called, and the spontaneous self. For I consider that argument, that unresolved conflict, to be at the heart of her difficulties. I even agree that such an argument may well be successfully solved in other probabilities, and that in larger terms that's an entirely acceptable way for things to work within nature's larger scheme of things. But that, then, still leaves us with the challenge of coping

with something much less than a successful solution here in this reality. And there must be resolutions possible here, too, I do believe. We have much to learn.)

DELETED SESSION
DECEMBER 3, 1981 8:20 PM THURSDAY

(Note that I managed to finish Tuesday's session last night after all, by working a bit later. Jane read it. By bedtime at midnight she had some things to say about the content of my notes—defending herself to some extent, naturally, and I told her to type her notes and add them to the session today. She made some good points, but I didn't agree on others. At least, I thought, while talking she showed more animation than she had in some time.

(Today, however, she didn't do the notes. She slept late, spent time at her table in the living room, read the mail—which contained some excellent pieces, by the way —but as far as I know did no notes or other writing.

(One of the letters, from a doctor in Canada, referred us to an article in Scientific American *in which a discussion of the many-worlds view of quantum mechanics clearly vindicated a number of Seth's ideas. We had the magazine on hand but I hadn't noticed the article, in the December/81 issue. However, I doubt if the author, a professional philosopher, had any idea of backing up Seth; pardon my skepticism.*

(With a bit more speed and animation than usual:

(Softly:) Good evening.

("Good evening.")

Now: this session follows your discussion of later afternoon *(today).*

I would like to make a few comments regarding "programs"—that is, certainly it must seem to you both that you begin many therapeutically designed programs only to have them disappear. There is a rhythm to such programs, however, and it is natural for the self to rouse at certain times, begin such activity, then <u>apparently</u> (underlined) discard them.

They begin with a certain impetus, give you a certain kind of progress, and regardless of how great or small that progress may be, there is a necessary time of assimilation—that is, the stimulation over a period of time is more effective when it is in a fashion intermittent, when certain methods are tried out, applied and so forth, but by the very nature of the healing process there is also the necessity of letup, diversion and looking away.

Left alone, the self knows how to utilize such rhythms. If you trusted the characteristics of the basic natural person, you would not need such sessions as ours, generally, in the world at all—for such knowledge would be part of it and implied in its cultural organizations, and the daily habits of the people.

(This material was very similar to thoughts I'd had while painting this morning. My ideas had been triggered by an article I'd read yesterday in a recent Science Digest *article, which I'll file: At first glance, I'd told Jane later, the article seemed very good. It dealt with the idea that imperfections in the universe gave birth to life and all we know—that if the "big bang" had expanded perfectly uniformly there would be no life in the universe, merely a perfectly uniform cloud of lifeless hydrogen gas. It took me a while to realize that the author had said nothing at all about the idea of life as we know it being latently present all the while in the primordial cloud before it began to expand. Then I thought that in the perfectly expanding, uniform hydrogen cloud, nothing would be needed, in those terms [the author's]—not even life itself. "There's something very wrong with that guy's thinking," I told Jane. Probably that there is no such thing in nature as perfection, and that although we think we can conceive of such a quality, we really cannot—hence the way is left open for such messy manifestations as "life," etc.)*

In your circumstances, in one way or another you have to build up that feeling of trust or confidence, often, again, in the face of old conflicting beliefs. *(Pause.)* Therefore Ruburt's idea of a new program is a quite natural therapeutic one.

Reading the sessions of the *Magical Approach* with some consistency is now in order, where for example I might counsel at another time that they be set aside for a while. In this case at this time, however, they can serve as valuable springboards to release from your own creative areas new triggers for inspiration and understanding, and hence for therapeutic development. That should be a part of the program, in other words, regardless of what Ruburt intends to do bookwise with those sessions.

Another point: regardless of any seeming contradictions, the beneficial aspects of any particular creative activity far outweigh any disadvantages. *(Long pause.)* The nature of creativity, regardless of any given specific manifestation, is shown in an overall generalized fashion that automatically increases the quality of life, and such benefits are definite regardless of what other conditions also become apparent. I mean to make clear here that regardless of any complications that may seem only too apparent to you, in the production and distribution of my last book, and Ruburt's, *Mass Events*—the benefits far outweigh any disadvantages.

You cannot know what would have happened, for example, had it not been produced, or distributed, so the question might seem moot. In the same fashion, the publication of my next book, or rather the one we are working on, is bound to bring you greater advantages than disadvantages. Expression is far preferred of course to repression, but more than this, the matter of repression cannot be solved by adding further repression as a therapeutic measure. That is, the problem would have popped up in a different fashion regardless of the apparent trigger.

(*Long pause at 8:48.*) If the apparent trigger of a difficulty is a creative accomplishment, then the difficulty itself is "loaded" also with its own natural therapeutic solutions. I am trying to make this point as clear as I can to you, because I know it has concerned you both.

(*Long pause at 8:51.*) Give us a moment.... In a like manner, it may seem childish—or worse, futile—when after all this time Ruburt still has the feeling that changing his room around will somehow help bring about the overall solution to any problem. Yet the feeling is the result of the natural person's knowledge of the symbolic nature both of objects and thoughts, and of the rhythmic patterns that both follow, so that, again, on such occasions such activities do trigger new unconscious activity and set up new patterns of organization.

Now in chronic disorders each new program may seem to be somewhat effective, ineffective, or whatever. Some may show exciting signs that then it seems are only abandoned. In all cases, however, therapeutic benefits "pile up" at other levels, so on occasion only one small trigger here may then release or make effective the very therapeutic benefits that have not shown themselves in practical terms to that point (*intently*).

The thing is, of course, that I have only been able to describe the surface of such activities. On the other hand, there is no reason why when you are ready you cannot enjoy the fruits of that abundance. You use energy without understanding how it works, so obviously you do not need a detailed map of the inner world to obtain its benefits. You do need a faith in the existence of that reality, however, therefore I suggest that your program once again includes your helping Ruburt change his working space, and that this time you both try it with a kind of loving play, if that is possible. But the attempt, to whatever degree you achieve it, will be of benefit.

(*9:04.*) The main issue, again, must be away from a concentration on the proposition that Ruburt's condition constantly worsens. Any alternative, small or large, of daily habit is also quite effective, and should be mentioned as a part of such a program. In such ways you allow yourselves the largest possible areas for creative expression and creative changes. In the overall, again, the reasons behind Ruburt's difficulty should be encouraged to rise to the surface of the mind, where they can be encountered—but the idea is not to concentrate upon those reasons but to let them be one part of a larger therapeutic motion or movement in which they show themselves in order to be orchestrated away.

Concentration upon them will rise and fall naturally in the entire proce-dure. Each time they will be understood more and more, become less detri-mental, until they are mere annoyances. In the same manner, a few suggestions or reminders, such as those Ruburt already has on tape, should be a portion of the program.

The habitual nature of the programming that you give your own minds helps continue the chronic condition. *(Long pause.)* Such a program, to be effec-tive, must also include Ruburt's initiative, so that he rouses himself and defi-nitely begins to take advantage of those energies that he has—that is, energy exercises for himself. These should be done on a regular basis.

The emphasis should be upon arousing your own individual and joint cre-ative healing abilities—in other words, magical properties of your own minds and hearts, and such intent is bound to put you ahead of the game.

As it naturally occurs to him, Ruburt should read over material he has of the Sinful Self, and it will with its own rhythm lead toward further therapeutic adjustments. You should begin such a program as soon as possible, regarding it, however, as not a last desperate approach toward an unsolvable problem, but as a proper step of development in your understanding of the magical approach to life.

(Long pause at 9:20.) New sentence: if you cannot put your disillusion-ment aside, then you can at least use the idea of such a program as a creative exercise, a creative game that you play with one portion of your consciousness —a game that might just possibly have some creative benefits whose effects might just <u>possibly</u> crop up in the middle of your more practical considerations.

I will give you further pointers, and continue also with whatever regular-ity toward the completion of our book, unless either of you make other deci-sions. You can, however, change your lives for the better in the twinkling of an eye. You can certainly add to life's enjoyment and bring about some improve-ment at the very least in Ruburt's condition. You also have the ability to com-pletely alter the nature of your days.

End of session. At my level of operation, of course, I seem to be far more aware of your individual and joint creative propensities than you are, but I assure you that you have them and that they are ready for your use. End of ses-sion and a fond good evening.

(9:27 PM. I for one <u>was</u> disillusioned, no doubt about it, I thought as Seth spoke. Yet I could agree with Seth in tonight's session. We slept well and got up early as usual. When we finished breakfast I read the session to Jane. I was still down, but when she described how good the idea of changing things around made her feel, I had

to smile. When she asked me what I thought about the session I replied that "we had no choice" but to try to implement it. So we spent the day rearranging her things in the back room, and finished by nap time. The place looks good, and Jane said it gave her a good feeling, although she had no time to make notes or read. Frank Longwell dropped in as I began moving furniture in the morning, and helped greatly as we repositioned a couple of heavy tables. His visit cheered us up, and seemed to do him some good also. [We paid him the balance due on the front glassed-in porch.])

DELETED SESSION
DECEMBER 9, 1981 8:49 PM WEDNESDAY

(We'd postponed last night's regularly scheduled session until Thursday because Jane had a dental problem [relining,] to resolve—but then tonight after supper she decided to have a session now "because you don't know what might happen tomorrow....")

Now *(with a smile)*—Good evening.

("Good evening, Seth.")

(With pauses:) Ruburt is truly beginning to understand that the Magical Approach is indeed the natural approach to life's experience.

It is the adult's version of childhood knowledge, the human version of the animal's knowledge, the conscious version of "unconscious" comprehension. I told you that Frameworks 1 and 2 were actually united. They seemed to be so <u>disunited</u> that it was almost impossible to discuss them using any other terms. To understand that much alone, to comprehend the simple idea of Framework 2's indisputable existence is strongly important, however.

(Long pauses.) You do not have to worry in an overly strained way about putting the new principles of life into practical experience at once. You do not need to worry or deride yourselves for stupidity if it appears *(very long pause, eyes closed, at 9:04)*, looking over the long annals of work that we have done together, that it should have been obvious that our ideas were leading in certain directions—for not only have I been trying to divest you of official ideas, but to prepare you for the acceptance of a new version of reality: A version that could be described in many fashions. It has been during the annals of history, but many of those fashions also indisputably, and with the best of intentions, managed to give a faulty picture: you ended up with your gods and demons, unwieldy methods and cults, and often with the intellect downgraded. I hope of course that our "model" avoids many of those pitfalls.

(9:10.) In those annals there is legend after legend, tale after tale, history

after history describing civilizations that have come and gone, kings risen and fallen, and those stories have always represented cultures (*spelled*) of the psyche, and described various approaches used by man's psyche as it explored its intersection with earthly experience.

Some mountain climbers, when asked why they climb a certain peak, respond "because the mountain is there to be climbed," so the natural approach, the magical approach, is to be used because it exists—and because it represents an open doorway into a world of reality that is always present, always at the base of all of your cultures and experience. Theoretically at least, the magical approach should be used because it represents the most harmonious method of life (underlined). It is a way of living that automatically enhances all of your abilities and accelerates your comprehensions.

To some extent tonight's relatively brief session should remove senses of urgency on your parts, or of self-criticism, that make you question when or how can you "learn to make" the magical approach work in any specific way—that is, why can you not learn to make the approach work in, say, helping Ruburt's condition in a faster, more effective fashion?

(*9:24.*) You should understand that the approach is the best one to use in life, generally speaking, but it will improve all conditions, even if you still have difficulties in certain areas (*pause*), and that its use cannot help but promote the overall quality of your lives. That recognition takes the pressure off, so that you can to some extent relax your old attitudes enough so that you allow the magical approach (*long pause*) to work in those areas that have been a bone of contention.

The magical approach puts you in harmony with your own individual knowledge of the universe. It puts you in touch with the magical feeling of yourself that you had as a child, and that is familiar to you at levels usually beyond your physical knowledge of yourself. It is better then, say, to use the approach because you recognize it for what it is, than to use it specifically in order to get something that you want, however beneficial. There is no doubt at my level that use of the approach can clear up Ruburt's difficulties naturally and easily. If it is used because you recognize its inherent rightness in yourself, its inherent "superior stance," then it automatically puts you in a position of greater trust and faith. It opens your options, enlarges your vista of comprehension, so that the difficulties themselves are simply no longer as important—and vanish from your experience in, again, a more natural manner (*all intently*).

(*Long pause at 9:37.*) In a fashion, all of the material that I have given you in the annals of our relationship was meant to lead you in one way or another to a place where the true nature of reality could at least be glimpsed. You are at that point now. In a manner of speaking Ruburt's physical condition represents the bruises, the wounds inflicted upon any individual in his or her long journey *(long pause)* toward a greater comprehension of life's experience. In religious terms you begin to glimpse a promised land—a "land" of psyche and reality that represents unimpeded nature *(again all intently.)*

(Now very slowly—that is, with many long pauses until the end of the session, eyes closed often:)

Can I enter that land is not the "proper" question to ask. The land is here, where you are, and it always has been. The methods, the ways, the beliefs, the modes of travel to a destination create the destination itself. *(Over a one-minute pause.)* It is impossible for you to operate without beliefs in your present mode of existence *(another minute)*, "for beyond" those glittering packages of beliefs, however, there exists the vast reservoir of sensation itself, the land that does indeed exist "beyond beliefs."

(9:55.) The universe is not dependent upon your belief in it in order that it can exist. It contains within itself its own comprehension of its own knowledge, its own magical recognition of itself, its own harmonious laws and orders, its own cabinetry. It possesses and holds intact even the smallest probability, so that no briefest possible life or creature or being is ever lost in the shuffle of a cosmic mechanics.

To even sense the existence of that kind of reality, however, you must already have "opened the doorway" to Framework 2, and begun to use the magical approach as your natural instinctive way of dealing with experience.

End of session and a fond good evening *(smile again).*

("Good night."

(10:05 PM. "Gee, that was pretty weird in some fashion," Jane said as soon as she was out of trance, "to sense all kinds of things that were really different." She paused. "I want to put my finger on it. I didn't expect anything different tonight, but I have a feeling that whether you can take advantage of it or not, it represents a kind of turning point...."

(Jane said she did know she was taking the very long pauses. At first she was "alarmed, wondering if I'd gone to sleep like that. It was a lapse of consciousness — that's what bothered me. I was aware of each one, but after I came out of the first one I felt something else was involved, but I'm not sure what. I seemed to go someplace while speaking for Seth...."

(She said that she also had images that she didn't describe during the session: "I saw the Jews marching across the desert like in the Bible, and Moses leading them to the Promised Land. Only he saw it before he got there, and wondered if he could get his people there. I think probabilities were involved.")

DELETED SESSION
DECEMBER 15, 1981 8:58 PM TUESDAY

Now: as I believe I have told you often, your creativity is one of your best clues as to how you operate, yourselves, in inner reality.

The approach that you use in the production of art is instinctively "magical." It is quite natural for children to play creatively with the various states of their own consciousnesses, to explore the "us-ness" of a seemingly single identity. They play at being historic known characters. They play at being trees or animals or stars. They play at being all of those things. They understand the multiplicity that resides within the idea of single personhood.

From their parents they learn to pare down the dimensions of their own practically accepted personhood. To that extent they cut themselves off from large portions of their own subjectivity. The "us-ness" of a single identity is experienced less and less. It exists, nevertheless. (Long pause.) I told you that at certain levels contradictions would certainly seem to appear, but the us-ness of the self represents an important psychic characteristic. The child's explorations of its environment are in a fashion quite different from its later adolescent explorations of the world. A child's curiosity goes out in all directions. In a fashion it psychologically multiplies itself as it goes. Its consciousness spreads out to include all that it perceives, while still retaining a sense of its own singularity.

(9:13.) A child may think "We will go to sleep now"—meaning quite happily that (pause) its own single consciousness also participates in the conscious life and activities of everything else in its environment, so it and the creatures of the night, say, sleep together, and waken together to greet the dawn. In such a way the child actively participates in the consciousness of nature—and I am not speaking of an imaginative or symbolic participation alone, but of an awareness of the multiplicity within itself and of other creatures.

To some extent, particularly at certain levels, that participation brings about a far greater sense of sympathy and power than adults ever realize, particularly in your cultural times. The child does not have to cry out or address or search for a particular kind of God, because it understands through such subjective behavior that its own precious singularity is also a part of the greater us-ness of all other creatures, and that its singularity is automatically assured, as is its own us-ness within that larger context.

The child understands that it is itself, and yet that it is simultaneously a portion of its parents, alive within their lives (intently), as well as within its own. In calling out to them, the child calls out to a quality of its own us-ness. The child expects the parents to come to its support in the same way that it expects its own fingers and toes to support its various positions and decisions. The child understands that in a certain fashion (underlined) the parents are an extension of its own identity. At the same time it knows that the parents are equally independent, and that its own identity is a part of extensions that are the parents'.

The concepts themselves are difficult verbally to express. *(Pause at 9:32.)* The children participate in their own dimensions of natural divinity to a large-enough extent that they feel themselves automatically supported within the presence of an ever-acting comprehensive trust and love. It is only when the us-ness of the self begins to fade that a sense of relative personal helplessness begins to mar the picture of subjective experience.

At that point the us-ness is ever projected outward. The dimensions of the self begin to shrink enough, and it is at that point, in your terms, that the search for a private God or religion begins to emerge. Everyone has at least some nebulous memories of the earlier state of comprehension, however.

(Very long pause at 9:37.) Give us a moment.... The creative abilities in one way or another deal with the us-ness, with the inner intersections that everywhere occur within the most singular seeming aspects of your reality. The creative abilities join the creator and created *(long pause)* in a behavior in which for example, now, the painting that is to be affects the creator of it before its inception and before its form, so that the two are connected in a kind of behavior in which at deeper levels the ideas of cause and effect can have no meaning. The painting-to-be pushes against the awareness of its creator *(all intently)*.

In the same fashion the consciousness of the individuals pushes against the consciousness of All That Is.

In a fashion, all prayers are answered. In a fashion *(long pause)*, the entire structure of reality *(long pause)* results from "divine characteristics," and levels of relatedness.

Now there are important insights in tonight's material particularly for Ruburt, but for you also, for it is that inner feeling of contact and awareness that is so amazingly productive in the creation of art and in the creation of any phys-ical aspects that you want to change in the physical world.

End of session and a fond good evening.

("This isn't book material, then?")

This is not book dictation. You can use it as a part of the book if you prefer. It is material to help you fill out your "program."

("Good night.")

(9:51 PM.)

SESSION 939 (DELETED PORTION)
JANUARY 25, 1982 9:48 PM MONDAY

(The following material is from the 939th session.

(10:39.) Give us a moment....

(Very long pause.) The small directions I have just given also in their way serve as excellent prescriptions, of course, for daily living.

Involved with this simple statement, however, as background, all of the material I have given you should be at least somewhat understood, particularly the sessions Ruburt is working with in the late summer of 1980 onward.

I keep trying to clear up certain matters for you, in the manner of a teacher, without offending your sensibilities, spurring you onward, but not wanting you to become despairing or dissatisfied overall with the state of your progress. At one level Ruburt's physical difficulties exist as you learn a richer, more complex and profound expression. They exist as a kind of faulty sentence construction in a paragraph of living experience that you keep going back to, persistently trying to improve it.

I would like you for the moment to clear the board, as much of course as possible. I would like you to <u>attend</u> to your lives as they otherwise appear before you, for a period of time to return to sessions because of your natural living curiosity and involvement with them, and to attend most of all to creative thought as it naturally makes itself known. And let the stressful episode momentarily rest, as if you were saying "Oh yes, there is indeed a most undesirable twisted group of sentences. But we will let it go for the moment, refresh ourselves and allow the energy of creativity to work upon the paragraph till we return to it."

Such an approach at this time is a good one. In the meantime the massage can indeed benefit *(long pause)*, for the two women do indeed allow a free expression of healing love to direct their lives, so that their touch is of itself soothing and healing, and carries certain important messages.

Let Ruburt attend, not to his book so much as to the ideas within it that give it meaning—and I bid you a fond good evening.

("The same to you."

(10:58 PM. A brief note: The two women Seth referred to are Dorothy [George Rhoads' lady] and Cathy Poklinkowski. Cathy teaches massage at BOCES, and was introduced to Jane through Dorothy. They gave Jane her first massage last Sunday afternoon. A program has been worked out whereby Cathy is to see Jane on Sunday and Thursday evenings for regular massages for a while, to see if they help her. Cost: $25.00 per week. Dorothy will not be down from Harford Mills very

often, especially in the wintertime, but she is to see Jane every few weeks to give her a haircut, etc.

(This grand idea soon petered out. Dorothy never did come down to see Jane for the reasons Seth mentioned—Cathy saw Jane a few times and that was that — Jane ended up in the hospital in a few weeks.)

DELETED SESSION
JANUARY 27, 1982 8:32 PM WEDNESDAY

("Our dentist, Paul O'Neill, visited us after lunch today, as I'll explain in the notes following the session. The session itself springs from Paul's visit also.)

Now—good evening.

("Good evening.")

A personal session that has of course some overall general merit.

I would heartily suggest that you and Ruburt consider (underlined) the possibility of buying Paul's cottage. The consideration itself is what I am after —the willingness to explore a probability that has come into your attention— because in so doing you remind yourselves of the freedoms that are (underlined) available in your terms, and because such a consideration, among other things, will allow you to automatically see your beliefs from a different focus, through another picture frame.

The same ingredients of your lives, yes, but with different light thrown upon them, so that newer understandings can sometimes appear that were not clear before. Such a possibility is feasible, containing in fact many desirable— and most desirable—elements; the presentation of a second frame of reference, a second environment that would still be your own. Period. The probability is in fact most intriguing, since it would offer you a home away from home that would still represent largely an investment rather than primarily an expenditure —as would, say, a series of vacations. A place of relative privacy, and yet one in which you would not be unknown or isolated, one in which in fact the 458 West Water Street connections would continue to operate, with Paul of course as mediator. *(We had lived at 458, three blocks from downtown Elmira.)*

In a fashion this would indeed represent a very desirable arrangement over a period of years, one that Ruburt could take advantage of, one that could serve you by also presenting you with a different framework through which to view your painting and visual world, one in which the idea of water as motion was always present.

Such a consideration, however, immediately shakes old beliefs and fears in a kind of clamor. Some old beliefs would rise to the forefront of attention that until now have remained generally in the background. Ideas of virtue, spareness and artistic single attentiveness as opposed to the idea of extravagance, the scattering of energies, or pleasure as a tempting disruptive force; all such beliefs are suddenly shaken up in a new bag, so to speak, so that you can distinguish between them with some new understanding.

Such a consideration brings also to mind gears about changing the status quo, of adding to life's ordinary distractions. *(Pause.)* Now in many ways you and other people close your eyes to such probabilities when they do present themselves, so that fears overall predominate, while any desirable characteristics or benefits of whatever quality largely remain unexplored and inactive.

I am of course quite aware of the danger of flooding that can occur under such circumstances, but I would like you both, as freely as you can, to explore that consideration. It does represent a rather significant probable development. Any decision is of course your own—but the overall willingness to explore the creativity possible in such a probability is perhaps more important than any choice you make.

The entire affair is highly intriguing. There are elements in it quite evocative of man camped about any lake, of his relationship with nature and with water, and with his sometimes seemingly contradictory desire to be apart from his fellows while still united somehow with a larger fellowship. It would give you the chance to explore different aspects of nature, quite simply, some different species of plants or animals, but one in which water itself is the ever-pervading main element.

(9:00 during a rather steady, emphatic delivery.) Man has within him the need to rest and to explore, to stay by "the hills of home," *(from Thomas Wolfe),* and to explore beyond them, but such a relatively accessible second environment does have certain advantages for you and Ruburt over those it sometimes presents for others, and such a willingness to explore the probability alone can give you some excellent results by providing a new elasticity of attitude, and in a fashion by bringing home in a different way the idea that the present is the point of power.

That is, you increase the feeling and intent of power by considering it in such action, whether or not in your world you pursue that particular issue—and I do not mean to consider the issue hypothetically either, but as a quite possible desirable course of action that you may or may not pursue. This means also that you are bringing such an issue into conscious light, that you are not afraid of making such a choice, and that you are thankful that the choice itself is available to you.

Many habits of repression come about because you are afraid to make conscious decisions, or simply do not want to be bothered with them, and certainly all probable events do not attract you to any important degree. It is, however, an excellent policy to seek out the available conscious decisions that can be made in your lives, for you see your own situations then in a newer clearer light. Period.

(Long pause.) Animals massage each other, and also use touch healing, and these activities represent the natural characteristics available in the "animal family," as well as occurring naturally in the family of man. Animals playing are always exchanging healing transformations of energy from one to the other. Your own feelings connecting your hands, therefore, are quite pertinent and significant. Some people are more aware than others of such connections. They have been frowned upon in your society, however, so they are most often repressed.

(Pause at 9:15.) It is quite healthy, particularly at certain stages, for young children to sleep together in the same room or even in the same bed, as long as some opportunity for seclusion is provided to them when they want it—for at night the ancient families did indeed refresh and heal themselves. You can consciously retrain yourself to use the ability more freely and directly, and in many instances one individual can help heal another easier than the person can himself. That is, the suffering person, to whatever degree, already mistrusts or distrusts the nature of his own abilities, but usually can and will accept such a loving attention from another family member, or even from a friend. I meant to mention these points in particular.

There are many different ways that people use such energy. Ruburt received another letter today *(which I have yet to read)*, from someone experimenting with the kundalini version of energy, in which the final results were poor, leading to a fear of energy itself. It is highly important then that you realize the vitality and natural right to such energy, as it is available not only to yourself but to the plant and animal kingdoms themselves. Since your bodies constantly heal themselves, and since all nature is basically cooperative, so the exchange of such healing energy is freely effortless.

(Long pause at 9:27. Much slower now:) It is best, beginning, to deal with specifics, working with any given small area—actually somewhat in the same manner that an animal might lick the fur of another. You have both made some rather important connections lately *(long pause)*, that can only serve to remind you of an important point: Ruburt's "symptoms" should not be regarded as one black blot of a certainly reprehensible quality, sometimes seen in a quite hopeless light, but as a combination or result of quite changeable, quite moveable,

quite separate characteristics that can also be dealt with separately, moved around and so forth, relieved or dissolved.

That is enough for now. My heartiest wishes and a fond good evening.

("Good evening.")

(9:36 PM. Jane's dictation had been the most fluid and even in some time, with few pauses until the near end.

(Seth's material on Paul O'Neill's cottage came about because of our conversation with Paul this noon as he checked Jane's lower teeth here at the house. It seems he and his wife are buying a larger cottage close by their old one, which they plan to rent. The price of the older cottage is around $35,000, I believe, and I don't recall Paul saying outright that they wanted to sell the cottage. Rather, the O'Neill's plan to rent it out for "the season" at a healthy sum, as is the custom at Lake Keuka.

(The session subject matter was quite unexpected by me, though Jane had had plenty of intimations beforehand, it developed, without telling me. This afternoon as she worked answering mail she began to get "stuff pretty strong on it from Seth." At the same time, she rather wished Seth would forget about it—probably because she knew what our reactions to it would be.

(Of course, I was nonplussed, thinking at once of the extra work involved in first purchasing, then second running a second establishment, when it seems that I barely manage to find the time to do what I'm doing now. I understood Seth's material on the subject, and even agreed with it, I told Jane after the session. I added that it wasn't a question of money, meaning that I thought the money would be provided should we decide to undertake such a project. But the time.... and I did fear that the extra work couldn't but help cut into painting time, or typing time, or whatever. Jane agreed....)

DELETED SESSION
APRIL 12, 1982 8:56 PM MONDAY

(Yesterday marked the beginning of Jane's third week home from the hospital, and lately I've been trying to gently encourage her to begin a series of private sessions in an effort to learn what we can about the whole hospital-health-establishment belief system, and our part in it through and with the Seth material. I was eager to get Jane started on a program of self-therapy through the Seth material in order to help her counter—or at least supplement—the standard rigid medical framework we've been encountering for the last month, or since she went into the hospital on February 26, 1982. [She was discharged on March 28.]

(I'm also trying to whip up some enthusiasm to begin work on Seth's latest

book, Dreams, "Evolution," and Value Fulfillment, *for which we recently signed the contract, and took money. [The contract was countersigned on March 22.] "Don't worry," I said to Jane in the hospital, "I know who's going to do the rest of the work on the book...." Meaning that I could see she wasn't going to be able to contribute much physical work on it at this time. Therefore, actually producing the physical work for the publisher was going to be up to me, and I was anxious to begin work on this once we've established some sort of viable daily routine revolving around Jane's nursing care, sleeping schedule, medication, etc.*

(We have had two short "sessions," during which Jane dictated passages for the intro to Dreams *while I wrote down her words. Not Seth trances, by the way. She did this work herself, presumably in a sort of altered state, and has made a good start here. I have yet to type that material, but will start it after finishing this session.*

(A note: Jane has mentioned several times since returning home that Seth may dictate a biography of her—presumably including her hospital experiences, etc. It took me a few days to realize that this is a unique idea—certainly it hasn't been done before. "Every so often I get ideas about it," she said, but not from Seth, at least yet.... that when you're a kid you pick up certain ideas about what kind of a person you want to be—from a photograph, a corner of life, an edge, and you put all those little things together into a personality. You draw upon the people you share your new environment with. Everybody does this, and it's much more forceful a thing in the formation of personality that people realize...."

(Jane still nods off as she sits in her chair, especially after supper, which we take to be an indication that her thyroid is still below par, although she's much improved in that regard over her condition before she entered the hospital. The drifting off worries her, however. Even as I sat beside her at the round card table in the living room, writing these notes, she kept nodding off into sleep. I'd spent some little time trying to talk her into a short session to begin with, and she'd finally agreed to try for one. It was 8:52 when she really fell asleep in her chair, for perhaps the tenth time. I could see that we'd get no session tonight. Yet she woke up. "I'm just waiting—I feel so funny...."

(The contradictory thing was, as I'd told her the other day, that I didn't think we were going to get anywhere in solving our dilemmas until we tapped into the session routine again. Otherwise, we'd be left to struggle within the establishment just as everyone else did. Yet each time I wanted to try something, Jane was having difficulty focusing. Just as I was about to give up for this evening, Jane came awake again and said rather firmly, "I've passed a certain point, Bob, and now I can do it...." meaning that she'd have a session after all. "But it'll be a real short one." And I knew it would be good.

(Jane went easily into trance as usual. Her Seth voice was stronger than I'd

expected it to be, yet with an underlying tremor that I'd noticed on a number of other
occasions since Jane had returned from the hospital.)

Now: a very brief discourse.

For all of his and your complaining, you understand in rather good measure the decisions and actions that motivate your lives, so that Ruburt is more than usually aware of the manipulations that psychologically and physically lie just beneath the material usually carried by what is ordinarily called the conscious mind.

Therefore, a kind of momentary gap appeared between his life <u>and his living of it</u>—a pause and a hesitation *(pause)* became obvious between his life and what he would do with it, as his condition showed just before the hospital hiatus.

I will help you still further understand those manipulations. For many people—<u>most</u> people—carry on the same kind of procedures while making important decisions as to whether or not they will continue life at any given time—but they hide the issues from themselves far more than Ruburt did.

(Long pause at 9:05.) Give us a moment.... The entire issue had been going on for some time. And the argument—the argument being somewhat in the nature of a soul facing its own legislature, or perhaps standing as a jury before itself, setting its own case in a kind of private yet public psychic trial. Life decisions are often made in just such a fashion. With Ruburt they carried a psychic and physical logic and economy, being obvious at so many different levels of actuality. In such a way buried issues were forced into the light, feared weaknesses or inadequacies were actively played out where they could be properly addressed, assorted and assessed. To whatever degree possible, given your time requirements, I will try to explain such matters.

(Pause at 9:10.) To such a degree, of course, the affair was, then, therapeutic. *(Pause.)* Ruburt is now far more willing to make certain changes in his life than he was earlier, and he sees himself more as one of a living congregation of creatures—<u>less</u> isolated than before, stripped down from the superperfect model, and therefore no more under the compulsion to live up to such a psychological bondage *(all with some emphasis)*. He need not try to be the perfect self, then, the super-image—and in fact to some extent found himself the supplicative *(self?)*, knocking upon creaturehood's earthly door, as any creature might ask aid from another who found himself wounded through misadventure. He found a mixed world—one hardly black or white, one with some considerable give-and-take, in which under even the most regrettable of circumstances there <u>was</u> (underlined) room for some action, for some improvement, for some decision, for some creative response. The rules of the game have there-

fore been automatically altered. The issues are clearer, dramatically etched.

(Long pause at 9:18.) Give us a moment.... The arthritis situation is as I gave it, but you are still faced with the medical interpretation of that situation, so that it is up to Ruburt to set it aside. He is returning to activity at his creative, naturally therapeutic pace, no longer afraid that he is going too fast—or will — but shown only too clearly that activity and motion represent the only safe, sane, and creative response.

We do not want long drawn-out discussions of why and what exactly happened, simply to understand the dynamics of the activity. Ruburt can work with the self-image he has now. It is imperfect, but it is pliable and willing to change.

There will be more. This is to give you a starter—and as always to you both my heartiest regards.

("Thank you very much, Seth. Good night."

(9:25 PM. Jane's pace had generally been okay, considering the circumstances. "I felt like when I got slow there a couple of times that it didn't have anything to do with dozing off," she said, referring to a few longer pauses. "It was just a normal, I don't know, thing...." I told her she'd done well. "It was more than I thought I could do," she said, "but I really got worried tonight when I started dozing off like that." I replied that all along I'd felt she could do more than she'd thought she could, and such had been the case.

(We were both very pleased with the session: It contains many important clues. The arthritis diagnosis, Jane said, would be the only one the medical profession could offer, with its very limited insights and viewpoint—whereas Seth has insisted all along that she didn't have arthritis per se. I'd wanted him to at least refer to the arthritis subject tonight, hoping that the reinforced suggestions would help Jane mobilize her own strong creative powers. Equally important, too was Seth's idea that Jane no longer needed to try to be "the perfect self." Very important.

(Seth's reference, above, to Jane's fear of going too fast is a reference to an excerpt from the deleted session for January 28, 1981. I keep this excellent excerpt in the current notebook where I see it each time I open the book. It seems to me that it very neatly sums up the core of Jane's difficulties—that one, along with a longer excerpt from the deleted session for January 26, 1981 just previous. That one concerns Jane's fear of the spontaneous self, and how she regarded her immobility as a form of protection.

(A note: I haven't answered fan mail since bringing Jane home from the hospital on March 28, and already it is beginning to pile up. I kept up with it religiously while visiting Jane each day for the month she was in the hospital. Since returning to the house, though, I've had absolutely no time at all for the mail, and have stopped answering it except for business and an occasional exceptional letter, or a request for

a visit, etc. I don't know whether I regret my actions or not. Now the mail has retreat-
ed way into the background, even though I don't forget what it means, that we get
such a response from what we do, and that each of those writers is sincere, and in my
opinion deserving of an answer.

(Sue Watkins has offered to help with the mail, but I don't know what to do
—guess I'm afraid that once it's out of our house and hands the situation would turn
into a mess. I also don't want to give up physical possession of the letters, I notice. One
option we've considered is having a temporary postcard printed up referring to our
hassles with Jane's illness, that we can't answer mail at this time except to say thanks,
and that later we may be able to. I think that at the moment that's our best way to
go, even if it means broadcasting the fact of Jane's troubles. At least the replies would
be from us....)

DELETED SESSION
APRIL 16, 1982 7:39 PM FRIDAY

(After last Monday's session, Jane told me that she'd try to hold private sessions
when she could, but that at this time she'd rather be free of any expected routine, say
of Monday and Wednesday nights. I agreed, of course. While waiting for the next ses-
sion to develop, then, I'd busied myself working on her intro and my notes for Seth's
Dreams. *I like the way it's going, although Jane plans some revisions. But it's a*
unique piece of work, and as I told her, we can use it to lay the foundation for much
future work. Certainly I know of nothing else like it on the market.

(In other words, I'm happy to say, our creativity is on the rise, showing itself
more and more in spite of—or perhaps because *of—all that's happened with us late-*
ly. Very comforting.

(However, I've also discovered that I'll have to watch my time if I want to get
anything done—for "time" can slip away like smoke as I do chores, help nurses take
care of Jane, or cook meals or take care of the cats or run errands. [Soon the grass,
which is turning green, will need cutting, too.] I became quite concerned over the
time element this afternoon when I saw that it was 2:45 before I could get back to
the typewriter, when I'd quit work at 11:30 AM. By the time I could go back to
work, I was in a half-angry, dejected mood. Jane picked this up, of course. I ended
up taking a nap.

(After supper we talked about whether she might want to resume dictation for
her intro to Dreams. *By then I'd answered two of the three letters we'd received today,*
for both writers wanted to come here—one from California, the other from
Australia. [We'd also had an unannounced visitor—a Korean woman lawyer—from

Los Angeles the other day.] Naturally we're turning away all visitors because of the time element.

("Well, I guess I'll do a Seth thing tonight," Jane finally said, and rather to my surprise, "but it won't be long at all...." When she did go into trance as we sat at the living room table, her voice had a distinct tremor—more so than on Monday night [April 12] and a farther-away or more distant feeling or sound. With many long pauses:)

Now—

("Good evening.")

The same process involving the thyroid gland has happened several times in his life, and in each of those cases it has <u>repaired</u> itself.

(This information came through because Jane's doctor, Marsha Kardon, had told her in the hospital that tests showed Jane's thyroid gland had quit working altogether—with the concomitant fact that Jane would have to take a synthetic thyroid extract—Synthroid—daily for the rest of her life.)

If earlier, however, Ruburt had the erroneous idea that he was going too fast—or would or could—and had to restrain himself and to exert caution, now he received the medical prognosis, the "physical proof" that such was not the case—and in fact that the opposite was true: he was too slow. If our words could not convince him, or his own understanding grasp the truth, then you had the "truth" uttered with all the medical profession's authority—and if once a doctor had told him years ago how excellent was his hearing, the medical profession now told him that his slowness *[his thyroid deficiency]*, helped impair his hearing to an alarming degree.

Moreover, here is the medication necessary—the Synthroid—that will right that balance. And so it will.

(Long pause at 7:46, one of many.) If Ruburt once found himself imagining that he must be strong and perfect enough to help solve everyone else's problems, now he found himself relatively helpless, and "undefended" —that is, his physical condition put him in a situation certainly where he felt helpless. The super-perfect, impractical self-image simply fell away: it could not survive such a situation.

(Very long pause at 7:50.) So <u>contrary</u> to its own beliefs, and helpless or not, Ruburt was holding his own.

There was a certain comradeship existing between himself and others, desires and impulses became more immediate, clearer cut, easier to identify.

(7:58.) The discomforts of a physical nature led to instant responses. He could enjoy the cooling drink *(Coke)*, the change of position, the sudden relief of turning from one hip to another. His weaknesses were out in the open, dra-

matically presented, and from that point, unless he chose death he could only go forward: for suddenly he felt that there was after all <u>some</u> (underlined) room to move, that achievements were possible, where before all achievements seemed beside the point in the face of his expected superhuman activity.

(And as Jane and I had discussed while she was in the hospital, she had indeed explored quite seriously the possibility of physical death—much more so than either of us had realized on conscious levels before her admittance to the hospital.)

He will, then, continue to improve, because he has allowed himself some room for <u>motion</u>, for change of value fulfillment. Trust the body's rhythms as these changes occur, however. Going out in the yard *(this afternoon in a wheelchair, accompanied by her nurse)* was an excellent case in point, important on practical and symbolic levels.

(Long pause at 8:00.) In a manner of speaking, the Sinful Self created the superhuman self-image that demanded so much, and it encased Ruburt's body as if in concrete. Well, that image cracked and crumbled in the hospital experience, leaving Ruburt with his more native, far more realistic image of himself. It is one he can work with.

All of that <u>was</u> (underlined) exhausting, and you had your own role to play in those developments. Do, when you can, look over my magical approach material. Ruburt kept turning down his thermostat, so to speak. Now his desires and intents have set it upon a healthy, reasonable setting, and the inner processes are automatically activated to bring about the normal quickening of his body, as before his intent led to the body's automatic slowness.

Enough for this evening. I bid you a fond good evening—and know that you have taken, both of you, important new strides.

("Good night," I said after a moment's pause.

(8:10 PM. Jane's Seth voice had strengthened somewhat as the session progressed. "I felt a little strange before the session," she said, "but it was no problem.... My hands have been better and better, especially eating, but they're sore, you know?" She does have somewhat less trouble using a fork, say, but still does about all of her eating with her left hand.

(We were very encouraged by two points especially that Seth had mentioned this evening: that Jane's thyroid had repaired itself before—which event now could free her from dependence upon medication—and that the Sinful Self's superhuman image had "cracked and crumbled in the hospital experience."

(These represented key points, I told Jane. They were very important, for they'd leave the body free to heal itself. "We'll see what develops. I wonder what you'll be doing six months from now, if Seth's right?" I asked. "Pretty interesting.... The body finally became so desperate to free itself of that rigid Sinful-Self superhuman image

that it took itself into the hospital for a month—even if it did almost die in order to get itself in there. But it got rid of that image...." Jane agreed.

(I also had to wonder what Jane's "Sinful Self" would have to say now, in comparison to the material Jane had received from it beginning in June 1981. Those first 40 or 50 pages that had been so revealing to us at the time....)

DELETED SESSION
APRIL 28, 1982 32 PM WEDNESDAY

("I feel gaps in my consciousness," Jane said, worried. "I'll start to do something, then I'll find myself thinking that I've already done it—but that means that I've dozed off in the meantime, and didn't do it at all...."

(She said this, as she has several times lately, after supper tonight. Once again I asked her if she wanted to have a session, or do some dictation on her own. As soon as she finished eating she began to nap in her chair as she sat bundled up at the card table in the living room. The television ran on unheeded.

(At first Jane didn't know what she wanted to—or could—do. She's fallen into a regular, very narrow pattern of eating, watching TV, and sleeping, either in her chair or in bed, night and day. She reads a little but writes—or tries to—even less. "I'm scared," she said again. "That dozing off really worries me...."

(Once again, I tried to get through to her that the sessions or her own work could offer ways to get through that period, or at least offer greater insights into it. "If it was me," I said, and I probably shouldn't have, "I couldn't wait to get something on what's going on, in the hope that it would help." Lately I've more or less given up bugging her to have sessions, since it seemed that that activity was beyond her means at this time. I also tried to keep in mind Seth's recent reference to her own natural rhythms, thinking that if she didn't want sessions just now, that might actually be part of the healing process.

(Today Jane's nurse, Peggy Jowett, put her through a regimen of moving, washing, and changing dressings—a busy two hours that was all Jane could handle, we agreed. Was her later malaise simply the result of physical exhaustion? I didn't really think so while granting the possibility, for Jane also dozed in the mornings and on weekends when no nurses were present, and I changed her dressings on weekends within 20 minutes, so there was little strain involved there.

("The only other thing I can think of is the thyroid, that it's still below par," Jane said. I agreed that had something to do with it, but also felt other, psychological factors were involved. Mr. Wrigley, the physician's assistant who had called a couple of weeks ago, also visited today to check upon Jane's decubiti [which are doing

well, by the way], so he was here when Peggy arrived. The four of us talked in the bedroom. Mr. Wrigley said that the ulcer on Jane's coccyx was filling in with "grainy" flesh, which means it's on the mend also, if slowly. But the entire afternoon had been an active, tiring one for Jane.

(I'd also run errands to the post office, supermarket and drugstore while Peggy assisted Jane, and by the time I got back Peggy had managed to get Jane from the bed back into her chair—but it hadn't been easy, Jane said later, and she hadn't been able to describe to Peggy just how I did it myself with little effort.

(At my request Mr. Wrigley is going to ask Jane's doctor, Marsha Kardon, if the blood test she's due for May 3 can't be run here at the house instead. This would save a trip to St. Joseph's Hospital next Monday, and perhaps speed things up a bit, for I felt that Jane could now use a boost in thyroid activity through a stronger dose of supplement, Synthroid. Mr. Wrigley is to call this morning—Thursday—as I type this material, although I don't hold out too much hope that things will work out that easily. He said Dr. Kardon herself could take the blood from Jane; and she has promised to visit us here.

("I'm just waiting." Jane said now, smoking a cigarette as I sat with her at the card table. I'd brought the notebook, as she had suggested I do. Her eyes were heavy, but—"I almost feel something." she said at 7:25. "Anything," she said, rocking back and forth in her chair, meaning she was trying to stay awake and would accept whatever she could get. And once again, as we waited I thought that I was the one who'd initiated events this evening, whereas I had trouble understanding why Jane didn't do more of that herself.

("I do feel him slightly around," she said at 7:30. "I've been telling myself...." Her voice trailed off, and I could see that she was struggling to stay awake. Yet she did manage to let a session happen. She began speaking for Seth with her eyes closed —but her voice was quite strong, comparatively speaking, with a minimum of tremor. Her eyes were quite dark when they finally opened to stare at me.)

Good evening. Now briefly—

("Good evening, Seth.")

The upsetting alterations of consciousness occur mainly when Ruburt's energies are being utilized elsewhere. On physical levels is then when he becomes most aware of the lack of his usual energy, or of available needed resources, which are so connected with thyroid activity.

After a fairly large meal *(like we had tonight)*, for example, digestion begins. His available energy is therefore directed to that activity, and with the thyroid still in a defective state, he feels then unaroused, lapses, and largely by such means *(long pause)* holds the energy that he has left. I hope I have put that clearly.

The night situation will be somewhat improved by a snack later during the evening—or one or two—so that you have a regular intake of protein and nutriments, rather than say large amounts more or less quickly eaten. This will also help the balance of the thyroid, and help sleep—that is, induce it—and even improve muscular activity.

(During the night Jane has also more or less settled into a routine of laying down for a couple of hours, then sitting in her chair for an equal time, and even sleeping in it, then going back to bed. She sips Coke but doesn't eat. The TV set is on constantly. I usually get up at least three, and usually four, times during the night to help her change from chair to bed to chair, etc.)

Ruburt needs to talk over his fears with you, quite "normal" ones. It will help them fade faster—and if you can, lovingly reassure him rather than act like a fine professor with a stubborn student *(with some humor)*. The fears largely have to do with the medical establishment's prognosis.

(A case in point: When he visited today, Mr. Wrigley said Jane should wear support stockings or bandages around her feet and legs in the daytime, to help reduce the swelling in her feet and ankles. Otherwise, he said, ulcers could develop there also. This frightened Jane, but she didn't tell me until some hours later. Her feet are some- what swollen—edema—but look much better than they did last year, say, and their color is normal. She does wear my elasticized winter stockings, which offer some such protective support. These kinds of dilemmas are what bother us about the medical establishment: We don't know whether to completely ignore such advice, or to heed it and thus accept medicine's prognosis. I do personally credit the body with having ter- rific healing powers—especially if, as I said to Jane recently, the body is left alone to repair itself. But obviously, this leaving alone is often very difficult to achieve in that fashion. It may even be, I've often thought, that one cannot really leave the body alone, nor be meant to—for the physical body would be a portion of the reality each individual creates, and so is bound to be intimately involved with individual fears, desires, intents, successes, etc.)

He does respond to stimuli rather well. So brief conversations with you on that subject, or on your work in general, or on any subject whatsoever, will auto- matically quicken his mood and responses. He has of course improved, and in general strength, since returning home—but in the hospital nothing was demanded or expected of him.

(Long pause at 7:44.) Now, he more or less thinks that he must and should return to "work" immediately, where instead a more relaxed attitude would allow his natural feelings, his love of ideas and his interest in our work to natu- rally show their results again, with the most natural balance of recuperation. That is, a rhythm would be found, and so it shall as the pressure is off.

(Pause.) He can use also stimuli from you of suggestion and so forth, when momentarily he <u>feels</u>, at least, unable to rouse himself on his own behalf. That is, your <u>invitation</u>, your offer *(long pause)*, is more important than, say, any implied or spoken <u>accusation</u> that implied he <u>should</u> (underlined) work or whatever at any given time.

You are yourself to be quite commended for your behavior and your understanding. And generally for a far fuller range of personality characteristics than you were able to show in far earlier years. The emotions are like musical notes: the more of them you can play the richer your composition *(with emphasis)*—and your understanding, even when it is not fully conscious, has helped release the range of those emotional characteristics.

(I'll have to admit that when Seth was speaking I wasn't sure whether he was contradicting himself or not—first talking about my accusing Jane, then commending me....

(7:53.) Ruburt is coming along all right. Before long I will be giving you information again on a more regular basis. Your writing ideas are good. The two of you in fact together, briefly, even for a short time discussing those ideas, can generate some of the best creative work that either of you have ever known.

You were of great benefit, you see, tonight, in actively mentioning the session—providing that stimuli, when Ruburt thought at least that his energies would not allow it.

(Long pause.) This may be the end of the session. It is possible that after a break I could add more, but we will see about Ruburt's energies then. For now, I assure you of my own devout *(humorously)* sympathies—and also offer you my own assurances that your capacities and energies are more than able to see you through this episode triumphantly.

("Thank you.")

(7:59 PM. Jane leaned back in her chair, coming out of trance even though her eyes were closed. "Very good," I said, pleased. "I can't believe it: he offered to come back after a break. Do you remember that?"

("Yes.... I got thirsty.... I'm sure glad I did that."

(I'd planned to mow grass for a few minutes after the session—it was dusk by now—but I had to wait. So did Jane: "Now that he said that. I'll have to wait...." I lit a cigarette for her. I told her the session had lasted for 27 minutes, which pleased her, "since I didn't think I could get two words out of me to begin with." But I'd known she could do it.

(I scanned the local newspaper during "break." "I think I'll go to the john," Jane said at 8:17. "What I was getting from Seth was that any hospital serves as a terrific example of a belief system...." Abruptly, Jane broke off speaking in her nor-

mal voice and began delivering her material in a different, light, hesitant voice that was in between her own and Seth's: "....highlighted through the light of activity and interactions. That is, you have the medical beliefs themselves, with their appropriate props *immediately available, so that suggestion becomes remarkably effective."*

("All of the personnel, patients, the entire community or social structure of such an establishment reinforce and promote the inner belief system about which they all congregate," she continued. "With our ideas, however, there are no props available, just waiting to be used, no organizations that personify or represent the core of our beliefs—only the individual more or less stubbornly interacting with a private universe, trying to establish this new beachhead."

("I'm in a sort of transitory state," Jane said after a pause, "between my own level of consciousness and Seth's. There will be far more said on such issues, but in the same way, any organization devoted primarily to one large system of beliefs will always highlight the effectiveness with which belief systems operate. But what you see is the end product."

(A very long pause at 8:26. "I lapsed a little," Jane said. "Courthouses, for example, dealing primarily with the law, already relying upon their courts and legislatures, are another case in point.... You do not have to accept their versions of reality, of course: You can think of them merely as interpretations of events. In any case...."

("That's it," Jane said after another long pause.

(8:27 PM. "I don't know where that came from," Jane said. "I started to disappear from it, or go into another state or something." Certainly she hadn't sounded like she was giving her usual "own" dictation for the intro to Dreams, *and certainly not like Seth. "Gee. I don't know what that was. We'll probably get something more on it later."*

("You sure did a lot more tonight than you expected to, though, didn't you?"

("Yeah. I'm glad I did.... I don't know what I did with that last material. I felt like I could get a lot from Seth, but that was all I could do."

("Probably your energy level dropped," I said, "and that was as far or deep as you could carry the material's expression." Jane tentatively agreed.

DELETED SESSION
APRIL 29, 1982 12:09 PM THURSDAY

(This is the second session I've typed today. I was typing last night's deleted session this morning, when at about 10:00 AM Jane said she would like to lie down briefly. She felt like passing out, she said, but I took this to mean she'd soon want to get up, as usual. Instead, she slept heavily for over an hour. I'd placed the goose-down

pillow under her knees, following the suggestion given us yesterday by nurse Peggy Jowett. When I looked in on Jane at 10:30, thinking she'd want to get up, I found instead that she was sleeping heavily, with her knees and legs relaxed and "dumped" to her left in a more relaxed position than usual. I left her alone, then.

(I finished last night's session at 11:00 AM, filed the carbons, etc., and called Jane at about 11:15, thinking that I'd get to spend half an hour in the yard before lunch. [I'd begun to mow the grass.] Jane was waking—but she was in a surprisingly uncomfortable, "sore" state involving her legs and hips. Much more than usual, she said, breathing heavily through her mouth and half-crying at the same time. It was clear something had happened: Jane said her legs were more relaxed than they'd been in years—but at the same time they were so sore she was appalled. I massaged them, and she said that action felt great but at the same time almost unendurable, so I soon stopped. I got her in her chair and out to the living room table.

(She was still half-crying with pain and upset, but told me to go out at 11:45. At the same time she said she knew the unusually intense feelings were good ones, say, as opposed to a worsening of her situation.

(I mowed some grass and filled a coffee container with forsythia I clipped from our bush on our southeast corner of the lot. Jane loved it, but almost broke down crying as I came in at noon. She asked me to get my notebook. She hadn't read last night's session yet, by the way. She began speaking, or dictating, to me in her own voice—not Seth's, for instance—but it was wavering, choked with tears. Her head was bent over, her eyes closed often so that I was afraid she'd bump into her glass of Coke, and perhaps knock it over.

(12:09.) Like I said before you went out, I feel as if some ancient swarm of wasps' nests *(long pause)* have finally been touched upon or stirred up—or of angry energy that had been stored in those portions of my body. And certainly to some extent they also had a strongly sexual cast.

I feel as if this is the first sign that those psychological and physical areas are being touched or allowed to relax or release. That the soreness and so forth —really wild—was a reaction as the swirling energy was stirred *(very long pause at 12:13)* and allowed to escape at least partially—probably only as much as you could allow at once.

The weirdest thing, I thought quite emotionally afterward while you were out, while my ass still stung—it even does now—but I personify myself, I guess. Or maybe just that withheld anguish, out of all things, is real *(almost crying).*

The name simply seemed to stand for all of man's agonizing reach for greatness, and yet for the anguish that always seemed to separate himself. But in any case I felt like a divided Israel, crying out for the people to come together in peace. And what it meant was that Israel itself was a simile for the individual

—that is, one person—who was *(long pause)* composed of so many fantasies and dreams and prophecies and hopes and angers and fears.

So for a minute I even called myself Israel, I guess, but there's more connections here that I haven't got. I feel that my sleep with the pillow, and my later reactions of soreness, mean that I've touched upon, again, those areas I'd forsaken for some time, and shoved away or whatever, and that the release of tension itself was bound to be somewhat explosive, I suppose.

(Long pause at 12:21.) It was and is pretty wild. That's all....

(We had barely started talking when Jane broke off to resume her dictation at 12:23:)

I guess I feel that Israel.... *(long pause)....* that the tale of Israel, with all of its wars and so forth, and its historical and biblical past, represents some ancient brilliant knowledge that man once had, of the self being so diverse as to <u>behave</u> as a nation of a million individuals, each looking for their homeland.

(Long pause at 12:25.) But through the years the story itself lost its meaning for people. But the term Israel still stands for one individual, along with its multitudinous parts, and all of the colorful, feared, anguished or enticing heroes of the bible represent elements of each person's soul, personified, set momentarily alive in myth.

("I guess that's all," Jane said. "Odd thoughts for me, though, about 'Israel.'" She hasn't read last night's session yet, but said now, "Well, I suppose you can see why I came up with this material after last night's session," although she hadn't mentioned Israel.

(Israel is constantly in the news, of course, and we see the television reports while eating supper or later in the evening. It always seems to be bad news, full of strife and agony and grim determination to survive. In addition, a NYC station is running a serialized story called Golda, *with Ingrid Bergman. Jane has seen some of this, and could have identified with the Golda Meir character as representing the soul of Israel, and well as its individuals and its multitude. There was also much publicity until a couple of days ago, about Israel returning to Egypt the last portions it held of the Sinai peninsula, and how Israel destroyed the settlement of Yamit rather than hand it over intact to the Egyptians—a haggle over a price, I believe.*

(Jane could also have equated the Israel nation with the large belief systems— involving hospitals and/or the law that she discussed in last night's session.

(Most interesting, and perhaps a significant breakthrough, Jane felt better by the time Peggy Jowett came at 1:45, and we explained the situation to Peggy. "I'm exhausted," Jane said.)

DELETED SESSION
MAY 2, 1982 11:12 AM SUNDAY

(Like the last deleted session, this one is Jane's own dictation, not Seth's. She'd mentioned doing some yesterday, but it hadn't worked out. "I don't know what to talk about," she said at 11:05 AM, "now that you're here. Something on Rich Bed, *or just generally about those feelings I had yesterday after reading your introduction for* Dreams.... *" When I mentioned that she could dictate something for the intro she said she couldn't—not without reading it again. I didn't advise that, for yesterday morning she'd ended up very depressed after pursuing it right after breakfast. Her mood had been very despairing for most of the day. "It's devastating, I guess," she said about the intro.*

(She added: "Now I don't know whether the hospital experience was worth it or not." We agreed her energy wasn't any better than it had seemed before she went in, but at least Dr. Kardon's treatment was supposed to be in the process of remedying that. [Dr. K is to see us tomorrow, to take blood for a thyroid test that may signal that it's okay to raise the amount of supplement Jane is now getting.]

("And your hearing is better than it's been for what—years?" I continued. Jane agreed. "Yes—I can hear the birds now. Last year I started wondering where all the birds had gone." "And you've had the whole hospital experience to use in the years ahead in your work," I said. "Creatively. You've learned a lot about another way of life, met a lot of people: you've got a much wider base now from which to work...."

(Jane agreed again. "And I wish I'd written down all I've just told you," I said. I began these notes, only to be interrupted as Jane began dictation. I finished them later.

(11:12 AM.) Last night *(Jane said)* I felt great when Robbie kissed me, and actually I slept quite well, both in my chair and bed. I felt fairly hopeful this morning, for example, yet now I feel quite sad again *(with a tremolo)*, and I feel as if I want to express myself—but when I try there is some strange block.

I guess I really want to cry. *(Long pause.)* Maybe its actually when I feel most ambitious that I begin to feel most helpless, since I began to realize how little I'm actually doing. Just to look through a notebook is quite uncomfortable for me. I wonder if I could work with small ink sketches at all now. I could at least give that a try.

I guess I thought that I'd keep up some level of communication if I talked as I am now, and Robbie took the words down. Come to think of it, I did feel fairly hopeful this morning for brief snatches. I was going to record some memories that suddenly came to me yesterday morning. Of the last few months or so I spent at my mother's house—when <u>she</u> called <u>me</u> time after time during those spring and summer months of 1950: she wanted her pillows turned, she cried out in rage and pain—and here I was some 30 years later, calling out to Rob *(voice breaking)* to move my pillows or raise my head.

She called me all kinds of names. *(Long pause.)* I tried to understand but felt half-doped—indeed. Maybe even half-<u>duped</u>, because I could never figure out when her crying outrage, her screaming anguish, were real expressions of nearly unbearable moments, or when she was acting. She could do that too.

But I thought, "My God, I should be able to forgive my mother anything, being in that state, with a child beside." No wonder she raged and screamed and struck out—yet I certainly, as far as I know, don't hold myself to blame, since I understood as well as I could. And helped in whatever ways I could. But surely my attitude as well as hers must have helped build a wall between us.

It must have taken something for me, at 21, to leave her that summer. She attempted suicide again, this time by taking an overdose of phenobarbital. Instead of making her sleepy, however, it turned her into someone wild: she yelled and shouted and tried to get out of bed. I was afraid she'd fall on the floor. She was taken directly to the hospital when I called the doctor, and I went back home to that odd, nervous house that felt strangely vacant with her presence gone. I packed my clothes.

(11:28.) I had told her a few days before the suicide attempt that I was leaving. I'm not sure, but I <u>think</u> I told her. We had a salesman who used the place as a business address, and he was there that night. I don't remember much about him, except that he wouldn't help. He got in his car as fast as he could and drove away, leaving mother raging on the bedside.

I took off with Walt on the motorcycle, and all the way across the country in my mind I heard her yell, "bitch, bitch, bitch." Yet I'm certain I didn't feel guilty. I was scared to death of her. For that matter, I was somewhat frightened of Walt, who threatened to leave me when he got angry in a new town we happened to be in, but we made it to the west coast.

So I wonder how much of this started then. I honestly thought I'd put most of that behind me—yet my early novels all dealt with the relationship between my mother and others, in various guises, and I know I was afraid that somehow she'd end up turning me into her.

She had some jumbled psychic abilities, I suppose. She was great for reading tea leaves now and then, and I used to think how strange it was that she could do that yet couldn't walk. She told me that sometime she walked in the night, and that some night she'd turn on the gas jets and kill us both. I really don't know if it's such a good idea to go over such memories or not, but since they came to mind I decided finally to have Rob write them down for me.

(End at 11:35 AM.

(I told Jane that as I listened to it some of the material sounded contradictory. That is, the young girl must have had some feelings of guilt for leaving her prostrate mother, etc. I thought that was perfectly natural, but extending those feelings for the next 30 years would seem to be too much in nature's scheme—as I've said before, it doesn't seem to me that nature necessarily <u>wants</u> things to work that way, while making perfectly possible the fact that they can, if one chooses. This may be a case of things being redeemed on a "higher" level, I suppose—reminding me of material I've been dealing with recently in the intro for Seth/Jane's Dreams.

(I also said that I thought today's material was the result of Jane's reading that intro after breakfast yesterday, which had triggered her day-long black mood of despair. I thought the intro had triggered Jane's material about her mother—for here Jane was, creating—or at least <u>mimicking</u>—her mother's situation on her own. Jane's material this morning seemed to show that her buried feelings about her mother were much stronger than she's suspected, and more damaging. Perhaps we'll discover that they play as strong a role in Jane's dilemma presently, as my wife's Sinful-Self material. For Jane the two sets of material-beliefs could be very closely related—seems like this would be almost inevitable.

(How ironic....)

DELETED SESSION
MAY 10, 1982 8:23 PM MONDAY

(I'd stopped asking Jane for sessions, private or regular, since most of the time it seemed obvious that she wasn't up to it, so she rather surprised me after supper tonight by saying that if I "sat with her" for ten minutes or so she'd see if she could have a session. She added that she often thought of trying something that way, but that she hesitated to ask me to take the time to sit around in case nothing happened, since she knew I was trying to work as much as I could on the intro for Seth's Dreams. My answer was that I'd gladly do the sitting around if she wanted to, on the chance that we might get some helpful material—especially about her own condition.

("I've got that damned question-and-answer thing going on inside my head," she remarked now with some exasperation. She'd just spoken a phrase I didn't understand as I worked on these notes—something in answer to a question she'd thought I'd asked. I hadn't said anything. She has been doing this since suppertime, and has repeated it at other times. She was angry and concerned. "Jesus, now I just started to drift right off," she said.

(8:12. For several days now, at Dr. Kardon's suggestion, I've been giving Jane only the 50 mcg. Synthroid tablet, instead of that plus the 25 mcg., thus cutting her dosage by a third. I'd started this after Dr. K's visit to the house and examination of Jane last Wednesday. Thursday a nurse from Arnot-Ogden drew blood from Jane for the tests Dr. K wanted, including the thyroid. This morning Dr. K's nurse called and gave us the results of the tests—all but the thyroid, that is, which is to run this coming Wednesday. The eight tests that were run were all normal; I have a list of them. We do think Jane may be a little better off with the reduced Synthroid dose, although this may be hard to prove. Odd, since ordinarily the reduced dosage would seem to be the opposite course of treatment Jane would need, with an underactive thyroid gland....

(This course of action has been reminding me, of course, of Seth's assertion that Jane's thyroid has regenerated itself in the past.

("See, now, that really bothers me," Jane said at 8:16. "I've done nothing but doze off since I called you.... Maybe Seth's right—about dozing after eating.... I'm warm now, quite warm. Like now I'm afraid to pick up a cigarette—I think I've got one in my hand but I don't at all.... But I do have the feeling that Seth will give us considerable help once we get going. I half-assed feel him around...."

(Jane still dozed, but perhaps the dozing was qualified now, for how could it be related to her relaxing enough to go into trance? She sat dozing with her body tipping to her left in the chair as we sat at the card table in the living room.

(Jane has achieved more motion and movement in her legs—her knees especially—since we began propping her feet up on a box as she lays in bed. This promotes drainage of the edema in her lower legs and feet, and has been quite effective, since she responds quickly. At the same time the new motions have resulted in feelings of soreness in her knees, but she recognizes that they're positive responses.

("All right," I think I can do it very briefly...." Her voice was fairly steady, her eyes dark, and she took many pauses.

("Okay.")

Now: Ruburt's body is experimenting with its own metabolism. The gland is (underlined) activating itself by itself—off and on, so to speak, giving a sputtering effect. Overall, the body is exploring the best rhythm of metabolism, and fitting itself in with the medication. In some fashions it uses more energies at times than at others, and slowly begins to demand more energy, so there will be periods of unevenness—but he is (underlined) being provided for. He is (underlined) safe, secure, and protected. Remembering a few small but potent suggestions will of course be of greatest benefit—particularly to offset any negative hospital suggestions, which do of course exist. On the other hand, in such cases remember that often a doctor's or a nurse's negative suggestions or fears, voiced, simply give voice to the individual's own fears. And if he or she can understand this the individual can then counter such suggestions that seem to come from "outside," I will indeed, and before too long, begin again some therapeutic material, winding this in with other pertinent data. The two of you can best help each other above all *(long pause at 8:29)* by communicating as honestly and clearly as possible, for expressions of your love will then come to the surface where on both of your parts that certain emotional expression often goes <u>hungry</u>.

This kind of communication can also help both of you in many ways, because the verbal expressions themselves stand for and represent inner emotions and expressions and fulfillments, and rouse your beings, for in some ways your emotions do of course <u>move</u> you *(with emphasis.*

(Long pause.) I am watching out for Ruburt, and have been, and for you as well. Your own natural persons, however, yearn to express whatever emotions and needs they have at any given time, even if from the outside such expression may certainly seem most unfortunate, and bring up more problems.

(8:34.) I hope here merely to set up again the feel of the sessions, and then will gradually give you more material. Tonight's message is in the way of reassurance. I cannot impress upon you too much, however, the importance of those early sessions on the *Magical Approach*, for they will make even more sense to you now after the hospital experience. You will also, it seems, be far more willing to accept such ideas, not quite as stubborn in the retention of old belief.

(Long pause.) I am speaking primarily to Ruburt in this particular sentence, but to some extent this applies to both of you, particularly involving the projecting of negative beliefs into the future. There is no reason why, with proper attitudes, even within your situation, that the typing of my last book should not go easily, Joseph. Ruburt's hands <u>will</u> improve. Normal writing will become as real to him as his normal hearing is now.

Reading those sessions together is important, for it is the inner realities and the inner insights that will also release the thyroid's proper activity, and allow the resumption of more normal physical expression.

For now I bid you a fond good evening—but your policy of sitting and waiting is a good one, at least several times a week.... I did not suggest that you go to the medical profession, or suggest you <u>stay away</u> from it specifically, knowing that your own beliefs would lead toward the proper decision <u>whichever</u> way it fell.

That is enough for now. My heartiest regards, and a fond good evening.
("Thank you very much."
(8:44 PM. Jane felt much better. She'd marched along pretty well in the ses-

sion, with her voice being much stronger than in previous ones. She didn't remember much of what Seth had said—yet she also knew she'd told me various parts of the material through the day. It also fit in with some of my own recent ideas—that eventually the reviving thyroid gland would lead to the dispensation of medication while also rejuvenating the physical body in many ways—including the "arthritis."

("It would be a joke if [Dr.] Cummins turned out to be right after all," I said now. For of all the doctors she'd encountered while in the hospital, Jane had liked Dr. C the best, feeling intuitively drawn to him and his optimistic statements that once her thyroid began functioning again she'd find herself getting around much much better than she thought possible. Cummins's opinion had been largely negated by Dr. K., especially after Dr. K's friend from Ithaca, the rheumatologist Dr. Sobel had examined Jane at Dr. K's request early in Jane's hospital stay. He'd evidently given Dr. K a very negative report on Jane. When we'd told Dr. K. what Dr C. had said, Dr K. had remarked that Dr C. "hadn't seen as many cases of arthritis as Dr. S. had" —meaning of course that Dr C. wasn't that much of an expert, and that his opinion could be discounted....)

THE SETH AUDIO COLLECTION

RARE RECORDINGS OF SETH SPEAKING through Jane Roberts are now available on audiocassette and CD. These Seth sessions were recorded by Jane's student, Rick Stack, during Jane's classes in Elmira, New York, in the 1970's. The majority of these selections have never been published in any form. Volume I, described below, is a collection of some of the best of Seth's comments gleaned from over 120 Seth Sessions. Additional selections from The Seth Audio Collection are also available. For information ask for our free catalogue.

Volume I of The Seth Audio Collection consists of six (1-hour) cassettes plus a 34-page booklet of Seth transcripts. Topics covered in Volume I include:

- Creating your own reality – How to free yourself from limiting beliefs and create the life you want.
- Dreams and out-of-body experiences.
- Reincarnation and Simultaneous Time.
- Connecting with your inner self.
- Spontaneity–Letting yourself go with the flow of your being.
- Creating abundance in every area of your life.
- Parallel (probable) universes and exploring other dimensions of reality.
- Spiritual healing, how to handle emotions, overcoming depression and much more.

FOR A FREE CATALOGUE of Seth related products including a detailed description of The Seth Audio Collection, please send your request to the address below.

ORDER INFORMATION:
If you would like to order a copy of The Seth Audio Collection Volume I, please send your name and address, with a check or money order payable to New Awareness Network, Inc. for $60 (Tapes), or $70 (CD's) plus shipping charges. United States residents in New York State must add sales tax.

Shipping charges: U.S.—$6.50, Canada—$8, Europe—$20, Australia/Asia—$22 Rates are UPS for U.S. & Airmail for International—Allow 2 weeks for delivery Alternate Shipping—Surface—$9.00 to anywhere in the world—Allow 5-8 weeks

Mail to: **NEW AWARENESS NETWORK INC.**
P.O. BOX 192,
Manhasset, New York 11030
(516) 869-9108 between 9:00-5:00 p.m. Monday-Friday EST
Visit us on the Internet—www.sethcenter.com

Books by Jane Roberts from Amber-Allen Publishing

Seth Speaks: The Eternal Validity of the Soul. This essential guide to conscious living clearly and powerfully articulates the furthest reaches of human potential, and the concept that each of us creates our own reality.

The Nature of Personal Reality: Specific, Practical Techniques for Solving Everyday Problems and Enriching the Life You Know.. In this perennial bestseller, Seth challenges our assumptions about the nature of reality and stresses the individual's capacity for conscious action.

The Individual and the Nature of Mass Events. Seth explores the connection between personal beliefs and world events, how our realities merge and combine "to form mass reactions such as the overthrow of governments, the birth of a new religion, wars, epidemics, earthquakes, and new periods of art, architecture, and technology."

The Magical Approach: Seth Speaks About the Art of Creative Living. Seth reveals the true, magical nature of our deepest levels of being, and explains how to live our lives spontaneously, creatively, and according to our own natural rhythms.

The Oversoul Seven Trilogy (The Education of Oversoul Seven, The Further Education of Oversoul Seven, Oversoul Seven and the Museum of Time). Inspired by Jane's own experiences with the Seth Material, the adventures of Oversoul Seven are an intriguing fantasy, a mind-altering exploration of our inner being, and a vibrant celebration of life.

The Nature of the Psyche. Seth reveals a startling new concept of self, answering questions about the inner reality that exists apart from time, the origins and powers of dreams, human sexuality, and how we choose our physical death.

The "Unknown" Reality, Volumes One and Two. Seth reveals the multidimensional nature of the human soul, the dazzling labyrinths of unseen probabilities involved in any decision, and how probable realities combine to create the waking life we know.

Dreams, "Evolution," and Value Fulfillment, Volumes One and Two. Seth discusses the material world as an ongoing self-creation—the product of a conscious, self-aware and thoroughly animate universe, where virtually every possibility not only exists, but is constantly encouraged to achieve its highest potential.

The Way Toward Health. Woven through the poignant story of Jane Roberts' final days are Seth's teachings about self-healing and the mind's effect upon physical health.

Available in bookstores everywhere.